Body Image, Eating Disorders, and Obesity in Youth

Body Image, Eating Disorders, and Obesity in Youth

Assessment, Prevention, and Treatment

Edited by J. Kevin Thompson and Linda Smolak

American Psychological Association
Washington, DC

Published by
American Psychological Association
750 First Street, NE
Washington, DC 20002
www.apa.org

To order
APA Order Department
P.O. Box 92984
Washington, DC 20090-2984
Tel: (800) 374-2721
Direct: (202) 336-5510
Fax: (202) 336-5502
TDD/TTY: (202) 336-6123
Online: www.apa.org/books/
Email: order@apa.org

In the UK and Europe, copies may be ordered from
American Psychological Association
3 Henrietta Street
Covent Garden, London
WC2E 8LU England

Typeset in Goudy by World Composition Services, Inc., Sterling, VA

Printer: United Book Press, Baltimore, MD
Cover designer: Nini Sarmiento, NiDesign, Baltimore
Editor/Project Manager: Debbie K. Hardin, Charlottesville, VA
Technical/Production Editor: Catherine Hudson

The opinions and statements published are the responsibility of the authors, and such opinions and statements do not necessarily represent the policies of the APA.

Library of Congress Cataloging-in-Publication Data

Body image, eating disorders, and obesity in youth : assessment, prevention, and treatment / edited by J. Kevin Thompson and Linda Smolak.
    p. cm.
  ISBN 1-55798-758-0
  1. Body image in children. 2. Body image in adolescence. 3. Obesity in children. 4. Eating disorders in children. 5. Eating disorders in adolescence. 6. Obesity in adolescence. 7. Children—Mental health. 8. Teenagers—Mental health. I. Thompson, J. Kevin. II. Smolak, Linda, 1951–
  RA777.B59   2001
  618.92′8526—dc21

                                                    2001022124

Printed in the United States of America
First Edition

CONTENTS

PREFACE

It is not unusual for a personal experience to capture the essence of an issue more fully than the use of a carefully planned analytical strategy. Such was the case when we were writing and editing this book. For instance, Kevin's son Jared, at the age of 4, declared to him, "Dad, you need to lift weights." A bit stunned, Kevin recovered sufficiently to ask him, "Where did you get that?" Jared smiled, "I saw it on television." In a moment, the issues we had been writing about—body image concerns in young children, media pressures regarding attractiveness standards, and the role of interpersonal feedback on body dissatisfaction—coalesced in one unique familial interaction.

Similarly, when Linda was collecting data on teasing in a sample of middle-school students, she naively asked her size-4 daughter, "Well, no one teases you about being fat, right?" She gave her one of the mom-how-can-you-be-so-ignorant looks that middle-schoolers have and said, "It doesn't matter whether or not you are fat." Continuing in her naivete, Linda said, "Well, why don't you just tell them you are not fat and that you are happy with the way you look?" This advice produced more eye rolling and this response: "Mom. You can't say that. Everyone will think you are stuck up." When Mimi Nichter introduced the term "fat talk" a few years later, Linda knew exactly what she meant. She also had a new understanding of the pressure young girls face regarding their appearance.

Indeed, these experiences are not unique to us, nor to the authors who contributed the chapters in this book. Increasingly, clinicians, academicians, teachers, and parents of diverse backgrounds and occupations are finding that their children are reporting and experiencing a wide variety of concerns related to appearance, eating, and weight. Once thought to be clinical problems of adulthood or, at least, the latter teenage years, researchers are now confirming what anecdote suggests: Eating disorders, obesity, and body image problems now affect a significant number of children of all ages and adolescents.

Examination of such issues as risk factors, prevention programs, assessment strategies, and treatment options for individuals of these ages (6–17) is now perhaps the most active area of inquiry in the interrelated fields of obesity, eating disorders, and body image. There has been such tremendous progress over the past 10 to 15 years that it now seems a good time to distill and summarize the findings into a manageable review for practitioners and researchers. It has been our good fortune to recruit successfully many of the leading figures in the field to contribute to this volume, with wide-ranging expertise areas, from eating regulation in infancy to the emerging (and controversial) field of plastic surgery in childhood and adolescence.

We believe that we have succeeded not only in producing a volume that covers many of the salient topic areas but also offers in each chapter a review based on the empirical research with accompanying guidelines for the clinician and indications for future inquiry. Beginning clinicians or graduate students will find it as readable, we believe, as the seasoned researcher who desires a succinct summary of current work in the field.

In the development and editing of this book, we are indebted to many individuals for their guidance, wisdom, and patience. This volume is the cumulative product not only of our formulation but also the constructive input from many individuals at the American Psychological Association, including Margaret Schlegel, Ed Meidenbauer, and Julia Frank-McNeil. We would also like to thank several individuals for providing careful critiques of early drafts of certain chapters, including David Allison, Leslie J. Heinberg, Stacey Tantleff-Dunn, Thomas F. Cash, and Ruth Striegel-Moore. Linda is also grateful to the person who makes her professional work possible, Sonja Gallagher, secretary to the Science Division at Kenyon College. Her Kenyon colleagues, Michael Levine and Sarah Mumen, are continual sources of support, information, and wisdom. We would like to thank Diane Dwyer and Patricia van den Berg for their excellent technical assistance and production efforts. Finally, we would like to thank our families for their support, patience, and good humor in dealing with papers all over the house. It is friends and family who make this kind of endeavor possible and rewarding.

CONTRIBUTORS

David B. Allison, New York Obesity Research Center, Saint Luke's-
   Roosevelt Hospital, Columbia University College of Physicians and
   Surgeons

Leann L. Birch, The Pennsylvania State University, University Park

Mary E. Connors, Illinois School of Professional Psychology, Chicago

Marjorie Crago, University of Arizona College of Medicine, Arizona
   Health Sciences Center, Tucson

Jennifer Zoler Dounchis, Center for Eating and Weight Disorders,
   San Diego, CA

Myles S. Faith, New York Obesity Research Center, St. Luke's-Roosevelt
   Hospital, Columbia University College of Physicians and Surgeons

Jennifer O. Fisher, The Pennsylvania State University, University Park

Rick M. Gardner, University of Colorado—Denver

Stacy A. Gore, University of Alabama—Birmingham

Helen A. Hayden, Center for Eating and Weight Disorders,
   San Diego, CA

Kelly Hill, University of Kentucky, Lexington

Joel D. Killen, Stanford University School of Medicine, Palo Alto, CA

Michael P. Levine, Kenyon College, Gambier, OH

Susan B. Netemeyer, Baton Rouge, LA

Vicky Phares, University of South Florida, Tampa

Claire Pomeroy, University of Kentucky, Lexington

Thomas N. Robinson, Stanford University School of Medicine,
   Palo Alto, CA

Brian E. Saelens, San Diego State University/University of California,
   San Diego Joint Doctoral Program in Clinical Psychology

David B. Sarwer, University of Pennsylvania, Philadelphia

Catherine M. Shisslak, University of Arizona College of Medicine, Tucson

Linda Smolak, Kenyon College, Gambier, OH

Ari B. Steinberg, University of South Florida, Tampa

Mark H. Thelen, University of Missouri, Columbia

J. Kevin Thompson, University of South Florida, Tampa

Denise E. Wilfley, Center for Eating and Weight Disorders, San Diego, CA

Jillon S. Vander Wal, University of Illinois—Chicago

Donald A. Williamson, Pennington Biomedical Research Center, Baton Rouge, LA

INTRODUCTION:
BODY IMAGE, EATING DISORDERS, AND OBESITY IN YOUTH— THE FUTURE IS NOW

J. KEVIN THOMPSON AND LINDA SMOLAK

Consider the following three cases:

> When I was 12, I stopped eating . . . everybody teased me because I was so tall, so I thought if I stopped eating I'd stop growing. . . . I was really skinny and I just wanted to stop growing. . . . I didn't eat lunch at all any time. I wouldn't eat much breakfast or dinner . . . (My parents) sort of thought I just didn't feel well with breakfast and dinner . . . they didn't know about me not eating lunch till one day I left about two days' lunches in my bag and Mum found them and I got blasted. . . . I do that regularly now. . . . Sometimes I think I'm fat, which I'm not, I think. I just get these feelings where I think I'm revolting in the public eye. . . . You see on TV lots of people who are tall and glamorous and skinny, and that's probably what you're meant to look like, so you feel odd and you don't fit in and just feel revolting.—A 12-year-old Australian girl (cited in Wertheim, Paxton, Schutz, & Muir, 1997, p. 351)

> Harold is a 12-year-old boy who is obese. His presenting problems of social withdrawal and depressive symptoms appeared to be related primarily to being teased frequently about his overweight status. "Fatso" and "tubby" were two of the names that he was called. He seemed to be particularly negatively affected by teasing that occurred in the locker room before and after gym class. The teasing seemed to worsen his already negative view of his appearance and also decreased his overall self-esteem. He avoided physical activities with peers if at all possible. Treatment for Harold included imaginal exposure to teasing situations, strategies to cope with teasing incidents, development of alternative responses to social avoidance, and cognitive reframing. (M. Faith, personal communication, June 1999)

> Jan is a 15-year-old girl with bulimia nervosa. Her concerns with eating began when she was five, when her mother put her and her older sister on diets. Her grandmother on her mother's side is very weight conscious and frequently makes comments about her daughter's weight (Jan's mother). Jan's mother is currently quite thin, and Jan reports that her

mother rarely eats in front of other people. Jan is terrified of becoming fat and purges, on average, about three times each day. During therapy, she was initially hesitant to consider "giving up" her disorder. A focus on her feminist views and discussion of unrealistic societal pressures on women regarding appearance had positive effects and, at termination, her purging activity was greatly reduced. (S. Gilbert, personal communication, August 1999)

These three cases offer compelling examples of the gravity of eating and weight-related disturbances in childhood and adolescence. Young girls and boys are no longer immune from the pressures engendered by peers, parents, and media to meet appearance standards once demanded only of adults. Those of us who have followed the research in the closely connected fields of obesity, eating disorders, and body image disturbances have witnessed a substantial, and necessary, redirection of research efforts from adults to children and adolescents. In just the past 10 years, the progress in our understanding of risk factors, development of assessment methods, and production of innovative preventive and treatment strategies has been phenomenal. Unfortunately, such enthusiasm is tempered by angst when we encounter the individual pain and agony that so many young persons, especially girls, experience as a product of their weight and shape concerns.

This introductory chapter is designed to provide a context for the wide-ranging information that follows in the areas of basic research, risk factors, models of disturbance, assessment methodologies, and prevention–treatment approaches. Initially, a brief and highly selective overview of prevalence data will be provided, followed by a discussion of research highlighting the negative psychological and physical factors associated with eating problems, obesity, and body image concerns. Recent work focusing on prospective studies concerning the developmental course of eating disorders will then be discussed, with a goal of noting the importance of predictive work for prevention and treatment.

DETERMINING HOW MANY CHILDREN AND ADOLESCENTS ARE AFFECTED

A brief review of prevalence data may give some indication of the number of children and adolescents who experience clinical or subclinical symptoms of eating disturbance. Scores of descriptive studies and surveys have been conducted detailing levels of appearance dissatisfaction, restrictive eating practices, bulimic symptoms, and related symptoms of body image disturbance and eating disorders. In addition, well-designed investigations have yielded data on the prevalence of children and adolescents who meet agreed on criteria for obesity or an eating disorder. Dieting, a behavior common to eating disorders as well as obesity, may be a good place to begin this discussion.

Three investigations provide quite comprehensive surveys of dieting levels and practices. The Heart, Lung, and Blood Institute sampled 2379 Black and White 9- and 10-year-old girls (Schreiber et al., 1996). Among 9-year-olds, 42% of the Black girls and 37% of the White girls reported that they were trying to lose weight; the corresponding numbers for 10-year-olds were 44% and 37%. However, the differences in percentage between the two ethnicities were not significant. In a second study, a large sample of girls (5882) and boys (5585) in the 9th through 12th grades was surveyed (Serdula et al., 1993). Participants were classified as White, Black, Hispanic, and "Other." For females, the following percentages were trying to lose weight: White (47.4%), Black (30.4%), Hispanic (39.1%), and Other (45.6%). Comparable statistics for boys were as follows: White (16.2%), Black (10%), Hispanic (16.7%), and Other (13.7%). Participants were also asked if they were trying to gain weight. Summary numbers across ethnicities indicated the greater concern in this weight direction for boys (26.0%) versus girls (6.6%).

Field and her colleagues (1999) surveyed a sample of more than 16,000 9- to 14-year-old boys and girls (Whites composed 93% of the sample). Although 20% of the 9-year-old girls were trying to lose weight, 44% of the 14-year-old girls were. Girls were more likely to exercise than diet to lose weight. For example, 4.2% of the 13-year-old girls were always on a diet to lose weight while 11% exercised daily to lose weight. Among the boys, 17% of the 9-year-olds and 19% of the 14-year-olds were trying to lose weight. Again, boys were more likely to exercise than diet to lose weight.

There are numerous studies that have measured the body satisfaction or some related aspect of body image in young girls and boys. For instance, Wood, Becker, and Thompson (1996) evaluated 8- to 10-year-olds and found that 55% of the girls and 35% of the boys were dissatisfied with their size. Ranges across a variety of different countries are quite consistent, indicating that around 30 to 50% of child and adolescent girls are weight-dissatisfied or dieting (Devaud, Jeannin, Narring, Ferron, & Michaud, 1998; Lunner et al., 2000; Perezmitre, 1997; Sasson, Lewin, & Roth, 1995; chapter 2, this volume). Weight concern has even been found to exist in 21% of 5-year-old girls (Davison, Markey, & Birch, 2000). In addition, recent work suggests that, in contrast to girls' dissatisfaction, which generally reflects a desire to be thinner, boys may be unhappy because they desire a larger and more muscular appearance (McCreary & Sasse, 2000; Smolak, Levine, & Thompson, 2001). Gender differences indicating that girls are more dissatisfied than boys may emerge early, even in the 8- to 10-year range (Cusumano & Thompson, 2001; Parkinson, Tovee, & Cohen-Tovee, 1998). Ethnicity and level of obesity may also moderate dissatisfaction level. Striegel-Moore et al. (2000) found that White girls had higher levels of dissatisfaction than Black girls, and the levels increased as a function of body mass index (BMI; (see Figure I-1. For more information on body image disturbance levels and the moderating influences of gender, age, and ethnicity see chapters 2 and 3, this volume.)

Dieting, body dissatisfaction, and a desire for reduced weight (or greater muscularity) may be caused by a variety of influences, including such factors as comparing one's self to media ideals or peers, internalizing unrealistic media images of attractiveness, being teased about one's appearance, modeling peers' or parents' weight practices or attitudes, sexual abuse or harassment, and early pubertal maturation (Muir, Wertheim, & Paxton, 1999; Stice & Agras, 1998; Thompson & Heinberg, 1999; Thompson & Stice, in press; Vander Wal & Thelen, 2001; Wertheim et al., 1997; chapters 4, 5, and 6, this volume). In fact, research into the delineation of these upstream influences that predict the onset of body image problems and dieting is among the most active areas of inquiry in the field of eating disorders (Thompson, Heinberg, Altabe, & Tantleff-Dunn, 1999; chapter 4, this volume).

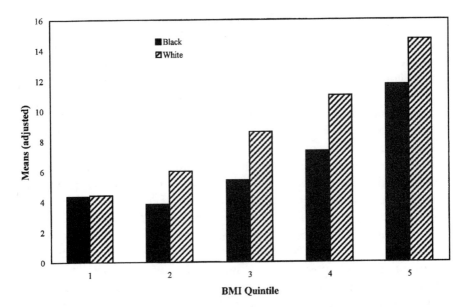

Body Dissatisfaction

Figure I-1. Adjusted mean scores for body dissatisfaction in Black and White girls, by body mass index (BMI) quintile (means are adjusted for age and maximum parental education). From Striegel-Moore et al. (2000). Reprinted by permission of Wiley-Liss, Inc., a subsidiary of John Wiley & Sons, Inc.

The extremely high rates of dieting and body dissatisfaction may not necessarily indicate that a clinical disorder exists that warrants intervention. However, there is emerging evidence that some individuals who have weight concerns may engage in extreme behaviors (e.g., excessive restriction or binge–purge activity). These persons may have (or develop) a more serious eating disorder such as anorexia nervosa or bulimia nervosa. In addition, some boys or girls may have a severe disparagement of appearance, perhaps indicative of the presence of a body dysmorphic disorder. It is interesting to note that disturbed eating behaviors, including use of appetite suppressants, laxatives, vomiting, and binge eating, have even been found to predict increased risk for obesity in adolescent girls (Stice, Cameron, Killen, Hayward, & Taylor, 1999). With these issues in mind, we now turn to a brief overview of the prevalence data for eating disorders, body dysmorphic disorder, and obesity.

Eating Disorders and Body Dysmorphic Disorder

Table I-1 contains the *DSM-IV* diagnostic criteria for these disorders (American Psychiatric Association, 1994). The existence of a diagnosable *DSM*-related disorder is always of concern when the individual is a child or adolescent. In the case of anorexia nervosa and bulimia nervosa, the issue of prevalence statistics for the 6- to 17-year range is a bit more complex than it is with adults. The high percentage of dieting and body dissatisfaction seen in ages 6 through 17, especially among girls, does not translate into a high rate of *DSM* diagnoses of anorexia nervosa or bulimia nervosa. In fact, the prevalence rate for adolescents has generally been found to be in the .5 to 1.0% range for anorexia nervosa and probably around 1.0% for bulimia nervosa (Doyle & Bryant-Waugh, 2000; Fairburn & Beglin, 1990; Lucas, Beard, O'Fallon, & Kurland, 1991; Rosenvinge, Borgen, & Boerresen, 1999; Steiner & Lock, 1998). Rosenvinge, Borgen, and Sundgot Boerresen, 1999, recently found a prevalence rate of 1.0% for binge eating disorder. The rates for prepubertal children are even lower than those found for adolescents (Lask & Bryant-Waugh, 2000). It is interesting to note, however, that these prevalence rates do not include the percentage of youth who might receive a diagnosis of eating disorder not otherwise specified, which may be 50% of such cases (Nicholls, Chater, & Lask, 2000). Also, the rates are just a bit below that found for adults (1.0% for anorexia nervosa and 1 to 3% for bulimia nervosa), and the mean age of onset for anorexia nervosa is 17 years of age, with peaks at 14 and 18 (American Psychiatric Association, 1994. As with adults, girls are diagnosed with an eating disorder at a much higher rate than boys, with the gender ratio approaching 10 to 1 (Lask, in press).

TABLE I-1
Diagnostic Criteria for Anorexia Nervosa, Bulimia Nervosa, and Body Dysmorphic Disorder

Anorexia Nervosa:
- Refusal to maintain a body weight at or above a minimally normal weight for age and height (e.g., weight loss leading to maintenance of body weight less than 85% of that expected; or failure to make expected weight gain during period of growth, leading to body weight less than 85% of that expected).
- Intense fear of gaining weight or becoming fat, even though underweight.
- Disturbance in the way in which one's body weight or shape is experienced, undue influence of body weight or shape on self-evaluation, or denial of the seriousness of the current low body weight.
- In postmenarcheal females, amenorrhea, i.e., the absence of at least three consecutive menstrual cycles. (A woman is considered to have amenorrhea if her periods occur only following hormone, e.g., estrogen, administration.)

Bulimia Nervosa:
- Recurrent episodes of binge eating. An episode of binge eating is characterized by both of the following:
    Eating, in a discrete period of time (e.g., within any two-hour period), an amount of food that is definitely larger than most people would eat during a similar period of time and under similar circumstances.
    A sense of lack of control over eating during the episode (e.g., a feeling that one cannot stop eating or control what or how much one is eating).
    Recurrent inappropriate compensatory behavior to prevent weight gain, such as self-induced vomiting, misuse of laxatives, diuretics, enemas, or other medications; fasting; or excessive exercise.
    The binge eating and inappropriate compensatory behaviors both occur, on average, at least twice a week for three months.
    Self-evaluation is unduly influenced by body shape and weight.
    The disturbance does not occur exclusively during episodes of Anorexia Nervosa.

Body Dysmorphic Disorder:
- Preoccupation with an imagined defect in appearance. If a slight physical anomaly is present, the person's concern is markedly excessive.
- The preoccupation causes clinically significant distress or impairment in social, occupational, or other important areas of functioning.
- The preoccupation is not better accounted for by another mental disorder (e.g., dissatisfaction with body shape and size in Anorexia Nervosa).

Reprinted with permission from the Diagnostic and Statistical Manual of Mental Disorders, *Fourth Edition, Washington, DC, American Psychiatric Association, 1994.*

Because reports of disordered eating (excessive dieting or the presence of bulimic behaviors) occur at a much higher level than the previously mentioned prevalence rate for diagnoses, researchers have adopted a "spectrum" or continuum model and advocated a method of classifying referred to as "partial syndrome" eating disturbance (Shisslak, Crago, & Estes, 1995). "Partial syndrome" may also be referred to by various investigators as "subclinical, subdiagnostic, subthreshold, subfrequency, atypical and eating disorders not otherwise specified" (Shisslak et al., 1995, pp. 209–210). A partial syndrome diagnosis might be considered if some of the following symptoms are present: Recurrent binge episodes, periodic use of purgative methods (laxatives, vomiting), feeling a lack of control over eating during a binge or persistent body image problems (Killen et al., 1994). Empirical evidence supporting the continuity between subthreshold and full-syndrome bulimia nervosa (BN) argues for the importance of a focus on the prevalence of these partial syndrome cases (Stice, Killen, Hayward, & Taylor, 1998b).

Although not strictly meeting *DSM* criteria, individuals with a partial syndrome may suffer significant social and occupational or educational impairment and may benefit from clinical intervention. An analysis of the prevalence data indicates that a large number of child and adolescent cases with eating problems may meet the criteria for a partial syndrome. Killen et al. (1994) found that only 1% of their sample of 11- and 12-year-old girls met criteria for diagnosis of bulimia nervosa, but 4% met their standard for partial syndrome (referred to as "symptomatic" in their study; p.357). Shisslak et al. (1995) reviewed studies that assessed adolescent girls and found a prevalence rate of partial syndrome that ranged from 1.78 to 13.3%. Gender and ethnicity distributions concerning partial syndromes have not been well-investigated, although individual symptoms, such as dieting and purging, do show gender and ethnic group differences (Smolak & Murnen, 2001; Smolak & Striegel-Moore, 2001; chapters 2 and 3, this volume).

A second diagnostic area that has received recent attention is body dysmorphic disorder. This *DSM* disorder, housed in the somatoform section, has as its primary characteristic a severe disparagement of "an imagined defect . . . or a slight physical anomaly" in appearance (American Psychiatric Association, 1994, p. 468; see Table I-1). In other words, an objective observer might not discern evidence of an appearance problem, yet the young girl or boy is obsessed with the site of concern. The disorder has received a great deal of attention in adults in recent years (Phillips, 1996), and its relevance for children and adolescents is now apparent. Mean age of onset in a large sample of adults was found to be 16.0 years, and symptoms began for 70% of this sample before the age of 18 (Phillips & Diaz, 1997). Albertini and Phillips (1999) recently reported on a series of 33 cases; 31 were between the ages of 12 and 17 and two were aged 6 to 11. The great majority of cases were female (91%) and White (97%). As with other eating and body shape disorders, the low percentage of ethnic minority clients may reflect their lack of access to or use of mental health facilities. There is evidence, for example, that many Asian Americans are deeply dissatisfied with their eyes and undergo plastic surgery to change them (Hall, 1995). Although preliminary, the findings of body dysmorphic disorder (BDD) in childhood and adolescence are of great concern given the potential profound effects on social and emotional development.

Obesity

The prevalence of obesity among youth and adults has increased dramatically in recent years (Heinberg, Thompson, & Mateson, 2001; chapter 3, this volume). More than 50% of adult Americans are either overweight or obese (Flegal, Carroll, Kuczmarski, & Johnson, 1998), and this represents a 30% increase within a 10-year time period. Alarmingly, the percentages are also increasing in children and adolescents. Troiano and Flegal (1998) noted that approximately 25% of children and adolescents are either obese or at risk for becoming obese, and the trend is on the rise: Average rates for obesity increased from 6.7% during the period of 1976 to 1980 to 11% during the period of 1988 to 1994 (Neumark-Sztainer, 1998). Furthermore, obesity is a greater problem among Blacks and Hispanics than among Asian American and White children. Recent data compiled by the U.S. Centers for Disease Control (*www.cdc.gov*, 5/31/00) are reproduced in Figures I-2 and I-3, illustrating the tremendous increase in rates of obesity over the past few decades in the youth of the United States and the different rates found by gender and ethnicity. The presence of such high levels of obesity (with its associated health risks; see the next section) poses a significant health concern that warrants aggressive treatment efforts (chapter 13, this volume).

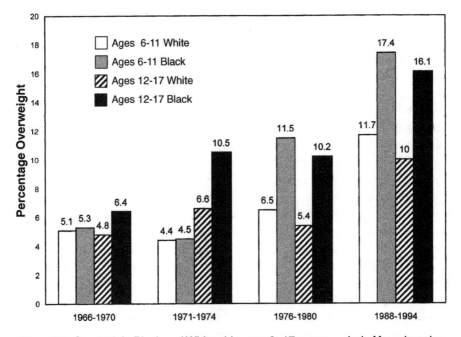

Figure I-2. Overweight Black and White girls ages 6–17 over a period of four decades. From the Centers for Disease Control, May 2000.

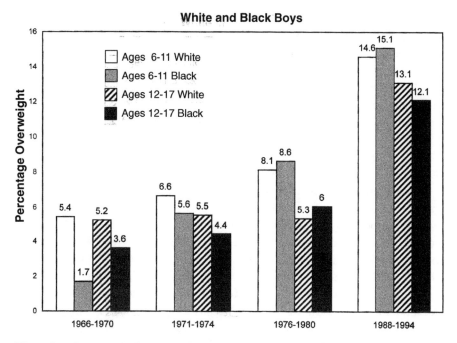

Figure I-3. Overweight Black and White boys ages 6–17 over a period of four decades. From the Centers for Disease Control, May 2000.

Summary

The available data suggest that a large number of individuals between the ages of 6 and 17 are unhappy with their weight. Many of these individuals report that they are dissatisfied with their appearance or diet to modify weight level. A relatively small percentage actually have an eating disorder, but a substantial proportion of youth may exhibit enough signs to be labeled "at-risk" or possess a "partial syndrome." In addition, recent actuarial statistics compiled by the Centers for Disease Control indicate that an alarming and increasing number of children and adolescents meet criteria for having a significant problem with excess weight. Perhaps there is one more recent, and also disturbing trend, that reflects the problems and pressures our youth feel from growing up in a world increasingly focused on the importance of attractiveness—the use of surgical procedures to alter appearance.

An analysis of plastic surgery data indicates that many adolescents have decided to opt for a relatively radical method of modifying appearance dissatisfaction. Sarwer (chapter 14, this volume) provides a wealth of statistical data reflective of the 134% increase from 1994 to 1998 in the use of cosmetic procedures by persons under the age of 18. He details a variety of procedures and findings—the 370% increase in breast augmentation surgeries surely deserves discussion in some context. For our purposes, however, with this book's focus on weight-related body image issues, the findings for such procedures as liposuction are perhaps more relevant. In 1994, 511 girls had this procedure nationwide; in 1998, the number had increased to 1645, a 222% increase. In addition, procedures such as thigh lift, tummy tuck, and upper arm lift are currently being done on young girls, whereas the procedures were simply not performed on this age group in previous years. It is also likely that these numbers are an underestimate of the total level of such surgeries because the data are based only on a survey of members of the American Society of Plastic Surgeons.

Prevalence statistics offer a starting point for understanding the possible importance of child and adolescent eating and shape-related problems. However, the associated physical and psychological problems of these conditions provide more direct cause for concern. The question of whether eating or body image disturbances in childhood portend the development of a higher level of such problems in adolescence is a significant question. As well, it is pertinent to determine if such disturbances in adolescence lead to further problems in adulthood and whether obesity in childhood and adolescence is a predictor of adult obesity. We now turn to these issues, with an initial exploration of the physical and psychological factors that are associated with eating problems and obesity.

ASSOCIATED FEATURES: PHYSICAL AND PSYCHOLOGICAL FACTORS

Obesity in young persons is a very serious matter. Contemporaneous health risks include hypertension, respiratory disease, diabetes mellitus, and orthopedic disorders (Gortmaker, Dietz, & Cheung, 1990; chapter 7, this volume). In addition, obese children are more likely to become obese adults (Dietz, 1998) with associated health problems that include such conditions as cardiovascular disease, hypertension, insulin resistance, and diabetes mellitus (Neumark-Sztainer, 1999). The psychosocial problems confronting the overweight or obese youth are also problematic. The negative verbal feedback that these individuals receive in the form of teasing is well-documented (Heinberg, 1996), and such experiences play a direct role in producing body image problems and eating disturbances (Thompson, Coovert, Richards, Johnston, & Cattarin, 1995). Neumark-Sztainer, Story, and Faibisch (1998) found that only 2 of 50 overweight girls had not been subjected to some negative interpersonal experience related to their weight. A recent meta-analysis of weight level and self-esteem found that lower self-esteem was associated with a heavier weight (Miller & Downey, 1999). In addition, psychosocial stressors in childhood and adolescence are predictive of weight gain (Mellbin & Vaille, 1989).

The physical problems associated with eating disorders are given a thorough examination by Hill and Pomeroy (chapter 7, this volume; see also Nicholls & Stanhope, 2000). Included among the many biological and physiological problems associated with anorexia nervosa are overall growth retardation, bone mass reduction, and cardiac disregulation. Death as a result of medical complications or suicide (approximately half of the cases) is estimated in 6 to 15% percent of individuals with anorexia nervosa (Steiner & Lock, 1998). Esophageal tears, gastric disturbances, and blood pressure perturbations are conditions of bulimia nervosa that often require immediate medical attention.

Eating disorders are associated with significant psychological distress. Family relationships are routinely disrupted (see chapter 5, this volume). Depression is commonly a problem and it appears to be prospectively predicted by levels of body dissatisfaction and eating disturbance (Stice, Hayward, Cameron, Killen, & Taylor, 2000; Wichstrom, 1999). In fact, weight dissatisfaction, along with other developmental factors related to pubertal and sex-role development, appear to account for the fact that girls become more depressed than boys at 13 to 14 years of age (Wichstrom, 1999). Eating disorders also show comorbidity with a variety of personality and anxiety disorders (Godart, Flament, Lecrubier, & Jeammet, 2000).

Determining If Early Problems Predict Later Problems

Early detection and prevention are extremely important considerations when dealing with childhood and adolescent disorders because of a concern that current problems are related to the development of later clinical conditions. In the case of eating and weight-related disturbances, evidence strongly suggests that such a fear is valid. Whitaker, Wright, Pepe, Seidel, and Dietz (1997) found that obese children over the age of 6 had a 50% higher risk of adult obesity. In addition, having an obese parent significantly increases the chance that an obese child will become an obese adult—79% of obese 10- to 14-year-olds with at least one obese parent were at risk to become an obese adult (Whitaker et al., 1997). Disconcertingly, there is even evidence that obesity in childhood and adolescence is associated with increased morbidity and mortality after a 50-year follow-up, even if adult weight is factored out (Must, Jaques, Dallal, Bajema, & Dietz, 1992). Thus, prevention of obesity is a paramount public health issue (Neumark-Sztainer, 1999; chapter 11, this volume).

In terms of eating and body image problems, the evidence is relatively clear that such disturbances in the younger years predict the development of severe disturbances in later years. For instance, in a four-year prospective study, Killen et al. (1996), in a sample of 14- to 18-year-old girls, divided the participants into quartiles based on weight concerns (at Time 1). Approximately 10% of the girls in the upper quartile of this measure developed a partial or full syndrome eating disturbance, whereas none of the sample in the lower quartile developed the more severe disturbance. Cattarin and Thompson (1994), in a three-year prospective study of adolescent girls, followed participants from early to midadolescence (mean age at Time 2 of testing was 15.3). Using regression analyses and controlling for the effects of age and weight status, they found that body dissatisfaction predicted Time 2 level of restrictive eating behaviors. In addition, bulimic behaviors predicted Time 2 level of overall psychological functioning (self-esteem, depression, anxiety).

Stice, Killen, Hayward, and Taylor (1998a), in a four-year prospective study, evaluated 543 females (mean age of 14.9 years) and found that dieting level and negative affectivity predicted onset of binge eating and purging. They also found that among initially asymptomatic participants, 5% reported onset of objective binge eating, 4% developed subjective binge eating, and 4% began purging. The peak age of binge eating was 16, whereas purging developed at age 18. Calam and Waller (1998) followed 63 women from an age of 12.8 to 19.8 and found that bulimic attitudes predicted subsequent bulimic features; restrictive attitudes were closely connected to purging behaviors. Marchi and Cohen (1990) assessed boys and girls (ages 1 to 10) and their mothers on three occasions over a 10-year period and found that eating problems in early childhood were predictive of anorexic and bulimic characteristics in adolescence.

A variety of other studies, including several using covariance structure modeling, could be added to those just recounted to support the view that there is a developmental trend for eating and body image problems to lead to more serious disturbances as children and adolescents mature (Thompson et al., 1999; chapters 2 and 4, this volume). In addition, the data are clear that obesity in childhood and adolescence is related to overweight status in adulthood, with its accompanying health risks. It is worth noting that dieting, as practiced by community-based adolescents, predicts the onset of later obesity (Stice et al., 1999). In terms of body dysmorphic disorder, there is not the empirical support for early problems leading to later disturbances that we have for eating disorders and obesity. However, as noted earlier, the great majority (70%) of adult cases onset before the age of 18, and emerging research suggests that very young persons may meet *DSM* criteria for the disorder (Albertini & Phillips, 1999). In sum, although much more research on developmental trends is needed, the extant evidence is compelling that efforts must be directed in the preventive and early intervention arenas (chapters 10 and 11, this volume).

A ROADMAP FOR THIS BOOK

The triad of body image problems, eating disorders, and obesity has been recognized for several years as an interrelated set of shape and weight-connected disturbances that cause significant distress for adults (Thompson, 1996). In recent years, researchers and clinicians have begun to believe and document that a similar situation exists for our youth, individuals who also experience weight and body image concerns that are associated with physical and psychological sequalae. We have reached the point wherein a substantial database exists for understanding not only the development of such disturbances but for offering an analysis of assessment, prevention, and treatment.

Our book is necessarily limited in scope. Our focus on body image will center on the disturbances associated with weight and size dissatisfaction. (For a more detailed discussion of other facets of body image disturbance, see Thompson et al., 1999.) We do not attempt to cover binge eating disorder, which is currently listed in an appendix of the *DSM-IV* as one of many disorders in need of further study. Studies are rapidly emerging on this disorder with adults; however, there is not enough information with children and adolescents to include coverage in this volume, which focuses on youth. We also do not review material on some of the atypical eating disorders of childhood, such as functional dysphagia, pervasive refusal syndrome, food avoidance emotional disorder, and selective eating (see Lask, 2000; see also chapter 9, this volume). These syndromes, by definition, do not include the disturbed body image and preoccupation with weight–shape characteristics required for a diagnosis of anorexia nervosa or bulimia nervosa. In addition, unless otherwise noted, *childhood* will refer to individuals between the ages of 6 and 11; *adolescence* will include ages 12 to 17 (when younger and older youth are considered, ages are noted). When possible, when referring to specific investigations, reference to certain ages or grade levels will be provided in this and subsequent chapters.

This book is divided into four sections: Foundations, Risk Factors, Assessment, and Prevention and Treatment. Before each section, a detailed guide to the arrangement and content of chapters is provided by a section introduction. Our hope is that these notes will provide a unifying framework for reading the subsequent chapters. Throughout, we have collaborated with our contributing authors to provide a nonpartisan review of the literature, with a focus on research studies that use traditional empirical scientific methodologies. The book is written and organized to be accessible to the wide range of individuals interested in the fields of body image disturbance, eating disorders, and obesity. As such, the beginning graduate student should find it readable and offering not only a review of the extant data but also directions for future research. Clinicians will find an up-to-date detailing of the current measures and methods for assessment and intervention. Researchers will find cutting-edge summaries of findings and critical discussions of methodological issues offered by the leading scientists in their topic areas. Although research is growing at a fast and furious pace, we also understand that the field, although well past the nascent stage, has yet to fully mature. We are confident, however, that the chapters contained herein provide a distillation of the current state of knowledge, and also offer directions for future research endeavors.

REFERENCES

Albertini, R. S., & Phillips, K. A. (1999). Thirty-three cases of body dysmorphic disorder in children and adolescents. *Journal of the American Academy of Child and Adolescent Psychiatry, 38*, 453–459.

American Psychiatric Association. (1994). *Diagnostic and statistical manual of mental disorders.* Washington, DC: Author.

Calam, R., & Waller, G. (1998). Are eating and psychosocial characteristics in early teenage years useful predictors of eating characteristics in early adulthood? A 7-year longitudinal study. *International Journal of Eating Disorders, 24*, 351–362.

Cattarin, J. A., & Thompson, J. K. (1994). A three-year longitudinal study of body image, eating disturbance and general psychological functioning in adolescent females. *Eating Disorders: The Journal of Treatment and Prevention, 2*, 114–125.

Cusumano, D. L., & Thompson, J. K. (2001). Media influence and body image in 8-11 year old boys and girls: A preliminary report on the Multidimensional Media Influence Scale. *International Journal of Eating Disorders, 29*, 37–44.

Davison, K. K., Markey, C. N., & Birch, L. L. (2000). Etiology of body dissatisfaction and weight concerns in 5-year-old girls. *Appetite, 35*, 143–151.

Devaud, C., Jeannin, A., Narring, F., Ferron, C., & Michaud, P.-A. (1998). Eating disorders among female adolescents in Switzerland. Prevalence and associations with mental and behavioral disorders. *International Journal of Eating Disorders, 24*, 207–216.

Dietz, W. H. (1998). Health consequences of obesity in youth: Childhood predictors of adult disease. *Pediatrics, 101*, 518–525.

Doyle, J., & Bryant-Waugh, R. (2000). Epidemiology. In B. Lask & R. Bryant-Waugh (Eds.), Anorexia nervosa and related eating disorders in childhood and adolescence (2nd ed.) (pp. 41–79). East Sussex, UK: Psychology Press

Fairburn, C. G., & Beglin, S. J. (1990). Studies of the epidemiology of bulimia nervosa. *American Journal of Psychiatry, 147*, 401–408.

Field, A., Camargo, C., Taylor, C. B., Berkey, C., Frazier, L., Gillman, M., & Colditz, G. (1999). Overweight, weight concerns, and bulimic behaviors among girls and boys. *Journal of the American Academy of Adolescent Psychiatry, 38*, 754–760.

Flegal, K. M., Carroll, M. D., Kuczmarski, R. J., & Johnson, C. L. (1998). Overweight and obesity in the United States: Prevalence and trends, 1960–1994. *International Journal of Obesity, 22*, 39–47.

Godart, N. T., Flament, M. F., Lecrubier, Y., & Jeammet, P. (2000). Anxiety disorders in anorexia nervosa and bulimia nervosa: Comorbidity and chronology of appearance. *European Psychiatry, 15*, 38–45.

Gortmaker, S. L., Dietz, W. H., & Cheung, L. W. (1990). Inactivity, diet, and the fattening of America. *Journal of the American Dietetic Association, 90*, 1247–1255,

Hall, C. (1995). Asian eyes: Body image and eating disorders of Asian and Asian American women. *Eating Disorders: The Journal of Treatment and Prevention, 3*, 8–18.

Heinberg, L. J. (1996). Theories of body image disturbance: Perceptual, developmental and sociocultural factors. In J. K. Thompson (Ed.), *Body image, eating disorders, and obesity: An integrative guide for assessment and treatment* (pp. 27–47). Washington, DC: American Psychological Association.

Heinberg, L. H. Thompson, J. K., & Matson, J. L. (2001). Body image dissatisfaction as a motivator for healthy lifestyle change: Is some distress beneficial? In R. Striegel-Moore & L. Smolak (Eds.), Eating disorders: Innovative directions for research and practice (pp. 215–232). Washington, DC: American Psychological Association.

Killen, J. D., Taylor, C. B., Hayward, C., Haydel, K. F., Wilson, D. M., Hammer, L. D., Kraemer, H. C., Blair-Greiner, A., & Strachowski, D. (1996). Weight concerns influence the development of eating disorders: A 4-year prospective study. *Journal of Consulting and Clinical Psychology, 64*, 936–940.

Killen, J. D., Taylor, C. B., Hayward, C., Wilson, C. M., Hammer, L. D., Robinson, T. N., Litt, I., Simmonds, B. A., Haydel, F., Varady, A., & Kraemer, H. C. (1994). The pursuit of thinness and onset of eating disorders symptoms in a community sample of adolescent girls: A three-year prospective analysis. *International Journal of Eating Disorders, 16*, 227–238.

Lask, B. (2000). Eating disturbances in childhood and adolescence. *Current Paediatrics, 10*, 254–258.

Lask, B., & Bryant,-Waugh, R. (2000). *Anorexia nervosa and related eating disorders in adolescence*. East Sussex, UK: Psychology Press.

Lucas, A. R., Beard, C. M., O'Fallon, W. M., & Kurland, L. T. (1991). Fifty-year trends in the incidence of anorexia nervosa in Rochester, Minnesota: A population-based study. *American Journal of Psychiatry, 148*, 917–922.

Lunner, K., Wertheim, E. H., Thompson, J. K., Paxton, S. J., McDonald, F., & Halvaarson, K. S. (2000). A cross-cultural examination of weight-related teasing, body image, and eating disturbance in Swedish and Australian samples. *International Journal of Eating Disorders, 28*, 430–435.

Marchi, M., & Cohen, P. (1990). Early childhood eating behaviors and adolescent eating disorders. *Journal of the American Academy of Child and Adolescent Psychiatry, 29*, 112–117.

McCreary, D. R., & Sasse, D. K. (2000). An exploration of the drive for muscularity in adolescent boys and girls. *Journal of America College Health, 48*, 297–304.

Mellbin, T., & Vuille, J. C. (1989). Rapidly developing overweight in school children as an indicator of psychological stress. *Acta Pediatrica Scandinavica, 78*, 568–575.

Miller, C. T., & Downey, K. T. (1999). A meta-analysis of heavyweight and self-esteem. *Personality and Social Psychology Review, 3*, 68–84.

Muir, S. L., Wertheim, E. H., & Paxton, S. J. (1999). Adolescent girls' first diets: Triggers and the role of multiple dimensions of self-concept. *Eating Disorders: The Journal of Treatment and Prevention, 7*, 259–270.

Must, A., Jaques, P. F., Dallal, G. E., Bajema, C. J., & Dietz W. H. (1992). Long term morbidity and mortality of overweight adolescents: A follow-up of the Harvard Growth Study of 1922-1935. *New England Journal of Medicine, 327*, 1350–1355.

Neumark-Sztainer, D. (1999). The weight dilemma: A range of philosophical perspectives. *International Journal of Obesity, 23* (Suppl. 2), S31–S37.

Neumark-Sztainer, D., Story, M., & Faibisch, L. (1998). Perceived stigmatization among African American and Caucasian adolescent girls. *Journal of Adolescent Health, 23*, 264–270.

Nicholls, D., Chater, R., & Lask, B. (2000). Children into DSM don't go: A comparison of classification systems for eating disorders in childhood and early adolescence. *International Journal of Eating Disorders, 28*, 317–324.

Nicholls, D., & Stanhope, R. (2000). Medical complications of anorexia nervosa in children and young adults. *European Eating Disorders Review, 8*, 170–180.

Parkinson, K., Tovee, M., & Cohen-Tovee, E. (1998). Body shape perceptions of preadolescent and young adolescent children. *European Eating Disorders Review, 6*, 126–135.

Perezmitre, G. G. (1997). Body image disturbances in a Mexican sample of preadolescent students. *Revista Mexicana de Psicologia, 14*, 31–40.

Phillips, K. A. (1996). *The broken mirror: Understanding and treating body dysmorphic disorder*. New York: Oxford University Press.

Phillips, K. A., & Diaz, S. (1997). Gender differences in body dysmorphic disorder. *Journal of Nervous and Mental Disease, 185*, 570–577.

Rosenvinge, J. H., Borgen, J. S., & Boerresen, R. (1999). The prevalence of psychological correlates of anorexia nervosa, bulimia nervosa and binge eating among 15-yr-old students: A controlled epidemiological study. *European Eating Disorders Review, 7*, 382–391.

Sasson, A., Lewin, C., & Roth, D. (1995). Dieting behavior and eating attitudes in Israeli children. *International Journal of Eating Disorders, 17*, 67–72.

Schreiber, G. B., Robins, M., Striegel-Moore, R., Obarzanek, E., Morrison, J. A., & Wright, D. J. (1996). Weight modification efforts reported by Black and White preadolescent girls: National Heart, Lung, and Blood Institute Growth and Health Study. *Pediatrics, 98,* 63–70.

Serdula, M. K., Collins, M. E., Williamson, D. F., Anda, R. F., Pamuk, E., & Byers, T. E. (1993). Weight control practices of U.S. adolescents and adults. *Annals of Internal Medicine, 119,* 667–671.

Shisslak, C. M., Crago, M., & Estes, L. S. (1995). The spectrum of eating disturbances. *International Journal of Eating Disorders, 18,* 209–219.

Smolak, L., Levine, M., & Thompson, J. K. (2001). Body image in adolescent boys and girls as assessed with the Sociocultural Attitudes Towards Appearance Scale. *International Journal of Eating Disorders, 29,* 216–223.

Smolak, L., & Murnen, S. K. (2001). Gender and eating disorders. In R. Striegel-Moore & L. Smolak (Eds.), *Eating disorders: Innovative directions for research and practice* (pp. 91–110). Washington, DC: American Psychological Association.

Smolak, L., & Striegel-Moore, R. (2001). The myth of the golden girl: Ethnicity and eating disorders. In R. Striegel-Moore & L. Smolak (Eds.), *Eating disorders: Innovative directions for research and practice* (pp. 111–132). Washington, DC: American Psychological Association.

Steiner, H., & Lock, J. (1998). Anorexia nervosa and bulimia nervosa in children and adolescents: A review of the past 10 years. *Journal of the American Academy of Child and Adolescent Psychiatry, 37,* 352–359.

Stice, E., & Agras, W. S. (1998). Predicting onset and cessation of bulimic behaviors during adolescence: A longitudinal grouping analysis. *Behavior Therapy, 29,* 257–276.

Stice, E., Cameron, R., Killen, J., Hayward, C., & Taylor, C. B. (1999). Naturalistic weight-reduction efforts prospectively predict growth in relative weight and onset of obesity among female adolescents. *Journal of Consulting and Clinical Psychology, 67,* 967–974.

Stice, E., Hayward, C., Cameron, R., Killen, J., & Taylor, C. (2000). Body image and eating disturbances predict onset of depression among female adolescents: A longitudinal study. *Journal of Abnormal Psychology, 109,* 438–444.

Stice, E., Killen. J. D., Hayward, C., & Taylor, C.B. (1998a). Age of onset for binge eating and purging during late adolescence: A 4-year survival analysis. *Journal of Abnormal Psychology, 107,* 671–675.

Stice, E., Killen, J., Hayward, C., & Taylor, C. B. (1998b). Support for the continuity hypothesis of bulimic pathology. *Journal of Consulting and Clinical Psychology, 66,* 784–790.

Striegel-Moore, R., Schreiber, G. B., Lo, A., Crawford, P., Obarzanek, E., & Rodin, J. (2000). Eating disorder symptoms in a cohort of 11 to 16-year-old Black and White girls: The NHLBI Growth and Health Study. *International Journal or Eating Disorders, 27,* 49–66.

Thompson, J. K. (Ed.). (1996). *Body image, eating disorders, and obesity: An integrative guide for assessment and treatment*. Washington, DC: American Psychological Association.

Thompson, J. K., Coovert, M., Richards, K. J., Johnson, S., & Cattarin, J. (1995). Development of body image, eating disturbance, and general psychological functioning in female adolescents: Covariance structure modeling and longitudinal investigations. *International Journal of Eating Disorders, 18,* 221–236.

Thompson, J. K., & Heinberg, L. J. (1999). The media's influence on body image disturbance and eating disorders: We've reviled them, now can we rehabilitate them? *Journal of Social Issues, 55,* 339–353.

Thompson, J. K., Heinberg, L. J., Altabe, M., & Tantleff-Dunn, S. (1999). *Exacting beauty: Theory, assessment and treatment of body image disturbance*. Washington, DC: American Psychological Association.

Thompson, J. K., & Stice, E. (in press). Internalization of the thin-ideal: Mounting evidence for a new risk factor for body image disturbance and eating pathology. *Current Directions in Psychological Science*.

Troiano, R. P., & Flegal, K. M. (1998). Overweight children and adolescents: Description, epidemiology, and demographics. *Pediatrics, 101,* 497–504.

Vander Wal, J. S., & Thelen, M. H. (2001). Predictors of body image dissatisfaction in elementary-age school girls. *Eating Behaviors, 1,* 1–18.

Wertheim, E. H., Paxton, S. J., Schutz, H. K., & Muir, S. L. (1997). Why do adolescent girls watch their weight? An interview study examining sociocultural pressures to be thin? *Journal of Psychosomatic Research, 42,* 345–355.

Wichstrom, L. (1999). The emergence of gender differences in depressed mood during adolescence: The role of intensified gender socialization. *Developmental Psychology, 35,* 232–245.

Whitaker, R. C., Wright, J. A., Pepe, M. S., Seidel, K. D., & Dietz, W. H. (1997). Predicting obesity in young adulthood from childhood and parental obesity. *New England Journal of Medicine, 337,* 869–873.

Wood, K. C., Becker, J. A., & Thompson, J. K. (1996). Body image dissatisfaction in preadolescent children. *Journal of Applied Developmental Psychology, 17,* 85–100.

I
FOUNDATIONS

There seems to be little doubt that eating disorders and problems begin to develop well before a clinical diagnosis is made. Furthermore, there appears to be real reason to be concerned about body dissatisfaction and weight and shape regulation by children and adolescents.

The goal of the first section of this book is to lay the groundwork for a discussion of eating-related problems among children and adolescents. Jennifer Fisher and Leann Birch begin by discussing the earliest sources and indicators of eating preferences and problems. Their work, including descriptions of prenatal and infancy patterns and influences, will be new to most eating disorder researchers. Eating for neonates is primarily an issue of survival, a response to physiological hunger signals. It is a bit startling to realize how early children lose this survival basis of eating. They did have it; that is one reason why we are so comfortable with the idea of "demand-feeding" infants (Hirschmann & Zaphiropoulos, 1993). Fisher and Birch present substantial empirical information about why and how eating becomes an event imbued with social and personal meaning. The developmental perspective that informs their work does much to help us formulate questions about the meaning of these early phenomena for later development.

Linda Smolak and Michael Levine then provide an overview of body image in children under age 12. Their review makes it clear that body dissatisfaction not only exists among children, particularly among White girls, but that it may also be associated with dangerous behaviors such as dieting both concurrently and prospectively. Indeed, by adolescence, some measure of body dissatisfaction or weight concerns is frequently found to be one of the best predictors of the later development of eating problems (e.g., Killen et al., 1994; Leon, Fulkerson, Perry, & Early-Zaid, 1995; Wertheim, Koerner, & Paxton, in press). Understanding the roots of body dissatisfaction is crucial, then, if we are to ever prevent eating problems and disorders. It is important, therefore, that Smolak and Levine present a model of how body dissatisfaction might develop among young children. This model may help to guide future research to improve our understanding of body image development.

The perspective that sociocultural influences are critical in the etiology of eating problems and disorders is not unusual. Indeed, both Fisher and Birch's and Smolak and Levine's contributions appear to be written from such a perspective. If it is indeed the case that eating problems are heavily rooted in sociocultural influences, it is not surprising that there are ethnic group differences in the rates, and, perhaps, the causes of various eating problems. Jennifer Zoler Dounchis, Helen Hayden, and Denise Wilfley provide an exhaustive review of the rates and features of obesity, body image problems, and eating disorders among children and adolescents from ethnic minority groups. Two messages seem very clear in their chapter. First, there are many studies of ethnic minority children and adolescents. Dounchis and her colleagues have identified more than 60 studies looking at body image and eating problems in these populations and there are additional studies of obesity. There are, of course, many unanswered questions and there is much work to be done. But Dounchis and her colleagues have clearly established a starting point for research and theorizing on ethnic group differences in the development of eating problems.

Their second message is that ethnic minority status does not constitute a homogenous, single variable in the etiology of eating problems. This is clearly very consistent with a sociocultural perspective. There certainly are some similarities among ethnic minority groups—for example, obesity is more of a problem in Black and Hispanic than in White communities. In all groups studied, eating problems appear to be more common in girls than in boys (though research does not always fully address the possible body image problems among boys, including steroid abuse or the overuse of damaging muscle-building techniques). On the other hand, there are important differences among the ethnic minority groups. Black adolescent girls seem to have a somewhat better body image than either Hispanic or White girls. Native American teenage girls seem to have particularly high rates of purging, though the data are admittedly limited. Thus cultural influences, which are as yet poorly delineated, do appear to play a role in the etiology of body image and eating problems.

These three chapters give us a starting point for our discussions of risk factors, assessment, and prevention and treatment of obesity, body image problems, and eating problems by providing basic developmental information. In doing so, they raise provocative and important questions for future research in the etiology of eating problems and disorders.

REFERENCES

Hirschmann, J., & Zaphiropoulos, L. (1993). *Preventing childhood eating problems*. Carlsbad, CA: Gurze.

Killen, J., Taylor, C., Hayward, C., Wilson, D., Haydel, K., Hammer, L., Simmonds, B., Robinson, T., Litt, I., Varady, A., & Kraemer, H. (1994). Pursuit of thinness and onset of eating disorder symptoms in a community sample of adolescent girls: A three year prospective analysis. *International Journal of Eating Disorders*, *16*, 227–238.

Leon, G., Fulkerson, J., Perry, C., & Early-Zaid, M. (1995). Prospective analysis of personality and behavioral vulnerabilities and gender influences in the later development of disordered eating. *Journal of Abnormal Psychology*, *104*, 140–149.

Wertheim, E., Koerner, J., & Paxton, S. (in press). Longitudinal predictors of restrictive eating and bulimic tendencies in three different age groups of adolescent girls. *Journal of Youth and Adolescence*.

1

EARLY EXPERIENCE WITH FOOD AND EATING: IMPLICATIONS FOR THE DEVELOPMENT OF EATING DISORDERS

JENNIFER O. FISHER AND
LEANN L. BIRCH

Throughout early development, food intake patterns reflect interaction between biological processes directed toward growth and conditions of the environment. In fact, the acquisition of food acceptance patterns may be characterized by a responsiveness to dietary exposure and eating experience. Eating patterns develop through repeated exposure to foods and repeated experience with the factors that regulate when eating begins and ends. Dietary experiences differ for each child. These differences, in turn, may serve as a basis for individual differences in the development of eating patterns. We shall see that these environmental influences shape multiple aspects of food acceptance, including the type of food consumed and the amount of food eaten, as well as the period of time separating eating occasions.

In this chapter, we will examine behavioral factors influencing the development of food acceptance patterns from infancy through early childhood. Principal sources of dietary experience will be described at several points of development and discussed in terms of their meaning for food preferences, selection, and the regulation of food intake. Throughout our discussion, we will focus on the pivotal role that parents play in providing early dietary experiences, eating interactions, and in shaping the contexts in which eating occurs. We will present the perspective that familial eating influences serve as a basis for individual differences among children in food selection and food intake regulation patterns. The role of these factors for the development of eating problems will be considered.

THE ROLE OF MATERNAL DIET IN EARLY TASTE
AND FLAVOR EXPERIENCES

When we think of the beginnings of dietary experience, the transition to solid foods or perhaps the decision to breast- or formula-feed, may come to mind. The first influences on dietary experience, in fact, appear to act well before birth, during the period in which nutritionists have traditionally been focused on the role of maternal nutrition in promoting optimal fetal growth. Growing evidence suggests, however, that the influence of maternal nutrition on fetal development extends beyond physical growth and includes effects on dietary experience. We shall see that the dietary environment of the developing fetus is sensitive to changes in maternal dietary patterns and that this source of exposure may set the stage for infants' later acceptance of solid foods.

Amniotic fluid surrounds the fetus to maintain fetal temperature, to serve as a buffer and a vehicle for fetal movement. With the emergence of swallowing and taste mechanisms between the 12th and 14th weeks of gestation, the amniotic fluid also becomes a rich source of sensory exposure for the fetus (Liley, 1972). In addition to a variety of metabolic substrates and by-products, such as glucose, lactic acid, proteins, and urea, the amniotic fluid appears to be sensitive to sensory properties of the maternal diet. For example, Mennella, Johnson, and Beauchamp (1995) found that a sensory panel of adults detected the odor of garlic in the amniotic fluid of four out of five women who consumed capsules containing oil of garlic shortly before undergoing a routine amniocentesis. Although these "transmittable" flavors of the maternal diet are not well characterized, this evidence suggests that experience with dietary flavors begins as the fetus is exposed to tastes and flavors of the maternal diet in utero.

THE INFLUENCE OF BREAST FEEDING
AND FORMULA FEEDING

At first glance, infant dietary experience during the first few months of life appears to be relatively straightforward because milk, provided by either breast milk or formula, constitutes the sole source of infant nutrition. Despite the relative simplicity of options, however, the choice to breast- or formula-feed may initiate very different trajectories with respect to influences on infants' flavor experiences, as well as their control of food intake.

Mothers' breast milk carries flavors of the maternal diet that appear in amniotic fluid. In one study, a sensory panel detected a garlic odor in samples of breast milk from women who consumed garlic capsules two hours before testing (Mennella & Beauchamp, 1991a). Comparable results were obtained when alcohol (Mennella & Beauchamp, 1991b) and vanilla extract (Mennella & Beauchamp, 1996a) were ingested by lactating women. Exposure to these flavors results in systematic alteration of infants' sucking rate and milk intake (Mennella & Beauchamp, 1991b, 1993, 1994, 1996a). These findings indicate that the earliest infant diet, consisting solely of human breast milk, does not provide a fixed and unidimensional dietary experience. Rather, breast milk appears to expose the infant to a changing taste environment that, in turn, results in modified feeding behavior. In contrast, the flavor experiences of the formula-fed infant may be much more constant and less varied. As we shall see, breast- and formula-fed infants may have very different experiences with flavors of the adult diet at the start of the weaning period.

In addition to its influence on flavor experience and food acceptance, breast versus bottle feeding may provide very different experiences in terms of the balance in control of feeding between mother and infant. Infants eat primarily to satisfy energy needs, and infants are responsive to the energy density of their diet. Limited evidence indicates that infants have some ability to self-regulate caloric intake by adjusting the volume of milk consumed to maintain a relatively constant energy intake (Fomon, 1993; Fomon, Filer, Thomas, Anderson, & Nelson, 1975). For instance, Fomon et al. (1975) observed that infants consumed more of a dilute formula in comparison to a more concentrated formula preparation. Because the breast-feeding mother does not have visual cues regarding the volume of any given feed, she may be much more dependent on and responsive to cues from the infant to initiate or terminate feeding. In this case, feeding is likely to end when the infant's sucking rate slows or stops, and the mother assumes that the infant is satiated. This perspective is consistent with the finding that the volume of feeding in breast-fed infants is not constrained by milk availability (Dewey, Heinig, Nommsen, & Lonnerdal, 1991). In contrast, bottle feeding provides the mother with relatively more information about her infant's intake. The amount of milk remaining in the bottle may not only give the mother an accurate idea of how much the infant has consumed at each feeding but also how much the infant consumes over the course of a day. As a natural consequence, mothers who choose to bottle feed may assume a more active role in determining when feeding begins and ends, as well as how much is consumed at each meal. These differences in mothers' approach to breast and bottle feeding may impart very different information to the infant about satiety; namely, the conditions under which feeding is terminated. For the breast-fed infant, meal termination may align closely with infant cues signaling fullness. In contrast, formula-fed infants may feed past fullness to the extent that infant cues about fullness are secondary to the mothers' control of feeding.

Whether differences in maternal control that tend to covary with feeding regimen have consequences for infants' ability to regulate intake is unknown. The potential for later problems of energy balance may be introduced when infant cues regarding fullness are less influential determinants of meal termination than maternal feeding decisions (Wright, Fawcett, & Crow, 1980). A recent study (Fisher, Birch, Smiciklas-Wright, & Picciano, 2000) supports this view. Breast feeding through the first year of life was associated with lower levels of maternal control in feeding. In this case, mothers who breast fed through the first year tended to report that the timing and amount consumed during infant feeding should be less regulated by the parent and more regulated by the infant in comparison to those mothers who did not breast feed through the first year. Although additional research is needed to control for the confounding influence of feeding method with other factors, such as maternal education that covary with feeding practices, one study found a lasting protective effect of breast feeding on obesity status during adolescence (Elliott, Kjolhede, Gournis, & Rasmussen, 1997).

One area that is virtually unexplored with regard to early feeding interactions between infant and caregiver is how feeding may become involved in the infant's regulation of distress. Parents may experience considerable concern during the first months of life while attempting to identify and distinguish various sources of distress and discomfort in their infant. Sources of distress may be quite numerous, such as startle, fatigue, illness, physical discomfort in clothes or blankets, and sensory overstimulation. Some parents, however, may use feeding as a nonspecific response to varying types of infant distress. For example, pacifiers may be used to induce nonnutritive sucking behavior. Alternatively, food or a bottle may also be provided to quiet the distressed infant. Of interest is the extent to which eating is paired with distress cues other than hunger. Research should examine whether the use of eating to diminish non–hunger-related emotional distress imparts particular responsiveness to external factors in eating.

FOOD ACCEPTANCE PATTERNS DURING THE TRANSITION TO SOLID FOODS

Introduction to semisolid foods generally begins in the United States around the fourth month of life. During this time, the role of infant taste preferences in dietary experience is highlighted. Infants are born with a preference for sweet, rejection of sour and bitter, and general indifference for the taste of salt (Bartoshuk & Beauchamp, 1994; Desor, Maller, & Anders, 1975; Desor, Maller, & Turner, 1973). These taste preferences are unlearned and consistent in their general effects on food intake. In general, sweet foods, such as juices or flavored yogurts, are more easily accepted relative to those containing bitter taste constituents. Taste acceptance, however, may not readily translate into food acceptance; infants and young children tend to initially reject new foods. This "neophobic" response is thought to originate from learned safety behavior, where a tentative approach to new foods serves an adaptive role to guard against poisoning. Work by Kalat and Rozin (1973) indicates that the initial neophobia is reduced and the food is accepted as safe when repeated opportunities to consume a new food are not followed by illness. The powerful role of experience in food acceptance is underscored by the fact that repeated exposure even facilitates acceptance of foods containing disliked tastes. For example, Mennella and Beauchamp (1996b) observed that infants who were exposed to the bitter components of protein hydrolysate formulas were more likely to accept that type of formula at later points in infancy than were those infants who had not been exposed to the taste.

Thus repeated exposure to flavors may play an important role in food acceptance during the transition to solid foods by modifying infants' response to novel foods. A recent study reveals that infants' exposure to a new food increases their acceptance of a similar food (Birch, Gunder, Grimm-Thomas, & Laing, 1998). These findings are consistent with earlier work by Sullivan and Birch (1991) in which six-month-old infants' acceptance of foods was enhanced by providing those foods on repeated occasions. This effect was most notable for breast-fed infants, indicating that repeated exposure to flavors of the maternal diet may facilitate food acceptance by providing the infant with varied flavor experiences. Differences in flavor experience between the formula and breast-fed infant form the basis of individual differences of early food acceptance patterns. Research with animals indicates that repeated exposure to flavors of the maternal diet experienced by the infant in mothers' milk fosters preferences for similarly flavored foods during weaning. Flavors of the maternal diet ingested during nursing tend to be preferred in diets of weanling animals (Capretta & Rawls, 1974; Galef & Henderson, 1972; Galef & Sherry, 1975). Thus breast-fed infants may more readily accept solid foods than formula-fed infants because of greater exposure to the flavors of the maternal diet in breast milk. In addition, animals exposed to a greater variety of flavors in breast milk are subsequently more likely to accept novel flavors during weaning (Capretta, Petersik, & Stewart, 1975). This route of transmission of flavor experience from mother to child also suggests the possibility that maternal dietary variety may affect the breadth of flavors experienced in utero, and in turn affect the variety of foods that are readily accepted by the infant.

The fact that breast feeding may facilitate the transition to solid foods raises the question of whether, in doing so, breast feeding may also influence maternal control of feeding during this period. To the extent that breast-fed infants more readily accept solid foods, less maternal control and encouragement may be required to facilitate toddlers' consumption of new foods during this period. This perspective is supported by the observation that breast feeding through the first year is associated with lower amounts of maternal control in feeding (Fisher et. al., 2000). In addition, infants who more readily accept new foods may be considered "easier" to feed, and elicit less maternal frustration and concern regarding feeding.

EARLY CHILDHOOD AND THE ROLE OF EATING SOCIALIZATION IN SHAPING FOOD ACCEPTANCE PATTERNS

As they make the transition to the adult diet of their culture, children are exposed to vast amounts of information regarding the meaning of food and eating. Although young children consume approximately 30% of their energy intake from snacks (Stanek, Abbott, & Cramer, 1990), an increasing percentage of eating takes place in meal-like settings. In these contexts, children learn where eating is acceptable—whether eating always takes place at a family table, or may occur in other settings such as in front of a television, in one's room, or at the grocery store. Children also receive information about the times of day when eating is appropriate, such as when dinner is eaten each night and whether eating a snack before bed is allowed. Information regarding the structure of eating occasions is also imparted and reinforced with the repeated experience of eating meals. Children learn manners and adopt cuisine rules regarding how foods are eaten—whether with a spoon or with their hands—and at what type of eating occasions those foods are consumed. For instance, children tend to prefer particular foods at the times of day when it is considered culturally appropriate to eat those foods (Birch, Billman, & Richards, 1984). Children also learn these food rules change in different environments, such as at a day care setting or at a friend's house.

For most children, eating alone is much more novel than eating among other children and family members; children's food preferences and eating patterns develop in social environments. Eating with others indicates which people are usually present at meals and how those individuals act and interact at meals. The impact of social influences on the development of children's food acceptance patterns is illustrated in work showing age-related changes in children's ideas about what foods are appropriate and inappropriate to eat. In work by Rozin and colleagues (Rozin, Hammer, Oster, Horowitz, & Marmara, 1986), older children were much less likely to consume culturally unacceptable combinations of foods, such as cookies with catsup, than their younger counterparts. In addition, older children found nonfood substances, such as grasshoppers and dirt, less acceptable than younger children.

Social influences may modify children's food acceptance patterns via observational learning as well as through the direct interaction that social experiences provide. Rozin and Kennel (1983) demonstrated the powerful role of observational learning in research on preference for chili peppers in monkeys. Although the taste of chili is accepted and liked by many humans, it is not accepted by other omnivores. Observing their keepers eating chili-flavored food was the only learning paradigm that facilitated acceptance of chili, a flavor rejected by nonhumans. Social learning was also involved in human acceptance of the chili taste. Exposure to older models consuming "hot" foods induced Mexican children to taste and eat small quantities of the foods (Rozin & Schiller, 1980). These findings suggest that young children may be quite sensitive to the preferences and eating behaviors of the individuals in their eating environment.

Parents and caregivers may serve as especially salient eating models because of their direct authority over the foods that come into the home, as well as many of the feeding decisions that affect the child. Children may also draw from the eating behavior of their siblings and peers as play behavior emerges and opportunities to eat with playmates and with peer groups in day care settings increase. Birch (1980) found that children's preferences and selection of a relatively disliked vegetable was facilitated by exposing the child to a peer group in which members displayed a preference for the "disliked" vegetable.

PARENTAL CONTROL IN CHILD FEEDING

At the same time that children learn about eating by observing the eating behavior of others, changes begin to occur in the dynamics of their social interactions surrounding eating. In particular, growing children become more independent and strive for greater autonomy and control over their eating. The developing ability to verbally articulate needs and wants about eating facilitates children's participation in eating decisions. As a consequence, children are increasingly able to provide input about when and what kinds of foods they want to eat, as well as when eating should begin and end. Although these changes reflect a growing self-sufficiency on the part of the child, the feeding interactions brought about with this stage of development do not necessarily make child-feeding easier for parent or child.

Because children eat frequently throughout each day, eating can become a focal context for parent–child control issues. For instance, parents may encounter more conflict over routine feeding decisions that were previously made without negotiation. The balance of parent–child control in feeding appears to have a formative influence on children's eating; the ability to self-regulate eating is determined, in part, by the extent to which parents provide structure in eating while also allowing the child a degree of autonomy in eating.

At any point in development, large differences may exist among parents in the extent to which they allow the child to control eating, including the timing of meals, as well as what and how much is eaten. Costanzo and Woody (1985) have contended that excessive control is imposed in feeding when that area of child behavior is important to the parent and potentially problematic for either parent or child. For example, societal values on thinness in females may cause parents of young girls to be particularly aware of what their own eating as well as that of their daughter means for the child's "risk" of developing eating or weight problems (Costanzo & Woody, 1984). As a consequence, parental influence in their daughters' eating may be especially heightened when parents perceive "risk." This perspective is supported by empirical work indicating that mothers' own restrained eating and their preschool-aged daughters' overweight is positively associated with maternal control in feeding (Birch & Fisher, 2000; Francis & Birch, 1999).

Differences among parents in control of child feeding have important implications for the development of children's food preferences, selection, and intake regulation. Young children possess the ability to adequately self-regulate energy intake within a meal (Birch & Deysher, 1985, 1986) and over the course of the day (Birch, Johnson, Andresen, Peters, & Schulte, 1991; Birch, Johnson, Jones, & Peters, 1993; Shea, Stein, Basch, Contento, & Zybert, 1992). However, large individual differences in children's ability to regulate energy intake are apparent by the preschool period. These differences among children are traceable, in part, to differences among their parents in the amount of control imposed in child feeding. Johnson and Birch (1994) found that high levels of parental control in child feeding were negatively associated with children's ability to regulate energy intake. These findings are consistent with the perspective that increasing amounts of parental control in feeding decrease children's opportunities to exercise and develop self-control in eating (Costanzo & Woody, 1985).

EXCESSIVE CONTROL IN FEEDING: CREATING FOOD DISLIKES, FORBIDDEN FRUIT, AND PROBLEMS OF SELF-CONTROL

Recent survey data indicates that parents often have good reason to exert control over their child's eating behavior; most children aged 2 to 19 fail to meet all guidelines specified by the food guide pyramid and have diets containing too much fat and sugar and few fruits and vegetables (Krebs-Smith et al., 1996; Muñoz, Krebs-Smith, Ballard-Barbash, & Cleveland, 1997). Indeed, parental attempts to increase children's intake of nutrient-rich foods, such as fruits and vegetables, may be directed at ensuring adequate nutrition to promote growth and well-being. Conversely, feeding practices that restrict children's intake of foods high in fat and sugar may occur in response to parents' awareness of an increasing focus on health risks associated with overweight and dieting behavior in children. Although these approaches may seem like straightforward means of creating healthful eating patterns in their children, mounting evidence indicates that excessive pressure and restriction in child feeding may have unintended and paradoxical effects on children's eating. Restriction may enhance children's preferences for and intake of restricted foods, whereas parental directives to eat may result in food dislike and refusal to eat. Both aspects of control may generally (a) decrease children's eating choices, (b) focus children on "external" eating cues (such as the amount left on the plate), and (c) devalue children's own hunger and fullness as the primary determinants of when eating begins and ends.

Restricting children's access to foods appears paradoxically to turn those foods into "forbidden fruits" in children's eating. Children's preferences are enhanced for foods that are offered as a reward for the completion of another task (Birch, Zimmerman, & Hind, 1980; Lepper, Sagotsky, Dafoe, & Greene, 1982). In addition, placing a preferred food in sight, but out of reach, decreases children's capacity to exercise self-control over obtaining that food (Mischel & Ebbesen, 1970; Mischel, Shoda, & Rodriguez, 1989). Although children's intake of restricted foods is limited while parental restriction is imposed, recent work by Fisher and Birch (1999a, 1999b) indicates that restriction may cause children to have difficulties in controlling their eating when restriction is not in effect and "forbidden" foods are present. Mothers' reports of restricting their preschool-aged daughters' access to palatable snack foods were positively associated with daughters' intakes when given free access to those foods immediately after a meal (Fisher & Birch, 1999a). In experimental research, Fisher and Birch (1999b) observed that restricting children's access to a snack food increased their subsequent behavioral response to that food and promoted its selection and intake. These studies indicate that restriction may diminish children's ability to self-control food intake if their own hunger and satiety cues take a secondary role to the availability of palatable, "forbidden" foods. Finally, parental restrictions imposed in child feeding may result in negative self-evaluation among children. Children as young as two years of age appear to be able to compare their behavior with parental standards (Burhans & Dweck,

1995). Work by Klesges and colleagues (Klesges, Stein, Eck, Isbell, & Klesges, 1991) illustrates that even young children understand parental expectations for the limited consumption of certain foods; young children decreased food choices that were high in sugar when told that their mothers would be evaluating their food selections. A recent study from our laboratory suggests that restriction may cause children to equate their consumption of a "forbidden" or "bad for you" food with "bad" behavior (Fisher & Birch, 2000). Parents' restriction predicted their 5-year-old daughters' intake when provided free access to restricted foods. In addition, parental restriction independently predicted how their daughters felt about their eating; high levels of restriction were associated with daughters' perceptions of eating too much and feeling bad about it. Thus restricting children's access to foods may create an eating environment in which children are overtly focused on the restricted foods and their responses to restriction. Although conveying a behavioral expectation to avoid particular foods, parents' use of restriction may also set children up for failure by increasing children's desire to obtain and consume those "forbidden" foods when present.

In contrast to the effects of restriction on children's eating, much less is known about how parents' pressure on children to eat may modify children's eating behavior. One study suggested that pressure may increase intake in the short-term. Behavioral observations of young children eating with their mothers indicated that children's food refusals were usually followed by parental prompts to eat and, in turn, a higher probability that the child would eat the food (Klesges et al., 1983). Limited evidence, however, suggests that pressure in feeding may ultimately discourage children's intake of "encouraged" foods. For instance, children's preferences decrease for foods that are used instrumentally (Birch, Marlin, & Rotter, 1984). Thus pressuring children to eat their vegetables to leave the table or have dessert ultimately may serve to only decrease children's liking of those vegetables. Other research suggests that parental pressure may reduce children's responsiveness to internal cues of hunger and satiety. Birch and colleagues (Birch, McPhee, Shoba, Steinberg, & Krehbiel, 1987) demonstrated that children's ability to respond to the energy density of the foods they consume was diminished by adult directives to "clean their plates." Finally, recent work from our laboratory showed a negative association between parents' pressure to eat and daughters' calcium intake (Birch, Fisher, Smiciklas-Wright, & Mitchell, 1999). In this study, parents with low calcium intakes reported using more pressure in feeding their 5-year-old daughters but had daughters with lower calcium intakes. In contrast, parents' calcium intake was positively related to their daughters' calcium intake through similarities in milk consumption; parents reporting more frequent milk intake had daughters who consumed more milk.

MODELING AND PARENTING EFFECTS ON CHILDREN'S EATING: TRANSFER OF PROBLEMATIC CONTROL OF EATING AND WEIGHT FROM PARENT TO CHILD AS A BASIS FOR FAMILY RESEMBLANCES

Parental influences on children's eating may not only affect children's eating experience and development but may also promote intergenerational transfer of eating behavior. Spouses tend to have similar nutrient intakes (Grimm-Thomas, Hoefling, & Birch, 1999; Lee & Kolonel, 1982; Patterson, Rupp, Sallis, Atkins, & Nader, 1988), and children's nutrient intakes reflect the diets of their parents (Laskarzewski et al., 1980; Oliveria et al., 1992; Patterson et al., 1988). Parents have the potential to shape these similarities by making the foods they consume available to their children, by serving as influential eating models, and by exerting control in child feeding. Studies examining multiple avenues of parental influence are needed to shed light on how eating behavior is transferred from one generation to the next.

Several recent studies from our laboratory indicate that parent–child similarities in problematic regulation of intake are present at an early point in development and particularly apparent for mothers and daughters. One recent study, by Cutting, Fisher, Grimm-Thomas, and Birch (1999) provided evidence that mothers' influence on their preschool-aged daughters' eating behavior may also convey information about how food intake is regulated. In that study, mothers' reports of their own disinhibited eating were positively associated with their preschool-aged daughters' intake of foods eaten beyond fullness. In this procedure, daughters were given free access to a variety of energy-dense snack foods immediately after having eaten lunch. Daughters' intakes in this setting resembled their mothers' reports of disinhibited eating: an enhanced responsiveness to external cues in eating. Information about eating that is transferred from mother to child appears to extend well beyond that of what and how much is eaten. For example, two studies have observed similarities in mother–daughter levels of dietary restraint (Hill, Weaver, & Blundell, 1990; Ruther & Richman, 1993). Research currently being conducted in our laboratory on the emergence of early dieting in girls shows a similar pattern of findings. Mothers who engaged in unhealthy dieting behaviors had 5-year-old daughters who reported higher weight concerns and were twice as likely to possess awareness of and knowledge about dieting (Abramovitz & Birch, 2000). These findings suggest that mothers shape their daughters' orientation to weight issues as well as to the dieting "tools" used to act on those concerns.

Modeling and parenting influences on children's eating and weight problems may be particularly pronounced when energy-dense foods are involved. Consider the example of parents' intake of high-fat desserts. Parents who enjoy high-fat desserts may tend to keep those types of foods in the home and exhibit particular habits of eating these foods. Children may observe that high-fat desserts constitute a focal part of the family dinner or of family time together, such as watching movies or playing board games. In addition, children may observe that parents not only express like for high-fat desserts but preferentially consume those foods. Because children readily form preferences for energy-dense foods (Johnson, McPhee, & Birch, 1991; Kern, McPhee, Fisher, Johnson, & Birch, 1993), repeated opportunities to consume high-fat desserts may enhance the effects of parental modeling on children's intake of such desserts. Research is needed to understand how the "family" diet interacts with parents' eating behavior and feeding practices to shape eating and weight problems in their children.

IMPLICATIONS FOR PREVENTION OF CHILDHOOD EATING PROBLEMS

Parents provide children with a model of eating behavior, the eating environment in which children's eating patterns emerge, and the feeding strategies used to structure children's eating. Converging evidence indicates that healthful patterns of eating develop in environments that provide children with diverse experiences with flavors and foods, exposure to eating models who exhibit healthful eating patterns, and repeated opportunities to make choices regarding what and how much to eat. Prevention efforts aimed at avoiding childhood eating problems should involve parenting skills that encourage variety and moderation, as well as those that help children make reasonable choices about what and how much to consume. At first glance, pressure and restriction in child feeding might appeal to parents as an effective means of guiding children's eating. These types of overly controlling strategies, however, may produce antithetical effects on children's food liking and intakes when children are given the opportunity to make their own choices. Thus prevention efforts should not focus solely on the quality of the choices that children make but rather on the overall quality of the choices that are made available to children. Ample opportunities should be provided in which children can experience and consume the foods that should be consumed in greatest proportion, such as fruits, vegetables, and grains. Parents should provide a model for their children of healthy eating patterns, including eating a variety of foods, particularly fruits and vegetables, and eating energy-dense foods in moderation. Finally, children's internal cues should be the primary determinant of child feeding decisions regarding when to begin and finish eating.

CONCLUSION

In conclusion, food acceptance patterns are shaped by eating experiences that begin well before birth and extend throughout early childhood. Experiences with tastes, foods, and factors that determine how eating is regulated may shed light on how individual differences in eating behavior are established. Progression toward an adult-like diet of the culture occurs as children learn about the meaning of food and eating. This learning occurs as children observe and interact with the people in their eating environments. Parents play a crucial role in the development of children's eating by providing foods, serving as eating models, and establishing control dynamics in feeding. Parental control in child feeding may have unintended effects on the development of eating patterns: emphasis on "external" cues in eating and decreased opportunities for the child to experience *self*-control in eating. Excessive parental influence on the factors that regulate meal initiation and termination may result in problems of energy balance throughout infancy and childhood. In addition, parental pressure to eat may result in food dislikes and refusal, and restriction may enhance children's liking and consumption of restricted foods. The amount of control imposed in child feeding can be linked to parent and child "risk" factors for weight and eating problems. Because thinness and restrained eating are particularly valued in females, parents may perceive greater risk for their daughters than for their sons. Parental control in feeding as well as parental eating behaviors may result in similarities between parent and child in the regulation of eating and weight. This view suggests that the etiology of eating problems may be found in children's earliest experiences with food and eating.

REFERENCES

Abramovitz, B. A., & Birch, L. L. (2000). Five-year-old girls' ideas about dieting are predicted by mothers' dieting. *Journal of The American Dietetic Association*, 100, 1157–1163.

Bartoshuk, L. M., & Beauchamp, G. K. (1994). Chemical senses. *Annual Review of Psychology*, 45, 414–449.

Birch, L. L. (1980). Effects of peer models' food choices and eating behaviors on preschoolers' food preferences. *Child Development*, 51, 489–496.

Birch, L. L., Billman, J., & Richards, S. (1984). Time of day influences food acceptability. *Appetite*, 5, 109–112.

Birch, L. L., & Deysher, M. (1985). Conditioned and unconditioned caloric compensation: Evidence for self-regulation of food intake by young children. *Learning and Motivation*, 16, 341–355.

Birch, L. L., & Deysher, M. (1986). Caloric compensation and sensory specific satiety: Evidence for self-regulation of food intake by young children. *Appetite, 7*, 323–331.

Birch, L. L., & Fisher, J. O. (2000). Mothers' child-feeding practices influence daughters' eating and weight. *American Journal of Clinical Nutrition, 71*, 1054–1061.

Birch, L. L., Fisher, J. O., Smiciklas-Wright., & Mitchell, D. (1999). Eat as I do not as I say: Parental influences on young girls' calcium intakes. *The FASEB Journal, 13*, A593.

Birch, L. L., Gunder, L., Grimm-Thomas, L., & Laing, D. G. (1998). Infants' consumption of a new food enhances acceptance of a similar food. *Appetite, 30*, 283–295.

Birch, L. L., Johnson, S. L., Andresen, G., Peters, J. C., & Schulte, M. C. (1991). The variability of young children's energy intake. *The New England Journal of Medicine, 324*, 232–235.

Birch, L. L., Johnson, S. L., Jones, M. B., & Peters, J. C. (1993). Effects of a non-energy fat substitute on children's energy and macronutrient intake. *The American Journal of Clinical Nutrition, 58*, 326–333.

Birch, L. L., Marlin, D. W., & Rotter, J. (1984). Eating as the "means" activity in a contingency: Effects on young children's food preference. *Child Development, 55*, 431–439.

Birch, L. L., McPhee, L., Shoba, B. C., Steinberg, L., & Krehbiel, R. (1987). "Clean up your plate": Effects of child feeding practices on the conditioning of meal size. *Learning and Motivation, 18*, 301–317.

Birch, L. L., Zimmerman, S. I., & Hind, H. (1980). The influence of social-affective context on the formation of children's food preferences. *Child Development, 51*, 856–861.

Burhans, K. K., & Dweck, C. S. (1995). Helplessness in early childhood: The role of contingent worth. *Child Development, 66*, 1719–1738.

Capretta, P. J., Petersik, J. T., & Stewart, D. J. (1975). Acceptance of novel flavours is increased after early experience of diverse taste. *Nature, 254*, 689–691.

Capretta, P. J., & Rawls, L. H. (1974). Establishment of a flavor preference in rats: Importance of nursing and weaning experience. *Journal of Comparative and Physiological Psychology, 86*, 670–673.

Costanzo, P. R., & Woody, E. Z. (1984). Parental perspectives on obesity in children: The importance of sex differences. *Journal of Social and Clinical Psychology, 2*, 305–313.

Costanzo, P. R., & Woody, E. Z. (1985). Domain-specific parenting styles and their impact on the child's development of particular deviance: The example of obesity proneness. *Journal of Social and Clinical Psychology, 3*, 425–445.

Cutting, T. M., Fisher, J. O., Grimm-Thomas, K., & Birch, L. L. (1999). Like mother, like daughter: Familial patterns of overweight are mediated by mothers' dietary disinhibition. *American Journal of Clinical Nutrition, 69*, 608–613.

Desor, J. A., Maller, O., & Anders, K. (1975). Ingestive responses of human newborns to salt, sour, and bitter stimuli. *Journal of Comparative and Physiological Psychology, 89,* 966–970.

Desor, J. A., Maller, O., & Turner, R. (1973). Taste in acceptance of sugars by human infants. *Journal of Comparative and Physiological Psychology, 84,* 496–501.

Dewey, K. G., Heinig, J., Nommsen, L. A., & Lonnerdal, B. (1991). Maternal versus infant factors related to breast milk intake and residual milk volume: The DARLING study. *Pediatrics, 87,* 829–837.

Elliott, K. G., Kjolhede, C. L., Gournis, E., & Rasmussen, K. M. (1997). Duration of breast-feeding associated with obesity during adolescence. *Obesity Research, 5,* 538–541.

Fisher, J. O., & Birch, L. L. (1999a). Restricting access to foods and children's eating. *Appetite, 32,* 405–419.

Fisher, J. O., & Birch, L. L. (1999b). Restricting access to palatable foods affects children's behavioral response, food selection and intake. *The American Journal of Clinical Nutrition, 69,* 1264–1272.

Fisher, J. O., & Birch, L. L. (2000). Parents' restrictive feeding practices are associated with young girls' negative self-evaluation about eating. *Journal of the American Dietetic Association, 100,* 1341–1346.

Fisher, J. O., Birch, L. L., Smiciklas-Wright, H., & Picciano, M. F. (2000). Breast-feeding through the first year predicts maternal control in feeding and subsequent toddler energy intakes. *Journal of the American Dietetic Association, 100,* 641–646.

Fomon, S. J. (1993). *Nutrition of normal infants.* St. Louis, MO: Mosby-Year Books.

Fomon, S. J., Filer, L. J., Thomas, L. N., Anderson, T. A., & Nelson, S. E. (1975). Influence of formula concentration on caloric intake and growth of normal infants. *Acta Pediatrica Scandinavica, 64,* 172–181.

Francis, L. A., & Birch, L. L. (1999). 5-year-old girls' overweight and dietary intake predicts maternal control of child feeding. *The FASEB Journal, 13,* A593.

Galef, B. G., & Henderson, P. W. (1972). Mother's milk: A determinant of the feeding preferences of weaning rat pups. *Journal of Comparative Physiological and Psychology, 78,* 213–219.

Galef, B. G., & Sherry, D. F. (1975). Mother's milk: A medium for transmission of cues reflecting the flavor of mother's diet. *Journal of Comparative Physiology and Psychology, 83,* 374–378.

Grimm-Thomas, K., Hoefling, G. D., & Birch, L. L. (1999). Similarities in spouses' intake and BMI: Implications for environmental influences. *The FASEB Journal, 13,* A264.

Hill, A. J., Weaver, C., & Blundell, J. E. (1990). Dieting concerns of 10-year-old girls and their mothers. *British Journal of Clinical Psychology, 29,* 346–348.

Johnson, S. L., & Birch, L. L. (1994). Parents' and children's adiposity and eating style. *Pediatrics, 94,* 653–661.

Johnson, S. L., McPhee, L., & Birch, L. L. (1991). Conditioned preferences: Young children prefer flavors associated with high dietary fat. *Physiology & Behavior, 50*, 1245–1251.

Kalat, J. W., & Rozin, P. (1973). "Learned safety" as a mechanism of long-delay taste aversion learning in rats. *Journal of Comparative and Physiological Psychology, 83*, 198–207.

Kern, D. L., McPhee, L., Fisher, J., Johnson, S., & Birch, L. L. (1993). The postingestive consequences of fat condition preferences for flavors associated with high dietary fat. *Physiology & Behavior, 54*, 71–76.

Klesges, R. C., Coates, T. J., Brown, G., Sturgeon-Tillisch, J., Moldenhauer-Klesges, L. M., Holzer, B., Woolfrey, J., & Vollmer, J. (1983). Parental influences on children's eating behavior and relative weight. *Journal of Applied Behavior Analysis, 10*, 371–378.

Klesges, R. C., Stein, R. J., Eck, L.H., Isbell, T. R., & Klesges, L. M. (1991). Parental influence on food selection in young children and its relationships to childhood obesity. *American Journal of Clinical Nutrition, 53*, 859–864.

Krebs-Smith, S. M., Cook, A., Subar, A. F., Cleveland, L., Friday, J., & Kahle, L. L. (1996). Fruit and vegetable intakes of children and adolescents in the United States. *Archives of Pediatric and Adolescent Medicine, 150*, 81–860.

Laskarzewski, P., Morrison, J. A., Khoury, P., Kelly K., Glatfelter, L., Larsen, R., & Glueck, C. J. (1980). Parent-child nutrient intake interrelationships in school children ages 6 to 19: The Princeton School District Study. *The American Journal of Clinical Nutrition, 33*, 2350–2355.

Lee, J., & Kolonel, L. N. (1982). Nutrient intakes of husbands and wives: Implications for epidemiologic research. *American Journal of Epidemiology, 115*, 515–525.

Lepper, M. R., Sagotsky, G., Dafoe, J. L., & Greene, D. (1982). Consequences of superfluous social constraints: Effects on young children's social inferences and subsequent intrinsic interest. *Journal of Personality and Social Psychology, 42*, 51–65.

Liley, A. W. (1972). Disorders of amniotic fluid. In N. S. Assali (Ed.), *Pathophysiology of gestation: Fetal placental disorders* (Vol. 2). San Diego, CA: Academic Press.

Mennella, J. A., & Beauchamp, G. K. (1991a). Maternal diet alters the sensory qualities of human milk and the nursling's behavior. *Pediatrics, 88*, 737–744.

Mennella, J. A., & Beauchamp, G. K. (1991b). The transfer of alcohol to human milk: Effects on flavor and the infant's behavior. *New England Journal of Medicine, 325*, 981–985.

Mennella, J. A., & Beauchamp, G. K. (1993). The effects of repeated exposure to garlic-flavored milk on the nursling's behavior. *Pediatric Research, 34*, 805–808.

Mennella, J. A., & Beauchamp, G. K. (1994). The infant's response to flavored milk. *Infant Behavior and Development, 17*, 819.

Mennella, J. A., & Beauchamp, G. K. (1996a). The infant's responses to vanilla flavors in mother's milk and formula. *Infant Behavior and Development, 19*, 13–19.

Mennella, J. A., & Beauchamp, G. K. (1996b). Developmental changes in the acceptance of protein hydrolysate formula. *Journal of Developmental & Behavioral Pediatrics, 17,* 386–391.

Mennella, J. A., Johnson, A., & Beauchamp, G. K. (1995). Garlic ingestion by pregnant women alters the odor of amniotic fluid. *Chemical Senses, 20,* 207–209.

Mischel, W., & Ebbesen, E. B. (1970). Attention in delay of gratification. *Journal of Personality and Social Psychology, 16,* 329–337.

Mischel, W., Shoda, Y., & Rodriguez, M. L. (1989). Delay of gratification in children. *Science, 244,* 933–938.

Muñoz, K. A., Krebs-Smith, S. M., Ballard-Barbash, R., Cleveland, L. E. (1997). Food intakes of US children and adolescents compared with recommendations. *Pediatrics, 100,* 323–329.

Oliveria, S. A., Ellison, R. C., Moore, L. L., Gillman, M. W., Garrahie, E. J., & Singer, M. R. (1992). Parent-child relationships in nutrient intake: The Framingham children's study. *American Journal of Clinical Nutrition, 56,* 593–598.

Patterson, T. L., Rupp, J. W., Sallis, J. F., Atkins, C. J., & Nader, P. R. (1988). Aggregation of dietary calories, fats, and sodium in Mexican-American and Anglo families. *American Journal of Preventive Medicine, 4,* 75–82.

Rozin, P., Hammer, L., Oster, H., Horowitz, T., & Marmara, V. (1986). The child's conception of food: Differentiation of categories of rejected substances in the 1.4 to 5 year age range. *Appetite, 7,* 141–151.

Rozin, P., & Kennel, K. (1983). Acquired preferences for piquant foods by chimpanzees. *Appetite, 4,* 69–77.

Rozin, P., & Schiller, D. (1980). The nature and acquisition of a preference for chili pepper in humans. *Behavior and Emotion, 4,* 77–101.

Ruther, N. M., & Richman, C. L. (1993). The relationship between mothers' eating restraint and their children's attitudes and behaviors. *Bulletin of the Psychonomic Society, 31,* 217–220.

Shea, S., Stein, A. D., Basch, C. E., Contento, I., & Zybert, P. (1992). Variability and self-regulation of energy intake in young children in their everyday environment. *Pediatrics, 90,* 542–546.

Stanek, K., Abbott, D., & Cramer, S. (1990). Diet quality and the eating environment of preschool children. *Journal of the American Dietetic Association, 90,* 1582–1584.

Sullivan, S. A., & Birch, L. L. (1994). Infant dietary experience and acceptance of solid foods. *Pediatrics, 93,* 271–277.

Wright, P., Fawcett, J., & Crow, R. (1980). The development of differences in the feeding behaviour of bottle and breast fed human infants from birth to two months. *Behavior Processes, 5,* 1–20.

2

BODY IMAGE IN CHILDREN

LINDA SMOLAK AND MICHAEL P. LEVINE

Body image disturbances are clearly implicated in eating disorders, including bulimia nervosa (BN), anorexia nervosa (AN), and binge eating disorder (BED). These eating disorders, even in their subthreshold forms, are quite rare among prepubescent children (Stein, Chalhoub, & Hodes, 1998). The greater concern about body image disturbance among children is that it might be a risk factor for the later development of eating disorders (Koff & Rierdan, 1991; Stice, 2001). Furthermore, at least among adolescent and adult females, body image problems are associated with the use of weight control techniques, including dieting and compulsive exercising, which may have short- and long-term negative effects, including increasing the risk for the later development of eating disorders and obesity (C. Davis, Kennedy, Ravelski, & Dionne, 1994; D. Davis, Apley, Fill, & Grimaldi, 1978; Shisslak et al., 1998; Stice, Cameron, Killen, Hayward, & Taylor, 1999). Finally, body image problems may be related to poor self-esteem and impaired psychosocial functioning, including the onset of adolescent depression (Button, 1990; Hill & Pallin, 1998; Stice, Hayward, Cameron, Killen, & Taylor, 2000; Wichstrom, 1999).

Thus body image disturbances among young children deserve substantial theoretical and empirical attention. This chapter focuses on body image among children ages 11 and younger. The chapter examines the data concerning the relationship of body image to weight management, eating problems, and eating disorders, but the emphasis is on body image not the eating pathologies. It is divided into three sections: (a) a description of the findings concerning rates of body image problems among children; (b) a discussion of factors that might contribute to the development of negative body image, as well as a model of those relationships; and (c) a consideration of the potential relationship between childhood body image and later eating disorders.

The term *body image* is a broad one, encompassing behavioral, perceptual, cognitive, and affective phenomena (Thompson, Heinberg, Altabe, &

Tantleff-Dunn, 1999). In this chapter the term is used to signify this broad construct. Given the constraints of the extant literature, we concentrate on the body esteem and body dissatisfaction components of body image. More specifically, *body esteem* refers to global ratings of how much the child likes her or his body. This is sometimes measured with a single question (e.g., agreement with the statement "I like the way my body looks") and sometimes with a scale such as Mendelson and White's (1993) Body Esteem Scale. The commonality among these measures is that they are phrased such that children might say they like or dislike their bodies based on weight and shape or on other factors (e.g., hair or face).

Body dissatisfaction measures tend to focus on body build. Body dissatisfaction is often operationalized as the difference between an ideal and self-perceived current figure selected from a group of drawings (e.g., Candy & Fee, 1998; Collins, 1991). Measures of weight and shape concern are even more clearly focused on issues of body fat and shape (chapter 8, this volume, for a discussion of the validity of various child body image measures).

DESCRIBING BODY IMAGE IN CHILDHOOD

Many studies indicate that a significant minority of White American children are dissatisfied with their body shapes or weights (see Smolak, Levine, & Schermer, 1998, for a review; see also chapter 3, this volume). For example, 33% of the girls and 17% of the boys in Gustafson-Larson and Terry's (1992) sample of Caucasian 9- to 11-year-olds were "very often" worried about being fat. In a study of 8- to 10-year-olds, 55% of the girls and 35% of the boys were dissatisfied with their size (Wood, Becker, & Thompson, 1996). In an Australian sample, 39% of the girls and 26% of the boys ages 8 through 12 wanted to be thinner, though this desire was related to actual body size (Rolland, Farnill, & Griffiths, 1996). It is interesting to note that in this sample, 10% of the girls (but no boys) in the underweight quartile wanted to be thinner.

Children as young as 6 express body dissatisfaction and weight concerns (Davison, Markey, & Birch, 2000; Flannery-Schroeder & Chrisler, 1997; Smolak & Levine, 1994). However, at least among girls, body dissatisfaction seems to increase with age (but see Tiggemann & Wilson-Barrett, 1998). Thelen, Powell, Lawrence, and Kuhnert (1992) found that, compared to second-grade girls, fourth- and sixth-grade girls were more concerned about being overweight and expressed a stronger desire to be thinner. Gardner, Sorter, and Friedman (1997) reported that body dissatisfaction among 12-year-old girls was greater than among 9-year-old girls, whose dissatisfaction was greater than that of 6-year-old girls. In Mellin, Irwin, and Scully's (1992) sample, 30% of the 9-year-olds, 55% of the 10-year-olds, and 65%

of the ll-year-olds worried about being too fat. These percentages among the older elementary school girls are comparable to those seen among adolescent and adult females and suggest that at least some components of disturbed eating may be internalized at fairly young ages (Shapiro, Newcomb, & Loeb, 1997).

Most studies of body image among girls have examined Caucasian samples. The sparse data available concerning African American girls, however, generally suggests that despite higher body mass indexes (BMIs), they suffer body dissatisfaction less than or equal to that of Caucasian girls. Lawrence and Thelen (1995), for example, reported that African American third and sixth graders reported less body dissatisfaction than did Caucasian children. In a large, national sample, Schreiber and colleagues (1996) reported that 9- and 10-year-old Black girls showed significantly lower body dissatisfaction than did White girls, despite the Black girls' heavier BMI and more advanced pubertal development. In fact, except in the lowest BMI quartile in which there were no significant differences, Black girls reported less body dissatisfaction at all levels of BMI.

S. Thompson, Corwin, and Sargent (1997) found that 46% of Black and 51% of White fourth-grade girls had thinner body ideals than their perceived current shape. It is interesting to note that 15% of the Black girls but only 8% of the White girls wanted to be *larger* than their current size. Indeed, Black girls generally indicated a larger ideal body size (S. Thompson et al., 1997). Similarly, Schreiber et al. (1996) found that 19% of the Black 9-year-olds but only 7% of the White girls expressed a desire to gain weight. On the other hand, Striegel-Moore, Schreiber, Pike, Wilfley, and Rodin (1995) did report that Black 9- to 10-year-old girls had a higher drive for thinness. However, this finding should be interpreted cautiously because Candy and Fee (1998) reported that body dissatisfaction was higher among 10-year-old than 11- or 12-year-old African American girls. In fact, the 10-year-old Black girls had greater body dissatisfaction than the 10-year-old White girls, whereas at ages 11 and 12 there were no ethnic group differences despite the Black girls' significantly higher average BMI. Why 10-year-olds would differ from other age groups is unclear, though temporary effects of early puberty should be investigated as a possibility. In general, the data suggest that, as in the adult literature (Striegel-Moore & Smolak, 1996, 2000), Black girls may be somewhat protected from developing eating problems because they espouse a less severely thin ideal body type. However, underscoring that Black is not the equivalent of ethnic or minority status (Smolak & Striegel-Moore, 2001), Gardner, Friedman, and Jackson (1999) found no differences in body dissatisfaction between Hispanic and White girls aged 7 through 13.

Among boys, body esteem may also decrease throughout the elementary school years, though not all studies find this (Gardner et al., 1997). Several issues must be considered in interpreting this trend, however. First, following puberty there may be a plateauing or even an increase in body esteem for boys but a continued decrease for girls (Abramowitz, Petersen, & Schulenberg, 1984; Gardner et al., 1997; Gardner, Friedman, Stark, & Jackson, 1999; Richards, Casper, & Larson, 1990; Wichstrom, 1999). This suggests that growth may be viewed more positively by boys. This raises a second issue. Some of the body dissatisfaction seen among boys may reflect feeling too small rather than too big. For example, Thelen et al. (1992) and Schur, Sanders, and Steiner (2000) found that second through sixth grade boys wanted to be bigger, although others have not found this effect (e.g., S. Thompson et al., 1997). It is interesting to note that Parkinson, Tovee, and Tovee-Cohen (1998) similarly reported that elementary schoolboys were more likely than girls to want to be bigger but that this gender difference was not evident among older children. Many researchers fail to differentiate direction of dissatisfaction. This brings up a third issue: There is less research on body image among boys than girls. It is, therefore, more difficult to draw definitive conclusions about body esteem development among boys.

Data concerning body image among ethnic minority males are extremely limited. S. Thompson et al. (1997) reported comparable levels of body satisfaction among Black and White fourth-grade boys. About 60% of both groups selected an ideal body that matched their own current body size. Whereas 32% of the Black boys wanted to be thinner, 28% of the White boys did. The remainder of the boys wanted to be heavier. Black and White boys in this study showed similar levels of concern with their weight. Data also suggest no difference between Hispanic and White boys in terms of body dissatisfaction (Gardner et al., 1999).

Given the adolescent and adult trends, it is surprising that some researchers report no gender differences in *overall* body esteem among elementary school children (e.g., Hill, Draper, & Stack, 1994; Hill & Pallin, 1998; Smolak & Levine, 1994). There do, however, appear to be gender differences in satisfaction and concerns with weight and shape, such that boys are more satisfied (Field, Camargo, et al., 1999; Gustafson-Larson & Terry, 1992; Lawrence & Thelen, 1995; Parkinson et al., 1998; S. Thompson et al., 1997; Tiggeman & Wilson-Barrett, 1998; Wardle, Volz, & Golding, 1995; Wood et al., 1996; but see Jacobi, Agras, & Hammer, 2000). This appears to be true among Black as well as White children. S. Thompson et al. (1997) found that Black and White boys were more satisfied with their body shapes and less concerned about their weight, but this main effect was tempered by an interaction showing that White girls were more concerned about their weights than were Black girls. Unfortunately, the data are too limited to draw firm conclusions about gender differences generally, much less within specific ethnic groups.

CONTRIBUTORS TO BODY IMAGE PROBLEMS

Any model of the development of body image problems needs to explain at least two things. First, there are developmental trends in body dissatisfaction, body esteem, and weight concerns. At least among White girls, there are fairly steady decreases in body esteem and body satisfaction accompanied by an increase in weight concerns throughout the elementary school years and immediately following puberty. Second, these trends vary by gender and ethnic group. These trends are important because they presage those of eating disorders. Sociocultural models of eating problems have given more attention to these patterns than have the biological models.

Biological Contributors

Several major theorists and researchers have recently argued that biological factors are central to the etiology and maintenance of eating disorders (e.g., Kaye & Strober, 1999). It is not currently clear precisely how genetic and biochemical mechanisms may contribute to the development of eating problems. It is, however, important to generate hypotheses concerning the potential role of biological contributors at various points in the pathways to eating disorders.

BMI

It is unlikely that there are any direct biological contributors to body image problems. However, given that body weight and shape have a strong genetic basis *and* that heavier body weights and shapes are seen as socially undesirable (especially for females), BMI may well act as an indirect biological contributor to negative body image, one that operates through social psychological mechanisms.

By age 6, and probably earlier, children are aware of the societal bias against fat people and will frequently express this bias themselves (Lerner & Jovanovic, 1990), although this prejudice may increase with age (Wardle et al., 1995). Not surprisingly, young children who are heavy begin to internalize this message. Overweight children as young as 5 years have lower body esteem than do normal weight children (Davison et al., 2000; Gardner et al., 1997; Mendelson & White, 1985; Phillips & Hill, 1998; Vander Wal & Thelen, 2001). Overweight children also express the wish to be thinner. In one study of children aged 8 to 12 years, 76% of the overweight girls and 56% of the overweight boys wanted to be thinner (Rolland et al., 1996). Nearly 80% of the overweight 9-year-olds in a study of British children wished to be thinner, compared to roughly 40% of the normal weight girls and 20% of the normal weight boys (Hill et al., 1994). Although overweight children appear to be unhappy with their bodies, this does not necessarily reduce their overall self-esteem. Mendelson and White (1985) reported no self-esteem differences between overweight versus normal weight 8-year-olds, although differences did appear by early adolescence. Phillips and Hill (1998) also reported differences between overweight and other 9-year-old girls in terms of Physical Appearance and Athletic Competence subscale scores but on no other Harter subscales, including global self-esteem. Even among nonobese fourth- and fifth-grade girls, there is a positive relationship between BMI and weight concerns (Taylor et al., 1998).

The correlation between BMI and body esteem is probably created by a third variable: societal attitudes toward fat people. Fat people are not inherently more prone to psychopathology or poor mental health (Yuker & Allison, 1994). Furthermore, the relationship between BMI and body esteem varies by gender and probably by ethnicity, even in childhood, further suggesting that societal attitudes may moderate this relationship.

Temperament

Some prominent theorists have suggested that personality predispositions for severe body image disturbances and eating disorders, including depressive tendencies, impulsivity, and harm avoidance, may be genetically mediated or a result of a neurochemical (e.g., serotonin) imbalance (Cloninger, 1987; Kaye & Strober, 1999; Strober, 1991). Because this work primarily deals with pathological states, it falls beyond the scope of this chapter. However, if we assume a continuum of eating problems, beginning with body dissatisfaction and weight concerns and culminating in eating disorders (Shisslak, Crago, & Estes, 1993; Stice, Killen, Hayward, & Taylor, 1998), then it becomes reasonable to at least acknowledge the potential contribution of these personality characteristics to body image problems.

Several studies have examined the relationship between these personality characteristics and body esteem in adolescents (e.g., Leon, Fulkerson, Perry, & Cudeck, 1993). Among children, depression has received some attention. Cattarin and Thompson's (1994) variable titled "psychological functioning" included measures of depression and anxiety as well as self-esteem. This measure, assessed when the girls were ages 10 to 15, did not predict scores on the Eating Disorder Inventory (EDI) subscales of body dissatisfaction, bulimia, or drive for thinness three years later. Adams, Katz, Beauchamp, Cohen, and Zavis (1993) reported that depression scores correlated significantly with scores on two eating inventories. However, they combined children and adolescents in their cross-sectional sample to calculate these correlations. This makes the correlations difficult to interpret because there were age, gender, and age-by-gender effects for all three measures. Wood et al. (1996) assessed depression and two measures of body dissatisfaction in 8-, 9-, and 10-year-old boys and girls. Depression scores were not significantly correlated with the current-ideal body figures assessment of body satisfaction in any of the groups but were significantly correlated with EDI-body dissatisfaction among 9-year-old boys and 10-year-old girls.

Thus the research on the relationship between depression and body image among children deserves more attention, but given the mix of findings, it is premature to draw conclusions about the genetic basis of this link, at least as it might emerge in childhood. The well-established findings that gender differences in depression do not emerge until adolescence (Nolen-Hoeksema & Girgus, 1994), whereas those in body image are evident in elementary school, will need explanation if depression and body image disturbance are to be linked by genetics. It is possible that the gender differences in body image contribute to the later developing gender difference in depression (Wichstrom, 1999).

Developmental data also challenge the applicability of temperament information. There are early appearing, individual differences in negative affect (Bates, 1987; Lemery, Goldsmith, Klinnert, & Mrazek, 1999). However, gender differences are not clearly evident, although some research suggests that infant boys may show less self-regulatory behavior, and hence more negative affect, during social interactions (Weinberg, Tronick, Cohn, & Olson, 1999). So models will need to explain how gender differences in depression and eating problems, as well as in their relationship, are formed from early behavioral predispositions that do not show a predominance of girls.

This challenge is highlighted by a recent study by Martin et al. (2000). They reported significant relationships between negative emotionality during the preschool and elementary school years and early adolescent girls' EDI drive for thinness scores. Lower persistence scores, another measure of preschool and elementary school temperament, were related to higher EDI bulimia scores among the early adolescent girls. However, no significant relationships emerged between preschool or even elementary school temperament and EDI scores among the boys. Might temperament be a risk factor for eating problems in girls but not boys? Or might the meaning of the temperament and eating measures differ by gender?

In general, then, although clinical theorists such as Strober and Kaye have raised provocative questions about the potential biological bases of body image and eating problems, the literature on child body image development and temperament simply is inadequate to allow an evaluation of this perspective. The picture is further complicated by suggestions that early trauma may significantly alter neurochemistry and hence coping styles (Perry, Pollard, Blakley, Baker, & Vigilante, 1995). These are clearly important areas for future research.

Sociocultural Influences

Gender, ethnicity, cross-cultural, historical, and age differences in levels of body esteem all suggest that culture and society play a major role in the construction and hence the development of body image (Silverstein & Perlick, 1995; Smolak & Murnen, 2001; Smolak & Striegel-Moore, 2001). In the late 20th- and early 21st-century United States, the most likely sociocultural influences include media, peers, and parents.

Parents

Children may learn certain elements of body image from their parents. The younger the child, the more likely that parents are influential in most areas of life. Parents select and comment on children's clothing and appearance, and may require the child to look certain ways and to eat or avoid certain foods (see chapter 1, this volume). Although peers and media gain in influence throughout the elementary school years, it is probably not until early adolescence that they become the primary arbitrators of appearance and style.

Many parents do comment on their children's weight, noting, for example, whether the children are too fat or too thin. They might also actively encourage their children to slim down. This is true for both mothers and fathers, for boys and girls, and in Black and White families (Hill, Weaver, & Blundell, 1990; Schreiber et al., 1996; Smolak, Levine, & Schermer, 1999; Striegel-Moore & Kearney-Cooke, 1994; Thelen & Cormier, 1995), although some researchers have suggested that African American mothers may place less emphasis on body shape (Parker, Nichter, Vuckovic, Sims, & Ritenbaugh, 1995). Some studies, surprisingly, have found that daughters are not more likely than sons to be encouraged to control their weight (Striegel-Moore & Kearney-Cooke, 1994; Thelen & Cormier, 1995).

In general, parents are satisfied with the appearance of their elementary school children. However, satisfaction decreases as children gets older (Striegel-Moore & Kearney-Cooke, 1994). The child's body weight is also a factor in parental comments. There was a linear relationship between BMI and maternal comments to their 9- and 10-year-old girls that they were too fat (Schreiber et al., 1996). Black mothers were more likely than White mothers to say that their daughters were too fat (Schreiber et al., 1996). In the same study, nearly one third of the mothers of girls categorized as underweight told their daughters they were too thin.

Parental comments do appear to be related to body image. Thelen and Cormier (1995) reported a significant correlation between the parents' reports of their encouragement to their daughters to lose weight and their daughters' desire to lose weight. Smolak and her colleagues (1999) reported significant correlations between maternal comments to children and the children's scores on the Body Esteem Scale. Taylor et al. (1998) reported that maternal concerns about their fourth- and fifth-grade daughters' body shape were related to the girls' level of weight concerns.

In addition to direct comments, parental modeling of weight concerns may contribute to body esteem problems in children. Parents might remark on the appearance of their own bodies or might engage in calorie-restrictive dieting or exercise solely for the purpose of weight loss. Davison et al. (2000) reported a small but significant correlation between the weight concerns of 5-year-old girls and their mothers. Hill et al. (1990) found that mothers with high dietary restraint scores tended to have 10-year-old daughters with high dietary restraint scores (but see Hill & Franklin, 1998). Parental complaints about their own weight were correlated with daughters' body esteem in a sample of fourth and fifth graders, as were mother's weight loss attempts (Smolak et al., 1999). However, Thelen and Cormier (1995) reported no significant correlations between parents' and Children's Eating Attitudes Test (EAT; Garfinkel & Garner, 1982) scores or dieting frequency. Sanftner, Crowther, Crawford, and Watts (1996) also found no relationship between mother's and prepubertal daughter's EDI drive for thinness or body dissatisfaction scores.

The Sanftner et al. (1996) study emphasizes the importance of examining *childhood* relationships rather than simply extending *adolescent* findings to children. These researchers found significant correlations between mother and daughter eating behaviors and attitudes in their sample of pubertal girls but not in a separate sample of prepubertal girls. The cross-sectional nature of this study limits interpretation of the data. Nonetheless, it appears that pubertal changes may alter the impact of maternal modeling of weight and shape concerns. Whether this is a result of changes in the mother's behavior or in the daughter's sensitivity to the input is unclear. It may also be because the general pressure to look a certain way—from peers, potential boyfriends, media, and teachers—intensifies (Levine, Smolak, & Hayden, 1994).

Despite the fact that parents do not clearly encourage weight control in their prepubertal daughters more than their sons, daughters may be more affected by parental weight-related behavior than sons are. For example, Smolak et al. (1999) reported that of 30 possible parent–child correlations concerning body esteem and weight loss attempts, 14 out of 30 of the girls' correlations, but only 5 out of 30 of the boys reached statistical significance. Girls appeared to be particularly affected by their mothers' behavior, and direct comments appeared to be more powerful than parental modeling (as measured, for example, by the EAT or EDI). Thelen and Cormier (1995) also found that daughters', but not sons', desire to be thinner was related to parental input. In a study using retrospective report, childhood levels of parental teasing and comments about appearance were more related to women's than men's body dissatisfaction (Schwartz, Phares, Tantleff-Dunn,

& Thompson, 1999). Among middle-school girls, living in a "culture of dieting" in which peers, parents, and media combine to send a strong antifat message to girls may increase the risk of eating problems (Levine et al., 1994). Perhaps elementary school girls, but not boys, also receive the message from multiple sources. Elementary school girls do report more peer interactions concerning body and eating issues than boys do (Oliver & Thelen, 1996). The consistency of the messages may result in their greater internalization among girls, which may make girls more susceptible to parental comments. These issues require additional research.

Peers

Although peers are less influential during the elementary school than adolescent years, they are not irrelevant to children's development. Social comparison appears as a factor by very early elementary school (Ruble, 1983). This is probably one reason why even young children are aware of whether they are overweight and why they feel badly about it. It probably also contributes to children's awareness of the negative stereotypes associated with body fat. Thus it is reasonable to expect that peer messages concerning body shape might affect children's body esteem. Oliver and Thelen (1996) reported such a correlation in third and fifth graders. Furthermore, girls' belief that they would be better liked if they were thinner was related to their weight concerns. This was not true for boys. Taylor et al. (1998) also reported that fourth- and fifth-grade girls who thought peers would like them better if they were thinner had higher weight concerns. In this regard, teasing about weight and shape may also influence body esteem (Heinberg, 1996). For example, Fabian and Thompson (1989) reported that teasing was related to body dissatisfaction in a sample of premenarcheal girls. Apparently some girls take such teasing more to heart; these girls appear to have higher levels of weight concerns (Taylor et al., 1998). Vander Wal and Thelen (2001) reported peer modeling and teasing to be more strongly related to body dissatisfaction in third- through fifth-grade girls than was perceived parental concern about the girls' weight. Clearly, peer influences in childhood deserve much more research attention, particularly given their potential role in prevention programs (Paxton, 1999).

In addition, teasing may be considered part of the cultural objectification of the female body, which feminists and others argue contributes to the development of eating disorders (Bordo, 1993; Fredrickson & Roberts, 1997; Larkin, Rice, & Russell, 1996). More specifically, treating women as sexual objects in a way that is threatening, dehumanizing, or demeaning might focus girls on their bodies, including comparisons to the cultural ideal and to other women. This might result in body dissatisfaction and low body esteem (Fredrickson & Roberts, 1997). In elementary schoolchildren such objectification might take the form of peer teasing that resembles later sexual harassment. For example, boys might prevent girls from walking in the halls, flip up their skirts, stare at them and comment on their appearance, and call them ugly. Murnen and Smolak (2000) used vignettes about such incidents to ask elementary school children not only whether they had experienced similar events but also how a child might react to such an experience. They found that about 75% of the third- through fifth-grade girls indeed reported similar experiences. Boys reported comparable levels of such incidents. However, frequency of sexual harassment was negatively correlated with body esteem for girls but not for boys. Furthermore, girls were more likely than boys to report that victims of harassment would be scared. Those girls who thought victims would be frightened had lower levels of body esteem as did girls who were not sure how victims would feel. There were no comparable findings for boys. These data can be interpreted within the objectification theory framework to explain how some girls, for example, those who are more frightened or silenced by harassment, might become more negatively focused on their bodies. Much more research is needed on this issue.

Media and Toys

Even among adolescents and adults, the influence of media images on body esteem is a complex and confusing issue (Levine & Smolak, 1996, 1998). It is even more complicated in children, partially because, again, research is severely limited.

Like adults, children see skewed gender roles on television, including the presentation of the "ideal" and, perhaps, even the typical, woman as slender. By late elementary school, girls may start reading the teen magazines that sell a particular appearance as well as appearance concerns. Up to half of late elementary school girls may read these magazines at least occasionally, with as many as 25% reading them twice a week (Field, Cheung, et al., 1999). The use of magazines to obtain beauty and weight information has been related to body image in late elementary and early adolescent girls (Field, Cheung, et al., 1999; Levine et al., 1994). Late elementary school girls (ages 8 to 11) do compare themselves to fashion models and other media images and feel badly about the comparison (Martin & Kennedy, 1993, 1994). Girls who make comparisons may have higher levels of weight concerns (Taylor et al., 1998).

Furthermore, Barbie, a doll owned by about 90% of girls aged 3 to 11, has a very unrealistic body (Nichter & Nichter, 1991). Indeed, fewer than 1 in 100,000 women are likely to have body proportions similar to Barbie's (Norton, Olds, Olive, & Dank, 1996). It is not only Barbie's appearance that may increase young girls' weight and shape consciousness. The primary way girls play with a Barbie is to change its clothes (Wolf, 1997). This focuses girls even more on the importance of appearance and of "looking good" in clothes. Research has not clearly examined the link between Barbie and body image issues. As with other sociocultural influences, the relationship is likely to be moderated, and perhaps mediated, by the girl's beliefs about thinness and success as well as her exposure to other sources that emphasize thinness.

A similar statement might be made about the action figures played with by boys. These male action figures have become unrealistically muscular during the past 20 or so years (Pope, Olivardia, Gruber, & Borowiecki, 1999) and may be presenting boys with a dangerously unattainable body ideal.

A MODEL OF INFLUENCES OF BODY IMAGE IN CHILDREN

In many studies (e.g., Attie & Brooks-Gunn, 1989; Killen et al., 1996) and theories (e.g., Huon & Strong, 1998; Smolak & Levine, 1996a) of the etiology of eating problems, body dissatisfaction appears as the first step in the process. Little or no attempt to trace the childhood roots of body dissatisfaction is made. Figure 2-1 presents a model of influences on the development of body image in children. The model focuses on sociocultural factors, including the way the cultural beliefs about fat and thin people and gender roles might affect both the nature and impact of environmental messages about body shape. It is loosely based on a model of the initiation and maintenance of dieting by adolescents developed by Huon and Strong (1998). This is not a model of eating pathology; it is a model of one of the potential precursors of eating disorders.

The model begins by suggesting that certain children are more likely to hear comments in their proximal environment (typically parents, siblings, and peers) about body shape and appearance. These are children who are heavier and girls, especially overweight girls. Empirical evidence clearly suggests that overweight children are the targets of such comments (Cattarin

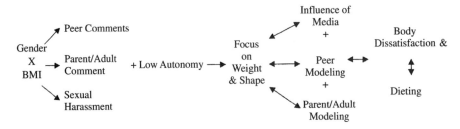

Figure 2-1. A model of sociocultural influences on the development of body dissatisfaction.

& Thompson, 1994). Whether girls receive more comments from parents is unclear, but they do appear to talk more with peers about weight and shape. The combination of these proximal influences is important, because it may intensify the salience of the message, a critical issue with young children.

It is important to emphasize that gender is not simply a one-time, additive influence within this model (Garcia-Coll et al., 1996). Gender influences all components. For example, a reduced sense of autonomy may be related to the feminine gender role and to girls' experience of silencing themselves to be accepted. Media portrayals are clearly gendered. Peer comments may be part of a general trend to objectify girls' bodies (Fredrickson & Roberts, 1997).

Comments about weight and shape, including teasing, have also been correlated with body esteem in young children and adolescents (see the earlier discussion). Some children also may be more susceptible to these messages because they are particularly interested in pleasing others and being well-liked (Huon & Strong, 1998). If these children think, based on messages that they have received, that being a certain weight will increase their likeability, they may be more concerned with weight and shape and hence be more prone to body dissatisfaction. This need to be liked or to please others has often been cited as a mediator in the eating-problems literature to explain why nearly universal influences (e.g., media messages) have differential effects. It has been called by a variety of names, including lack of voice (Steiner-Adair, 1986), sociotropy (Friedman & Whisman, 1998), need for social approval (Striegel-Moore, Silberstein, & Rodin, 1993), and low autonomy (Huon & Strong, 1998).

The combination of the proximal influences and the lack of autonomy are hypothesized to increase a girl's focus on weight and shape. This, in turn, facilitates the influences of media and parental and peer modeling by increasing the girl's attention to weight and shape messages. Because most girls will not meet the sociocultural image of a perfect body, these girls are likely to suffer from negative body images and weight concerns. Empirical testing of this model may yield an understanding of the source of body dissatisfaction and weight preoccupation. This is an important endeavor because by middle school these become powerful predictors of eating problems and disorders (e.g., Attie & Brooks-Gunn, 1989; Killen et al., 1996; Leon, Fulkerson, Perry, & Early-Zald, 1995).

BODY IMAGE AND EATING PROBLEMS

It is not clear how body image problems in childhood might be related to eating problems in adolescents and adults. It is widely assumed that poor body image in childhood is a risk factor for the development of eating disorders. This perspective is supported by data suggesting that children who are problem eaters (e.g., picky eaters) and obese children are more likely to develop eating disorders later in life (Marchi & Cohen, 1990). There are, however, only a handful of longitudinal prospective studies of eating disorders that begin in childhood, though several large-scale investigations are underway (e.g., Shisslak et al., 1998). Thus much of the available data concerns only concurrent relationships between body image and eating problems or disorders.

Concurrent Relationships

Eating disorders themselves are quite rare among prepubertal children. Thus most of the studies looking at body image and its concomitants have measured behaviors and attitudes that may be related to eating disorders rather than the disorders themselves. These typically include measures of dieting or weight-loss techniques, drive for thinness, or an overall score on a measure of disordered eating such as the Children's Eating Attitudes Test (ChEAT; Maloney, McGuire, & Daniels, 1988).

Even among young children, negative body image may be related to the use of weight loss techniques and to indicators of eating pathology. For example, body dissatisfaction was related to weight loss attempts among 9- and 10-year-old Black and White girls (Schreiber et al., 1996), although Striegel-Moore and her colleagues (1995) found a relationship between body esteem and drive for thinness among White, but not Black, girls. Hill, Oliver, and Rogers (1992) reported that 9-year-old girls showing high dietary restraint had lower body esteem and greater body dissatisfaction. Shisslak et al. (1998), however, did not find body esteem to be a significant correlate of weight control behaviors in fourth- and fifth-grade girls.

These relationships are more common among girls than boys. Smolak and Levine (1994) reported that girls who were unhappy with their weight and shape were more likely to have tried to lose weight than were boys. Thelen and Cormier (1995) found that girls who wanted to be thinner were significantly more likely to be dieting and to have elevated ChEAT scores; this was not true of the boys. Lawrence and Thelen (1995) found that White third- and sixth-grade girls, but not Black children or White boys, with lower Harter Physical Appearance (Harter, 1985) scores were more likely to engage in dieting behavior. In another study of 9-year-olds, body esteem, a desire to be thin, and dietary restraint were interrelated, but this pattern was stronger for girls (Hill et al., 1994). Kelly, Ricciardelli, and Clarke (1999) also reported a stronger relationship between body esteem and dieting in Australian elementary school girls than boys. Wood et al. (1996) found that virtually all of the body-dissatisfied girls in their study wanted to be thinner, whereas only about half of the boys did. This again raises the possibility that some body-dissatisfied boys want to be heavier.

This does not mean that boys who are concerned about weight do not suffer. Among Australian boys poorer body image was associated with emotional concerns about eating (Kelly et al., 1999). Tiggeman and Wilson-Barrett (1998) reported that body dissatisfaction and general self-esteem were significantly negatively correlated for boys but not for girls. Wood and colleagues (1996) report a similar finding for 8- and 9-, but not 10- year-olds. They interpret this as indicating that body dissatisfaction may be a "normative discontent" (Rodin, Silberstein, & Striegel-Moore, 1985), even among young girls, and hence it does not significantly affect their global self-esteem.

There is a possibility that these various elements of eating problems—body dissatisfaction, drive for thinness, and dieting—may be less strongly intercorrelated in children than in adults (Shisslak et al., 1998; Smolak & Levine, 1994; Smolak et al., 1998). For example, in a study of 5-year-old girls and their parents, Davison et al. (2000) reported a correlation of .17 between the girls' BMI and body dissatisfaction and a correlation of .19 between the girls' body dissatisfaction and weight concerns. The comparable correlations for the mothers' data were .77 and .52. Even the fathers showed stronger relationships between BMI, body dissatisfaction, and weight concerns than the girls did. For the fathers, the correlation between BMI and body dissatisfaction was .61 and between body dissatisfaction and weight concerns was .37. Striegel-Moore et al. (1995) found no correlation between drive for thinness and calorie restriction in their 9- to 10-year-old sample. Hill et al. (1994) found correlations between body dissatisfaction and dietary restraint in 9-year-olds roughly half that frequently found with older samples (e.g., Stice, Nemeroff, & Shaw, 1996). Shisslak et al. (1998) reported that body image was not a significant predictor of weight control behaviors in their late elementary school group but was in their middle school sample. If there is indeed a weaker relationship among such variables, the elementary school years may present an especially good time to implement prevention programs (Smolak, 1999; Smolak & Levine, 1994).

Longitudinal Studies

Cattarin and Thompson (1994) followed a sample of 10- to 15-year-old girls over a three-year period. Unfortunately, because their analysis did not separate the prepubertal or elementary school girls from the postpubertal or older girls, it is possible that their results have been affected by the presence of older girls. Nonetheless, for the entire sample, they found that baseline body dissatisfaction was a strong predictor of later body dissatisfaction and was also a significant predictor of later drive for thinness.

Smolak and Levine (1996b, 1996c) followed a group of children ages 6 to 11 over a two-year period. For the purposes of analyses, they divided the children into two groups: those who were in grades 1 and 2 at Time 1 (baseline) and those who were in grades 3 to 5 at Time 1. The former group was still in elementary school at the time of the follow-up and were assumed to still be prepubertal.

In the younger sample, there was a significant decline in body esteem from Time 1 to Time 2 (follow-up), but body esteem at Time 1 was not significantly related to body esteem at Time 2. Only a few of the children had reported trying to lose weight at Time 1. These children did not differ from the other children on any measures of weight concerns or eating pathology at Time 2. It is interesting to note that the belief that a "good body" is important to attractiveness, as measured at Time 1, was significantly related to girls' Time 2 concerns about weight and to boys' Time 2 body esteem.

In the older sample of 85 children, Time 1 body esteem scores were significantly correlated with Time 2 body esteem scores, ChEAT scores, and use of weight management techniques. These correlations were generally stronger for girls and generally remained significant even after controlling for BMI.

These results should be interpreted cautiously. The sample was relatively small and consisted only of White children in a rural school district. Nonetheless, these results raise the provocative possibility that body esteem in very early (first and second grade) elementary school may not be a substantial risk factor for later problems, even for poor body esteem. By late elementary school, however, poor body esteem may form a foundation for later eating problems.

IMPLICATIONS FOR PREVENTION AND TREATMENT

There can no longer be any doubt that many children aged 11 and younger do indeed have body esteem problems. Very limited research seems to suggest that these problems may be related to the development of more severe body image and eating-related problems. The elementary school years may, then, present an opportunity to nip eating problems in the bud (Smolak, 1999; Smolak & Levine, 1994, 1996a). Programs aimed at adolescents and adults face the difficulty of teaching a diverse audience; some students will be well on their way to an eating problem, others will be in the very early phases of developing risk factors, and still others will be on a path that it is not likely to culminate in eating problems. We might reasonably expect less variability among elementary school students, particularly those in early elementary school.

In addition, there is evidence to suggest that the "thinness schema" (Smolak & Levine, 1994) underlying eating problems may be more susceptible to intervention in children than in adolescents and adults. It appears that this schema is less consolidated in children, with weaker relationships among its behavioral, attitudinal, and affective components. Again, this means that elementary school audiences may be particularly affected by classroom programs.

The findings also suggest that young elementary school children may differ from older elementary school children, who in turn differ from adults and adolescents, in their likelihood of having body image issues, the causes of these problems, and the relationship of these problems to other problems. This implies that treatments developed for use with adolescents may need more than tinkering or simplifying to be useful with younger children. Treatments and prevention programs for children need to be based on the nature of childhood problems as well as on developmental level.

Assuming it is supported by empirical work, the model of body image development presented in this chapter also provides clues for prevention programs. The model's focus on sociocultural factors raises several possibilities for changing the school culture—in terms of sexual harassment, weight-related teasing and comments, and teacher modeling of body dissatisfaction—which might be addressed in a prevention program (Piran, 1995).

CONCLUSION

Although there are empirical data available concerning body image in children, there are still many gaps. Most of the extant data simply describe the rate of body dissatisfaction or body esteem among children. There is substantial disagreement among these studies (Smolak et al., 1998). Some of this is a result of measurement differences, but some discrepancies may be attributable to genuine sample differences. If sociocultural influences are as important as we have argued, it is likely that different groups of children will be exposed to different pressures and hence will show different levels of body dissatisfaction. These issues deserve more research attention.

More information is needed on the rates of eating problems in various ethnic groups, with age, social class, and gender taken into account. The literature on African Americans and body image raises the interesting possibility that traditional African American culture may be somewhat protective against body image problems (Striegel-Moore & Smolak, 1996; chapter 3, this volume). If this is so, understanding these factors may provide important information for those designing prevention programs (Smolak & Striegel-Moore, 2001).

More information is also needed about gender differences and gender roles. Boys' concern about overweight is likely quite a bit less than girls. However, they may be concerned about being too small. This may create a risk for steroid or nutritional supplement abuse or excessive weight training. The question of whether concern about smallness in boys poses a risk for healthy development deserves attention (Smolak, Levine, & Thompson, 2001). In addition, more information about what experiences females have that make them more vulnerable to concerns about overweight is also vitally important (Smolak & Murnen, 2001).

There are very few longitudinal data tracing body image concerns from childhood. Thus we can make no statements about either the factors that cause negative body esteem or the role of early body image problems in the development of eating disorders. The data looking at concurrent relationships raise some interesting questions that can only be answered in prospective studies. These will require both the development of new measures (Smolak, 1996) and new models (e.g., Figure 2-1) to guide the research.

REFERENCES

Abramowitz, R., Petersen, A., & Schulenberg, J. (1984). Changes in self-image during early adolescence. In D. Offer, E. Ostrov, & K. Howard (Eds.), *Patterns of adolescent self-image* (pp. 19–28). San Francisco: Jossey-Bass.

Adams, P., Katz, R., Beauchamp, K., Cohen, E., & Zavis, D. (1993). Body dissatisfaction, eating disorders, and depression: A developmental perspective. *Journal of Child and Family Studies, 2,* 37–46.

Attie, I., & Brooks-Gunn, J. (1989). Development of eating problems in adolescent girls: A longitudinal study. *Developmental Psychology, 25,* 70–79.

Bates, J. (1987). Temperament in infancy. In J. D. Osofsky (Ed.), *Handbook of infant development* (2nd ed., pp. 1101–1149). New York: Wiley.

Bordo, S. (1993). *Unbearable weight: Feminism, western culture, and the body.* Berkeley: University of California Press.

Button, E. (1990). Self-esteem in girls aged 11–12: Baseline findings from a planned prospective study of vulnerability to eating disorders. *Journal of Adolescence, 13,* 407–413.

Candy, C., & Fee, V. (1998). Reliability and concurrent validity of the Kids' Eating Disorders Survey (KEDS) body image silhouettes with preadolescent girls. *Eating Disorders: The Journal of Treatment and Prevention, 6,* 297–308.

Cattarin, J., & Thompson, J. K. (1994). A three-year longitudinal study of body image, eating disturbance, and general psychological functioning in adolescent females. *Eating Disorders: The Journal of Prevention and Treatment, 2,* 114–125.

Cloninger, C. (1987). A systematic method for clinical description and classification of personality variants. *Archives of General Psychiatry, 44,* 573–588.

Collins, M. (1991). Body figure perceptions and preferences among preadolescent children. *International Journal of Eating Disorders, 10,* 100–108.

Davis, C., Kennedy, S., Ravelski, E., & Dionne, M. (1994). The role of physical activity in the development and maintenance of eating disorders. *Psychological Medicine, 24,* 957–967.

Davis, D., Apley, J., Fill, G., & Grimaldi, C. (1978). Diet and retarded growth. *British Medical Journal, 1,* 539–542.

Davison, K., Markey, C., & Birch, L. (2000). Etiology of body dissatisfaction and weight concerns among 5-year-old girls. *Appetite, 35,* 143–151.

Fabian, L., & Thompson, J. K. (1989). Body image and eating in young females. *International Journal of Eating Disorders, 8,* 63–74.

Field, A., Camargo, C., Taylor, C., Berkey, C., Frazier, L., Gillman, M., & Colditz, G. (1999). Overweight, weight concerns, and bulimic behaviors among girls and boys. *Journal of the American Academy of Child and Adolescent Psychiatry, 38,* 754–760.

Field, A., Cheung, L., Wolf, A., Herzog, D., Gortmaker, S., & Colditz, G. (1999). Exposure to the mass media and weight concerns among girls. *Pediatrics, 103,* e36.

Flannery-Schroeder, E., & Chrisler, J. (1997). Body esteem, eating attitudes, and gender-role orientation in three age groups of children. *Current Psychology: Developmental, Learning, Personality, Social, 15,* 235–248.

Frederickson, B. & Roberts, T. (1997). Objectification theory: Towards understanding women's lived experience and mental health risks. *Psychology of Women Quarterly, 21,* 173–206.

Friedman, M., & Whisman, M. (1998). Sociotropy, autonomy, and bulimic symptomatology. *International Journal of Eating Disorders, 23,* 439–442.

Garcia-Coll, C., Lamberty, G., Jenkins, R., McAdoo, H., Crnic, K., Wasik, B., & Garcia, H. (1996). An integrative model for the study of developmental competencies in minority children. *Child Development, 67,* 1891–1914.

Gardner, R., Friedman, B, & Jackson, N. (1999). Hispanic and White children's judgments of perceived and ideal body size in self and others. *Psychological Record, 49,* 555–564.

Gardner, R., Friedman, B., Stark, K., & Jackson, N. (1999). Body size estimations in children six through fourteen: A longitudinal study. *Perceptual & Motor Skills, 88,* 541–555.

Gardner, R., Sorter, R., & Friedman, B. (1997). Developmental changes in children's body images. *Journal of Social Behavior and Personality, 12,* 1019–1036.

Garfinkel, P., & Garner, D. (1982). *Anorexia nervosa: A multidimensional approach.* New York: Brunner/Mazel.

Gustafson-Larson, A., & Terry, R. (1992). Weight-related behaviors and concerns of fourth-grade children. *Journal of the American Dietetic Association, 92,* 818–822.

Harter, S. (1985). *Manual for the Self-Perception Profile for Children.* Denver, CO: University of Denver Press.

Heinberg, L. (1996). Theories of body image disturbance: Perceptual, developmental, and sociocultural factors. In J. K. Thompson (Ed.), *Body image, eating disorders, and obesity: An integrative guide for assessment and treatment* (pp. 27–48). Washington, DC: American Psychological Association.

Hill, A., Draper, E., & Stack, J. (1994). A weight on children's minds: Body shape dissatisfactions at 9-years-old. *International Journal of Obesity, 18*, 383–389.

Hill, A., & Franklin, J. (1998). Mothers, daughters, and dieting: Investigating the transmission of weight control. *British Journal of Clinical Psychology, 31*, 95–105.

Hill, A., Oliver, S., & Rogers, P. (1992). Eating in the adult world: The rise of dieting in childhood and adolescence. *British Journal of Clinical Psychology, 31*, 95–105.

Hill, A., & Pallin, V. (1998). Dieting awareness and low self-worth: Related issues in 8-year-old girls. *International Journal of Eating Disorders, 24*, 405–414.

Hill, A., Weaver, C., & Blundell, J. (1990). Dieting concerns of 10-year-old girls and their mothers. *British Journal of Clinical Psychology, 29*, 346–348.

Huon, G., & Strong, K. (1998). The initiation and the maintenance of dieting: Structural models for large-scale longitudinal investigations. *International Journal of Eating Disorders, 23*, 361–370.

Jacobi, C., Agras, S., & Hammer, L. (2000). *Do parents' eating disturbances predict children's eating disturbances? Differential influences and emerging gender differences at 8 years.* Manuscript submitted for publication.

Kaye, W., & Strober, M. (1999). Neurobiology of eating disorders. In D. Charney, E. Nestler, & W. Bunney (Eds.), *Neurobiological foundations of mental illness.* New York: Oxford.

Kelly, C., Ricciardelli, L., & Clarke, J. (1999). Problem eating attitudes and behaviors in young children. *International Journal of Eating Disorders, 25*, 281–286.

Killen, J., Taylor, C., Hayward, C., Haydel, K., Wilson, D., Hammer, L., Kraemer, H., Blair-Greiner, A., & Strachowski, D. (1996). Weight concerns influence the development of eating disorders: A four year prospective study. *Journal of Consulting and Clinical Psychology, 64*, 936–940.

Koff, E., & Rierdan, J. (1991). Perceptions of weight and attitudes toward eating in early adolescent girls. *Journal of Adolescent Health, 14*, 433–439.

Larkin, J., Rice, C., & Russell, V. (1996). Slipping through the cracks: Sexual harassment, eating problems, and the problem of embodiment. *Eating Disorders: The Journal of Treatment and Prevention, 4*, 5–26.

Lawrence, C., & Thelen, M. (1995). Body image, dieting, and self-concept: Their relation in African-American and Caucasian children. *Journal of Clinical Child Psychology, 24*, 41–48.

Lemery, K., Goldsmith, H., Klinnert, M., & Mrazek, D. (1999). Developmental models of infant and childhood temperament. *Developmental Psychology, 35*, 189–204.

Leon, G., Fulkerson, J., Perry, C., & Cudeck, R. (1993). Personality and behavioral vulnerabilities associated with risk status for eating disorders in adolescent girls. *Journal of Abnormal Psychology, 102*, 438–444.

Leon, G., Fulkerson, J., Perry, C., & Early-Zald, M. (1995). Prospective analysis of personality and behavioral vulnerabilities and gender influences in the later development of disordered eating. *Journal of Abnormal Psychology, 104*, 140–149.

Lerner, R., & Jovanovic, J. (1990). The role of body image in psychosocial development across the life span: A developmental contextual perspective. In T. Cash & T. Pruzinsky (Eds.), *Body images: Development, deviance, and change* (pp. 110–127). New York: Guilford Press.

Levine, M. P., & Smolak, L. (1996). Media as a context for the development of disordered eating. In L. Smolak, M. P. Levine, & R. Striegel-Moore (Eds.), *The developmental psychopathology of eating disorders* (pp. 235–257). Mahwah, NJ: Erlbaum.

Levine, M. P., & Smolak, L. (1998). The mass media and disordered eating: Implications for primary prevention. In W. Vandereycken & G. Van Noordenbos (Eds.), *Prevention of eating disorders* (pp. 23–56). London: Athlone.

Levine, M. P., Smolak, L., & Hayden, H. (1994). The relation of sociocultural factors to eating attitudes and behaviors among middle school girls. *Journal of Early Adolescence, 14*, 471–490.

Maloney, M., McGuire, J., & Daniels, S. (1988). Reliability testing of a children's version of the Eating Attitudes Test. *Journal of the American Academy of Child and Adolescent Psychiatry, 5*, 541–543.

Marchi, M., & Cohen, P. (1990). Early childhood eating behavior and adolescent eating disorders. *Journal of the American Academy of Child and Adolescent Psychiatry, 29*, 112–117.

Martin, G., Wertheim, E., Prior, M., Smart, D., Sanson, A., & Oberklaid, F. (2000). A longitudinal study of the role of childhood temperament in the later development of eating concerns. *International Journal of Eating Disorders, 27*, 150–162.

Martin, M. C., & Kennedy, P. F. (1993). Advertising and social comparison: Consequences for female preadolescents and adolescents. *Psychology & Marketing, 10*, 513–530.

Martin, M. C., & Kennedy, P. F. (1994). Social comparison and the beauty of advertising models: The role of motives for comparison. *Advances in Consumer Research, 21*, 365–371.

Mellin, L., Irwin, C., & Scully, S. (1992). Prevalence of disordered eating in girls: A survey of middle-class children. *Journal of the American Dietetic Association, 92*, 851–853.

Mendelson, B., & White, D. (1985). Development of self-body-esteem in overweight youngsters. *Developmental Psychology, 21*, 90–96.

Mendelson, B. & White, D. (1993). *Manual for the Body-Esteem Scale for Children.* Montreal, Canada: Center for Research in Human Development, Concordia University.

Murnen, S., & Smolak, L. (2000). The experience of sexual harassment among grade-school students: Early socialization of female subordination? *Sex Roles, 43,* 1–17.

Nichter, M., & Nichter, M. (1991). Hype and weight. *Medical Anthropology, 13,* 249–284.

Nolen-Hoeksema, S., & Girgus, J. (1994). The emergence of gender differences in depression during adolescence. *Psychological Bulletin, 115,* 424–443.

Norton, K., Olds, T., Olive, S., & Dank, S. (1996). Ken and Barbie at life size. *Sex Roles, 34,* 287–294.

Oliver, K., & Thelen, M. (1996). Children's perceptions of peer influence on eating concerns. *Behavior Therapy, 27,* 25–39.

Parker, S., Nichter, M., Vuckovic, N., Sims, C., & Ritenbaugh, C. (1995). Body image and weight concerns among African American and white adolescent females: Differences that make a difference. *Human Organization, 54,* 103–114.

Parkinson, K., Tovee, M., & Cohen-Tovee, E. (1998). Body shape perceptions of preadolescent and young adolescent children. *European Eating Disorders Review, 6,* 126–135.

Paxton, S. (1999). Peer relations, body image, and disordered eating in adolescent girls: Implications for prevention. In N. Piran, M. P. Levine, & C. Steiner-Adair (Eds.), *Preventing eating disorders: A handbook of interventions and special challenges* (pp. 85–104). Philadelphia: Brunner/Mazel.

Perry, B., Pollard, R., Blakley, T., Baker, W., & Vigilante, D. (1995). Childhood trauma, the neurobiology of adaptation, and "use-dependent" development of the brain: How "states" become "traits". *Infant Mental Health Journal, 16,* 271–291.

Phillips, R., & Hill, A. (1998). Fat, plain, but not friendless: Self-esteem and peer acceptance of obese pre-adolescent girls. *International Journal of Obesity, 22,* 287–293.

Piran, N. (1995). Prevention: Can early lessons lead to a delineation of an alternative model? A critical look at prevention with schoolchildren. *Eating Disorders: The Journal of Treatment & Prevention, 3,* 28–36.

Pope, H., Olivardia, R., Gruber, A., & Borowiecki, J. (1999). Evolving ideals of male body image as seen through action toys. *International Journal of Eating Disorders, 26,* 65–72.

Richards, M., Casper, R., & Larson, R. (1990). Weight and eating concerns among pre- and young adolescent boys and girls. *Journal of Adolescent Health Care, 11,* 203–209.

Rodin, J., Silberstein, L., & Striegel-Moore, R. (1985). Women and weight: A normative discontent. In T. Sonderegger (Ed.), *Nebraska Symposium on Motiva-*

tion: Vol. 32. Psychology and gender (pp. 267–308). Lincoln: University of Nebraska Press.

Rolland, K., Farnill, D., & Griffiths, R. (1996). Children's perceptions of their current and ideal body sizes and body mass index. *Perceptual and Motor Skills, 82*, 651–656.

Ruble, D. N. (1983). The development of social-comparison processes and their role in achievement-related self-socialization. In E. T. Higgins, D. N. Ruble, & W. W. Hartup (Eds.), *Social cognition and social development: A sociocultural perspective* (pp. 134–157). Cambridge: Cambridge University Press.

Sanftner, J., Crowther, J., Crawford, P., & Watts, D. (1996). Maternal influences (or lack thereof) on daughters' eating attitudes and behaviors. *Eating Disorders: The Journal of Treatment & Prevention, 4*, 147–159.

Schreiber, G., Robins, M., Striegel-Moore, R., Obarzanek, E., Morrison, J., & Wright, D. (1996). Weight modification efforts reported by Black and White preadolescent girls: National Heart, Lung, and Blood Institute Growth and Health Study. *Pediatrics, 98*, 63–70.

Schur, E., Sanders, M., & Steiner, H. (2000). Body dissatisfaction and dieting in young children. *International Journal of Eating Disorders, 27*, 74–82.

Schwartz, D., Phares, V., Tantleff-Dunn, S., & Thompson, J. K. (1999). Body image, psychological functioning, and parental feedback regarding physical appearance. *International Journal of Eating Disorders, 25*, 339–344.

Shapiro, S., Newcomb, M., & Loeb, T. (1997). Fear of fat, disregulated-restrained eating, and body-esteem: Prevalence and gender differences among eight- to ten-year-old children. *Journal of Clinical Child Psychology, 26*, 358–365.

Shisslak, C., Crago, M., & Estes, L. (1993). The spectrum of eating disturbances. *International Journal of Eating Disorders, 18*, 209–219.

Shisslak, C., Crago, M., McKnight, K., Estes, L., Gray, N., & Parnaby, O. (1998). Potential risk factors associated with weight control behaviors in elementary and middle school girls. *Journal of Psychosomatic Research, 44*, 301–314.

Silverstein, B., & Perlick, D. (1995). *The cost of competence: Why inequality causes depression, eating disorders, and illness in women.* New York: Oxford University Press.

Smolak, L. (1996). Methodological implications of a developmental psychopathology approach to the study of eating problems. In L. Smolak, M. P. Levine, & R. H. Striegel-Moore (Eds.), *The developmental psychopathology of eating disorders: Implications for research, prevention, and treatment* (pp. 37–55). Mahwah, NJ: Erlbaum.

Smolak, L. (1999). Elementary school curricula for the primary prevention of eating problems. In N. Piran, M. P. Levine, & C. Steiner-Adair (Eds.), *Preventing eating disorders: A handbook of interventions and special challenges* (pp. 85–104). Philadelphia: Brunner/Mazel.

Smolak, L., & Levine, M. P. (1994). Toward an empirical basis for primary prevention of eating problems with elementary school children. *Eating Disorders: The Journal of Treatment and Prevention, 2*, 293–307.

Smolak, L., & Levine, M. P. (1996a) Adolescent transitions and the development of eating problems. In L. Smolak, M. P. Levine, & R. Striegel-Moore (Eds.), *The developmental psychopathology of eating disorders: Implications for research, prevention, and treatment* (pp. 207–234). Mahwah, NJ: Erlbaum.

Smolak, L., & Levine, M. P. (1996b). *Body esteem and eating problems in young children: A longitudinal approach.* Presented at the International Society for the Study of Behavioral Development, Quebec City, Canada.

Smolak, L., & Levine, M. P. (1996c, March). *Childhood attitudes and behaviors as predictors of early adolescent eating attitudes, behaviors, and problems.* Paper presented at the Society for Research in Adolescence, Boston.

Smolak, L., Levine, M. P., & Schermer, F. (1998). Lessons from lessons: An evaluation of an elementary school prevention program. In W. Vandereycken & G. Noordenbos (Eds.), *The prevention of eating disorders* (pp. 137–172). London: Athlone Press.

Smolak, L., Levine, M. P., & Schermer, F. (1999). Parental input and weight concerns among elementary school children. *International Journal of Eating Disorders, 25,* 263–272.

Smolak, L., Levine, M. P., & Thompson, J. K. (2001). The use of the Sociocultural Attitudes towards Appearance Questionnaire with middle school boys and girls. *International Journal of Eating Disorders, 29,* 216–223.

Smolak, L., & Murnen, S. K. (2001). Gender and eating problems. In R. Striegel-Moore & L. Smolak (Eds.), *Eating disorders: Innovative directions for research and practice* (pp. 91–110). Washington, DC: American Psychological Association.

Smolak, L., & Striegel-Moore, R. (in press). Challenging the myth of the golden girl: Ethnicity and eating disorders. In R. Striegel-Moore & L. Smolak (Eds.), *Eating disorders: Innovative directions for research and practice* (pp. 111–132). Washington, DC: American Psychological Association.

Stein, S., Chalhoub, N., & Hodes, M. (1998). Very early-onset bulimia nervosa: Report of two cases. *International Journal of Eating Disorders, 24,* 323–327.

Steiner-Adair, C. (1986). The body politic: Normal female adolescent development and the development of eating disorders. *Journal of the American Academy of Psychoanalysis, 14,* 95–114.

Stice, E. (2001). Risk factors for eating pathology: Recent advances and future directions. In R. Striegel-Moore & L. Smolak (Eds.), *Eating disorders: New direction for research and practice* (pp. 57–73). Washington, DC: American Psychological Association.

Stice, E., Cameron, R., Killen, J., Hayward, C., & Taylor, C. (1999). Naturalistic weight-reduction efforts prospectively predict growth in relative weight and onset of obesity among female adolescents. *Journal of Consulting and Clinical Psychology, 67,* 967–974.

Stice, E., Hayward, C., Cameron, R., Killen, J., & Taylor, C. (2000). Body image and eating disturbances predict onset of depression among female adolescents: A longitudinal study. *Journal of Abnormal Psychology, 109,* 438–444.

Stice, E., Killen, J., Hayward, C., & Taylor, C. (1998). Support for the continuity hypothesis of bulimic pathology. *Journal of Consulting and Clinical Psychology*, 66, 784–790.

Stice, E., Nemeroff, C., & Shaw, H. (1996). A test of the dual pathway of bulimia nervosa: Evidence for dietary restraint and affect regulation mechanisms. *Journal of Social and Clinical Psychology,15*, 340–363.

Striegel-Moore, R., & Kearney-Cooke, A. (1994). Exploring parents' attitudes and behaviors about their children's physical appearance. *International Journal of Eating Disorders, 15*, 377–385.

Striegel-Moore, R., Schreiber, G., Pike, K., Wilfley, D., & Rodin, J. (1995). Drive for thinness in black and white preadolescent girls. *International Journal of Eating Disorders, 18*, 59–69.

Striegel-Moore, R., Silberstein, L., & Rodin, J. (1993). The social self in bulimia nervosa: Public self-consciousness, social anxiety, and perceived fraudulence. *Journal of Abnormal Psychology, 102*, 297–303.

Striegel-Moore, R., & Smolak, L. (1996). The role of race in the development of eating disorders. In L. Smolak, M. Levine, & R. Striegel-Moore (Eds.) *The developmental psychopathology of eating disorders: Implications for research, prevention, and treatment* (pp. 259–284). Mahwah, NJ: Erlbaum.

Striegel-Moore, R., & Smolak, L. (2000). The influence of ethnicity on eating disorders in women. In R. Eisler & M. Hersen (Eds.), *Handbook of gender, culture, and health* (pp. 227–254). Mahwah, NJ: Erlbaum.

Strober, M. (1991). Family-genetic studies of eating disorders. *Journal of Clinical Psychiatry, 52*, 9–12.

Taylor, C., Sharpe, T., Shisslak, C., Bryson, S., Estes, L., Gray, N. McKnight, K., Crago, M., Kraemer, H., & Killen, J. (1998). Factors associated with weight concerns in adolescent girls. *International Journal of Eating Disorders, 24*, 31–42.

Thelen, M., & Cormier, J. (1995). Desire to be thinner and weight control among children and their parents. *Behavior Therapy, 26*, 85–99.

Thelen, M., Powell, A., Lawrence, C., & Kuhnert, M. (1992). Eating and body image concerns among children. *Journal of Clinical Child Psychology, 21*, 41–46.

Thompson, J. K., Heinberg, L., Altabe, M., & Tantleff-Dunn, S. (1999). *Exacting beauty: Theory, assessment, and treatment of body image disturbance*. Washington, DC: American Psychological Association.

Thompson, S., Corwin, S., & Sargent, R. (1997). Ideal body size beliefs and weight concerns of fourth-grade children. *International Journal of Eating Disorders, 21*, 279–284.

Tiggemann, M., & Wilson-Barrett, E. (1998). Children's figure ratings: Relationship to self-esteem and negative stereotyping. *International Journal of Eating Disorders, 23*, 83–88.

Vander Wal, J. S., & Thelen, M. (2001). Predictors of body image dissatisfaction in elementary-age school girls. *Eating Behaviors, 1*, 1–18.

Wardle, J., Volz, C., & Golding, C. (1995). Social variation in attitudes to obesity in children. *International Journal of Obesity, 19,* 562–569.

Weinberg, M., Tronick, E., Cohn, J., & Olson, K. (1999). Gender differences in emotional expressivity and self-regulation during early infancy. *Developmental Psychology, 35,* 175–188.

Wichstrom, L. (1999). The emergence of gender differences in depressed mood during adolescence: The role of intensified gender socialization. *Developmental Psychology, 35,* 232–245.

Wolf, N. (1997). *Promiscuities: The secret struggle for womanhood.* New York: Random House.

Wood, C., Becker, J., & Thompson, J. K. (1996). Body image dissatisfaction in preadolescent children. *Journal of Applied Developmental Psychology, 17,* 85–100.

Yuker, H., & Allison, D. (1994). Obesity: Sociocultural perspectives. In L. Alexander-Mott & D. B. Lumsden (Eds.), *Understanding eating disorders: Anorexia nervosa, bulimia nervosa, and obesity* (pp. 243–270). Washington, DC: Taylor & Francis.

3

OBESITY, BODY IMAGE, AND EATING DISORDERS IN ETHNICALLY DIVERSE CHILDREN AND ADOLESCENTS

JENNIFER ZOLER DOUNCHIS,
HELEN A. HAYDEN, AND
DENISE E. WILFLEY

Into the 21st century, as populations throughout the world become more and more ethnically diverse, the study of ethnicity will continue to have ever-increasing importance. In addition, with the consumption of fatty, sugar-laden convenience foods and higher levels of sedentary behavior, the rates of obesity, body dissatisfaction, and eating disorder symptomatology among ethnically diverse children and adolescents will also continue to rise. This chapter reviews the ways in which obesity and body dissatisfaction are related to the development of eating disorders among ethnically diverse youth within the United States,[1] with a focus on treatment implications. Our goals are to (a) identify important culture-related constructs; (b) examine the prevalence of obesity by ethnicity as a context within which eating and weight-related problems arise; (c) review the literature on body image, body type preference, body dissatisfaction, and eating disorder symptomatology among ethnically diverse children and adolescents; (d) identify methodological limitations of the current literature; and (e) suggest future directions and implications for modifying treatment for these often neglected populations.

The authors would like to thank R. Robinson Welch and Brian E. Saelens for their thoughtful feedback on this manuscript.
[1]Of note, there also have been within country as well as across-country studies of ethnicity among children and adolescents conducted outside the United States which are unfortunately beyond the scope of this chapter (for a review, see e.g., Davis & Yager, 1992; Pate, Pumariega, Hester, & Garner, 1992).

ASPECTS OF ETHNIC DIVERSITY

Understanding the development of ethnic identity and the process of cultural adaptation are important, because the degree to which individuals depart from the values and behaviors of their culture of origin appears to play a crucial role in their risk for eating and weight disorders.

Ethnicity

Ethnicity refers to the designation of group differences on the basis of race (i.e., genetic makeup) as well as by culture (i.e., heritage influencing attitudes, values, and beliefs) of origin (Phinney, 1996). The majority of United States-based studies use the broad ethnic classifications of White, Black, Hispanic, Asian and Pacific Islander, and American Indian and Alaskan American. In turn, each of these groups comprises further racially and culturally distinct subgroups. For example, *Hispanic American* encompasses individuals with origins from Mexico, Puerto Rico, Cuba, Central America, Latin American, and Spain (Kumanyika, 1995). Although it may be difficult to obtain adequate numbers of research participants within each subclassification, collapsing across diverse subgroups necessarily blurs important ethnic distinctions and life circumstances.

Ethnic Identity

Additional differences among individuals of the same ethnicity are determined by ethnic identity. Ethnic identity is the degree to which an individual identifies with his or her own ethnic group, as well as the type and extent of involvement that he or she has. Ethnic identity encompasses one's experiences, preferences, attitudes (i.e., cultural beliefs about lifestyle, mental illness, and health care), and behaviors involving one's ethnicity. In this manner, ethnic identity provides a framework for acquiring a view of the self and interpreting one's experiences. Identity formation is a dynamic process that is modified throughout development (Langner et al., 1974). As an individual progresses into adolescence, a developmental crisis may result if views from another culture conflict with one's ethnic identity. It has been hypothesized that the struggle involving the acceptance of a body type preferred by one's culture of origin and the development of eating disorders is linked to ethnic identity confusion (Harris & Kuba, 1997).

Acculturation

Like ethnic identity, acculturation is a useful framework for understanding intracultural variance. A multidimensional construct (Cuellar, Arnold,

& Maldonado, 1995), acculturation involves a change in orientation from one's culture of origin toward a new culture. Differences in acculturation are a function of the age and length of time in contact with a new culture (Szapocznik, Scopetta, Kurtines, & Aranalde, 1978). Furthermore, the outcome of the acculturation process depends on the extent of an individual's ethnic identity. An individual with low ethnic identification can either remain marginalized from both cultures or become assimilated into the new one. However, an individual with high identification can remain identified with his or her culture of origin or become integrated into both (Berry & Kim, 1988).

Obesity, body dissatisfaction, and eating disorder symptomatology among ethnically diverse children and adolescents can be explained in part by the degree to which individuals are acculturated toward U.S. societal behaviors, attitudes, and values (e.g., Winkleby, Albright, Howard-Pitney, Lin, & Fortmann, 1994). The issue of culture change is helpful in establishing an individual's framework of stressors and pressures to conform (Falicov, 1996). The unfortunate effects of racial discrimination are reflected in multiple levels of acculturative stress, including those occurring chronically (e.g., poverty), as major life events (e.g., traumas and other undesirable events), and as day-to-day hassles (e.g., strain from attempting to fill prescribed social roles; Anderson, 1991). Although these stressors are recognized to affect both health and emotional well-being (Anderson, 1991), no published studies have yet examined the interaction between racial discrimination, acculturation, and distress about eating and weight.

OBESITY

Multiple factors contribute to the widespread problem of obesity among ethnically diverse youth.

Prevalence Rates

The prevalence of obesity in children and adolescents differs significantly by ethnic group (Rosner, Prineas, Loggie, & Daniels, 1998; Troiano, Flegal, Kuczmarski, Campbell, & Johnson, 1995). Data from the largest set of normative height and weight for ethnically diverse children (aged 5 to 11) and adolescents (aged 12 to 17) in the United States indicate that among females aged 5 to 17, Blacks and Hispanics have the highest measures of body mass index (BMI; Rosner et al., 1998). These rates are substantially higher than those of White and Asian females, and differences are especially apparent after age 9 (see Figure 3-1 for percentage of girls meeting 95th

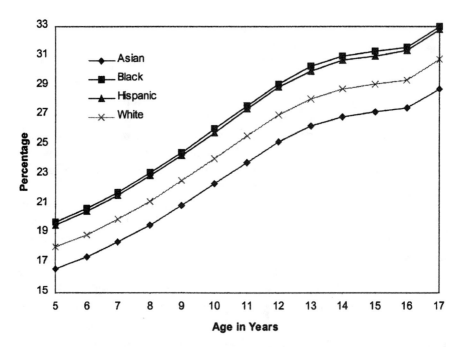

Figure 3-1. Ages 5–17: Percentage of Girls Meeting 95th and Above Percentile BMI (based on studies published between 1976 and 1994, compiled by Rosner et al., 1998).

percentile BMI).[2] Ethnic differences among males aged 5 to 17 are less distinct, but Hispanic boys have significantly higher BMIs than the other groups (see Figure 3-2). American Indians as a whole consistently have high rates of obesity (Kumanyika, 1993).

High rates of obesity are especially prevalent in certain ethnic subgroups. For example, data from the National Center for Health Statistics—Center for Disease Control reveal rates of obesity for American Indian schoolchildren ranging from 17 to 23% (Gallaher, Hauck, Yang-Oshida, & Serdula, 1991). BMI levels among Cuban preschool children have been found to be six times that which is expected, and Hmong preschoolers have been disproportionately obese as well (Kumanyika, 1993). A high prevalence of obesity has also been found in Puerto Rican schoolchildren and Native Hawaiian adolescents (Kumanyika, 1993), as well as by tribal and geographic regions (e.g., American Indians of the Midwest, Southeast, and Southwest; Davis, Gomez, Lambert, & Skipper, 1993; Knowler et al., 1991; Story, Tompkins, Bass, & Wakefield, 1986).

---

[2] Similar patterns of increasing BMI by ethnic group were found in the 85th through 95th, and 95th and above percentiles for girls and boys, respectively. Although Rosner and colleagues (1998) use the definition of greater than or equal to 95% for percent overweight, the more common use of this percentage for obesity (i.e., 95%) will be adhered to for the rest of this chapter.

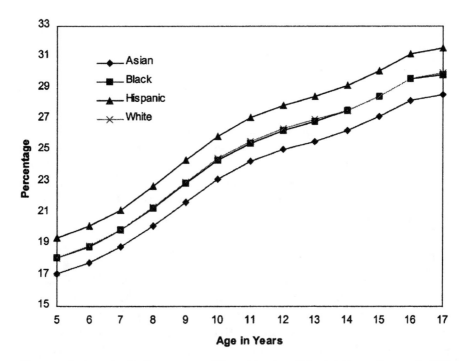

Figure 3-2. Ages 5–17: Percentage of Boys Meeting 95th and Above Percentile BMI (based on studies published between 1976 and 1994, compiled by Rosner et al., 1998).

Risk and Protective Factors

The high rates of obesity in certain ethnic groups as well as in specific subgroups can be explained by the interaction of several culturally and biologically based risk and protective factors.

Socioeconomic Status

In adulthood, there is a strong inverse relation between obesity and socioeconomic status (Sobal & Stunkard, 1989). This problem is especially apparent among ethnic minority families (e.g., Gerald, Anderson, Johnson, Hoff, & Trimm, 1994; Kumanyika, 1987), whose socioeconomic status is likely to be lower than that of Whites (Kumanyika, 1994) because of discrimination, lower levels of education, and more single-parent families (McLoyd, 1998). The relation between socioeconomic status and weight is bidirectional (Sobal, 1995). Furthermore, socioeconomic status appears to influence weight through health-related behaviors and values, such as education about nutrition. Saturated fat and cholesterol avoidance increases with increased socioeconomic status in both Mexican American and White families (Knapp, Hazuda, Haffner, Young, & Stern, 1988). In turn, weight appears to influence socioeconomic status through factors such as discrimination (Gortmaker, Must, Perrin, Sobol, & Dietz, 1993) and social mobility (Jeffery, French, Forster, & Spry, 1991).

Physical Activity

Increased obesity among ethnically diverse youth may be a result of reduced energy expenditure resulting from decreased nonsedentary behavior (Andersen, Crespo, Bartlett, Cheskin, & Pratt, 1998; Tucker, 1986). However, as studied among a primarily non-White sample of students, higher rates of television viewing appear to be only weakly associated with decreases in physical activity and increases in BMI (Robinson & Killen, 1995).

Eating Behaviors

Eating habits vary by ethnic group. Hispanic children consume the most fast food (Williams, Achterberg, & Sylvester, 1993). Higher rates of television watching, especially for Hispanic children and Asian girls (including Pacific Islanders), are associated with increased dietary fat intake (Robinson & Killen, 1995). In addition, lower levels of maternal education appear to serve as a risk factor for obesity; Mexican American mothers with less formal education serve less healthy food and monitor their children's food consumption less than those with more education (Olvera-Ezzell, Power, & Cousins, 1990).

Acculturative factors provide valuable information about the process of dietary change. Higher levels of acculturation toward U.S.-majority culture generally correspond to less healthy eating behaviors, such as increased consumption of fat (Winkleby et al., 1994). For example, second- and third-generation Asian and Hispanic adolescents are more likely to be obese than their first-generation peers (Popkin & Udry, 1998). However, the relationship between acculturation and dietary composition does not always function in this direction. The diet of Navajo Indians living on reservations is characterized by higher levels of fat than those living off of them; this is reflected in lower rates of overweight for American Indian adolescents living off reservations (Gruber, Anderson, Ponton, & DiClemente, 1995).

Genetics

There are several genetically based hypotheses for the high rates of obesity among specific ethnic groups. As even minor decreases in metabolic rates would result in sizable weight differences over the long-term, one possible explanation is lower metabolisms among individuals of certain ethnic groups. Although findings have been inconsistent, Black women and girls have been shown to have lower resting energy expenditures than

White girls (Foster, Wadden, & Vogt, 1997; Yanovski, Reynolds, Boyle, & Yanovski, 1997).

Other untestable explanations, such as the thrifty genotype hypothesis (Neel, 1962), attempt to provide an evolutionary explanation for the genetic basis of excess body fat among certain ethnic subgroups. According to such theories, the ability to retain excessive fat may have initially served an adaptive function. However, the interactions of these once invaluable traits with current conditions of overabundant dietary fat (Aluli, 1991) and more sedentary lifestyles (Davis et al., 1993) results in excessive weight. In support of such hypotheses, when returning to foods of their native culture (despite eating until fullness), Native Hawaiians have been successful in losing excess fat (Shintani, Hughes, Beckham, & O'Connor, 1991).

Puberty

Racial differences in physical maturation and sexual development are also associated with differential rates of overweight among ethnically diverse populations (Patterson et al., 1997). For example, onset of puberty is earlier for Black than for White females (Doswell, Millor, Thompson, & Braxter, 1998). Recent National Heart, Lung, and Blood Institute (NHLBI) data suggest that pubertal milestones (e.g., pubic hair distribution, areolar development, breast maturation) are strongly related to fat cell count (Kimm, Barton, Obarzanek, & Crawford, 1997), with adiposity both a cause and consequence of menstruation (Brown, Koenig, Demorales, McGuire, & Mersai, 1996).

Preferred Body Type

Research supports the existence of a larger preferred body type among Black and Hispanic females as compared to their White counterparts (Lopez, Blix, & Blix, 1995; Thompson, Corwin, & Sargent, 1997). A substantial benefit of this larger body type preference is the protection it affords to self-esteem in the face of greater levels of overweight (Kumanyika, Wilson, & Guilford-Davenport, 1993). However, a notable drawback of this protection to self-esteem is its failure to serve as a protective mechanism against obesity (Parnell et al., 1996).

BODY IMAGE

Obesity is a major risk factor for the development of eating disorders (Fairburn, Welch, Doll, Davies, & O'Connor, 1997). In addition, body image plays an essential role in this equation, because the risk for eating disorders is moderated by body dissatisfaction. Body image is the internal, subjective representation of physical appearance and bodily experience (Fisher, 1990). Thus body image largely determines body satisfaction. Regardless of ethnicity, obesity among children is consistently viewed negatively (Goldfield & Chrisler, 1995; Pierce & Wardle, 1997; see Richardson, Goodman, Hastorf, & Dornbusch, 1961, for a classic study), especially among girls. Very little research is available examining the combined impact of discrimination for both weight and ethnicity on body satisfaction and the development of eating disorders. Therefore, this chapter more generally examines the impact of ethnicity on body type preference and body satisfaction among ethnically diverse youth.

Body Type Preference

Body type preference is the ideal against which one measures or compares one's own body's size and shape. As referred to earlier, culture is a powerful determinant of body preference (Sobal, 1995). For example, in general Black females tend to associate positive characteristics (e.g., power, health, and well-being) with heavier women (Flynn & Fitzgibbon, 1996). Black females appear to be much less rigid in their conceptualization of their self-worth than their White counterparts, such that they derive a greater sense of identity from individuality, personal style, and attitude than from body shape alone (Parker et al., 1995). Preferred body shapes among Black adolescent females have been found to be more strongly influenced by immediate family members and adult role models than those of White adolescent females, which were more influenced by peers and the media (Parnell et al., 1996). Furthermore, rather than desiring thinner body shapes, nonobese black girls have been shown to hold body ideals that are actually heavier than their own current weights (e.g., Kemper et al., 1994; Parnell et al., 1996). As an additional consideration, age and degree of exposure to U.S. culture also affects preference for a thinner body type. Among Hispanic females of Latin American descent, adolescents who immigrated to the United States before age 17 were more likely to espouse a thinner body type than those immigrating after age 16 (Lopez, et al., 1995).

Body Satisfaction

Body type preference affects the degree of satisfaction with one's body. The smaller the discrepancy between ideal and actual body image, the more body satisfaction. Overall, as compared to other ethnic groups, White children are most likely to be dissatisfied with their weight or shape (Adams, Katz, Beauchamp, Cohen, & Zavis, 1993; Joiner & Kashubeck, 1996; Kemper et al., 1994; Neff, Sargent, McKeown, Jackson, & Valois, 1997; Robinson et al., 1996; Smith & Krejci, 1991; Story, French, Resnick, & Blum, 1995; Thelen, Lawrence, & Powell, 1992). Perhaps as a result of higher body weight acceptance among Black children and adolescents (Pritchard, King, & Czajka-Narins, 1997; Thompson, Corwin, & Sargent, 1997), Black females are more likely than White females to report being satisfied with their weight (Brown, Schreiber, McMahon, Crawford, & Ghee, 1995; Doswell et al., 1998; Schreiber et al., 1996; Story et al., 1995). The evidence is mixed, however, for American Indian girls, who have been shown to be more (Bronner, 1996) and less likely (Story et al., 1995) to be satisfied with their body image when compared to White girls.

Research suggests that body dissatisfaction is more pervasive in non-White females within the United States than originally thought. American Indian girls have been found to report equal body dissatisfaction when compared to White girls (Snow & Harris, 1989). Although Black adolescent females have reported being more proud of their bodies than those among other ethnic groups, including Asian American, Hispanics, and American Indians (Story et al., 1995), they have also endorsed a high drive for thinness. Drive for thinness is significantly related to overweight, and in fact Black girls have endorsed a higher drive for thinness than White girls before controlling for overweight status (Striegel-Moore, Schreiber, Pike, Wilfley, & Rodin, 1995). It should be noted, however, that when controlling for age, parental education, and BMI, White girls were more dissatisfied with their bodies than Black girls (Striegel-Moore, Schreiber, Lo, Crawford, Obarzanek, & Rodin, 2000). In Mexican American media, fashion magazines and television advertisements reflect similar thinness-equals-beauty equation that has been well-documented within the White American media (Joiner & Kashubeck, 1996). Although they may prefer a larger body type, research supports that Mexican American female adolescents idealize and desire a shape thinner than their current figure (Joiner & Kashubeck, 1996; see the appendix at the end of the chapter for specific information about body image by ethnicity).

Given the discrepant study findings at present, it cannot be assumed that one's ethnicity serves as a protective factor against body dissatisfaction among ethnically diverse female youth. Unfortunately, the field has only begun to systematically explore the risk and protective factors associated with underlying differences in body image among children and adolescents from different ethnic groups (Parker et al., 1995). Across race, increased body fat associated with the onset of puberty is related to a decrease in body satisfaction among females (Doswell et al., 1998; Duncan, Ritter, Dornbusch, Gross, & Carlsmith; 1985). More research is needed to determine the interacting influences of ethnic identity and puberty.

EATING DISORDERS

The pattern of eating disorder symptoms and syndromes among ethnically diverse youth is complex and also requires the consideration of culture-related constructs. Although little research yet exists, it can be hypothesized that children and adolescents with the strongest ethnic identification with their culture of origin may benefit the most from the protective factors of accepting a larger body size and increased body satisfaction (Kemper et al., 1994).

Eating Disorder Symptomatology

Disturbed eating behaviors and attitudes, most often stemming from maladaptive efforts to manage weight, also occur among children and adolescents across ethnicity (Crago, Shisslak, & Estes, 1996; Lachenmeyer & Muni-Brander, 1988). Conclusions have been mixed, however, with regard to whether specific eating disorder symptoms occur with equal frequency by ethnic group (see appendix for eating disorder symptomatology for females by ethnicity). Overall, dieting appears to occur most frequently in Hispanic females and least frequently in Black females (Story et al., 1995). Some research has shown that American Indians engage in greater or equal levels of self-induced vomiting than Hispanics, Blacks, Asian Americans (Smith & Krejci, 1991) and Whites (Story et al., 1995). Binge eating may be equally common or greater in Black (Childress, Brewerton, Hodges, & Jarrell, 1993) and American Indian (Smith & Krejci, 1991) than in White adolescents and appears to be more prevalent in Asian than White females (Story et al., 1995). Black (Mintz & Betz, 1988) and Hispanic (Story et al., 1995) females have endorsed using laxatives more frequently than females of other ethnic groups.

Aside from differences among individuals, differences in rates of eating disturbance across ethnic groups may reflect differences in symptoms. In turn, different risk factors may be related to differences in rates of the specific eating disorder (e.g., binge eating disorder may be more common among Black individuals because of their high rates of binge eating). In males, where less research has been conducted, conclusions are even more tentative.

As well, differences in prevalence of eating disorder symptomatology among ethnically diverse youth can be explained in large part to widely varying criteria for operationalizing and assessing disordered attitudes and behavior (Lachenmeyer & Muni-Brander, 1988). Differences can also be accounted for by controlling for other important variables. For example, in a study among high school students, differences in eating attitudes across ethnicity disappeared once weight was controlled for (Smith & Krejci,

1991). Refinements in research will help produce a more accurate picture of the exact distribution of symptomatology by age and gender across ethnicity.

Syndromal Eating Disorders

Data for the prevalence of diagnosable eating disorders is not widely available. First, few large-scale community studies have been conducted in the United States with sufficiently diverse samples. Second, Western health care is typically underused among ethnically diverse populations (Cheung & Snowden, 1990). Rather than seeking professional help for their children, Black and Hispanic families, for example, may be more likely to rely instead on family members and community resources (McMiller & Weisz, 1996). Thus the extent of these disorders among ethnically diverse children and adolescents are most likely underreported (Striegel-Moore & Smolak, 1996).

Anorexia Nervosa

Given that anorexia nervosa is typically of low prevalence in White populations, an epidemiological assessment examining anorexia nervosa by race may necessitate extremely large samples (Striegel-Moore & Smolak, 1996). However, no studies of this magnitude have been conducted (Pike & Walsh, 1996). Although little mention of race has been made within the anorexia nervosa treatment literature, the number of ethnically diverse patients in treatment has been estimated to be less than 5% of all anorexia nervosa patients (Pike & Walsh, 1996).

Bulimia Nervosa

Similar to anorexia nervosa, accurate prevalence data among ethnically diverse populations is yet unavailable. Nevertheless, interesting preliminary data have been published. Although findings among adults and college students are more mixed, it appears that the prevalence of bulimia nervosa in ethnically diverse youth are more comparable to those of White youth (e.g., Lachenmeyer & Muni-Brander, 1988; Snow & Harris, 1989), although perhaps lower among Black youth (Gross & Rosen, 1988).

Binge Eating Disorder

No large-scale community-based studies exist regarding rates of binge eating disorder among ethnically diverse children and adolescents. Binge eating and bulimia nervosa may be increasing for ethnically diverse school-children in the United States (Pike & Walsh, 1996), which is not surprising given that increases in weight are associated with increases in eating disturbances. Indeed, as noted by Pike and Walsh (1996), the addition of binge eating disorder, which frequently occurs among obese individuals, broadens the spectrum of eating disorders within which individuals struggling with overweight may fall. Although fewer children and adolescents have binge eating disorder than adults, it would be expected that ethnically diverse youth with increased overweight and obesity in childhood and adolescence will be more likely to be diagnosed with this disorder in the future. Thus it will be important to examine the specific factors involved in the development and maintenance of binge eating disorder in ethnically diverse individuals to formulate both effective and culturally appropriate treatments.

LIMITATIONS AND FUTURE DIRECTIONS

Several methodological refinements will help foster a better understanding of the nature and complexity of eating and weight concerns in ethnically diverse groups, moving the research beyond its current limitations.

Standardization by Age

Given that rates of obesity and eating disorders among ethnically diverse youth tend to vary by age (e.g., Broussard et al., 1991; Howat & Saxton, 1988), age-matched comparisons are needed. In addition, examining distributions of weight by ethnicity will provide a clearer picture of developmental trends as children grow, as well as facilitate age comparisons across ethnic groups.

Determining Weight Status

Differences in body size and the distribution of body fat by ethnic group (Anonymous, 1992; Malina, Huang, & Brown, 1995; Malina, Zavaleta, & Little, 1986) call into question present methods of overweight status determination (Dietz & Robinson, 1998). Body mass index has traditionally been considered to be the best metric to determine whether or not a child was overweight. However, as population differences in BMI are evident across ethnic groups, although slightly discrepant for boys, it has been further recommended that ethnically specific BMI percentiles be used to determine youth's overweight status (Rosner et al., 1998). Beyond merely the evaluation of weight status, however, more research is required to determine the relation between weight status and morbidity by ethnic group. Indeed, the establishment of morbidity and mortality risk for various ethnic groups based on the degree of overweight could help focus weight loss and health interventions to the most at-risk populations. As suggested by Obarzanek (1993), a solution may lie in developing new ethnically specific prediction equations, with cut-points of elevated disease risk.

Assessing Body Image Disturbance and Eating Symptomatology

New assessment measures are needed to explore body image within ethnically diverse populations. First, the current measures of body image disturbance have been designed and tested on primarily White samples (Riley et al., 1998). Ethnically specific instruments (e.g., silhouettes depicting predominant body fat distribution patterns for a particular ethnic group) are needed to assess body image concerns. Until this happens, it cannot be assumed that body image or eating disturbance is being measured from an unbiased, nonunidimensional perspective (Parker et al., 1995). In addition, identifying and controlling for additional independent contributors to body dissatisfaction (e.g., socioeconomic status; Caldwell, Brownell, & Wilfley, 1997) or eating disorder symptoms (e.g., weight status) will provide a more direct picture of the relation between eating disorders and ethnicity. Finally, rates of eating disorders symptomatology differ across studies as a result of a lack standardization (Smith & Krejci, 1991).

Assessing Acculturation

Refined methodological tools are being developed that will be helpful to assess acculturative factors in relation to body image perception (Singh, 1994) and disordered eating. An example of a promising new tool is the Scale of Ethnic Experience (Malcarne, Chavira, & Liu, 1996), which measures acculturation to and from any culture, rather than being culture-specific. With improved assessments, more research regarding the relation between ethnic identity, acculturation, and eating and weight concerns will follow.

IMPLICATIONS FOR TREATMENT

Cultural differences in program content and delivery have been shown to be strong determinants of treatment outcome. In a weight-loss study involving Black and White women, controlling for many of the participant characteristics (e.g., food preferences, exercise and dietary patterns, and biological factors associated with lower metabolic activity) did not fully explain differences in weight loss between Black and White women (Kumanyika, Obarzanek, Stevens, Hebert, & Whelton, 1991). These findings illustrate the need to examine cultural assumptions underlying existing program content and delivery, as well as the need to reconsider components of treatment.

Collectivism

Given the collectivistic orientation of Hispanic, American Indian, and Asian cultures (Marin & Marin, 1991; Triandis, 1995), protocols directed at the individual may be less appropriate than those targeting the extended family as the unit of treatment (Kumanyika & Morssink, 1997). As learned through Black, Hispanic, American Indian, and Asian child intervention research, families are the primary agents through which changes can be made (Vraniak & Pickett, 1993). For example, in a behavior weight control program targeting Black adolescents, as well as a school education program for Mexican American schoolchildren, additional family involvement resulted in more weight lost and improved dietary habits, respectively (Nader et al., 1989; Wadden et al., 1990). Although these findings do not only apply to ethnically diverse families, they nonetheless point to the need to make group therapy, family meetings, and intergenerational interventions part of eating and weight control management (Foreyt & Goodrick, 1995). Furthermore, prevention and treatment programs can be designed to capitalize on the presence of a strong sense of community by also intervening at the community level (e.g., Riley et al., 1998).

Diversity

Aside from adapting treatments for collectivistic orientations, recognizing within-group heterogeneity (McGinnis & Ballard-Barbash, 1991) can aid the development of culturally appropriate interventions. Discussions about an extended family or tribe's unique foods, activities, sedentary behaviors, rewards, parenting skills, and praise yields information that can be used to develop treatments (Tharp, 1991). As mentioned, a "pre-Western-contact" diet intervention was successfully used for Native Hawaiians to reduce obesity and cardiovascular risk. The excellent adherence appeared to be a result of the cultural appropriateness of this treatment, driven by participants' cultural pride in returning to their native foods (Shintani et al., 1991).

Treatments can easily be contextualized within family and community structures of meaning and language. Qualitative, ethnographic techniques (e.g., sorting out which foods are considered healthy versus unhealthy) can be used to determine current belief systems, and have resulted in improved, culturally specific targets for intervention in American Indian communities (Gittelsohn et al., 1996). In addition, delivering treatments through storytelling, role-playing, and linking positive eating and activity habits with folk beliefs (Foreyt & Goodrick, 1995) appear to be also of great use. Finally, as hypothesized by Williamson (1998), focusing on the function of the problem (i.e., the obesity or the eating disorder symptomatology) within the larger ethnic identification and acculturative perspective may provide important insight toward its onset, maintenance, and treatment.

Timely Interventions

The development of ethnic identity during adolescence is also a time of great risk for the development of eating disorders and obesity (Harris & Kuba, 1997). Thus this developmental stage may serve as an ideal point for effective intervention. Providing body-satisfaction-enhancing interventions and helping adolescents develop a healthy sense of one's ethnic identity may protect against future eating disorder symptomatology as well as the further onset of obesity (Jackson, Proulx, & Pelican, 1991; National Task Force on Prevention and Treatment of Obesity, 1994).

Patterns of Health Care Use

Given the lower health care use among many ethnically diverse individuals, it is crucial to reduce barriers to treatment (Cheung & Snowden, 1990). A focused approach of outreach into ethnically diverse communities could facilitate participation. Recruitment methods such as providing information to families, teachers, and schools, and using community health advisors as liaisons, may also increase the use of services by ethnically diverse patients (e.g., Eng & Young, 1992).

Acknowledging Limited Resources

Interventions must be feasible. The limited accessibility of costly fresh fruits and vegetables, low-fat foods, and safe streets and playgrounds are all realistic barriers to a healthy lifestyle for families with very limited financial resources (Foreyt & Cousins, 1993). Clinics in remote locations may be inaccessible by public transportation, and programs that operate during normal business hours inaccessible for families with working parents. Although school-based programs may appear to be an ideal solution, school populations may not include an adequate portion of the youth requiring intervention as a result of high drop-out rates among youth with mental health problems (Hoberman, 1992).

Overcoming False Assumptions

Unfortunately, ethnically diverse youth with eating disorder or body image concerns who seek treatment are at risk for not being properly diagnosed. The myth that eating disorders occur exclusively in upper-class Caucasian females may result in treatment delay and a higher threshold for diagnosis among non-White individuals (Silber, 1986). Similarly, it is recommended that public health researchers and clinicians exercise caution in assuming that ethnically diverse females are inoculated against body dissatisfaction (Williamson, 1998). The unhealthy aspects of American culture are strong and far-reaching. Therefore, it is critical that the possibility of eating and body image concerns are considered for all individuals, regardless of ethnic background.

CONCLUSION

The widespread prevalence of obesity among ethnically diverse youth is multidetermined. Genetic factors, such as parental BMI, lower resting metabolic rates, and early puberty clearly make up key components in the predisposition for obesity. On the other hand, low socioeconomic status and the predilection for modernized and sedentary fast-food lifestyles play important roles in the increased overweight among children and adolescents. Westernized values are in one sense dictated, and another sense chosen, through the process of cultural identification. Through identification with one's culture of origin and rejection of a modernized lifestyle by decreased fat consumption, decreased television viewing, and increased physical activity, the development of obesity may be mitigated.

Overall, body type preference differs by ethnic group. The general preference for a heavier body type among Black and Hispanic people may serve as a protective factor for some individuals against body dissatisfaction, which is in itself a risk factor for eating disorders. Similarly, ethnically diverse youth may be less likely to perceive themselves as overweight than White youth and tend to be more accepting of their own bodies. However, there is substantial variation by ethnic group, with the most body satisfaction reported in Black individuals, followed by Hispanics, American Indians, and Asians.

Research findings are mixed about whether the rates of eating disorder symptoms in ethnic minorities are equal to those in Whites, and if any profiles are specific to particular ethnic groups. Little or no epidemiological research has been conducted to determine the prevalence of eating disorders among ethnically diverse youth. Nonetheless, it is unmistakably evident that disturbed eating behaviors and attitudes occur across ethnicity.

Designing culturally and developmentally appropriate interventions requires an examination of the eating and weight-related beliefs, practices, and values of ethnically diverse individuals, as well as questioning our assumptions about the nature, form, and content of treatment. Interventions for Black, Hispanic, American Indian, or Asian youth may be more successful when based on the larger cultural contexts in which the problems occur.

Interventions with individuals can be tailored to particular levels of acculturation and orientation to collectivistically or individualistically based cultures. Knowledge of the acculturative heterogeneity within ethnic groups and as well as culture-specific beliefs, practices, and values can help shape the focus and content of treatment. Finally, planning interventions to correspond with the formation of ethnic identity, working within the framework of health care utilization patterns among targeted individuals, and foreseeing limited resources in communities may all assist in the thoughtful design of treatments which are more likely to be valued, valuable, and used.

REFERENCES

Adams, P., Katz, R., Beauchamp, K., Cohen, E., & Zavis, D. (1993). Body dissatisfaction, eating disorders, and depression: A developmental perspective. *Journal of Child & Family Studies, 2*, 37–46.

Anderson, L. P. (1991). Acculturative stress: A theory of relevance to Black Americans. *Clinical Psychology Review, 11*(6), 685–702.

Andersen, R. E., Crespo, C., Bartlett, S. J., Cheskin, L., & Pratt, M. (1998). Relationship of physical activity and television watching with body weight and level of fatness among children. *JAMA, 279*(12), 938–942.

Aluli, N. E. (1991). Prevalence of obesity in a Native Hawaiian population. *American Journal of Clinical Nutrition, 53*, 1556S–1560S.

Anonymous. (1992). Obesity and cardiovascular disease risk factors in black and white girls: The NHLBI Growth and Health Study. *American Journal of Public Health, 82*, 1613–1620.

Berry, J. W., & Kim, U. (1988). Acculturation and mental health. In P. R. Dasen & J. W. Berry (Eds.), *Health and cross-cultural psychology: Toward applications.* (pp. 207–236). Newbury Park, CA: Sage.

Bronner, Y. L. (1996). Nutritional status outcomes for children: Ethnic, cultural, and environmental contexts. *Journal of the American Dietetic Association, 96*, 891–903.

Broussard, B. A., Johnson, A., Himes, J. H., Story, M., Fichtner, R., Hauck, F., Bachman-Carter, K., Hayes, J., Frohlich, K., & Gray, N. (1991). Prevalence of obesity in American Indians and Alaska Natives. *American Journal of Clinical Nutrition, 53*, 1535S–1542S.

Brown, D., Koenig, T., Demorales, A., McGuire, K., & Mersai, C. (1996). Menarche age, fatness, and fat distribution in Hawaiian adolescents. *American Journal of Physical Anthropology, 99*, 239–247.

Brown, K. M., Schreiber, G. B., McMahon, R. P., Crawford, P., & and Ghee, K. (1995). Maternal influences on body satisfaction in Black and White girls aged 9 and 10: The NHLBI Growth and Health Study (NGHS). *Annals of Behavioral Medicine, 17*(3), 213–220.

Caldwell, M. B., Brownell, K. D., & Wilfley, D. E. (1997). Relationship of weight, body dissatisfaction, and self-esteem in African American and White female dieters. *International Journal of Eating Disorders, 22*(2), 127–130.

Candy, C. M., & Fee, V. E. (1998). Reliability and concurrent validity of the Kids' Eating Disorders Survey (KEDS) body image silhouettes with preadolescent girls. *Eating Disorders: The Journal of Treatment & Prevention, 6*(4), 297–308.

Cheung, F. K., & Snowden, L. R. (1990). Community mental health and ethnic minority populations. *Community Mental Health Journal, 26,* 277–291.

Childress, A. C., Brewerton, T. D., Hodges, E. L., & Jarrell, M. P. (1993). The Kids' Eating Disorders Survey (KEDS): A study of middle school students. *Journal of the American Academy of Child & Adolescent Psychiatry, 32*(4), 843–850.

Collins, M. E. (1991). Body figure perceptions and preferences among preadolescent children. *International Journal of Eating Disorders, 10*(2), 199–208.

Crago, M., Shisslak, C. M., & Estes, L. S. (1996). Eating disturbances among American minority groups: A review. *International Journal of Eating Disorders, 19,* 239–248.

Cuellar, I., Arnold, B., & Maldonado, R. (1995). Acculturation Rating Scale for Mexican Americans-II: A revision of the original ARSMA Scale. *Hispanic Journal of Behavioral Sciences, 17*(3), 275–304.

Davis, C., & Yager, J. (1992). Transcultural aspects of eating disorders: A critical literature review. *Culture, Medicine & Psychiatry, 16*(3), 377–394.

Davis, H., & Gergen, P. (1994). Self-described weight status of Mexican-American adolescents. *Journal of Adolescent Health, 15,* 407–409.

Davis, S., Gomez, Y., Lambert, L., & Skipper, B. (1993). Primary prevention of obesity in American Indian children. *Annals of the New York Academy of Sciences, 699,* 167–180.

Dietz, W. H., & Robinson, T. N. (1998). Use of the body mass index (BMI) as a measure of overweight in children and adolescents [editorial; comment]. *Journal of Pediatrics, 132,* 191–193.

Doswell, W., Millor, G., Thompson, H., & Braxter, B. (1998). Self-image and self-esteem in African-American preteen girls: Implications for mental health. *Issues in Mental Health Nursing, 19,* 71–94.

Duncan, P. D., Ritter, P. L., Dornbusch, S. M., Gross, R. T., & Carlsmith, J. M. (1985). The effects of pubertal timing on body image, school behavior, and deviance. Special Issue: Time of maturation and psychosocial functioning in adolescence: I. *Journal of Youth & Adolescence, 14*(3), 227–235.

Emmons, L. (1992). Dieting and purging behavior in black and white high school students. *Journal of the American Dietetic Association, 92,* 306–312.

Eng, E., & Young, R. (1992). Lay health advisors as community change agents. *Family & Community Health, 15*(1), 24–40.

Fairburn, C. G., Welch, S., Doll, H. A., Davies, B. A., & O'Connor, M. E. (1997). Risk factors for bulimia nervosa. A community-based case-control study. *Archives of General Psychiatry, 54,* 509–517.

Faith, M., Manibay, E., Kravitz, M., Griffith, J., & Allison, D. (1998). Relative body weight and self-esteem among African Americans in four nationally representative samples. *Obesity Research, 6,* 430–437.

Falicov, C. J. (1996). Mexican families. In M. McGoldrick, J. Giordano, & J. Pierce (Eds.), *Ethnicity and family therapy.* New York: Guilford Press.

Field, A. E., Colditz, G. A., & Peterson, K. E. (1997). Racial/ethnic and gender differences in concern with weight and in bulimic behaviors among adolescents. *Obesity Research, 5,* 447–454.

Fisher, S. (1990). The evolution of psychological concepts about the body. In T. F. Cash & T. Pruzinsky (Eds.), *Body images: Development, deviance, and change* (pp. 3–20). New York: Guilford Press.

Flynn, K., & Fitzgibbon, M. (1996). Body images and obesity risk among Black females: A review of the literature. *Annals of Behavioral Medicine, 20*(1), 13–24.

Foreyt, J. P., & Cousins, J. H. (1993). Primary prevention of obesity in Mexican-American children. *Annals of the New York Academy of Sciences, 699,* 137–146.

Foreyt, J. P., & Goodrick, G. K. (1995). Prediction in weight management outcome: Implications for practice. In D. B. Allison. & F. X. Pi-Sunyer. (Eds.), *Obesity treatment: Establishing goals, improving outcomes, and reviewing the research agenda* (pp. 199–205). New York: Plenum Press.

Foster, G. D., Wadden, T. A., & Vogt, R. A. (1997). Resting energy expenditure in obese African American and Caucasian women. *Obesity Research, 5,* 1–8.

Gallaher, M. M., Hauck, F. R., Yang-Oshida, M., & Serdula, M.K., (1991). Obesity among Mescalero preschool children. Association with maternal obesity and birth weight. *American Journal of Diseases of Children, 145,* 1262–1265.

Gerald, L. B., Anderson, A., Johnson, G. D., Hoff, C., & Trimm, R. F. (1994). Social class, social support and obesity risk in children. *Child Care, Health, & Development, 20,* 145–163.

Gittelsohn, J., Harris, S. B., Burris, K. L., Kakegamic, L., Landman, L. T., Sharma, A., Wolever, T. M., Logan, A., Barnie, A., & Zinman, B. (1996). Use of ethnographic methods for applied research on diabetes among the Ojibway-Cree in northern Ontario. *Health Education Quarterly, 23,* 365–382.

Goldfield, A., & Chrisler, J. C. (1995). Body stereotyping and stigmatization of obese persons by first graders. *Perceptual & Motor Skills, 81*(3), 909–910.

Gortmaker, S., Must, A., Perrin, J., Sobol, A., & Dietz, W. (1993). Social and economic consequences of overweight in adolescence and young adulthood. *New England Journal of Medicine, 329,* 1008–1012.

Gross, J., & Rosen, J. C. (1988). Bulimia in adolescents: Prevalence and psychosocial correlates. *International Journal of Eating Disorders, 7*(1), 51–61.

Gruber, E., Anderson, M. M., Ponton, L., & DiClemente, R. (1995). Overweight and obesity in native-American adolescents: Comparing nonreservation youths with African-American and Caucasian peers. *American Journal of Preventive Medicine, 11*, 306–310.

Guinn, B., Semper, T., Jorgensen, L., & Skaggs, S. (1997). Body image perception in female Mexican-American adolescents. *The Journal of School Health, 67*, 112–115.

Harris, D. J., & Kuba, S. A. (1997). Ethnocultural identity and eating disorders in women of color. *Professional Psychology: Research & Practice, 28*(4), 341–347.

Hoberman, H. M. (1992). Ethnic minority status and adolescent mental health services utilization. *Journal of Mental Health Administration, 19*, 246–267.

Howat, P. M., & Saxton, A. M. (1988). The incidence of bulimic behavior in a secondary and university school population. *Journal of Youth & Adolescence, 17*(3), 221–231.

Jackson, M. Y., Proulx, J. M., & Pelican, S. (1991). Obesity prevention. *American Journal of Clinical Nutrition, 53*, 1625S–1630S.

Jeffery, R., French, S., Forster, J., & Spry, V. (1991). Socioeconomic status differences in health behaviors related to obesity: The Healthy Worker Project. *International Journal of Obesity, 15*, 689–696.

Joiner, G., & Kashubeck, S. (1996). Acculturation, body image, self-esteem, and eating-disorder symptomatology in adolescent Mexican American women. *Psychology of Women Quarterly, 20*(3), 419–435.

Kemper, K. A., Sargent, R. G., Drane, J. W., Wanzer, J., Valois, R. F., & Hussey, J. R. (1994). Black and white females' perceptions of ideal body size and social norms. *Obesity Research, 2*(2), 117–126.

Kimm, S. Y., Barton, B. A., Obarzanek, E., & Crawford, P. (1997) Changes in adiposity in a biracial cohort during puberty: NHLBI Growth and Health Study (NGHS). *Canadian Journal of Cardiology, 13*(SB), 218B.

Knapp, J. A., Hazuda, H. P., Haffner, S. M., Young, E. A., & Stern, M. P. (1988). A saturated fat/cholesterol avoidance scale: Sex and ethnic differences in a biethnic population. *Journal of the American Dietetic Association, 88*(2), 172–177.

Knowler, W. C., Pettitt, D. J., Saad, M. F., Charles, M. A., Nelson, R. G., Howard, B. V., Bogardus, C., & Bennett, P. H. (1991). Obesity in the Pima Indians: Its magnitude and relationship with diabetes. *American Journal of Clinical Nutrition, 53*, 1543S–1551S.

Kumanyika, S. (1987). Obesity in black women. *Epidemiologic Reviews, 9*, 31–50.

Kumanyika, S. (1993). Ethnicity and obesity development in children. Prevention and treatment of childhood obesity. *Annals of the New York Academy of Sciences, 699*, 81–92.

Kumanyika, S. (1994). Obesity in minority populations: An epidemiologic assessment. *Obesity Research, 2*(2), 166–182.

Kumanyika, S. (1995). Obesity in minority populations. In K. D. Brownell & C. F. Fairburn (Eds.), *Eating disorders and obesity: A comprehensive handbook* (pp. 431–437). New York: Guilford Press.

Kumanyika, S., & Morssink, C. (1997). Cultural appropriateness of weight management programs. In S. Dalton (Ed.), *Overweight and weight management: The health professional's guide to understanding and practice* (pp. 69–106). Gaithersburg, MD: Aspen.

Kumanyika, S., Obarzanek, E., Stevens, V. J., Hebert, P. R., & Whelton, P. K. (1991). Weight-loss experience of black and white participants in NHLBI-sponsored clinical trials. *American Journal of Clinical Nutrition, 53,* 1631S–1638S.

Kumanyika, S., Wilson, J. F., & Guilford-Davenport, M. (1993). Weight-related attitudes and behaviors of black women. *Journal of the American Dietetic Association, 93,* 416–422.

Lachenmeyer, J. R., & Muni-Brander, P. (1988). Eating disorders in a nonclinical adolescent population: Implications for treatment. *Adolescence, 23*(90), 303–312.

Langner, T. S., Gersten, J. C., Greene, E. L., Eisenberg, J. G., Herson, J. H., & McCarthy, E. D. (1974). Treatment of psychological disorders among urban children. *Journal of Consulting and Clinical Psychology, 42,* 170–179.

Lopez, E., Blix, G., & Blix, A. (1995). Body image of Latinas compared to body image of non-Latina White women. *Health Values: The Journal of Health Behavior, Education & Promotion, 19*(6), 3–10.

Malcarne, V. L., Chavira, D. A., & Liu, P-J. (1996, August). *The Scale of Ethnic Experience: A measure for use across ethnic groups.* Paper presented at the annual convention of the American Psychological Association, Toronto, Canada.

Malina, R. M., Huang, Y. C., & Brown, K. H. (1995). Subcutaneous adipose tissue distribution in adolescent girls of four ethnic groups. *International Journal of Obesity and Related Metabolic Disorders, 19,* 793–797.

Malina, R. M., Zavaleta, A. N., & Little, B. B. (1986). Estimated overweight and obesity in Mexican American school children. *International Journal of Obesity, 10,* 483–491.

Marin, G., & Marin, B. V. (1991). *Research with Hispanic populations.* Newbury Park, CA: Sage.

McGinnis, J. M., & Ballard-Barbash, R. M. (1991). Obesity in minority populations: Policy implications of research. *American Journal of Clinical Nutrition, 53,* 1512S–1514S.

McLoyd, V. C. (1998). Socioeconomic disadvantage and child development. *American Psychologist, 53*(2), 185–204.

McMiller, W. P., & Weisz, J. R. (1996). Help-seeking preceding mental health clinic intake among African-American, Latino, and Caucasian youths. *Journal of the American Academy of Child & Adolescent Psychiatry, 35*(8), 1086–1094.

Mintz, L. B., & Betz, N. E. (1988). Prevalence and correlates of eating disordered behaviors among undergraduate women. *Journal of Counseling Psychology, 35*(4), 463–471.

Nader, P., Sallis, J., Patterson, T., Abramson, I., Rupp, J., Senn, K., Atkins, C., Roppe, B., Morris, J., Wallace, J., & Vega, W. (1989). A family approach to cardiovascular risk reduction: Results from the San Diego Family Health Project. *Health Education Quarterly*, 16(2), 229–244.

National Task Force on Prevention and Treatment of Obesity. (1994). Towards prevention of obesity: Research directions. *Obesity Research*, 2(6), 571–584.

Neel, J. V. (1962). Diabetes mellitus: A "thrifty" genotype rendered detrimental by "progress"? *American Journal of Human Genetics*, 14, 353–362.

Neff, L. J., Sargent, R. G., McKeown, R. E., Jackson, K. L., & Valois, R. F. (1997). Black-white differences in body size perceptions and weight management practices among adolescent females. *Journal of Adolescent Health*, 20, 459–465.

Neumark-Sztainer, D., Story, M., French, S. A., & Resnick, M. D. (1997). Psychosocial correlates of health compromising behaviors among adolescents. *Health Education Research*, 12(1), 37–52.

Obarzanek, E. (1993). Methodological issues in estimating the prevalence of obesity in childhood. *Annals of the New York Academy of Sciences*, 699, 278–279.

Olvera-Ezzell, N., Power, T. G., & Cousins, J. H. (1990). Maternal socialization of children's eating habits: Strategies used by obese Mexican-American mothers. Special Issue: Minority children. *Child Development*, 61(2), 395–400.

Parker, S., Nichter, M., Nichter, M., Vuckovic, N., Sims, C., & Ritenbaugh, C. (1995). Body image and weight concerns among African American and White adolescent females: Differences that make a difference. *Human Organization*, 54(2), 103–114.

Parnell, K., Sargent, R., Thompson, S., Duhe, S., Valois, R., & Kemper, R. (1996). Black and white adolescent females' perceptions of ideal body size. *Journal of School Health*, 66, 112–118.

Pate, J. E., Pumariega, A. J., Hester, C., & Garner, D. M. (1992). Cross-cultural patterns in eating disorders: A review. *Journal of the American Academy of Child & Adolescent Psychiatry*, 31(5), 802–809.

Patterson, M., Stern, S., Crawford, P., McMahon, R., Similo, S., Schreiber, G., Morrison, J., & Waclawiw, M. (1997). Sociodemographic factors and obesity in preadolescent black and white girls: NHLBI's growth and health study. *Journal of the National Medical Association*, 89, 594–600.

Phinney, J. S. (1996). When we talk about American ethnic groups, what do we mean? *American Psychologist*, 51(9), 918–927.

Pierce, J., & Wardle, J. (1997). Cause and effect beliefs and self-esteem in overweight children. *Journal of Child Psychology and Psychiatry & Allied Disciplines*, 38(6), 645–650.

Pike, K. M., & Walsh, B. T. (1996). Ethnicity and eating disorders: implications for incidence and treatment. *Psychopharmacology Bulletin*, 32, 265–274.

Popkin, B. M., & Udry, J. R. (1998). Adolescent obesity increases significantly in second and third generation U.S. immigrants: the National Longitudinal Study of Adolescent Health. *Journal of Nutrition*, 128, 701–706.

Pritchard, M. E., King, S. L., & Czajka-Narins, D. M. (1997). Adolescent body mass indices and self-perception. *Adolescence, 32*(128), 863–880.

Richardson, S. A., Goodman, N., Hastorf, A. H., & Dornbusch, S. M. (1961). Cultural uniformity in reaction to physical disabilities. *American Sociological Review, 26*, 241–247.

Riley, N. M., Bild, D. E., Cooper, L., Schreiner, P., Smith, D. E., Sorlie, P., & Thompson, J. K. (1998). Relation of self-image to body size and weight loss attempts in black women: The CARDIA study. Coronary Artery Risk Development in Young Adults. *American Journal of Epidemiology, 148*, 1062–1068.

Robinson, T. N., & Killen, J. D. (1995). Ethnic and gender differences in the relationships between television viewing and obesity, physical activity, and dietary fat intake. *Journal of Health Education, 26*(2), S94–S98.

Robinson, T. N., Killen, J. D., Litt, I. F., Hammer, L. D., Wilson, D. M., Haydel, K. F., Hayward, C., & Taylor, C. B. (1996). Ethnicity and body dissatisfaction: Are Hispanic and Asian girls at increased risk for eating disorders? *Journal of Adolescent Health, 19*(6), 384–393.

Rosner, B., Prineas, R., Loggie, J., & Daniels, S. R. (1998). Percentiles for body mass index in U.S. children 5 to 17 years of age. *Journal of Pediatrics, 132*, 211–222.

Schreiber, G. B., Robins, M., Striegel-Moore, R., Obarzanek, E., Morrison, J. A., & Wright, D. J. (1996). Weight modification efforts reported by black and white preadolescent girls: National Heart, Lung, and Blood Institute Growth and Health Study. *Pediatrics, 98*, 63–70.

Shintani, T. T., Hughes, C. K., Beckham, S., & O'Connor, H. K. (1991). Obesity and cardiovascular risk intervention through the ad libitum feeding of traditional Hawaiian diet. *American Journal of Clinical Nutrition, 53*, 1647S–1651S.

Silber, T. J. (1986). Anorexia nervosa in Blacks and Hispanics. *International Journal of Eating Disorders, 5*(1), 121–128.

Singh, D. (1994). Body fat distribution and perception of desirable female body shape by young Black men and women. *International Journal of Eating Disorders, 16*(3), 289–294.

Smith, J. E., & Krejci, J. (1991). Minorities join the majority: Eating disturbances among Hispanic and Native American youth. *International Journal of Eating Disorders, 10*(2), 179–186.

Snow, J. T., & Harris, M. B. (1989). Disordered eating in South-western Pueblo Indians and Hispanics. *Journal of Adolescence, 12*(3), 329–336.

Sobal, J. (1995). Social influences on body weight. In K. D. Brownell & C. F. Fairburn (Eds.), *Eating disorders and obesity: A comprehensive handbook* (pp. 73–77). New York: Guilford Press.

Sobal, J., & Stunkard, A. J. (1989). Socioeconomic status and obesity: A review of the literature. *Psychological Bulletin, 105*(2), 260–275.

Stevens, J., Alexandrov, A. A., Smirnova, S. G., Deev, A. D., Gershunskaya Y. B., Davis, C. E., & Thomas, R. (1997). Comparison of attitudes and behaviors related to nutrition, body size, dieting, and hunger in Russian, Black-American, and White-American adolescents. *Obesity Research, 5,* 227–236.

Stevens, J., Story, M., Becenti, A., French, S. A., Gittelsohn, J., Going, S. B., Juhaer, Levin, S., & Murray, D. M. (1999). Weight-related attitudes and behaviors in fourth grade American Indian children. *Obesity Research, 7*(1), 34–42.

Story, M., French, S. A., Resnick, M. D., & Blum, R. W. (1995). Ethnic/racial and socioeconomic differences in dieting behaviors and body image perceptions in adolescents. *International Journal of Eating Disorders, 18*(2), 173–179.

Story, M., Hauck, F. R., Broussard, B. A., White, L. L., Resnick, M. D., & Blum, R. W. (1994). Weight perceptions and weight control practices in American Indian and Alaska Native adolescents. A national survey. *Archives of Pediatric and Adolescent Medicine, 148,* 567–571.

Story, M., Tompkins, R. A., Bass, M. A., & Wakefield, L. M. (1986). Anthropometric measurements and dietary intakes of Cherokee Indian teenagers in North Carolina. *Journal of the American Dietetic Association, 86,* 1555–1560.

Striegel-Moore, R. H., Schreiber, G. B., Lo, A., Crawford, P., Obarzanek, E., & Rodin, J. (2000). Eating disorder symptoms in a cohort of 11- to 16-year-old black and white girls: The NHLBI Growth and Health Study. *International Journal of Eating Disorders, 27*(1), 49–66.

Striegel-Moore, R. H., Schreiber, G. B., Pike, K. M., Wilfley, D. E., & Rodin, J. (1995). Drive for thinness in black and white preadolescent girls. *International Journal of Eating Disorders, 18,* 59–69.

Striegel-Moore, R., & Smolak, L. (1996). The role of race in the development of eating disorders. In L. Smolak, M. P. Levine, & R. Striegel-Moore (Eds.), *The developmental psychopathology of eating disorders: Implications for research, prevention, and treatment* (pp. 259–284). Mahwah, NJ: Erlbaum.

Szapocznik, J., Scopetta, M. A., Kurtines, W., & Aranalde, M. D. (1978). Theory and measurement of acculturation. *Revista Interamericana de Psicologia, 12*(2), 113–130.

Tharp, R. (1991). Cultural diversity and treatment of children. Special Section: Clinical child psychology: Perspectives on child and adolescent therapy. *Journal of Consulting and Clinical Psychology, 59,* 799–812.

Thelen, M. H., Lawrence, C. M., & Powell, A. L. (1992). Body image, weight control, and eating disorders among children. The etiology of bulimia nervosa: The individual and familial context. *Series in applied psychology: Social issues and questions,* 81–101.

Thompson, S. H., Corwin, S. J., & Sargent, R. G. (1997). Ideal body size beliefs and weight concerns of fourth-grade children. *International Journal of Eating Disorders, 21,* 279–284.

Triandis, H. C. (1995). *Individualism and collectivism.* Boulder, CO: Westview Press.

Troiano, R. P., Flegal, K. M., Kuczmarski, R. J., Campbell, S. M., & Johnson, C. L. (1995). Overweight prevalence and trends for children and adolescents.

The National Health and Nutrition Examination Surveys, 1963 to 1991. *Archives of Pediatric and Adolescent Medicine, 149,* 1085–1091.

Tucker, L. A. (1986). The relationship of television viewing to physical fitness and obesity. *Adolescence, 21*(84), 797–806.

Vraniak, D., & Pickett, S. (1993). Improving interventions with American ethnic minority children: Recurrent and recalcitrant challenges. *Handbook of psychotherapy with children and adolescents,* 502–540.

Wadden, T. A., Stunkard, A. J., Rich, L., Rubin, C. J., Sweidel, G., & McKinney, S. (1990). Obesity in black adolescent girls: A controlled clinical trial of treatment by diet, behavior modification, and parental support. *Pediatrics, 85,* 345–352.

Williams, J. D., Achterberg, C., & Sylvester, G. P. (1993). Target marketing of food products to ethnic minority youth. In C. L. Williams. & S. Y. Kimm. (Eds.), *Prevention and treatment of childhood obesity* (pp. 107–114). New York: New York Academy of Science.

Williamson, L. (1998). Eating disorders and the cultural forces behind the drive for thinness: Are African American women really protected? *Social Work in Health Care, 28,* 61–73.

Winkleby, M. A., Albright, C. L., Howard-Pitney, B., Lin, J., & Fortmann, S. P. (1994). Hispanic/white differences in dietary fat intake among low educated adults and children. *Preventive Medicine, 23,* 465–473.

Yanovski, S. Z., Reynolds, J. C., Boyle, A. J., & Yanovski, J. A. (1997). Resting metabolic rate in African-American and Caucasian girls. *Obesity Research, 5,* 321–325.

Appendix
Summary of Body Image and Eating Disorder Studies Within Ethnically Diverse Child and Adolescent Populations

Author(s)	Race	Age	Findings
Body Image			
Stevens et al., 1999	AI	4th grade	2nd thinnest figure (modified Stunkard ratings) chosen by 13% of girls, 3rd thinnest by 39% of girls, middle chosen by 38%
			Children who tried weight loss were more likely to have smaller desired vs. perceived body sizes and more likely to report being unhappy with weight
			48% AI girls endorsed ideal thinner than perceived body and 22% endorsed heavier ideal
			Overall, older tribal members preferred heavier body sizes; younger members preferred thinner figure
Guinn et al., 1997	H	8th grade	Sign. (−) association between body image (BI) and body fat composition; lower self-esteem related to poor BI and less feeling of control over body
David & Gergen, 1994	H	12–19	Concerns re: OW greater among adolescent females than males (19% vs. 2%)
Story et al., 1994	AI, AL	7th–9th grade	AI more likely to have body dissatisfaction (49.8% vs. 46.0%)
Snow & Harris, 1989	AI, H	High School	Majority of girls, regardless of ethnicity, endorsed being worried about weight Rural minority group individuals expressed concerns re: weight and disordered eating patterns similar to those found in urban W females
Candy & Fee, 1998	B, W	8–13	B girls indicated larger perceived body size than W girls and had sign. higher mean BMIs
			B girls (10-year-olds) were more dissatisfied with bodies and preferred smaller body size than both W girls and older B girls
Doswell et al., 1998	B, W	9–12	Prepubertal B girls had higher BI scores, greater tolerance for higher BMI, and more satisfied with nonthin body frame than prepubertal W girls
Williamson, 1998	B, W	**	Population defined as "women and girls" in this review paper
			May see higher acceptance of body shape, but Bs are not completely isolated from effects of mainstream; this should not be ignored in treatment
Neff et al., 1997	B, W	14–18	W female adolescents were more likely (41%) to perceive self as OW than B females (29%)
			W female adolescents had 1.57 times greater odds of perceiving self as OW than B female adolescents
			Association was sign. for body size perception and weight loss goals: 60% W, 34% B—with weight loss as goal
			W females were sign. more likely to want to lose weight than B females

Study		Age	Findings
Thompson et al., 1997	B, W	8–12	W females' greater desire for thinness than B females may predispose them to EDs
			Interaction of gender times race times SES has strong influence on selection of ideal body size and determination of body satisfaction
			38% B females and 41% W females hold same ideal as current body; W female weight concern greater than B weight concern, but SES interaction is important
			46% B vs. 51% W have ideal that is thinner current body; 15% B vs. 8% W hold ideal heavier than current body
			B children selected sign. heavier ideal size than W for self and ideal female child; B selected sign. heavier size perceived of self than W
Flynn & Fitzgibbon, 1996	B, W	9–12	Nonobese B girls idealize body sizes heavier than current weight; Approximately 25% of nonobese B girls endorsed "gain weight" preference
Schreiber et al., 1996	B, W	9–10	B girls were less dissatisfied with their body shape and body parts
Brown et al., 1995	B, W	9–10	Higher levels of body satisfaction in heavy B daughters compared to heavy W daughters
Parker et al., 1995	B, W	(13–18)	B attitude ("use what you got") differs from W rigid ideas of "perfect body"; more (-) BI attitudes and self-perception among W adolescent females
Parnell et al., 1996	B, W	(13–18)	B adolescent females selected ideal female body size sign. larger than W adolescent females
			B adolescent females perceived parents would select sign. larger ideal female body size than size perceived by W adolescent females of parents[a]
			B adolescent females believed female friends would select sign. larger ideal female body size than W adolescent females believed about their female friends
			B adolescent females believed male friends would select sign. ideal female body size than W adolescent females believed male friends would prefer
			B adolescent females were 5.3 times more likely to desire larger hip/buttocks size than W; B adolescent females were 4 times more likely to prefer larger thigh size than W
			B adolescent females were more influenced re: body size questions by immediate family members than W adolescent females
			W adolescent females were more influenced re: body size questions by their peers than B adolescent females

(*continued*)

Appendix (*Continued*)

Summary of Body Image and Eating Disorder Studies Within Ethnically Diverse Child and Adolescent Populations

Author(s)	Race	Age	Findings
Kemper et al., 1994	B, W	13–19	Both B & W females perceived social norms for body size as smaller than their ideal
			W more likely to perceive parents wanting them to lose weight; B perceived parents as wanting neither weight gain nor loss
			W females perceived greater disparity between ideal of parents than their ideal body weight
			B females desired less than W to be smaller; B females tended to feel size satisfactory for significant others
			B females were approximately 2 times more likely than W females to describe selves as thin and 7 times more likely to state as not OW
			W females were more dissatisfied with body size than B females; W wanted to be smaller, B tended to be more satisfied
			Body size ideal was larger for B; body size considered ideal by B was sign. larger than size selected by W females
Story et al., 1995	B, W	12–20	Lower perceptions of OW found in B than W; higher rates of body satisfaction among B than W females
			Overall, lower perception of OW in Bs than Ws; higher rates of body satisfaction among B than W females
Striegel-Moore et al., 1995	B, W	9–10	B girls reported sign. greater drive for thinness than W girls, but when controlling for OW status had equal drive for thinness
Childress et al., 1993	B, W	9–16	More W (46.4%) than B (29.2%) felt fat; more W (45.8%) wanted weight loss (B = 33.9%); more W (26.2%) were afraid of weight gain (B = 14.1%)
Thelen et al., 1992	B, W	≤12	W girls indicated more concern about being or becoming OW than B girls
			Bs desired figure that was larger than perceived current figure and Ws indicated desire to have thinner-than-current figure
Collins, 1991	B, W	9–12	B preadolescents consistently selected heavier figures than W for self and ideal self on Stunkard-figure-rating-type scale
			Desire for thinner ideal figures were same for B & W females; overall preference for thinness among both racial groups, even among preadolescents

Study	Groups	Age/Grade	Findings
Lopez et al., 1995	H, W	15–45	H more likely than non-H to consider selves OW; H had heavier ideal body size; H born in U.S. had smaller body size preference than those not U.S.-born Those immigrating to U.S. before age 17 were more like non-H; those immigrating after 16, not like non-H
Robinson et al., 1996	A, H, W	6th–7th grade	H girls reported sign. greater body dissatisfaction than W girls, A girls in between H and W; 3 groups didn't differ sign. in choices of desired body After adjustment for BMI, normal and OW W, H, A girls reported similar levels of body dissatisfaction Among leanest 25%, H and A reported sign. more body dissatisfaction than W girls
Field et al., 1997	AI, H, W	9th–12th grade	53.2% H girls wanted to lose weight compared to 40.6% W girls
Pritchard et al., 1997	B, H, W	15–19	B females had higher BMI than W females, but less likely to perceive selves as OW and had more positive self-concepts Overall those who judged selves as OW had higher BMIs; W females had most negative self-image; B females had most positive self-image Ws had lowest BMI of those who perceived selves as OW (19.4 vs. 20.43 for Bs; 20.06 for Hs) Being female was strongest predictor of (−) self-concept; with perception of OW came increased (−) self-concept
Anonymous, 1997	B, H, W	9th–12th grade	Hs (30.4%) more likely than Bs (23.5%) to perceive self as OW; All girls (33.5%) more likely than boys (22.2%) to perceive self as OW
Faith et al., 1998	B, H, O, W	13–20	Found no association between relative body weight and self-esteem in B
Joiner & Kashubeck, 1996	A, B, H, O, W	12–18	Dissatisfaction with BI common in all female adolescents—females perceive current body figure as heavier than figure perceived as ideal/most attractive to males
Adams et al., 1993	A, B, H, O, W	5th, 8th, 12th grade	All females more likely to prefer thinner-than-average body; W more dissatisfied with bodies (30%) than H (25%), A (17%), B (10%), or O (18%)
Smith & Krejci, 1991	A, AI, B, H, W	High School	Dissatisfaction with body shape: AI (24%), W (19.9%), H (13.8%)
Dieting			
Stevens et al., 1999	B, W	4th grade	37% W girls vs. 43% B girls tried to lose weight; studies with AI girls indicated eating disturbances and unhealthy weight loss practices common

(continued)

Appendix (Continued)
Summary of Body Image and Eating Disorder Studies Within Ethnically Diverse Child and Adolescent Populations

Author(s)	Race	Age	Findings
Neff et al., 1997	B, W	14–18	6 times greater odds of W teens taking diet pills than B; 3.8 times greater odds of diet and exercise to control weight than B
Schreiber, 1996	B, W	9–10	Attempts to gain weight much more frequent among B preadolescent girls than W girls; B girls more likely to report trying to gain weight than W girls
Story et al., 1995	B, W	12–20	Less dieting found in B than W; perhaps more tolerant of attitudes toward weight—i.e., less definition of attractiveness in terms of weight in B culture
Emmons et al., 1992	B, W	High School	61% of B girls dieted compared to 77% of W girls
Robinson et al., 1996	H, W	6th–7th grade	W and H females share similar attitudes concerning dieting and weight
Anonymous, 1997	B, H, W	9th–12th grade	H (46%), B (36%) trying to lose weight; W and H girls were sign. more likely than B women to try to lose weight
Story et al., 1994	A, AI, B, H, W	7th–9th grade	The prevalence of dieting lower in AI adolescents, but correlations of dieting are similar, suggesting common underlying mechanisms
OW, AI adolescents more likely to diet frequently and engage in unhealthy weight control practices than normal-weight adolescents
In all ethnic groups, dieting was associated with weight dissatisfaction, perceived OW and low body pride
AI girls less likely to have ever dieted to lose weight (48% vs. 66.8%); AI girls less likely to be chronic dieters to lose weight (6.6% vs. 12.8%)
Vomiting			
Stevens et al., 1999	AI	4th grade	AI did not report vomiting for weight loss
Story et al., 1994	AI, AL	7th–9th grade	AI girls more likely to vomit in general than W girls (27.1% vs. 12.6%)
Neff et al., 1997	B, W	14–18	W teens had 6.04 times odds of vomiting to manage weight than B, even when controlling for SES
Emmons et al., 1992	B, W	High School	More W girls than B girls self-induced vomiting (16% vs. 3%)
Neumark-Stzainer et al., 1997	AI, H, W	High School	AI and H girls were more likely than W girls to report purging
Anonymous, 1997	B, H, W	9th–12th grade	H girls more likely than B girls to have taken laxatives or vomited to lose weight or prevent weight gain (10.4% vs. 6.3%)
Field et al., 1997	B, H, W	9th–12th grade	Fewer W than B or H girls used vomiting to control their weight

			Results
Smith & Krejci, 1991	AI, H, W	High School	Self-induced vomiting: AI (10.7%), W (4.6%), H (4.3%)
Story et al., 1995	A, AI, B, H, W	12–20	B girls were more likely to have intentionally vomited after eating compared to W Rates of vomiting (% ever vomited): H (21.3%), AI (19.2%), B (17.9%), A (16.5%), W (12.6%)
Diuretics/Laxatives			
Story et al., 1994	AI, AL	7th–9th grade	AI girls less likely to use laxatives to lose weight than W girls (0.6% vs. 1.6%); AI girls less likely to use diuretics to lose weight (1.2% vs. 1.6%)
Emmons et al., 1992	B, W	High School	More B girls than W girls used laxatives (18% vs. 7%, respectively)
Anonymous, 1997	B, H, W	9th–12th grade	H more likely than B girls to have taken laxatives or vomited to lose weight or prevent weight gain (10.4% vs. 6.3%)
Story et al., 1995	A, B, H, W	12–20	Females endorsing laxative use: H (3.4%), AI (2.1%), W (1.9%), B (1.8%), A (1.6%) Females endorsing diuretic use: H (4.0%), AI (2.7%), W (1.8%), B (1.6%), A (0.4%) 2 times the number of H girls reported using diuretics or laxatives to lose weight than other ethnic females
Binge Eating			
Story et al., 1994	AI, AL	7th–9th grade	AI girls more likely to binge eat (41.7% vs. 33.2%)
Snow & Harris, 1989	AI, H	High School	Majority of girls reported being worried about weight and binge eating
Smith & Krejci, 1991	AI, H, W	High School	Binge eating behavior: AI (56.6%), W (46.1%), H (42.2%)
Story et al., 1995	A, B, H, W	12–20	% ever binged: A (33.6%), W (30.6%), AI (29%), H (25.2%), B (23%) girls % ever out of control eating: A (25.6%), W (17.7%), H (16%), AI (13.9%), B (10.2%) girls B less likely to have binged than W; A more likely to report binge eating and out-of-control eating than W
Eating Disorders—General			
Snow & Harris, 1989	AI, H	High School	No ethnic differences found; 9 girls reported eating habits consistent with *DSM-III* criteria for BN
Story et al., 1995	B, W	12–20	B less likely to have binged or feel out of control eating and more likely to have intentionally vomited after eating compared to W

(continued)

Appendix (Continued)
Summary of Body Image and Eating Disorder Studies Within Ethnically Diverse Child and Adolescent Populations

Author(s)	Race	Age	Findings
Smith & Krejci, 1991	AI, H, W	High School	AI scored highest on EDI; rate of disturbed eating patterns in H and AI comparable to those of W
			AI consistently scored highest on each of 7 items representing disturbed eating behaviors and attitudes
			Rate of disturbed eating patterns of AI and H youths are comparable to W youths
Lachenmeyer & Muni-Brander, 1988	A/O, B, H, W	13–19	More A/O and sign. fewer B met modified *DSM-III* criteria for BN
Story et al., 1994	A, AI, H, B, W	7th–9th grade	Compared with W girls, eating disturbances less frequent in B and A girls, as equally common in H girls, and more frequent than in AI girls
			Purging status in AI was sign. associated with perceived OW, weight dissatisfaction, peer acceptance concerns, emotional stress, and suicide risk
Howat & Saxton, 1988	A, AI, H, B, W	High School	More W females report bulimic behavior than Bs; more W females reported bulimic behaviors than B, H, or A
Gross & Rosen, 1988	A, AI, H, B, W	9th–12th grade	Girls reported as bulimic: W 58/536 (11%), B 3/100 (3%), A 2/14 (14%), H 2/22 (9%)
			Although not found statistically sign. it should be noted that BN was much less common in B females
Adams et al., 1993	A, AI, B, H, W	5th, 8th, 12th grade	Found EDs prevalent among ethnic groups (W = 30%; H = 25%; A = 17%; B = 10%)

Key: A = Asian, A/O = Asian/Other, AI = American Indian, AL = Alaskan Indian, B = black, H = Hispanic, O = Other, W = white; BI = body image; BMI = body mass index; BN = bulimia nervosa; ED = eating disorder; EDI = Eating Disorder Inventory; OW = overweight; SES = socioeconomic status; sign. = significant, significantly.
[a]With higher SES levels, adolescents perceived parents would choose smaller body size.

II

RISK FACTORS

Prospective research (e.g., Attie & Brooks-Gunn, 1989; Graber, Brooks-Gunn, Paikoff, & Warren, 1994; Killen et al., 1994; Leon, Fullkerson, Perry, & Early-Zald, 1995) indicates clearly that body image and eating problems in early to middle adolescence predict to more severe eating problems, and perhaps even eating disorders, in later adolescence. It is not particularly clear when this relationship emerges. In other words, we do not yet know that body image problems in early elementary school are related to adolescent or adulthood eating problems. Furthermore, we have only begun to identify risk factors that might contribute to the early adolescent body image and eating problems that in turn predict disordered eating. Even less information is available concerning protective factors.

Although there is some controversy over definitions (see, e.g., Leadbeater, Kuperminc, Blatt, & Hertzog, 1999), the term *risk factor* generally refers to influences that increase the likelihood that an individual will develop an eating problem, and *protective factors* are those characteristics and opportunities that decrease the chances that a problem will emerge. Catherine Shisslak and Marjorie Crago begin their chapter by discussing the meaning of risk and protective factors in more depth. They then provide an overview of the empirical research on risk and protective factors for subthreshold and clinical cases of eating disorders, with special attention to those influences that might be sufficiently malleable to be addressed in prevention and treatment programs. The chapter underscores the difficulty of research in this area because of the multiple factors and pathways that may lead to eating problems (equifinality).

The other two chapters in this section focus on specific risk factors that have received substantial attention in the adult literature. Ari Steinberg and Vicky Phares discuss family issues, including general family systems and family functioning issues. Their analysis underscores the fact that some of the risk factors for eating problems are not truly specific to eating problems—for example, family dysfunction may provide a backdrop for the development of any number of psychological disorders. However, Steinberg and Phares also discuss family influences such as teasing about weight and shape, factors that are likely to be specific contributors to eating disorders. This distinction raises important questions for the prevention and treatment of eating problems, particularly among young children who are not likely to be as able to shape or alter their family's behaviors as adults might be.

Mary Connors tackles the controversial and confusing area of child sexual abuse and its influence on body image. As with family influences, there is little doubt that child sexual abuse may increase the likelihood of a variety of disorders. This has created considerable controversy within the adult literature about whether child sexual abuse is really a risk factor of eating disorders (see, e.g., Connors & Morse, 1993; Wooley, 1994). Connors's chapter clearly emphasizes the need to investigate the relationship of childhood sexual abuse to childhood and adolescent (as opposed to adult) body image and eating problems. She also presents important ideas about the potential pathways of childhood sexual abuse's influence that should help to guide future research.

The formulation of research questions is one of the goals of this volume. Shisslak and Crago, Steinberg and Phares, and Connors all raise unanswered questions and point out gaps in the research that should help to guide future empirical work on eating problems. As such, these chapters are important contributions to our efforts to discover the root causes of body image and eating disturbances.

REFERENCES

Attie, I., & Brooks-Gunn, J. (1989). Development of eating problems in adolescent girls: A longitudinal study. *Developmental Psychology, 25*, 70–79.

Connors, M., & Morse, W. (1993). Sexual abuse and eating disorders: A review. *International Journal of Eating Disorders, 13*, 1–11.

Graber, H., Brooks-Gunn, J., Paikoff, R., & Warren, M. (1994). Prediction of eating problems: An 8-year study of adolescent girls. *Developmental Psychology, 30*, 823–834.

Killen, J., Taylor, C., Hayward, C., Wilson, D., Haydel, K., Hammer, L., Simmonds, B., Robinson, T., Litt, I., Varady, A., & Kraemer, H. (1994). Pursuit of thinness and onset of eating disorder symptoms in a community sample of adolescent girls: A three year prospective analysis. *International Journal of Eating Disorders, 16*, 227–238.

Leadbeater, B., Kuperminc, G., Blatt, S., & Hertzog, C. (1999). A multivariate model of gender differences in adolescents' internalizing and externalizing problems. *Developmental Psychology, 35*, 1268–1282.

Leon, G., Fulkerson, J., Perry, C., & Early-Zaid, M. (1995). Prospective analysis of personality and behavioral vulnerabilities and gender influences in the later development of disordered eating. *Journal of Abnormal Psychology, 104*, 140–149.

Wooley, S. (1994). The female therapist as outlaw. In P. Fallon, M. A. Katzman, & S. C. Wooley (Eds.), *Feminist perspectives on eating disorders* (pp. 318–338). New York: Guilford Press.

4

RISK AND PROTECTIVE FACTORS IN THE DEVELOPMENT OF EATING DISORDERS

CATHERINE M. SHISSLAK AND MARJORIE CRAGO

The purpose of this chapter is to provide an overview of the research that has been done on risk and protective factors for eating disorders (EDs) in children and adolescents and draw inferences from this research that can be applied to the treatment and prevention of EDs. It is beyond the scope of this chapter to provide a detailed critique of individual studies. The research discussed in this chapter includes studies of subclinical EDs as well as anorexia nervosa (AN), bulimia nervosa (BN), and binge eating disorder (BED).

The goals of risk factor research are to formulate etiological models for a particular disorder, design preventive or treatment interventions for the disorder, and identify those individuals or groups most at risk and, therefore, most likely to benefit from these interventions. Risk factor research involves the study of both risk and protective factors. *Risk factors* refer to "antecedent conditions associated with an increase in the likelihood of adverse, deleterious, or undesirable outcomes" and *protective factors* refer to "antecedent conditions associated with a decrease in the likelihood of undesirable outcomes or an increase in the likelihood of positive outcomes" (Kazdin, Kraemer, Kessler, Kupfer, & Offord, 1997, p. 377).

It is important to demonstrate that risk and protective factors precede the outcome of interest. If they do not, it is more appropriate to refer to them as correlates, concomitants, or consequences of the disorder (Kazdin et al., 1997). Risk factors have been categorized into three types: fixed markers, variable markers, and causal risk factors (Kazdin et al., 1997). A fixed marker is a risk factor that cannot be changed (e.g., race, gender, year of birth) and a variable marker is a risk factor that changes or can be changed but changing it does not affect the outcome. A causal risk factor, on the other hand, is one that is manipulable and, when manipulated, changes the outcome. Fixed and variable markers can be very useful in choosing a population to target for a preventive intervention or treatment program. However, in designing an intervention, it is essential to focus on causal risk factors because these are the only factors that are capable of altering the outcome. In addition to identifying risk and protective factors, it is also important to study those variables that mediate or moderate the effects of these factors. *Moderators* are variables that influence the direction and magnitude of the risk factor–outcome relationship, and *mediators* refer to the processes or mechanisms by which a factor, or set of factors, operates to produce an outcome (Kazdin et al., 1997).

Risk and protective factors for a particular disorder may vary as a function of age, gender, ethnicity, and social class (Kazdin et al., 1997; O'Connor & Rutter, 1996). Also, different factors may be responsible for the onset of a disorder than for maintenance, recovery, or relapse. In addition, risk and protective factors may be either general or specific. General factors are those associated with a variety of disorders, and specific factors are associated with one particular disorder. With many disorders, there is more than one causal pathway to the disorder, consisting of both general and specific factors. Finally, risk and protective factors may vary depending on whether the disorder is acute or chronic, pure or comorbid, partial or full syndrome, or a community versus clinic case (Attie & Brooks-Gunn, 1995; Wilfley, Pike, & Striegel Moore, 1997).

PUTATIVE RISK AND PROTECTIVE FACTORS FOR EATING DISORDERS

A variety of risk factor models for eating disorders have been proposed (e.g., Connors, 1996; Leung, Geller, & Katzman, 1996; Pike, 1995; Smolak & Levine, 1996; Stice, 1994; Striegel-Moore & Cachelin, 1999; Wilfley et al., 1997). These models include multiple putative risk factors for EDs that can be divided into three general categories: individual (biological, behavioral, personality), family, and sociocultural. Risk factors of an individual nature that have been proposed in these models include low self-esteem, perfectionism, body dissatisfaction, inadequate coping skills, weight concerns, impulsivity, being overweight, early maturation, dieting, affective dysregulation, and initiation of dating. Family risk factors that have been proposed include parental obesity, parental overprotection, parental neglect, family conflict, parental loss or absence, EDs in family members, family concerns about shape or weight, and parental psychopathology. Sociocultural risk factors include importance of appearance for success in women, thin beauty ideal for women, gender role conflict, teasing about weight or shape, media influences, weight concerns or EDs among friends, and physical or sexual abuse. It should be noted that most of these proposed risk factors were identified in cross-sectional studies, so they do not fit the definition of "risk factor" proposed by Kazdin et al. (1997) until they are found to be significant in longitudinal studies.

In contrast to risk factors for EDs, relatively little is known or has been written about protective factors that may increase resistance to EDs. Among the individual protective factors that have been proposed are (a) being self-directed and assertive (Rodin, Striegel-Moore, & Silberstein, 1990); (b) successful performance of multiple roles—for example, education, career, family, personal interests (Rodin et al., 1990); (c) coping well with stressful situations (Rodin et al., 1990; Striegel-Moore & Cachelin, 1999); (d) high self-esteem (Shisslak, Crago, Renger, & Clark-Wagner, 1998; Striegel-Moore & Cachelin, 1999); and (e) a genetic predisposition to be slender (Connors, 1996; Rodin et al., 1990). Family protective factors that have been suggested are (a) being a member of a family in which there is not an overemphasis on weight and attractiveness (Connors, 1996; Rodin et al., 1990); and (b) close, but not too close, relationships with parents (Smolak & Striegel-Moore, 1996). Protective factors of a sociocultural nature that have been proposed are (a) social acceptance of a diverse range of body shapes and sizes (Rodin et al., 1990); (b) participation in sports that encourage appreciation of the body for its performance more than just its attractiveness (Rodin et al., 1990; Smolak, Murnen, & Ruble, 2000); (c) close relationships with friends or romantic partners who are relatively unconcerned with weight (Rodin et al., 1990); and (d) social support (Striegel-Moore & Cachelin, 1999).

In one of the few studies of protective factors for EDs, Wertheim, Paxton, Schutz, and Muir (1997) interviewed 30 high school girls and identified several factors that appeared to protect girls from excessive weight concerns that can lead to EDs. These factors were self-acceptance, family acceptance, positive peer influences (e.g., being talked out of dieting or purging), and knowledge about the dangers of dieting. Although this study has several limitations (i.e., small sample size, qualitative data), it represents a beginning in the investigation of the effects of protective factors on the development of EDs. There is also some evidence suggesting that sports participation may have protective effects against the development of EDs in girls and young women (Crago, Shisslak & Ruble, 2001; Smolak et al., 2000).

RETROSPECTIVE STUDIES

In addition to cross-sectional studies, potential risk factors for EDs have also been assessed in a series of retrospective studies in which individuals were either asked about traumatic events that occurred before the onset of their ED or were asked what factors they thought had contributed to the onset or maintenance of the disorder once it had begun (Lacey, Coker, & Birtchnell, 1986; Margo, 1985; Mitchell, Hatsukami, Pyle, & Eckert, 1986; Morgan & Russell, 1975; Mynors-Wallis, Treasure, & Chee, 1992; Pyle, Mitchell, & Eckert, 1981; Rossotto, Rorty-Greenfield, & Yager, 1996; Strober, 1984). The factors identified in these studies as possible contributors to the onset of EDs included dieting, school difficulties, being teased about one's weight, physical illness, move to a new school or residence, conflict with parents or peers, separation from a significant person, pressure by family members or friends to lose weight, striving for perfection or control, and sexual change (e.g., onset of menses, becoming sexually active). However, none of these studies used control groups. Without control groups it is not possible to determine whether a risk factor is specific to EDs or whether it simply increases the risk for psychiatric disorders in general. The following studies included an ED group and one or more control groups that were compared on their levels of exposure to various risk factors prior to the age of onset in the ED group.

Horesh et al. (1995) compared the life events of 21 adolescent AN inpatients (17 girls, 4 boys), 79 adolescent psychiatric inpatients, and 40 healthy adolescents. All participants were Jewish and living in Israel. Based on a semistructured interview regarding the occurrence of 18 life events, only physical or emotional abuse by parents distinguished between the two patient groups, with these experiences being reported significantly more often by the AN patients. In another study, Horesh et al. (1996) interviewed 20 adolescent girls with EDs who were matched for age and socioeconomic status with 20 psychiatric patients and 20 healthy controls. All participants were Jewish females living in Israel. The only experience that was reported significantly more often by the ED group was inappropriate parental pressures (e.g., being forced to behave in an exaggerated feminine manner, being forced to engage in activities that reflected their parents' ambitions rather than their own).

Gowers, North, Byram, and Weaver (1996) compared the rate of negative life events in a group of 35 AN patients, 35 psychiatric control patients, and 35 community control research participants. There were 31 female adolescents and 4 male adolescents in each group. They found that the AN patients reported rates of extreme negative events at an intermediate level between the community control group (who reported the fewest) and the psychiatric control group (who reported the most). The most frequently reported negative events were death of a family member or friend, loss of a friendship, illness in the family, change of school, and departure of a family member—for example, marital separation.

In a study by Fairburn and associates (Fairburn, Welch, Doll, Davies, & O'Connor, 1997), exposure to a number of putative risk factors for EDs was compared in a group of 102 BN research participants, 204 healthy control participants, and 102 participants with psychiatric disorders other than EDs. The participants were British females between the ages of 16 and 35 who were recruited from a community sample and matched on age and parental social class. When compared to the healthy control participants, the BN participants reported significantly greater levels of exposure to 29 of the 58 risk factors that were assessed. However, when compared to the psychiatric control group, the BN group reported significantly greater levels of exposure to only 4 of the 58 factors. These factors included negative self-evaluation; childhood obesity; parental high expectations; and critical comments by family about weight, shape, or eating. On the basis of these findings, Fairburn et al. concluded that BN is the result of exposure to risk factors for psychiatric disorders in general as well as risk factors for dieting.

In another study, Fairburn and associates (1998) compared the BN research participants and psychiatric control participants from their previous study to 52 BED participants and 104 healthy control participants. Again, all participants were British females between the ages of 16 and 35. The BED participants reported significantly greater levels of exposure to 20 of the 56 risk factors that were assessed than did the normal control participants. In comparison to the psychiatric group, however, the BED participants reported significantly greater levels of exposure to only 5 of the 56 factors. These five factors were low parental contact; parental high expectations; severe personal health problems; childhood obesity; and critical comments by family members about shape, weight, or eating. There were no significant differences between the BED and BN groups in level of exposure to any of the 56 risk factors. Fairburn et al. concluded from these findings that BED is associated with exposure to two broad classes of risk factors: those that increase the risk for psychiatric disorders in general and those that increase the risk for obesity.

In general, the results of these studies suggest that ED patients, in contrast to other psychiatric patients, are more likely to have experienced before onset (a) greater parental pressure, high expectations, or abuse; (b) more health problems; (c) childhood obesity; (d) more familial criticism about their weight, shape, or eating habits; and (e) a more negative self-evaluation. Other adverse experiences such as the death of someone close to them, loss of a relationship with a friend or family member, and work or school problems were not reported significantly more often by ED patients than by other psychiatric patients.

Although less expensive and less time-consuming than longitudinal studies, retrospective studies are limited by the possibility of inaccuracy or bias in the recall of both stressful life events and the time of onset of ED symptoms. For example, certain events perceived to be antecedent to the onset of symptoms might actually have developed concurrently or as a result of the disorder. Also, individuals may differ in their tendency to over- or underreport the occurrence of stressful events. What is considered to be an extremely stressful situation by one person may not be considered so stressful by another person. However, Kazdin et al. (1997) emphasized that retrospective studies, as well as cross-sectional studies, are useful first steps in risk factor research. In spite of their limitations, they are efficient approaches for identifying possible risk factors that can then be investigated in prospective, longitudinal studies.

LONGITUDINAL STUDIES

The relationship between an antecedent event or condition and an outcome can only be firmly established by conducting prospective, longitudinal studies in which participants are evaluated at baseline and periodically reevaluated over a period of time. The results of longitudinal studies of ED risk factors in children and adolescents are summarized in Table 4-1.

As Table 4-1 indicates, in more than half of these longitudinal studies, participants were followed for three years or less. Participants in most of the studies ranged in age from 11 to 20. Only Gardner and associates (Gardner, 1999; Gardner, Friedman, & Jackson, 1998), Marchi and Cohen (1990), Martin et al. (2000), and Stice, Agras, and Hammer (1999) included participants younger than 11 in their sample. Because many girls younger than 11 prefer a body shape that is thinner than their current shape or have problematic eating attitudes and behaviors (Hill, Draper, & Stack, 1994; Rolland, Farnill, & Griffiths, 1997; chapter 2, this volume), it may be important in future longitudinal studies to collect baseline information before girls have developed weight concerns and a desire to be thinner. By initiating longitudinal studies when girls are younger, it may be possible to determine what some of the precursors are for risk factors such as body dissatisfaction and a desire for thinness.

Participants in the longitudinal studies were predominantly White, with the exception of Killen et al. (1994, 1996) and Stice, Killen, Hayward, and Taylor (1998) in which more than half of the participants were ethnic minorities. Because there is evidence that risk and protective factors may vary as a function of ethnicity (Crago, Shisslak, & Estes, 1996; also see chapter 3, this volume), it is important that future longitudinal studies include participants from different ethnic groups.

Across studies, risk factors that were identified in more than one longitudinal study included low self-esteem, weight concerns, dietary restraint, body dissatisfaction, depression, negative emotionality, early maturation, and being overweight. The significance of these findings in more than one study suggests that these may be some of the most potent risk factors for EDs. Four of the factors are specific to EDs (weight concerns, dietary restraint, body dissatisfaction, and being overweight) and the others are general factors (low self-esteem, depression, negative emotionality, and early maturation) that are associated with other psychiatric disorders as well as EDs. These results suggest that it is important to focus on both general and specific risk factors in the treatment and prevention of EDs. Also, by targeting general factors that are associated with more than one type of psychiatric disorder, the risk for the development of comorbid disorders is likely to be reduced as well.

Prospective, longitudinal studies have several limitations. Besides being expensive and time-consuming to conduct, attrition can easily reach 20% per year and, depending on the length of the study, the remaining sample can be biased as a result. Going one step beyond longitudinal studies is the randomized, controlled design in which a putative casual risk factor is manipulated to determine whether changing the factor results in a change in outcome (Kraemer, Stice, Kazdin, Offord, & Kupfer, 2000). Unfortunately, this approach is also both costly and time-consuming, and for this reason is usually a later step in the risk research process.

Stice and his colleagues (Stice, Mazotti, Weibel, & Agras, 2000) used the randomized, controlled design and found that a prevention program they developed aimed at modifying internalization of the thin ideal led to a decrease in thin-ideal internalization, body dissatisfaction, dieting, negative affect, and BN symptoms. Most of these changes remained significant at the one-month follow-up. These findings were later replicated in another randomized experimental study (Stice, Chase, Stormer, & Appel, in press). The results of these experimental studies provide further evidence that internalization of the thin ideal can be considered a causal risk factor for eating disturbances.

MULTIPLE FACTORS AND MULTIPLE PATHWAYS

Investigators have begun to empirically test models incorporating a number of the ED risk factors that have been proposed or identified thus far. In these models, different pathways to EDs are compared, consisting of various potential risk factors as well as potential mediators and moderators of these factors.

Based on a comprehensive review of ED research aimed at evaluating the role that sociocultural factors play in the development of BN, Stice (1994) proposed a dual pathway model of BN. According to this model,

TABLE 4-1
Longitudinal Studies of Risk Factors for Eating Disturbances in Children and Adolescents

Author(s)	Location of Study	Participants	Age/Grade at Baseline	Types of Measures	Length of Study	Predictors of Eating Disturbances
Attie & Brooks-Gunn, 1989	U.S.	193 girls	Grades 7–10	Questionnaires	2 years	Negative body image
Button, 1990; Button, Loan, Davies, & Sonuga-Barke, 1997; Button, Sonuga-Barke, Davies, & Thompson, 1996	England	397 girls	Age 11–12	Questionnaires	4 years	Low self-esteem
Calam & Waller, 1998	England	63 girls	Age 12	Questionnaires	7 years	Restrictive and bulimic attitudes, poor communication, and poor role differentiation in family
Cattarin & Thompson, 1994	U.S.	87 girls	Age 13–18	Questionnaires	3 years	Body dissatisfaction
Gardner, 1998; Gardner, 1999	U.S.	104 girls 112 boys	Age 6–13	Questionnaires	3 years	Depression, low body esteem, later born, parental concerns about body size (boys and girls). Being shorter and heavier, body dissatisfaction (girls only), teasing history (boys only)
Garner, Garfinkel, Rockert, & Olmstead, 1987	Canada U.S.	35 girls (ballet students)	Age 11–14	Questionnaires & interviews	2–4 years	Body dissatisfaction and drive for thinness
Graber, Brooks-Gunn, Praikoff, & Warren, 1994	U.S.	116 girls	Grades 7–9	Questionnaires	8 years	Early maturation, higher body fat, and depression

Study	Country	Sample	Age/Grade	Method	Duration	Risk factors
Keel, Fulkerson, & Leon, 1997	U.S.	80 girls 85 boys	Grades 5–6	Questionnaires	2 years	Early maturation and higher BMI (girls only); poor body image (boys only)
Killen et al., 1994	U.S.	887 girls	Grades 6–7	Questionnaires	3 years	Weight concerns
Killen et al. 1996	U.S.	825 girls	Grade 9	Questionnaires and interviews	4 years	Weight concerns
Leon, Fulkerson, Perry, & Early-Zald, 1995	U.S.	852 girls 815 boys	Grades 7–10	Questionnaires	3 years	Previous ED risk status, poor interoceptive awareness, and being White (girls only); previous ED risk status (boys only)
Leon, Fulkerson, Perry, Keel, & Klump, 1999	U.S.	726 girls 698 boys	Grades 7–10	Questionnaires and Interviews	4 years	Negative emotionality, depression, sense of ineffectiveness, lack of interoceptive awareness, and body dissatisfaction (both boys and girls)
Marchi & Cohen, 1990	U.S.	326 girls 333 boys	Age 1–10	Interviews with mothers	10 years	Picky eating and digestive problems
Martin et al., 2000	Australia	597 girls 631 boys	Birth to 13 years	Questionnaires	13 years	Negative emotionality and low persistance
Patton, Johnson-Sabine, Wood, Mann, & Walceling, 1990	England	176 girls	Age 14–16	Questionnaires and interviews	1 year	Past psychiatric history and mother's lack of self-confidence
Patton, Selzer, Coffey, Carlin, & Wolfe, 1999	Australia	1,000 girls 947 boys	Age 14–15	Questionnaires	3 years	Dieting and psychiatric morbidity (girls only)

(continued)

TABLE 4-1 (*Continued*)
Longitudinal Studies of Risk Factors for Eating Disturbances in Children and Adolescents

Author(s)	Location of Study	Participants	Age/Grade at Baseline	Types of Measures	Length of Study	Predictors of Eating Disturbances
Schleimer, 1983	Sweden	109 girls	Age 14–20	Interviews, physical exam, psychiatric exam and information from parents, school, and hospital records	10 years	Dieting combined with anxiety, low self-esteem, traumatic experiences, and/or relationship problems
Smolak, Levine, & Gralen, 1993	U.S.	79 girls	Grade 6	Questionnaires	2 years	Early maturation and initiation of dating
Stice & Agras, 1998	U.S.	218 girls	Age 16–18	Questionnaires	9 months	Perceived pressure to be thin, internalization of thin ideal, body dissatisfaction, dieting, and negative affect
Stice, Killen, 1998	U.S.	543 girls	Grade 9	Questionnaires and interviews	4 years	Dietary restraint and negative affectivity
Stice, 1999	U.S.	100 girls 116 boys	Birth to age 5	Physical measures (mother and child), observational data (child), questionnaires (mother)	5 years	Maternal and paternal BMI; infant BMI and feeding behavior; maternal body dissatisfaction, dieting, drive for thinness, and BN symptoms

Study	Country	Sample	Age	Method	Follow-up	Findings
Stice, Akutagawa, Gaggar, & Agras, 2000	U.S.	320 girls 311 boys	Age 16–19	Questionnaires	9 months	Dieting and negative affect
Swarr & Richards, 1996	U.S.	177 girls	Grades 5–9	Questionnaires and interviews	2 years	Poor relationship with parents and early maturation
Wichstrom, 2000	Norway	7751 (approximately half boys and girls)	Age 12–19	Questionnaires	2 years	Disordered eating at baseline, female gender, excessive exercise, unstable self-perceptions, perceived obesity, depressed mood, and idols with perfect bodies
Wlodarczyk-Bisaga & Dolan, 1996	Poland	747 girls	Age 14–16	Questionnaires and interviews	10 months	No predictors were identified because of small number of new cases that developed during follow-up period ($n = 7$)
Wood, Waller, & Goners, 1994	England	33 girls	Age 11–16	Questionnaires and interviews	2 years	Abnormal eating attitudes

sociocultural influences such as the emphasis on thinness and the importance of appearance for success in women can lead to body dissatisfaction in some women. Stice proposed that one of the pathways from body dissatisfaction to BN is through dietary restraint and the other pathway is through negative affect. Stice, Nemeroff, and Shaw (1996) tested the dual pathway model using data from a sample of 257 female undergraduates. Structural equation analyses indicated that the model accounted for 71% of the variance in BN symptomatology. Stice and his colleagues (Stice, 1998; Stice & Agras, 1998; Stice, Shaw, & Nemeroff, 1998) later tested the dual pathway model in a nine-month longitudinal study of 218 girls who were high school seniors. Time 1 perceived sociocultural pressure, body mass, ideal-body internalization, body dissatisfaction, dietary restraint, and negative affect were all significantly correlated with Time 2 BN symptoms (Stice et al., 1998). Overall, the model accounted for 33% of the variance in BN symptomatology, which was considerably less than the 71% of variance accounted for in the college student sample, suggesting that there are other BN risk factors for adolescent girls that were not assessed in this study. Methodological differences (cross-sectional versus longitudinal) may also have contributed to the difference in variance in BN symptomatology accounted for in the two studies.

Shepherd and Ricciardelli (1998) tested Stice's dual pathway model in a sample of 166 female high school students and 246 female college students. Because no significant differences between the high school and college students were found on any of the measures, multiple regression analyses were conducted with the two groups combined. These analyses demonstrated that body dissatisfaction accounted for 48% of the variance in BN symptomatology. The mediators, dietary restraint and negative affect, contributed an additional 8% of the variance.

In a study of 385 middle school girls conducted by Levine, Smolak, and Hayden (1994), multiple regression analyses revealed that the strongest predictor of drive for thinness, weight management, and eating disturbances was the extent to which girls reported that fashion and beauty magazines were an important source of information for them about diet, fitness, ideal shape, and beauty (accounting for 25% to 41% of the variance in the three criterion variables). The second strongest predictor was weight–shape-related teasing and criticism by family members (accounting for 6% to 8% of the variance).

Leung, Schwartzman, and Steiger (1996) used structural equation analyses to test a model they developed combining family and self-esteem variables in a sample of 918 high school girls in Montreal. Their findings indicated that family preoccupation with weight and appearance was a specific risk factor for ED problems and family dysfunction was a general risk factor. Family dysfunction had a direct effect on self-esteem, which was associated with both EDs and other psychiatric symptoms.

Pike (1995) designed a study to evaluate both general and specific risk factors for EDs in a sample of 410 high school girls. Regression analyses revealed that weight concerns among family members or friends was not a significant predictor of BN symptoms, but actual BN symptoms among family members or friends was a significant predictor of BN symptoms in the participants, as was difficulty in expressing conflict with friends. A sense of ineffectiveness and low interoceptive awareness were also specific risk factors for BN.

Neumark-Sztainer, Butler, and Palti (1996) tested a risk factor model using structural equation analyses to predict disordered eating among 341 Jewish high school girls living in Israel. The model included both personal and sociocultural factors. Personal factors (i.e., body dissatisfaction, drive for thinness, and low self-esteem) were the strongest predictors of disordered eating. Overall, the model explained 65.6% of the variance in disordered eating, with personal factors accounting for 64.6% of the variance and sociocultural factors (e.g., pressure for thinness from family and peers, number of close friends dieting, mother's weight concerns as perceived by daughter) accounting for only 1% of the variance. It should be noted that sociocultural factors did have an indirect effect on disordered eating via their effect on personal factors ($r = .29$), even though the direct effect of these factors was considerably lower ($r = .10$).

In a study of 148 girls aged 8 to 13, Veron-Guidry, Williamson, and Netemeyer (1997) tested a model that included social pressure for thinness, self-esteem, depression, and onset of menses as antecedent risk factors and body dysphoria (discrepancy between actual and ideal body size) as a mediating variable between these factors and ED symptoms. Controlling for body mass index (BMI), structural equation analyses showed that onset of menses was not significantly related to any of the other factors, so it was omitted from further analyses. In the revised model, 49% of the variance in body dysphoria was accounted for by the remaining three factors, and 16% of the variance in ED symptoms was accounted for by the body dysphoria variable.

In a study of 286 British schoolgirls aged 13 to 16, multiple regression analyses revealed that increased stress and maladaptive coping resulted in lower levels of self-esteem, which was associated with more disturbed eating attitudes (Fryer, Waller, & Kroese, 1997). Stressors were also directly associated with disturbed eating attitudes, indicating that the relationship between these two variables was imperfectly mediated by self-esteem.

Taylor et al. (1998) conducted a stepwise regression analysis of risk factors predicting weight concerns (considered to be a proximal risk factor for EDs) in a sample of 78 elementary schoolgirls and 333 middle schoolgirls.

In the elementary school sample, 57% of the variance in weight concerns was accounted for by four factors: the importance that peers put on weight and eating (34%), site differences (Arizona versus California, 7.9%), media influences (7.5%), and BMI (7.5%). In the middle school sample, 55% of the variance was accounted for by five factors: the importance that peers put on weight and eating (32.6%), self-confidence (11.2%), BMI (7.5%), media influences (2.3%), and being teased about one's weight (1.7%).

In general, these studies of different models and pathways to EDs indicate that low self-esteem may be an important risk factor for EDs, as is body dissatisfaction, weight-related teasing by family or friends, a desire to be thinner, a higher BMI, negative affect, and media influences.

IMPLICATIONS FOR TREATMENT AND PREVENTION

In the beginning of this chapter, we stated that ultimately risk factor research should lead to defining causal models for EDs and that by identifying antecedent conditions associated with the increased likelihood of EDs, we can design interventions that reduce or eliminate these factors. Simultaneously, by strengthening protective factors we can also increase the likelihood of behaviors that compete with unhealthy eating practices. In this review, we have delineated a number of risk factors that are manipulable (causal risk factors) and, therefore, capable of altering the development of an ED. Although many of these factors are general risk factors for other psychiatric disorders as well as EDs (e.g., low self-esteem, depression, family and relationship problems), some are more specific for EDs (e.g., weight concerns, body dissatisfaction, higher BMI). Because there is considerable research evidence that there are multiple, causal pathways to EDs including both general and specific factors, interventions need to encompass both of these sources. Also, the use of developmental models that are gender sensitive and that target risk factors for specific developmental phases is important in designing interventions because manifestations of symptoms can vary with developmental stage (Gralen, Levine, Smolak, & Murnen, 1990; Shisslak, Crago, Estes, & Gray, 1996).

The importance of focusing on general as well as symptom-specific factors in the treatment and prevention of EDs is supported by outcome research comparing the psychotherapeutic techniques of cognitive behavioral therapy (CBT) and interpersonal therapy (IPT). Both interventions have been found to provide long-term benefits for ED patients even though IPT focuses on general factors rather than on specific ED symptoms (Fairburn, Jones, Peveler, Hope, & O'Connor, 1993). Symptom-specific interventions for the core features of EDs (e.g., weight and shape concerns, self-worth based on body esteem) are probably most helpful in the acute phase of EDs in a patient population or for high-risk individuals in the general population. However, for the purposes of ED prevention in a younger population, or for low-risk individuals, it may be more beneficial in the long run to focus on general rather than symptom-specific factors. By focusing only on general factors in prevention programs for younger girls and low-risk girls, it may be possible to avoid inadvertently teaching girls unhealthy weight regulation practices, as seems to have happened in several ED prevention programs in the past (Cohn & Maine, 1998).

Low self-esteem emerged as a significant predictor of eating disturbances in many of the studies reviewed in this chapter. It is our contention that the role self-esteem plays in EDs can be better understood by focusing on the process of self-esteem building, which involves the actual experience of success in a particular domain or area of interest (Shisslak, Crago, Renger, et al., 1998). One needs the opportunity to develop skills that lead to a resilient sense of self-mastery in many settings and over an extended period of time. Also, it is important that interventions target areas that are of interest to the individual (Harter, 1993). The importance of a sense of mastery and competence for the prevention of EDs is emphasized by the results of a recent study in which it was found that women who reported experiencing more feelings of helplessness and lower levels of mastery in childhood were more likely to develop EDs in adulthood (Troop & Treasure, 1997).

Role models, peer support groups, mentors, and life skills training are all methods that have been used to enhance self-esteem (Shisslak, Crago, Renger, et al., 1998). Life-skills training enables girls to develop individualized skills in problem solving and communication that can not only change high-risk behaviors but build skills that can help prevent these high-risk behaviors from developing in the first place. In a recent review of ED prevention programs, Levine and Piran (1999) found that 85% of the prevention programs that included a life-skills training component were effective in promoting a positive change in attitudes or behaviors. We support interventions and treatment models that accomplish a change in risk status by providing opportunities to experience competency and success in domains that are valued and that one perceives others value as well. Providing individuals with structured opportunities to experience success in a valued area is also likely to decrease or prevent other comorbid disorders such as depression and anxiety.

CONCLUSION

From the research reviewed in this chapter, it is obvious that a number of potential risk factors for EDs in children and adolescents have been identified in a variety of studies using different methodologies (effectively countering the argument that we know too little about ED risk factors in children and adolescents to develop prevention programs for them). So many possible risk factors have been identified that it would be difficult to evaluate all of them in one study or to include interventions for all of them in one ED prevention program. Some of the factors that have been identified are general factors contributing to various psychiatric disorders (e.g., low self-esteem, poor relationships with family members, and negative emotionality) and others appear to be specific to EDs (e.g., weight concerns, dieting, body dissatisfaction). It is interesting to note that it is often general factors that are cited as distinguishing between girls whose weight concerns and eating problems are serious and may lead to an ED and those who are considered to have "normal" weight concerns that reflect the "normative discontent" about weight experienced by many girls and adult women in our society (Leung et al., 1996; Shisslak, Crago, & Estes, 1995). It is not known at this point whether psychopathology increases the risk for EDs or whether the same risk factors that cause EDs also cause other psychiatric disorders. Because of the comorbidity of EDs with other psychiatric disorders, it is important to develop broad-based prevention programs that address issues common to a variety of psychiatric disorders.

It appears that the potency of certain risk factors varies over time. Studies of age-related differences in risk factors indicate that certain factors are predictive of ED risk at younger ages (e.g., onset of menses, initiation of dating), but these factors are no longer predictive in later adolescence (Gralen et al., 1990). These findings emphasize the necessity for longer follow-up studies because the factors found to be predictive in a one-year follow-up may no longer be predictive if the participants are followed for a longer period of time. Ideally, participants would be assessed in elementary school, before abnormal eating attitudes and behaviors begin, and would then be followed through young adulthood. Longer follow-up studies that begin when participants are younger will enable researchers to evaluate the age effects of risk factors, which will facilitate the development of ED prevention programs designed for specific age groups. At this point, we know little about the precursors to such risk factors as weight concerns and body dissatisfaction. However, the longitudinal studies by Marchi and Cohen (1990) and Stice et al. (1999) suggest that parents' body weight, maternal eating attitudes and behaviors, and problematic feeding behaviors during infancy and childhood may play a role in the development of eating disturbances later on (also see chapter 1, this volume).

Because of yearly attrition rates, it is important that longitudinal studies begin with relatively large sample sizes at baseline. It is also important to include participants from different ethnic backgrounds because little ED risk factor research has been focused on these groups, and there may be ethnic differences in these risk factors (Crago et al., 1996; see chapter 3, this volume).

Additional empirical research aimed at identifying protective factors for EDs is much needed because it is likely that risk and protective factors involve different pathways and underlying mechanisms. Continuation of the work begun by Stice and others in evaluating different ED models and pathways is essential for determining not only risk and protective factors for EDs but the mediators and moderators of these factors as well. Because EDs in girls are often associated with other problems of adolescence such as depression, anxiety, and substance abuse (Killen et al., 1987), the inclusion of general protective factors such as self-esteem in preventive interventions would serve to decrease the likelihood not only of EDs but other emotional and behavioral problems as well. In addition, the inclusion of both risk and protective factors in preventive interventions for EDs may help to increase the overall effectiveness of these interventions.

REFERENCES

Attie, I., & Brooks-Gunn, J. (1989). The development of eating problems in adolescent girls: A longitudinal study. *Developmental Psychology, 25,* 70–79.

Attie, I., & Brooks-Gunn, J. (1995). The development of eating regulation across the life span. In D. Cicchetti & D. J. Cohen (Eds.), *Developmental psychopathology: Vol. 2. Risk, disorder, and adaptation* (pp. 332–368). New York: Wiley.

Button, E. (1990). Self-esteem in girls aged 11-12: Baseline findings from a planned prospective study of vulnerability to eating disorders. *Journal of Adolescence, 13,* 407–413.

Button, E. J., Loan, P., Davies, J., & Sonuga-Barke, E. J. S. (1997). Self-esteem, eating problems, and psychological well-being in a cohort of schoolgirls aged 15-16: A questionnaire and interview study. *International Journal of Eating Disorders, 21,* 39–47.

Button, E. J., Sonuga-Barke, E. J. S., Davies, J., & Thompson, M. (1996). A prospective study of self-esteem in the prediction of eating problems in adolescent schoolgirls: Questionnaire findings. *British Journal of Clinical Psychology, 35,* 193–203.

Calam, R., & Waller, G. (1998). Are eating and psychosocial characteristics in early teenage years useful predictors of eating characteristics in early adulthood? A 7-year longitudinal study. *International Journal of Eating Disorders, 24,* 351–362.

Cattarin, J. A., & Thompson, J. K. (1994). A three-year longitudinal study of body image, eating disturbance, and general psychological functioning in adolescent females. *Eating Disorders: Journal of Treatment and Prevention, 2,* 114–125.

Cohn, L., & Maine, M. (1998). More harm than good. *Eating Disorders: Journal of Treatment and Prevention, 6,* 93–95.

Connors, M. A. (1996). Developmental vulnerabilities for eating disorders. In L. Smolak, M. P. Levine & R. Striegel-Moore (Eds.), *The developmental psychopathology of eating disorders* (pp. 285–310). Mahwah, NJ: Erlbaum.

Crago, M., Shisslak, C. M., & Estes, L. S. (1996). Eating disturbances among American minority groups: A review. *International Journal of Eating Disorders, 19,* 239–248.

Crago, M., Shisslak, C. M., & Ruble, A. (2001). Protective factors in the development of eating disorders. In R. Striegel-Moore & L. Smolak (Eds.), *Eating disorders: Innovative directions for research and practice* (pp. 75–89). Washington, DC: American Psychological Association.

Fairburn, C. G., Doll, H. A., Welch, S. L., Hay, P. J., Davies, B. A., & O'Connor, M. E. (1998). Risk factors for binge eating. *Archives of General Psychiatry, 55,* 425–432.

Fairburn, C. G., Jones, R., Peveler, R. C., Hope, R. A., & O'Connor, M. (1993). Psychotherapy and bulimia nervosa: The longer-term effects of interpersonal psychotherapy, behaviour therapy and cognitive behaviour therapy. *Archives of General Psychiatry, 50,* 419–428.

Fairburn, C. G., Welch, S. L., Doll, H. A., Davies, B. A., & O'Connor, M. E. (1997). Risk factors for bulimia nervosa: A community-based case-control study. *Archives of General Psychiatry, 54,* 509–517.

Fryer, S., Waller, G., & Kroese, B. S. (1997). Stress, coping, and disturbed eating attitudes in teenage girls. *International Journal of Eating Disorders, 22,* 427–436.

Gardner, R. M. (1999). *Body images in children: Size estimations and predisposing factors for eating disorders.* Unpublished manuscript.

Gardner, R. M., Friedman, B. N., & Jackson, N. A. (1998, April). *Predictors for eating disorder tendencies in children ages six through fourteen.* Paper presented at the meeting of the International Conference on Eating Disorders, New York.

Garner, D. M., Garfinkel, P. E., Rockert, W., & Olmsted, M. P. (1987). A prospective study of eating disturbances in the ballet. *Psychotherapy and Psychosomatics, 48,* 170–175.

Gowers, S. G., North, C. D., Byram, V., & Weaver, A. B. (1996). Life event precipitants of adolescent anorexia nervosa. *Journal of Child Psychology and Psychiatry, 37,* 469–477.

Graber, J. A., Brooks-Gunn, J., Praikoff, R. L., & Warren, M. P. (1994). Prediction of eating problems: An 8-year study of adolescent girls. *Developmental Psychology, 30,* 823–834.

Gralen, S. J., Levine, M. P., Smolak, L., & Murnen, S. (1990). Dieting and disordered eating during early and middle adolescence: Do the influences remain the same? *International Journal of Eating Disorders, 9,* 501–512.

Harter, S. (1993). Causes and consequences of low self-esteem in children and adolescents. In R. F. Baumeister (Ed.), *Self-esteem: The puzzle of low self-regard* (pp. 87–116). New York: Plenum Press.

Hill, A. J., Draper, E., & Stack, J. (1994). A weight on children's minds: Body shape dissatisfaction at 9-years old. *International Journal of Obesity, 18*, 383–389.

Horesh, N., Apter, A., Ishai, J., Danziger, Y., Miculincer, M., Stein, D., Lepkifker, E., & Minouni, M. (1996). Abnormal psychosocial situations and eating disorders in adolescence. *Journal of the American Academy of Child and Adolescent Psychiatry, 35*, 921–927.

Horesh, N., Apter, A., Lepkifker, E., Ratzoni, G., Weizmann, R., & Tyano, S. (1995). Life events and severe anorexia nervosa in adolescence. *Acta Psychiatrica Scandinavica, 91*, 5–9.

Kazdin, A. E., Kraemer, H. C., Kessler, R. C., Kupfer, D. J., & Offord, D. R. (1997). Contributions of risk factor research to developmental psychopathology. *Clinical Psychology Review, 17*, 375–406.

Keel, P. K., Fulkerson, J. A., & Leon, G. R. (1997). Disordered eating precursors in pre- and early adolescent girls and boys. *Journal of Youth and Adolescence, 26*, 203–216.

Killen, J. D., Taylor, C. B., Hayward, C., Haydel, K. F., Wilson, D. M., Hammer, L. D., Kraemer, H. C., Blair-Greiner, A., & Strachowski, D. (1996). Weight concerns influence the development of eating disorders: A 4-year prospective study. *Journal of Consulting and Clinical Psychology, 64*, 936–940.

Killen, J. D., Taylor, C. B., Hayward, C., Wilson, D. M., Haydel, K. F., Hammer, L. D., Simmonds, B., Robinson, T. N., Litt, I., Varady, A., & Kraemer, H. (1994). Pursuit of thinness and onset of eating disorder symptoms in a community sample of adolescent girls: A three-year prospective analysis. *International Journal of Eating Disorders, 16*, 227–238.

Killen, J. D., Taylor, C. B., Telch, M. J., Robinson, T. N., Maron, D. J., & Saylor, K. E. (1987). Depressive symptoms and substance use among adolescent binge eaters and purgers: A defined population study. *American Journal of Public Health, 77*, 1539–1541.

Kraemer, H., Stice, E., Kazdin, A., Offord, D., & Kupfer, D. (2000). *How do risk factors work together to produce an outcome? Mediators, moderators, independent, overlapping and proxy-risk factors.* Manuscript submitted for publication.

Lacey, M., Coker, S., & Birtchnell, S. (1986). Bulimia: Factors associated with its etiology and maintenance. *International Journal of Eating Disorders, 5*, 475–487.

Leon, G. R., Fulkerson, J. A., Perry, C. L., & Early-Zald, M. B. (1995). Prospective analysis of personality and behavioral vulnerabilities and gender influences in the later development of disordered eating. *Journal of Abnormal Psychology, 104*, 140–149.

Leon, G. R., Fulkerson, J. A., Perry, C. L., Keel, P. K., & Klump, K. L. (1999). Three- to four-year prospective evaluation of personality and behavioral risk factors for later disordered eating in adolescent girls and boys. *Journal of Youth and Adolescence, 28*, 181–196.

Leung, F., Geller, J., & Katzman, M. (1996). Issues and concerns associated with different risk models for eating disorders. *International Journal of Eating Disorders, 19*, 249–256.

Leung, F., Schwartzman, A., & Steiger, H. (1996). Testing a dual-process family model in understanding the development of eating pathology: A structural equation modeling analysis. *International Journal of Eating Disorders, 20,* 367–375.

Levine, M., & Piran, N. (1999). *Approaches to health promotion in the prevention of eating disorders.* Manuscript submitted for publication.

Levine, M. P., Smolak, L., & Hayden, H. (1994). The relationship of sociocultural factors to eating attitudes and behaviors among middle school girls. *Journal of Early Adolescence, 14,* 472–491.

Marchi, M., & Cohen, P. (1990). Early childhood eating behaviors and adolescent eating disorders. *Journal of the American Academy of Child and Adolescent Psychiatry, 29,* 112–117.

Margo, J. L. (1985). Anorexia nervosa in adolescents. *British Journal of Medical Psychology, 58,* 193–195.

Martin, G. C., Wertheim, E. H., Prior, M., Smart, D., Sanson, A., & Oberklaid, F. (2000). A longitudinal study of the role of childhood temperament in the later development of eating concerns. *International Journal of Eating Disorders, 27,* 150–162.

Mitchell, J. E., Hatsukami, D., Pyle, R. L., & Eckert, E. D. (1986). The bulimia syndrome: Course of the illness and associated problems. *Comprehensive Psychiatry, 27,* 165–170.

Morgan, H. G., & Russell, G. F. M. (1975). Value of family background and clinical features as predictors of long-term outcome in anorexia nervosa: Four-year follow-up study of 41 patients. *Psychological Medicine, 5,* 355–371.

Mynors-Wallis, L., Treasure, J., & Chee, D. (1992). Life events and anorexia nervosa: Differences between early and late onset cases. *International Journal of Eating Disorders, 11,* 369–375.

Neumark-Sztainer, D., Butler, R., & Palti, H. (1996). Personal and socioenvironmental predictors of disordered eating among adolescent females. *Journal of Nutrition Education, 28,* 195–201.

O'Connor, T. G., & Rutter, M. (1996). Risk mechanisms in development: Some conceptual and methodological considerations. *Developmental Psychology, 32,* 787–795.

Patton, G. C., Johnson-Sabine, E., Wood, K., Mann, A. H., & Wakeling, A. (1990). Abnormal eating attitudes in London schoolgirls: A prospective epidemiological study, outcome at 12 months. *Psychological Medicine, 20,* 383–394.

Patton, G. C., Selzer, R., Coffey, C., Carlin, J. B., & Wolfe, R. (1999). Onset of adolescent eating disorders. Population based cohort study over 3 years. *British Medical Journal, 318,* 765–768.

Pike, K. M. (1995). Bulimic symptomatology in high school girls. *Psychology of Women Quarterly, 19,* 373–396.

Pyle, R. L., Mitchell, J. E., & Eckert, E. D. (1981). Bulimia: Report of 34 cases. *Journal of Clinical Psychiatry, 42,* 60–64.

Rodin, J., Streigel-Moore, R. H., & Silberstein, L. R. (1990). Vulnerability and resilience in the age of eating disorders: Risk and protective factors for bulimia nervosa. In J. Rolf, A. S. Masten, D. Cicchetti, K. H. Neuchterlein & S. Weintraub (Eds.), *Risk and protective factors in the development of psychopathology* (pp. 361–383). Cambridge: Cambridge University Press.

Rolland, K., Farnill, D., & Griffiths, R. A. (1997). Body figure perceptions and eating attitudes among Australian school children aged 8 to 12 years. *International Journal of Eating Disorders, 21,* 273–278.

Rossoto, E., Rorty-Greenfield, M., & Yager, J. (1996). What causes and maintains bulimia nervosa? Recovered and nonrecovered women's reflections on the disorder. *Eating Disorders: Journal of Treatment and Prevention, 4,* 115–127.

Schleimer, K. (1983). Dieting in teenage schoolgirls: A longitudinal prospective study. *Acta Paediatrica Scandinavica, 312* (Suppl.), 1–54.

Shepherd, H., & Ricciardelli, L. A. (1998). Test of Stice's dual pathway model: Dietary restraint and negative affect as mediators of bulimic behavior. *Behaviour Research and Therapy, 36,* 345–352.

Shisslak, C. M., Crago, M., & Estes, L. S. (1995). The spectrum of eating disturbances. *International Journal of Eating Disorders, 18,* 209–219.

Shisslak, C. M., Crago, M., Estes, L. S., & Gray, N. (1996). Content and method of developmentally appropriate programs. In L. Smolak, M. Levine, & R. Streigel-Moore (Eds.), *The developmental psychopathology of eating disorders* (pp. 341–363). Mahwah, NJ: Erlbaum.

Shisslak, C. M., Crago, M., Renger, R., & Clark-Wagner, A. (1998). Self-esteem and the prevention of eating disorders. *Eating Disorders: Journal of Treatment and Prevention, 6,* 105–117.

Smolak, L., & Levine, M. P. (1996). Adolescent transitions and the development of eating problems. In L. Smolak, M. P. Levine, & R. Striegel-Moore (Eds.), *The developmental psychopathology of eating disorders* (pp. 207–233). Mahwah, NJ: Erlbaum.

Smolak, L., Levine, M. P., & Gralen, S. (1993). The impact of puberty and dating on eating problems among middle school girls. *Journal of Youth and Adolescence, 22,* 355–368.

Smolak, L., Murnen, S. K., & Ruble, A. E. (2000). Female athletes and eating problems: A meta-analysis. *International Journal of Eating Disorders, 27,* 371–380.

Smolak, L., & Striegel-Moore, R. (1996). The implications of developmental research for eating disorders. In L. Smolak, M. Levine, & R. Striegel-Moore (Eds.), *The developmental psychopathology of eating disorders* (pp. 183–203). Mahwah, NJ: Erlbaum.

Stice, E. (1994). Review of the evidence for a sociocultural model of bulimia nervosa and an exploration of the mechanisms of action. *Clinical Psychology Review, 14,* 633–661.

Stice, E. (1998). Relations of restraint and negative affect to bulimic pathology: A longitudinal test of three competing models. *International Journal of Eating Disorders, 23,* 243–260.

Stice, E., & Agras, W. S. (1998). Predicting onset and cessation of bulimic behaviors during adolescence: A longitudinal grouping analysis. *Behavior Therapy, 29,* 257–276.

Stice, E., Agras, W. S., & Hammer, L. D. (1999). Risk factors for the emergence of childhood eating disturbances: A five-year prospective study. *International Journal of Eating Disorders, 25,* 375–387.

Stice, E., Akutagawa, D., Gaggar, A., & Agras, W. S. (2000). Negative affect moderates the relation between dieting and binge eating. *International Journal of Eating Disorders, 27,* 218–229.

Stice, E., Chase, A., Stormer, S., & Appel, A. (in press). A randomized trial of a dissonance-based eating disorder prevention program. *International Journal of Eating Disorders.*

Stice, E., Killen, J. D., Hayward, C., & Taylor, C. B. (1998). Age of onset for binge eating and purging during late adolescence: A 4-year survival analysis. *Journal of Abnormal Psychology, 107,* 671–675.

Stice, E., Mazotti, L., Weibel, D., & Agras, W. S. (2000). Dissonance prevention program decreases thin-ideal internalization, body dissatisfaction, dieting, negative affect, and bulimic symptoms: A preliminary experiment. *International Journal of Eating Disorders, 27,* 206–217.

Stice, E., Nemeroff, C., & Shaw, H. E. (1996). Test of the dual pathway model of bulimia nervosa: Evidence for dietary restraint and affect regulation mechanisms. *Journal of Social and Clinical Psychology, 15,* 340–363.

Stice, E., Shaw, H., & Nemeroff, C. (1998). Dual pathway model of bulimia nervosa: Longitudinal support for dietary restraint and affect-regulation mechanisms. *Journal of Social and Clinical Psychology, 45,* 129–149.

Striegel-Moore, R. H., & Cachelin, F. M. (1999). Body image concerns and disordered eating in adolescent girls: Risk and protective factors. In N. G. Johnson & M. C. Roberts (Eds.), *Beyond appearance: A new look at adolescent girls* (pp. 85–108). Washington, DC: American Psychological Association.

Strober, M. (1984). Stressful life events associated with bulimia in anorexia nervosa. *International Journal of Eating Disorders, 3,* 3–16.

Swarr, A. E., & Richards, M. H. (1996). Longitudinal effects of adolescent girls' pubertal development, perceptions of pubertal timing, and parental relations on eating problems. *Developmental Psychology, 32,* 636–646.

Taylor, C. B., Sharpe, T., Shisslak, C. M., Bryson, S., Estes, L. S., Gray, N., McKnight, K. M., Crago, M., Kraemer, H. C., & Killen, J. D. (1998). Factors associated with weight concerns in adolescent girls. *International Journal of Eating Disorders, 24,* 31–42.

Troop, N. A., & Treasure, J. L. (1997). Setting the scene for eating disorders, II. Childhood helplessness and mastery. *Psychological Medicine, 27,* 531–538.

Veron-Guidry, S., Williamson, D. A., & Netemeyer, R. G. (1997). Structural modeling analysis of body dysphoria and eating disorder symptoms in preadolescent girls. *Eating Disorders: Journal of Treatment and Prevention, 5,* 15–27.

Wertheim, E. H., Paxton, S. J., Schutz, H. K., & Muir, S. L. (1997). Why do adolescent girls watch their weight? An interview study examining sociocultural pressures to be thin. *Journal of Psychosomatic Research, 42,* 345–355.

Wichstrom, L. (2000). Psychological and behavioral factors unpredictive of disordered eating: A prospective study of the general adolescent population in Norway. *International Journal of Eating Disorders, 28,* 33–42.

Wilfley, D. E., Pike, K. M., & Striegel-Moore, R. (1997). Toward an integrated model of risk for binge eating disorder. *Journal of Gender, Culture, and Health, 2,* 1–32.

Wlodarczyk-Bisaga, K., & Dolan, B. (1996). A two-stage epidemiological study of abnormal eating attitudes and their prospective risk factors in Polish schoolgirls. *Psychological Medicine, 26,* 1021–1032.

Wood, A., Waller, G., & Gowers, S. (1994). Predictors of eating psychopathology in adolescent girls. *European Eating Disorders Review, 2,* 6–13.

5

FAMILY FUNCTIONING, BODY IMAGE, AND EATING DISTURBANCES

ARI B. STEINBERG AND VICKY PHARES

Since the beginning of the identification of eating disorders, researchers and clinicians have acknowledged that the family may play some role in the development and maintenance of maladaptive body image and eating disturbances. In the late 1800s, a number of scholars suggested that anorexic clients and their families should be kept apart during treatment to allow the client to separate from her family and to protect the client from maladaptive family functioning that could exacerbate the eating disorder (e.g., Gull, 1874/1964). In the 1970s, other scholars continued to suggest that eating disorders were largely related to family functioning and that family therapy was an essential component in the treatment of eating disorders (e.g., Minuchin, Rosman, & Baker, 1978). Although cognitive–behavioral models that focus on the individual client have taken center stage more recently, there has continued to be acknowledgment of the role of the family in the development and maintenance of body image and eating disturbances (Humphrey, 1994).

THEORIES OF FAMILY DYSFUNCTION IN BODY IMAGE DISTURBANCE AND EATING DISORDERS

There is a wealth of research supporting the idea that sociocultural factors are a strong influence on the development of body image concerns (Heinberg & Thompson, 1995). This chapter attempts to examine more intimate social factors such as parental influences on an individual's body and weight concerns. It is important to note that these parental influences

Preparation of this chapter was supported in part by National Institute of Mental Health Grant R29 MH49601-05.

exist within the larger sociocultural framework and thus may themselves be influenced by current societal standards. Unfortunately, it is almost impossible to separate these more intimate influences from the larger sociocultural influences.

Several lines of research have emerged regarding familial influences on the development of body image disturbance and eating disturbance. Some areas that have been investigated as possible risk factors for eating disorders or body image disturbance are the level of family functioning (Humphrey, 1994), communication patterns within the family (VanFurth et al., 1996), parental functioning (O'Kearney, 1996), parental modeling of dysfunctional eating attitudes and behaviors (Thelen & Cormier, 1995), and parents' influence over their children by direct communication of weight-related attitudes and opinions (Stein & Woolley, 1996). In addition, there is evidence of a possible genetic component in the development of eating disorders based on research with relatives of individuals with eating disorders (Strober & Humphrey, 1987) and with twins (Kendler et al., 1991). These factors are reviewed after a discussion of methodological issues in the assessment of family functioning.

METHODOLOGICAL ISSUES

Although assessment techniques for body image and eating disturbances have already been presented in this volume, it is important to understand the issues that are unique to the assessment of family functioning and dyadic relationships within the family. Just as it is imperative to understand normal developmental processes before understanding abnormal developmental processes (Smolak, 1996), it is also imperative to understand normal family functioning before attempting to identify abnormal family functioning. Thus both normative family functioning and abnormal family functioning are addressed throughout this chapter.

Another integral part of understanding functioning within families is to acknowledge the diversity of perspectives that different family members bring to the assessment of any issue. For example, in a classic meta-analysis, Achenbach, McConaughy, and Howell (1987) found that ratings of children's and adolescents' emotional–behavioral problems depended on which informants were used to assess the problems. The same issue of divergent perspectives has been evidenced in the use of diagnostic interviews for eating disorders. Cantwell, Lewinsohn, Rohde, and Seeley (1997) found that adolescent–parent reports of anorexia nervosa were highly related (with a kappa of .75), whereas adolescent–parent reports of bulimia nervosa had poorer correspondence (with a kappa of .53). Thus even with relatively objective constructs such as emotional–behavioral problems and eating disorders, divergent perspectives are often evident. Although it is difficult to interpret results from divergent perspectives, it is imperative for researchers to attempt to understand body image and eating disturbances from multiple perspectives to address these issues in the systems in which they are partially developed and maintained.

There are a number of assessment measures that can be helpful in understanding family functioning and dyadic relationships within the family to investigate the familial influences in body image and eating disturbances. Measures that focus on the family system tend to assess the family environment or family functioning from a global perspective, rather than focusing on any individual within the family. For example, the Family Environment Scale (FES; Moos, 1990), which contains scales such as expressiveness, conflict, and control, is a well-established measure that has been used to explore body image and eating disturbances (Hodges, Cochrane, & Brewerton, 1998). The Family Adaptability and Cohesion Evaluation Scale (FACES-III; Olson et al., 1985) is another well-established measure that has often been used to evaluate family functioning in relation to body image and eating disturbances (Johnson, Brownell, St. Jeor, Brunner, & Worby, 1997; Leung, Schwartzman, & Steiger, 1996).

These questionnaires allow for different family members to report on their experiences. A much more complex way of evaluating family functioning in the context of an eating disorder is to conduct direct observations with all family members present and to use structural analysis of social behavior to analyze the family's functioning (reviewed by Humphrey, 1994). Although this methodology is time-consuming and arduous, the resulting data can allow a much more comprehensive understanding of the complexity of family relationships.

In addition to assessing the family as a system, there are also a number of measures that explore dyadic relationships within the family. The Parental Bonding Inventory (PBI; Parker, Tupling, & Brown, 1979) has been used to assess eating-disordered young adults' retrospective memories of their mother's and father's care and overprotection during childhood (Calam, Waller, Slade, & Newton, 1990). The Children's Report of Parental Behavior Inventory (CRPBI; Schludermann & Schludermann, 1970) can also be used to assess retrospective or concurrent reports of a wide variety of parental behavior in childhood (including affection, control, intrusiveness, and discipline). Concurrent reports of children's and adolescents' experiences of the parent–child relationship can be assessed using the Lum Emotional Availability of Parents Scale (LEAP; Lum & Phares, 1999; Lum, Phares, & Roberts, 1996) and the Perceptions of Parents Scale (POP; Phares & Renk, 1998). Specifically, the LEAP assesses children's and adolescents' perceptions of how emotionally available their parents are to them and the POP measures the level of positive and negative affect that children and adolescents feel toward their mothers and fathers. In addition, parents can report on the parent–child relationship with the Parenting Scale (Arnold, O'Leary, Wolff, & Acker, 1993) and the Parental Stress Index (PSI; Abidin, 1990), which both assess parental discipline and parental functioning. Although many of these measures have not yet been used to explore the parent–child relationship related to body image and eating disturbances, these measures may prove to be valuable tools in furthering our understanding of the development and maintenance of body image and eating disturbances.

Although there has been some investigation into negative verbal commentary by siblings (see later section), few other investigations have explored the sibling relationship regarding the development and maintenance of body image and eating disturbances. An excellent measure that could be used for these purposes is the Sibling Inventory of Differential Experiences (SIDE; Dunn & Plomin, 1990). This measure could be used to help tease apart shared and nonshared environmental influences for siblings related to body image and eating disturbances.

Now that some of the methodological issues within family research have been covered, the following topics will be considered: family dysfunction, problem communication patterns, parental behavior, parental attitudes and perceptions toward weight, parental body image and eating issues, and negative verbal commentary within the family. Within each section, both body image disturbance and eating disorders will be covered when there is available research. Given the relative lack of research into the father–child relationship (Phares, 1996), research findings in relation to both mother–child and father–child functioning will be highlighted when available.

FAMILY FUNCTIONING

Minuchin and colleagues (1978) argued that "psychosomatic families" (i.e., families that are characterized as enmeshed, rigid, overprotective, and limited in conflict resolution) put adolescents at risk for an eating disorder. In a more recent summary of the research on family functioning and eating disorders, Humphrey (1994) surmised that there was more familial chaos, hostility, disturbance, and isolation, and less nurturance, empathy, and satisfaction in families with a bulimic or bulimic–anorexic child than in families with a restricting anorexic child. Conversely, families with a restricting anorexic child showed greater rigidity and dependency than families with a bulimic or bulimic–anorexic child. These results can have ramifications for self-esteem and psychological functioning as well as eating disturbances even in nonclinical samples. In a community sample of adolescent girls, family dysfunction appeared to be related directly to negative self-esteem and related indirectly to eating disturbances and psychological problems (Leung, Schwartzman, et al., 1996).

With regard to restrained eating, Hill and Franklin (1998) found that highly restrained 11-year-old girls from a nonclinical sample reported significantly less family cohesion than did nonrestrained girls. With regard to anorexia nervosa, Russell, Kopec-Schrader, Rey, and Beumont (1992) found that anorexic adolescents reported their parents' care and protection in ways that were more comparable to adolescents in the nonclinical control group, whereas adolescents in the psychiatrically disturbed control group reported less paternal and maternal caring and more maternal overprotection than did anorexic adolescents. This study points to the importance of including both a nonclinical control group and a clinical control group when comparing family functioning in the context of an eating disorder.

Family issues seem to be more salient for binge-eating adolescents when compared with nonclinical control adolescents. In a group of adolescent girls with binge eating disorder (purging type), parental overprotection and inappropriate parental pressures were significantly related to maladaptive eating patterns (Horesh et al., 1996). When an internalized family image was activated (i.e., by having the participant respond to both positive and negative statements about their family), binge eating participants reported a greater degree of hunger, more hostility, and a greater preoccupation with family issues than nonclinical controls (Villejo, Humphrey, & Kirschenbaum, 1997). In another study, binge-eating clients reported less family cohesion than anorexic clients, less family expressiveness than bulimic clients, and less active–recreational family functioning in comparison with both anorexic and bulimic clients (Hodges et al., 1998). In a seven-year longitudinal study, Calam and Waller (1998) found that lower levels of perceived role differentiation in the family when the daughter was 12 years old were associated with greater bulimic behaviors at age 19. In a review of the research literature, Shisslak, Crago, and Estes (1995) concluded that adolescents who experience binge eating showed lower family cohesion than did adolescents who were normal eaters.

Family issues also appear to be more salient for binge-eating adolescents and adolescents with bulimia nervosa when compared with non–binge-eating obese adolescents. Older adolescents with binge-eating disorder reported that their parents showed greater levels of affectionless control while they were growing up than did a control group of obese older adolescents who did not show symptoms of binge-eating disorder (Fowler & Bulik, 1997). Similarly, older adolescents and young adults with bulimia nervosa reported more troubled family functioning, a higher prevalence of previous physical and sexual abuse, higher levels of psychopathology within the family, and more self-directed hostility than older adolescents and young adults who were obese binge eaters (Friedman, Wilfley, Welch, & Kunce, 1997).

When compared with normal weight children and adolescents in a control group, however, significant findings often emerge for obese children and adolescents (Mendelson, White, & Schliecker, 1995). Vogt (1999) noted that obese children are significantly more likely to have obese parents than are normal-weight children. This pattern appears to be a result of genetic factors that influence metabolism and activity levels, but there are also social and family factors that appear to influence the connections between obese parents and children. It is interesting to note that obese adolescent girls as well as underweight adolescent boys reported lower family cohesion, expressiveness, and democratic family style when compared with their same-gender peers (Mendelson et al., 1995). There is some evidence that family functioning may be of even greater importance in the development of obesity in males than in females (Johnson et al., 1997). Note, however, that significant effects are not always found in samples of obese youth. Valtolina and Marta (1998) did not find any differences between obese and normal weight, nonclinical adolescents with regard to communication with their mothers and fathers and in the support that was received from their mothers and fathers.

There is some evidence that these patterns of findings may differ based on race and ethnicity. Although this area has not received a great deal of attention, there is evidence that family race–ethnicity, in addition to the family's cultural orientation, may be related to body image and eating disorder concerns (Crago, Shisslak, & Estes, 1996). Specifically, families with greater cultural orientation toward White, middle-class values tended to have children and adolescents who were at greater risk for eating disturbances. This pattern was found in samples of Hispanic/Latina Americans, African Americans, Asian Americans, and Native Americans (Crago et al., 1996), as well as British Asian girls (Hill & Bhatti, 1995). In addition, lower family connectedness was associated with binge-eating, more so in Caucasian American adolescents than in other racial and ethnic groups (French et al., 1997). In an Australian sample, lower levels of family adaptability were associated with more eating-related concerns, more so for Greek-Australian youth than for Anglo-Australian youth (Mildred, Paxton, & Wertheim, 1995).

Overall, there are clear connections between family dysfunction and eating disturbances. These connections seem to be more consistent for bulimia nervosa, binge-eating disorders, and obesity with less consistent evidence of the connection between restrictive anorexia nervosa and family dysfunction. Further research is needed to clarify the specificity of these results with regard to race–ethnicity and gender.

COMMUNICATION PATTERNS

Family communication style has been implicated in a number of psychological problems, including eating disorders. Family member's expressed emotion (EE) is most often evaluated in therapeutic outcome research, with a focus on criticism, hostility, emotional overinvolvement, warmth, and positive remarks. Outcome studies with eating disordered clients have suggested that mothers' and fathers' expressed emotion improves significantly over the course of treatment (Shugar & Krueger, 1995; VanFurth et al., 1996). Although this area of research focuses on primarily eating disordered clients who are in family therapy, the results suggest that it is an area worthy of further study.

PARENTAL FUNCTIONING

The three primary areas of research regarding parental functioning are parenting behavior as reflected through attachment styles of the child, parental psychopathology, and abuse in relation to the development and maintenance of body image and eating disturbances. There is growing evidence that disturbed patterns of parent–child attachment are linked to disturbances in body image and eating (O'Kearney, 1996). Specifically, children who showed insecure attachment reported higher levels of weight concerns than children who showed secure attachment (Sharpe et al., 1998).

Overall, there are limited findings to connect parental psychopathology (other than eating disorders) and eating disturbances in children and adolescents (reviewed by Leung, Geller, & Katzman, 1996). Garfinkel and colleagues (1983) found no differences in the psychological symptoms of mothers and fathers with an anorexic adolescent daughter and those with a nonclinical adolescent daughter. When comparing mothers and fathers of restricted eaters, binge eaters, dieters, nondieters, and psychiatrically distressed older adolescents, Steiger, Stotland, Ghadirian, and Whitehead (1995) found no differences between these groups related to affective instability, compulsivity, anxiousness, and narcissism. There were no differences in rates of parental substance abuse or other types of psychopathology when comparing older adolescents with binge-eating disorder and older adolescents who were obese (Fowler & Bulik, 1997; Lee et al., 1999). In addition, mothers' and fathers' psychopathological traits were related to their daughters' psychopathological traits, whether or not the daughter had an eating disorder (Steiger, Stotland, Trottier, & Ghadirian, 1996).

There is some evidence that clients with bulimia nervosa and a comorbid substance dependence are more likely to have first-degree relatives (including parents) diagnosed with psychopathology than clients with bulimia nervosa without a comorbid substance dependence and individuals in a nonclinical control group (Lilenfeld et al., 1997). In addition, adolescent girls whose parents misused alcohol (e.g., parents who ingested hard liquor on a daily basis) showed significantly higher rates of eating disordered symptoms when compared with adolescent girls whose parents did not misuse alcohol (Chandy, Harris, Blum, & Resnick, 1995).

There is conflicting evidence as to the connection between child sexual abuse and the development of an eating disorder, with evidence of a connection found in Austria but not in the United States (Mangweth, Pope, Hudson, & Biebl, 1996). In the United States, clients diagnosed with bulimia nervosa and a comorbid substance dependence showed significantly higher rates of childhood sexual abuse than clients with bulimia nervosa without a comorbid substance dependence, anorexic clients, and nonclinical control participants (Deep, Lilenfeld, Plotnicov, Pollice, & Kaye, 1999). Males' eating disordered behavior appeared to be related to family adversity (such as physical abuse and parental conflict) but not childhood sexual abuse (Kinzl, Mangweth, Traweger, & Biebl, 1997). In a nonclinical sample in the United States, older adolescents who met criteria for bulimia nervosa reported greater family conflict and less cohesion than normal controls. This difference was not significant, however, once sexual abuse was controlled statistically (Kern & Hastings, 1995). It appeared that chaotic and dysfunctional family systems were more connected to a history of sexual abuse than to a current diagnosis of bulimia nervosa. Overall, there is limited evidence of a history of childhood sexual abuse and the onset of an eating disorder (see chapter 6, this volume).

PARENTAL ATTITUDES AND PERCEPTIONS TOWARD WEIGHT

Although contradictory findings have emerged with respect to familial influences on the development of body image concerns (e.g., Sanftner, Crowther, Crawford, & Watts, 1996), the majority of present research supports a familial component to the development of body image disturbance. Most research in this area has overlooked the roles of fathers in the development of eating problems and body image concerns; however, several studies have included both mothers and fathers (Moreno & Thelen, 1993; Thelen & Cormier, 1995). Regardless of gender, adolescents reported that family members were the primary source of weight control and appearance-related information (Desmond, Price, Gray, & O'Connell, 1986). Thus it is possible that parents' attitudes and beliefs concerning eating, weight, and body shape directly influence (either through modeling or direct transmission) their children's and adolescents' eating behaviors and body image concerns (see also chapters 1 and 2, this volume).

This modeling and direct transmission of parents attitudes and beliefs about eating and weight begin very early in children's lives. In a series of studies, Birch and colleagues (Abramovitz & Birch, 2000; Carper, Fisher, & Birch, 2000; Davison & Birch, in press; Davison, Markey, & Birch, 2000; see also chapter 1, this volume) have shown that children as young as 5 years old are influenced by their parents' attitudes toward eating and weight. In nonclinical samples of 5-year-old girls, parents' weight concerns were associated with girls' weight concerns (Davison et al., 2000) and lower self-evaluations (Davison & Birch, in press). In addition, mothers were involved actively in dieting were more likely to have daughters who had strong ideas about dieting (Abramovitz & Birch, 2000).

Pike and Rodin (1991) provided additional support for the modeling theory in a sample of adolescents when they found that, in comparison to nonclinical controls, mothers of daughters with disordered eating exhibited greater eating disturbance, had a longer history of dieting, and thought their daughters should lose more weight. Levels of dietary restraint (Hill & Pallin, 1998) and body image disturbance (Rieves & Cash, 1996) were also found to correspond significantly for mothers and their older adolescent daughters.

Moreno and Thelen (1993) found that mothers of bulimic and subclinical bulimic older adolescent daughters were more likely to try to restrict their food intake and to encourage their daughters to exercise and to diet than were the mothers of the control daughters. Contrary to Pike and Rodin's (1991) results, there were no differences between the mothers of the three groups with respect to the frequency of dieting or regarding their own perceptions that they had ever been overweight. Moreno and Thelen proposed an alternative explanation, suggesting that mothers may not model dysfunctional eating behaviors but may directly communicate their beliefs about weight, dieting, and exercise, which are then internalized by their daughters. This conclusion is consistent with the work of Attie and Brooks-Gunn (1989), who found that maternal body image predicted problem eating in adolescent girls.

In a study using structural equation modeling, Leung, Schwartzman, and colleagues (1996) found that family preoccupation with eating and body shape had a direct effect on female adolescents' degree of body dissatisfaction and eating symptoms. Family preoccupation also indirectly influenced eating disturbance, negative self-esteem, and psychiatric symptoms (mediated by body dissatisfaction or negative self-esteem). It is interesting to note that a direct effect of dysfunctional family relations was not revealed. An indirect effect was shown for family dysfunction on eating and psychiatric symptoms mediated by negative self-esteem.

Overall, the relationship between parents' attitudes and beliefs concerning weight, eating, and body shape and the development of body image concerns and eating disturbance has been well-established. Further examination of the particular mechanisms (e.g., modeling, direct communication) of transmission of parental attitudes to their children is needed.

PARENTAL BODY IMAGE AND EATING ISSUES

Another line of research has focused on mothers suffering from eating disorders and the influences it has on their children. Unfortunately, most of the research to date is based on small sample sizes or is presented as a case study (e.g., Evans & leGrange, 1995). In addition, some work has focused on the effects of the mother's eating disorder on her infant's physical development, with the idea that infants are at risk of "anorexia by proxy" as a result of their mother's unhealthy attitudes toward food and weight (Honjo, 1996).

In an observational study, Stein, Woolley, Cooper, and Fairburn (1994) found that in comparison to control mothers, mothers with eating disorders expressed more negative emotions toward their infants during mealtimes and that infants of mothers with eating disorders weighed less than infants of control mothers. With older adolescents, Strober, Lampert, Morrell, Burroughs, and Jacobs (1990) found that daughters of anorexic mothers were five times more likely to develop an eating disorder than daughters with mothers in a nonclinical control group.

Stein and Woolley (1996) suggested five mechanisms of influence that parents with eating disorders may exert over their children: parents' maladaptive attitudes concerning eating, weight, and body shape that may directly affect their children; parents' inability to parent adequately because of their eating disorder; parents' unhealthy modeling of eating attitudes and behaviors; parents' interpersonal problems including marital problems that may have negative effects on their children; and parents' possible genetic transmission of eating disorders. Overall, minimal empirical research has been completed regarding the connections between parental eating disorders and the development of eating problems and body image disturbance in children.

NEGATIVE VERBAL COMMENTARY (TEASING)
WITHIN THE FAMILY

Shapiro, Baumeister, and Kessler (1991) examined the nature of teasing behavior and defined it as "a personal communication, directed by an agent toward a target, that includes three components: aggression, humor, and ambiguity" (p. 460). Cash (1995) reported that 72% of all college women recalled being teased as children usually with respect to their facial features or body weight and shape. Shapiro and colleagues (1991) found that most teasing is verbal in nature and that the most common contents of teasing refer to poor physical appearance (39%) and more specifically about being overweight (13%). Girls (48%) were more likely than boys (29%) to report appearance-related teasing.

Teasing, or negative verbal commentary, during childhood and adolescence has been shown to have a detrimental effect on body satisfaction (Cattarin & Thompson, 1994; Fabian & Thompson, 1989). It appears that teasing may have a strong influence on the development of eating and weight concerns (Thompson & Heinberg, 1993). Similar results concerning the effects of teasing were found for obese women (Grilo, Wilfley, Brownell, & Rodin, 1994).

Although most studies in this area do not specify the origins of teasing, a study by Rieves and Cash (1996) documented that family members and peers are most often the perpetrators of teasing and criticism during childhood and adolescence. The findings indicated that brothers (79%) were the most frequently reported perpetrator of teasing behaviors and were also reported as the "worst" perpetrator. Other immediate family members were reported to be frequent agents of teasing, including sisters (36%), mothers (30%), and fathers (24%). Other relatives (23%) were also noted for teasing. It was apparent that older adolescent college women perceived the family in general, as well as specific members within the family, as perpetrators of teasing behavior concerning weight and appearance during their childhood and adolescence.

Schwartz, Phares, Tantleff-Dunn, and Thompson (1999) examined the relationship between older adolescents' body image and parental teasing within the family. Using retrospective reports of parental teasing, the results suggested that for women, but not men, negative verbal commentary from parents resulted in body image dissatisfaction. Higher levels of teasing and appearance-related feedback were also related to increased psychological disturbance.

Although most studies regarding the relationship between teasing and body image disturbance have been limited to the United States and Great Britain, a recent cross-cultural study examined the effects of teasing by family members toward adolescents in Sweden and Australia (Lunner et al., 2000). In both samples, a strong relationship between teasing and body dissatisfaction was revealed. Specifically, the relationship between body mass index and body dissatisfaction was partially mediated by teasing. These findings were consistent with research within the United States (Thompson, Coovert, Richards, Johnson, & Cattarin, 1995).

Based on covariance structure modeling and longitudinal analyses, Thompson and colleagues (1995) found that negative verbal commentary by family members had a direct negative effect on body dissatisfaction, eating disturbances, and overall psychological functioning. In addition, negative verbal commentary was revealed as a mediator in the relationship between level of obesity and body image disturbance. More specifically, overweight status appeared to be a risk factor for teasing, but overweight status did not appear to exert a direct influence on body dissatisfaction. These findings suggest that an interactive relationship between a dispositional factor (obesity) and a sociocultural factor (teasing) both appear to have an influence on the development of body image disturbance.

In a retrospective study of appearance-related teasing, self-reported sibling social comparisons and maternal modeling of weight-related behaviors and attitudes, Rieves and Cash (1996) found that recollections of appearance-related teasing were negatively correlated with women's current body satisfaction, social comparisons with siblings were correlated with current body image perceptions, and women's perceptions of their mothers' body image concerns were related to current body and weight concerns. In addition, stepwise regression revealed that the combination of all three factors contributed between one fourth to one third of the unique variance in the explanation of women's body image concerns.

Overall, it is likely that teasing, or negative verbal commentary, especially within the family context, has a strong influence on the development of body image disturbance and eating problems. Additional research needs to examine teasing within the context of the family. In particular, very little work has explored the relations between siblings' teasing and functioning in children and adolescents.

IMPLICATIONS FOR PREVENTION AND TREATMENT

The research on family functioning in relation to body image and eating disturbances has clear implications for prevention and treatment of eating disorders. In terms of prevention, the family provides a point of prevention that could help children learn healthy eating habits, healthy attitudes about weight and body issues, and supportive communication styles. Chandy and colleagues (1995) identified a number of protective factors that have relevance for work with families. Specifically, adolescents who were not worried about being abused by their parents and adolescents who had parents who did not misuse alcohol were less likely to be at risk for the development of an eating disorder. In addition, parents who were supportive and who did not use body-related negative verbal commentary seemed to help protect children from the development of an eating disorder (Cattarin & Thompson, 1994). Berndt and Hestenes (1996) identified social support from the family and from peers as a protective factor against the development of body image and eating disturbances. It is possible that public awareness campaigns could be targeted for parents to understand the ramifications of their words and actions and to help parents find more beneficial ways of dealing with their children as well as living their own lives.

Family therapy seems to be an effective treatment strategy, especially for children and adolescents with body image and eating disturbances (reviewed in chapter 12, this volume; see also Diamond, Serrano, Dickey, & Sonis, 1996). Even with an intensive day hospital treatment program focusing on the individual client with concomitant therapy for the family, significant gains in family functioning and eating behaviors were reported over the course of treatment (Woodside et al., 1995). Consistent with issues related to multiple informants, clients with bulimia nervosa reported more family disturbance than their parents, but clients also reported greater gains in therapy with regard to improvements in family interactions (Woodside et al., 1995).

CRITIQUE

Although a thorough critique of the body image and eating disorder literature is beyond the scope of this chapter, a number of issues should be mentioned regarding research methodologies in studies of family functioning. An overwhelming majority of family studies that include participants who meet criteria for anorexia nervosa or bulimia nervosa focus solely on clients who are in treatment for these disorders (Wilson, Heffernan, & Black, 1996). This practice is problematic because different findings often emerge when disordered individuals who are receiving treatment are compared with disordered individuals who are not receiving treatment (Wilson et al., 1996). Samples, as well as research teams, are also often limited by the ethnic and racial diversity that is represented (Pumariega, 1997). Care should be taken to conduct research that is representative and thus generalizable to a larger community.

Another issue in studies of family functioning pertains to the usefulness of investigating the family history of psychopathology. Heightened rates of parental psychopathology are often found in samples of participants with diagnoses other than an eating disorder, so psychiatric control groups are necessary to ascertain the patterns of family history that are specific to eating disordered participants (Leung, Geller, et al., 1996; Lilenfeld et al., 1997). In addition, studying parental psychopathology in individuals with body image disturbance or eating disorders does not tease apart genetic and environmental influences (Wilson et al., 1996). These issues can often be addressed with studies of monozygotic and dizygotic twins, but even twin studies have limitations. Klump, Keel, Leon, and Fulkerson (1999) found that twins were not representative of the general population and they suggested that twin studies should not be generalized to nontwin samples.

Another issue that is salient in studies of families is the overreliance on retrospective reports of family functioning (e.g., having young adults report on their recollections of their parents' behavior during childhood). There is evidence that retrospective reports of parenting behavior can be influenced by current mood (Brewin, Andrews, & Gotlib, 1993) and level of psychopathology (Kendler et al., 1991) in a process that is often called recall bias. For example, Kendler and colleagues (1991) found that twins diagnosed with an eating disorder reported lower levels of paternal care than their twin siblings who were not diagnosed with any disorder. Although retrospective reports are thought to be valid, they should be interpreted with caution (Brewin et al., 1993).

Studies of family functioning are also limited by the lack of acknowledgment of reciprocity within the family (Foreyt, Poston, Winebarger, & McGavin, 1998). The assumption often appears to be that parents influence children, without acknowledging that children can influence parents. Because the majority of research in this area is cross-sectional, causality of effects cannot be assumed. Thus research on family functioning should be interpreted with caution because of the reciprocal nature of eating disordered offspring and their families.

Finally, there has been a history of writing in the area of family functioning that has been based on clinical observations with limited empirical evidence (e.g., Minuchin et al., 1978). Conflicting conclusions often arise when information from clinical experience is compared with information from empirical studies (Wilson et al., 1996). Thus care should be taken to interpret clinical writings that have not yet been substantiated through the empirical process.

CONCLUSION

Even with these limitations in research on family functioning, the studies in this chapter highlight the reciprocal nature of family dysfunction and eating disorders. That is, family dysfunction and problematic communication styles may serve to exacerbate eating disorders, but individual resolution of eating disorders may serve to lessen family dysfunction. As research on family functioning, body image disturbances, and eating disorders becomes more sophisticated, greater attention should be paid to the mechanisms that help develop and maintain these problems, in addition to a greater exploration of the directionality of these mechanisms. Greater attention should also be paid to understudied family members (such as fathers and siblings) and understudied populations (such as diverse racial and ethnic groups) to gain a better understanding of the complexity of the family in relation to body image and eating disturbances. Finally, more attention should be paid to protective factors that might lead to better prevention programs to prevent the onset of body image and eating disturbances. The family unit is an integral part of children's and adolescents' lives, and thus the family unit provides a compelling site for prevention and intervention efforts to deal with body image disturbances and eating disorders.

REFERENCES

Abidin, R. R. (1990). *Parenting Stress Index.* Charlottesville, VA: Pediatric Psychology Press.

Abramovitz, B. A., & Birch, L. L. (2000). Five-year-old girls' ideas about dieting are predicted by their mothers' dieting. *Journal of the American Dietetic Association, 100,* 1157–1163.

Achenbach, T. M., McConaughy, S. H., & Howell, C. T. (1987). Child/adolescent behavioral and emotional problems: Implications of cross-informant correlations for situational specificity. *Psychological Bulletin, 101,* 213–232.

Arnold, D. S., O'Leary, S. G., Wolff, L. S., & Acker, M. M. (1993). The Parenting Scale: A measure of dysfunctional parenting in discipline situations. *Psychological Assessment, 5,* 137–144.

Attie, I., & Brooks-Gunn, J. (1989). Development of eating problems in adolescent girls: A longitudinal study. *Developmental Psychology, 25,* 70–79.

Berndt, T. J., & Hestenes, S. L. (1996). The developmental course of social support: Family and peers. In L. Smolak, M. P. Levine, & R. Striegel-Moore (Eds.), *The developmental psychopathology of eating disorders* (pp. 77–106). Mahwah, NJ: Erlbaum.

Brewin, C. R., Andrews, B., & Gotlib, I. H. (1993). Psychopathology and early experience: A reappraisal of retrospective reports. *Psychological Bulletin, 113,* 82–98.

Calam, R., & Waller, G. (1998). Are eating and psychosocial characteristics in early teenage years useful predictors of eating characteristics in early adulthood? A 7-year longitudinal study. *International Journal of Eating Disorders, 24,* 351–362.

Calam, R., Waller, G., Slade, P. D., & Newton, T. (1990). Eating disorders and perceived relationships with parents. *International Journal of Eating Disorders, 9,* 479–485.

Cantwell, D. P., Lewinsohn, P. M., Rohde, P., & Seeley, J. R. (1997). Correspondence between adolescent report and parent report of psychiatric diagnostic data. *Journal of the American Academy of Child and Adolescent Psychiatry, 36,* 610–619.

Carper, J. L., Fisher, J. O., & Birch, L. L. (2000). Young girls' emerging dietary restraint and disinhibition are related to parental control in child feeding. *Appetite, 35,* 121–129.

Cash, T. F. (1995). Developmental teasing about physical appearance: Retrospective descriptions and relationships with body image. *Journal of Social Behavior and Personality, 23,* 123–130.

Cattarin, J. A., & Thompson, J. K. (1994). A three-year longitudinal study of body image, eating disturbance, and general psychological functioning in adolescent females. *Eating Disorders, 2,* 114–124.

Chandy, J. M., Harris, L., Blum, R. W., & Resnick, M. D. (1995). Female adolescents of alcohol misusers: Disordered eating features. *International Journal of Eating Disorders, 17,* 283–289.

Crago, M., Shisslak, C. M., & Estes, L. S. (1996). Eating disturbances among American minority groups: A review. *International Journal of Eating Disorders, 19,* 239–248.

Davison, K. K., & Birch, L. L. (in press). Weight status, parent reaction, and self-concept in 5-year-old girls. *Pediatrics.*

Davison, K. K., Markey, C. N., & Birch, L. L. (2000). Etiology of body dissatisfaction and weight concerns among 5-year-old girls. *Appetite, 35,* 143–151.

Deep, A. L., Lilenfeld, L. R., Plotnicov, K. H., Pollice, C., & Kaye, W. H. (1999). Sexual abuse in eating disorder subtypes and control women: The role of comorbid substance dependence in bulimia nervosa. *International Journal of Eating Disorders, 25,* 1–10.

Desmond, S. M., Price, J. H., Gray, N., & O'Connell, J. K. (1986). The etiology of adolescents' perceptions of their weight. *Journal of Youth and Adolescence, 15,* 461–473.

Diamond, G. S., Serrano, A. C., Dickey, M., & Sonis, W. A. (1996). Current status of family-based outcome and process research. *Journal of the American Academy of Child and Adolescent Psychiatry, 35,* 6–16.

Dunn, J., & Plomin, R. (1990). *Separate lives: Why siblings are so different.* New York: Basic Books

Evans, J., & leGrange, D. (1995). Body size and parenting in eating disorders: A comparative study of the attitudes of mothers towards their children. *International Journal of Eating Disorders, 18,* 39–48.

Fabian, L. J., & Thompson, J. K. (1989). Body image and eating disturbance in young females. *International Journal of Eating Disorders, 8,* 63–74.

Foreyt, J. P., Poston, W. S. C., Winebarger, A. A., & McGavin, J. K. (1998). Anorexia nervosa and bulimia nervosa. In E. J. Mash & R. A. Barkley (Eds.), *Treatment of childhood disorders (2nd ed.; pp. 647–691).* New York: Guilford Press.

Fowler, S. J., & Bulik, C. M. (1997). Family environment and psychiatric history in women with binge-eating disorder and obese controls. *Behaviour Change, 14,* 106–112.

French, S. A., Story, M., Neumark-Sztainer, D., Downes, B., Resnick, M., & Blum, R. W. (1997). Ethnic differences in psychosocial and health behavior correlates of dieting, purging, and binge eating in a population-based sample of adolescent females. *International Journal of Eating Disorders, 22,* 315–322.

Friedman, M. A., Wilfley, D. E., Welch, R. R., & Kunce, J. T. (1997). Self-directed hostility and family functioning in normal-weight bulimics and overweight binge eaters. *International Journal of Eating Disorders, 22,* 367–375.

Garfinkel, P. E., Garner, D. M., Rose, J., Darby, P. L., Brandes, J. S., O'Hanlon, J., & Walsh, N. (1983). A comparison of characteristics in the families of patients with anorexia nervosa and normal controls. *Psychological Medicine, 13,* 821–828.

Grilo, C. M., Wilfley, D. E., Brownell, K. D., & Rodin, J. (1994). Teasing, body image, and self-esteem in a clinical sample of obese women. *Addictive Behaviors, 19,* 443–450.

Gull, W. W. (1964). Anorexia nervosa. In R. M. Kaufman & M. Heiman (Eds.), *Evolution of psychosomatic concepts anorexia nervosa: A paradigm.* New York: International Universities Press. (Reprinted from *Transactions in the Clinical Society of London,* 1874, 7, 22–28)

Heinberg, L. J., & Thompson, J. K. (1995). Body image and televised images of thinness and attractiveness: A controlled laboratory investigation. *Journal of Social and Clinical Psychology, 14,* 325–338.

Hill, A. J., & Bhatti, R. (1995). Body shape perception and dieting in preadolescent British Asian girls: Links with eating disorders. *International Journal of Eating Disorders, 17,* 175–183.

Hill, A. J., & Franklin, J. A. (1998). Mothers, daughters and dieting: Investigating the transmission of weight control. *British Journal of Clinical Psychology, 37,* 3–13.

Hill, A. J., & Pallin, V. (1998). Dieting awareness and low self-worth: Related issues in 8–year-old-girls. *International Journal of Eating Disorders, 24,* 405–413.

Hodges, E. L., Cochrane, C. E., & Brewerton, T. D. (1998). Family characteristics of binge-eating disorder patients. *International Journal of Eating Disorders, 23,* 145–151.

Honjo, S. (1996). A mother's complaints of overeating by her 25-month-old daughter: A proposal of anorexia nervosa by proxy. *International Journal of Eating Disorders, 20,* 433–437.

Horesh, N., Apter, A., Ishai, J., Danziger, Y., Miculincer, M., Stein, D., Lepkifker, E., & Minouni, M. (1996). Abnormal psychosocial situations and eating disorders in adolescence. *Journal of the American Academy of Child and Adolescent Psychiatry, 35,* 921–927.

Humphrey, L. L. (1994). Family relationships. In K. A. Halmi (Ed.), *Psychobiology and treatment of anorexia nervosa and bulimia nervosa* (pp. 263–282). Washington, DC: American Psychiatric Press.

Johnson, B., Brownell, K. D., St. Jeor, S. T., Brunner, R. L., & Worby, M. (1997). Adult obesity and functioning in the family of origin. *International Journal of Eating Disorders, 22*, 213–218.

Kendler, K. S., Maclean, C. Neale, M. C., Kessler, R., Heath, A. C., & Eaves, L. (1991). The genetic epidemiology of bulimia nervosa. *American Journal of Psychiatry, 148*, 1627–1637.

Kern, J. M., & Hastings, T. (1995). Differential family environments of bulimics and victims of childhood sexual abuse: Achievement orientation. *Journal of Clinical Psychology, 51*, 499–506.

Kinzl, J. F., Mangweth, B., Traweger, C. M., & Biebl, W. (1997). Eating-disordered behavior in males: The impact of adverse childhood experiences. *International Journal of Eating Disorders, 22*, 131–138.

Klump, K. L., Keel, P. K., Leon, G. R., & Fulkerson, J. A. (1999). Risk for eating disorders in a school-based twin sample: Are twins representative of the general population for eating disorders behavior? *Eating Disorders: The Journal of Treatment and Prevention, 7*, 33–41.

Lee, Y. H., Abbott, D. W., Seim, H., Crosby, R. D., Monson, N., Burgard, M., & Mitchell, J. E. (1999). Eating disorders and psychiatric disorders in the first-degree relatives of obese probands with binge eating disorder and obese non-binge eating disorder controls. *International Journal of Eating Disorders, 26*, 322–332.

Leung, F., Geller, J., & Katzman, M. (1996). Issues and concerns associated with different risk models for eating disorders. *International Journal of Eating Disorders, 19*, 249–256.

Leung, F., Schwartzman, A., & Steiger, H. (1996). Testing a dual-process family model in understanding the development of eating pathology: A structural equation modeling analysis. *International Journal of Eating Disorders, 20*, 367–375.

Lilenfeld, L. R., Kaye, W. H., Greeno, C. G., Merikangas, K. R., Plotnicov, K., Pollice, C., Rao, R., Strober, M., Bulik, C. M., & Nagy, L. (1997). Psychiatric disorders in women with bulimia nervosa and their first-degree relatives: Effects of comorbid substance dependence. *International Journal of Eating Disorders, 22*, 253–264.

Lum, J. J., & Phares, V. (1999, August). *Assessing emotional availability of parents: Child, adolescent, and parent perceptions.* Poster presented at the Annual Convention of the American Psychological Association, Boston, Massachusetts.

Lum, J. J., Phares, V., & Roberts, A. K. (1996, August). *Development and validation of the Lum Emotional Availability of Parenting (LEAP) Scale.* Paper presented at the American Psychological Association annual meeting, Toronto, Canada.

Lunner, K., Wertheim, E. H., Thompson, J. K., Paxton, S. J., MacDonald, F., & Halvarsson, K. S. (2000). A cross-cultural examination of weight-related teasing, body image, and eating disturbance in Swedish and Australian samples. *International Journal of Eating Disorders, 28*, 430–435.

Mangweth, B., Pope, H. G., Hudson, J. I., & Biebl, W. (1996). Bulimia nervosa in Austria and the United States: A controlled cross-cultural study. *International Journal of Eating Disorders, 20,* 263–270.

Mendelson, B. K., White, D. R., & Schliecker, E. (1995). Adolescents' weight, sex, and family functioning. *International Journal of Eating Disorders, 17,* 73–79.

Mildred, H., Paxton, S. J., & Wertheim, E. H. (1995). Risk factors for eating disorders in Greek- and Anglo-Australian adolescent girls. *International Journal of Eating Disorders, 17,* 91–96.

Minuchin, S., Rosman, B. L., & Baker, L. (1978). *Psychosomatic families: Anorexia nervosa in context.* Cambridge, MA: Harvard University Press.

Moos, R. H. (1990). Conceptual and empirical approaches to developing family-based assessment procedures: Resolving the case of the Family Environment Scale. *Family Process, 29,* 199–208.

Moreno, A., & Thelen, M. H. (1993). Parental factors related to bulimia nervosa. *Addictive Behaviors, 18,* 681–689.

O'Kearney, R. (1996). Attachment disruption in anorexia nervosa and bulimia nervosa: A review of theory and empirical research. *International Journal of Eating Disorders, 20,* 115–127.

Olson, D. H., McCubbin, H. I., Barnes, H., Larsen, A., Muxem, M., & Wilson, M. (1985). *Family inventories.* St. Paul: University of Minnesota, Family Social Science.

Parker, G., Tupling, H., & Brown, L. B. (1979). A parental bonding instrument. *British Journal of Medical Psychology, 52,* 1–10.

Phares, V. (1996). *Fathers and developmental psychopathology.* New York: Wiley.

Phares, V., & Renk, K. (1998). Perceptions of parents: A measure of adolescents' feelings about their parents. *Journal of Marriage and the Family, 60,* 646–659.

Pike, K. M., & Rodin, J. (1991). Mothers, daughters, and disordered eating. *Journal of Abnormal Psychology, 100,* 198–204.

Pumariega, A. J. (1997). Body dissatisfaction among Hispanic and Asian-American girls. *Journal of Adolescent Health, 21,* 1–5.

Rieves, L., & Cash, T. F. (1996). Social developmental factors and women's body-image attitudes. *Journal of Social Behavior and Personality, 11,* 63–78.

Russell, J. D., Kopec-Schrader, E., Rey, J. M., & Beumont, P. J. (1992). The Parental Bonding Instrument in adolescent patients with anorexia nervosa. *Acta Psychiatrica Scandinavica, 86,* 236–239.

Sanftner, J. L., Crowther, J. H., Crawford, P. A., & Watts, D. D. (1996). Maternal influences (or lack thereof) on daughters' eating attitudes and behaviors. *Eating Disorders, 4,* 147–159.

Schludermann, S., & Schludermann, E. (1970). Replicability of factors in Children's Report of Parent Behavior (CRPBI). *Journal of Psychology, 76,* 239–249.

Schwartz, D. J., Phares, V., Tantleff-Dunn, S., & Thompson, J. K. (1999). Body image, psychological functioning, and parental feedback regarding physical appearance. *International Journal of Eating Disorders, 25,* 339–343.

Shapiro, J. P., Baumeister, R. F., & Kessler, J. W. (1991). A three-component model of children's teasing: Aggression, humor, and ambiguity. *Journal of Social and Clinical Psychology, 10,* 459–472.

Sharpe, T. M., Killen, J. D., Bryson, S. W., Shisslak, C. M., Estes, L. S., Gray, N., Crago, M., & Taylor, C. B. (1998). Attachment style and weight concerns in preadolescent and adolescent girls. *International Journal of Eating Disorders, 23,* 39–44.

Shisslak, C. M., Crago, M., & Estes, L. S. (1995). The spectrum of eating disturbances. *International Journal of Eating Disorders, 18,* 209–219.

Shugar, G., & Krueger, S. (1995). Aggressive family communication, weight gain, and improved eating attitudes during systemic family therapy for anorexia nervosa. *International Journal of Eating Disorders, 17,* 23–31.

Smolak, L. (1996). Methodological implications of a developmental psychopathology approach to the study of eating problems. In L. Smolak, M. P. Levine, & R. Striegel-Moore (Eds.), *The developmental psychopathology of eating disorders* (pp. 31–55). Mahwah, NJ: Erlbaum.

Steiger, H., Stotland, S., Ghadirian, A. M., & Whitehead, V. (1995). Controlled study of eating concerns and psychopathological traits in relatives of eating-disordered probands: Do familial traits exist? *International Journal of Eating Disorders, 18,* 107–118.

Steiger, H., Stotland, S., Trottier, J., & Ghadirian, A. M. (1996). Familial eating concerns and psychopathological traits: Causal implications of transgenerational effects. *International Journal of Eating Disorders, 19,* 147–157.

Stein, A. & Woolley, H. (1996). The influence of parental eating disorders on young children: Implications of recent research for some clinical interventions. *Eating Disorders, 4,* 139–146.

Stein, A., Woolley, H., Cooper, S. D., & Fairburn, C. G. (1994). An observational study of mothers with eating disorders and their infants. *Journal of Child Psychology and Psychiatry, 35,* 733–748.

Strober, M., & Humphrey, L. L. (1987). Familial contributions to the etiology and course of anorexia nervosa and bulimia. *Journal of Consulting and Clinical Psychology, 55,* 654–659.

Strober, M., Lampert, C., Morrell, W., Burroughs, J., & Jacobs, C. (1990). A controlled family study of anorexia nervosa: Evidence of familial aggregation and lack of shared transmission with affective disorders. *International Journal of Eating Disorders, 9,* 239–253.

Thelen, M. H., & Cormier, J. (1995). Desire to be thinner and weight control among children and their parents. *Behavior Therapy, 26,* 85–99.

Thompson, J. K., Coovert, M. D., Richards, K. J., Johnson, S., & Cattarin, J. (1995). Development of body image, eating disturbance, and general psychological functioning in female adolescents: Covariance structure modeling and longitudinal investigations. *International Journal of Eating Disorders, 18,* 221–236.

Thompson, J. K., & Heinberg, L. J. (1993). Preliminary test of two hypotheses of body image disturbance. *International Journal of Eating Disorders, 14,* 59–63.

Valtolina, G. G., & Marta, E. (1998). Family relations and psychosocial risk in families with an obese adolescent. *Psychological Reports, 83*, 251–260.

VanFurth, E. F., VanStrien, D. C., Martina, L. M. L., VanSon, M. J. M., Hendrickx, J. S., & VanEngeland, H. (1996). Expressed emotion and the prediction of outcome in adolescent eating disorders. *International Journal of Eating Disorders, 20*, 19–31.

Villejo, R. E., Humphrey, L. L., & Kirschenbaum, D. S. (1997). Affect and self-regulation in binge eaters: Effects of activating family images. *International Journal of Eating Disorders, 21*, 237–249.

Vogt, C. J. (1999). A model of risk factors involved in childhood and adolescent obesity. In A. J. Goreczny & M. Hersen (Eds.), *Handbook of pediatric and adolescent health psychology* (pp. 221–234). Boston: Allyn & Bacon.

Wilson, G. T., Heffernan, K., & Black, C. M. D. (1996). Eating disorders. In E. J. Mash & R. A. Barkley (Eds.), *Child psychopathology* (pp. 541–571). New York: Guilford Press.

Woodside, D. B., Shekter-Wolfson, L., Garfinkel, P. E., Olmsted, M. P., Kaplan, A. S., & Maddocks, S. E. (1995). Family interactions in bulimia nervosa I: Study design, comparisons to established population norms, and changes over the course of an intensive day hospital treatment program. *International Journal of Eating Disorders, 17*, 105–115.

6

RELATIONSHIP OF SEXUAL ABUSE TO BODY IMAGE AND EATING PROBLEMS

MARY E. CONNORS

Traumatic events such as child sexual abuse (CSA) have increasingly been viewed as potentially contributing to the development of later pathology (e.g., Herman, 1992). Questions concerning a possible relationship between CSA and eating disorder symptoms have received much attention in recent years (e.g., Connors & Morse, 1993). Early reports of this possible link between CSA and eating disorders were very confusing, with some studies reporting a highly significant relationship between the two and others suggesting no connection (Connors & Morse, 1993). On the basis of this earlier work Connors and Morse suggested that CSA seemed to be a risk factor for developing an eating disorder but was neither necessary nor sufficient for this outcome. However, several investigations of a possible link resulted in negative findings, leading some authors (e.g., Pope & Hudson, 1992; Pope, Mangweth, Negrao, Hudson, & Cordas, 1994) to conclude that CSA is not a significant risk factor in the etiology of eating disorders.

The advent of more sophisticated methodology and large sample sizes in some reports over the last several years has helped to clarify the proposed association. CSA does seem to be a nonspecific risk factor for the development of bulimia nervosa (BN), showing a stronger relationship with BN than with restricting anorexia nervosa (AN; see Wonderlich, Brewerton, Jocic, Dansky, & Abbott, 1997, for a review). However, these findings were based on studies consisting primarily of adults and tell us little about the developmental trajectories of abuse survivors who develop an eating disorder.

The impact of CSA on body image and eating disturbance in children and adolescents represents a challenging area for researchers, and few studies have examined this link specifically. The precursors of adult eating disorders are not completely understood, especially for younger children. Rosen (1996) noted that characteristics identified as important in adult eating disorders, such as lack of interoceptive awareness, may not appear in young children because of developmental limitations. Researchers may speculate about what behaviors, experiences, attitudes, and so forth in young children are particularly salient in predicting later eating disturbance, but knowledge in this area is incomplete. Literature on children who have been abused primarily refers to internalizing and externalizing symptoms, with uncertain relevance to eating disorders. Moreover, assessment of CSA is difficult and complex. Much research literature uses a yes–no dichotomous categorization about occurrence of CSA, but as Friedrich (1998) stated, this "obscures the heterogeneity, severity, and co-occurrence of maltreatment experiences" (p. 524).

Given these limitations, conclusions concerning the relationship of CSA and body image–eating disorder symptoms in children and adolescents must be regarded as preliminary. I shall review the available literature on abused children, adolescents, and adolescents–young adults in college, and briefly describe findings on adults. I shall also examine associated variables and offer suggestions for prevention, assessment and treatment, and further research.

IMPACT OF ABUSE ON CHILDREN

A number of studies have examined children's adjustment following sexual abuse, reporting initial effects that include anxiety, depression, fear, hostility, and inappropriate sexual behavior (e.g., Browne & Finkelhor, 1986). However, very little work has explored attitudes or behaviors related to body image and eating concerns in abused children. Thompson, Authier, and Ruma (1994) assessed foster parents' concerns about sexually abused children removed from their homes and placed in foster care. Three hundred questionnaires were analyzed about children whose ages ranged from preschool to adolescence. Foster parents were asked to rate whether a variety of behaviors occurred, and 77% of the foster parents reported that eating problems occurred either sometimes or frequently, and 23% reported that these were very bothersome. When different age ranges were examined separately, 61% reported eating problems in children up to age 5, 96% noted problems in children ages 6 through 10, and 79% reported eating problems in children 11 to 13. However, there is no further information concerning the nature of these eating problems, and children in this study were experiencing the displacement of foster care in addition to the stress of the abuse itself.

Wells, McCann, Adams, Voris, and Ensign (1995) analyzed results of a structured parent interview completed on three matched samples of girls: 68 nonabused, 68 abused girls whose perpetrator confessed, and 68 alleging abuse without a perpetrator confession. The girls' ages ranged from 2 to 11, with a mean of 7. As is typical in studies comparing abused children to controls, a variety of differences were found in areas of emotional, behavioral, and sexual functioning, but one that might be of particular relevance to body image and eating disorder issues is self-consciousness about one's body. No children in the nonabused group were reported to be unusually self-conscious about their bodies, but 18 girls in the alleged abuse group and 38 girls in the confessed abuse group were described in this fashion.

The very limited literature available on younger children thus may indicate some vulnerability for more problematic eating and increased bodily self-consciousness following CSA, but no conclusions can be drawn with any confidence until further research is conducted.

OLDER CHILDREN AND ADOLESCENTS

The literature on this age group is considerably more robust, and includes several reports that specifically assess eating disorder symptoms in abused individuals. In addition, continuity of some patterns of disturbed eating behavior is more well-established for this age group. For example, Calam and Waller (1998) found that measures of bulimic behaviors at age 12 were strong predictors of general eating psychopathology at age 19, whereas restrictive dieting behavior at age 12 predicted purging behaviors at 19.

Moyer, DiPietro, Berkowitz, and Stunkard (1997) compared 63 girls between ages 14 and 18 in treatment for CSA with high school student controls on measures of binge eating, satisfaction with body weight, body mass index (BMI), and other variables such as depression. CSA girls had significantly higher binge eating scores than controls ($p < .05$), although this difference was a result of individuals with a lower BMI; after simultaneously adjusting for all covariables, CSA was not independently associated with binge eating. The relationship between CSA and binge eating was influenced by higher levels of depression, more external locus of control, and lower self-esteem for the CSA group. Girls in the CSA group reported less satisfaction with their weight than controls ($p < .01$), despite no difference in BMI. Furthermore, in the control group, binge eating scores increased as body weight increased, reaching the highest level in the heaviest individuals, but in the CSA group binge eating occurred across the spectrum of weights, showing no regular relationship to BMI. The authors suggest that CSA seems to put thinner girls at higher risk for binge eating.

Three reports have detailed findings on a large sample of Minnesota adolescents who took part in a school-based health behavior survey in the late 1980s. French, Story, Downes, Resnick, and Blum (1995) reported on 33,393 students in grades 7 through 12 and focused on factors that correlated with frequent dieting. The sample consisted of 17,135 females and 16,258 males, and was approximately 86% White, 8% Black, 3% Asian American, 2% Native American, and 1% Hispanic. Dieting behavior was assessed with a question about how often the student had dieted during the past year, with five different frequency ranges possible. The survey also inquired about purging, binge eating, out of control eating, and sexual abuse as dichotomous variables. Both dieting frequency and purging status were independently associated with a variety of risk factors, including sexual abuse ($p < .00001$ for females, $p < .01$ for males). Sexual abuse increased in prevalence with increasing frequency of dieting for females. Female purgers were about twice as likely as nonpurgers to report a history of CSA. Similar patterns were observed in males, with CSA consistently associated with purging status.

Another report from this data set specifically focused on adolescents with a history of CSA. Chandy, Blum, and Resnick (1996) studied the 1011 females in the sample who reported a history of CSA. Respondents' average age was 15.3, and the racial composition of the group was similar to the overall sample described previously. The CSA group was compared to randomly selected control individuals from the study who did not report a CSA history. As in the French et al. report, sexual abuse was defined as "when someone in your family, or someone else, touches you in a place you did not want to be touched, or does something to you sexually which they shouldn't have done" (p. 506). Research participants in the abused group reported significantly more disordered eating than their nonabused counterparts. CSA participants described themselves as feeling overweight, as binge-eating, as engaging in nonstop eating, and as dieting more than 10 times in the previous year significantly more than controls (all at $p < 001.$). Participants reporting abuse also described purging more than controls ($p < .01$ for at least weekly self-induced vomiting and for diuretic use; $p < .05$ for laxative use).

Hernandez (1995) similarly reported on a data set gathered two years later from Minnesota students in grades 9 and 12. A random sample of 10% of students completing the survey was analyzed for this study, with a total of 6224 individuals, 3238 males and 2986 females. The sample consisted of 85% Whites, 8% Native Americans, and 7% African Americans. Sexual abuse was assessed in a bit more detail than in the previous reports, with two questions that inquired about sexually abusive experiences both inside and outside of the family. These questions also specified that the abuser was someone older or stronger (a typical procedure in abuse-related research to exclude reporting of consensual experiences with peers but one that was not done in French et al. and Chandy et al.). Students were also asked about binge eating, worries about weight, and purging. In this study, having an eating disorder was defined as reporting two of the following: binge eating, vomiting, and using laxatives (note that this definition taps a rather restricted range of eating pathology, excluding excessive dieting and binge eating without compensatory behavior). Males and females reporting CSA (incestuous or extrafamilial) were significantly more likely to endorse having an eating disorder than nonabused controls. Although only 2% of nonabused males reported an eating disorder, 18% of the extrafamilial abuse group and 20% of the incest group males endorsed having an eating disorder. For females, 9% responding in the negative to the question on extrafamilial sexual abuse reported an eating disorder, as did 10% of females reporting no history of incest, whereas 22% of females reporting extrafamilial sexual abuse and 21% of females reporting incest also endorsed having an eating disorder. Male and female abuse survivors (incestuous and extrafamilial) reported binge eating, vomiting, and using other compensatory behaviors significantly more than nonabused peers. Female abuse survivors also reported fasting, and male incest survivors endorsed worrying about weight significantly more than controls. Abused participants were more likely to be underweight or overweight than nonabused peers, with the greatest differences seen in males, but because nonnormal weight status was a dichotomous variable, the meaning of these deviations and in what direction they tended to be are not clear. This report did not provide separate analyses by racial group, so the potential importance of this variable is unknown.

These three studies are particularly important because they used a large sample size and were population-based; they also provided information about males as well as females. Limitations include the fact that Minnesota's population is not identical to the U.S. population in terms of racial and ethnic composition and that this sample is predominantly White. Moreover, only a relatively crude assessment of abuse status can be obtained with one or two questions. In contrast to the Moyer et al. (1997) study with a smaller clinical sample, these population-based studies found sexual abuse to be associated with frequency of dieting, feeling overweight, binge eating, fasting, and a variety of purging methods. The available literature on adolescents clearly suggests that sexual abuse is a risk factor for eating disturbance in this age group, for both females and males. However, it is important to note that this link is neither exclusive nor specific; physically abused individuals, for example, reported similar levels of eating pathology (French et al., 1995; Hernandez, 1995), and sexual abuse was associated with substance use, greater pregnancy risk, poor school performance, and suicidal thoughts and behaviors, in addition to eating pathology (Chandy et al., 1996).

OLDER ADOLESCENTS AND ADULTS

A number of studies have been conducted on undergraduate populations, which will be reviewed briefly to clarify any CSA–eating disorder associations in this late adolescent age group. These studies have typically involved administration of measures of eating disturbance and body dissatisfaction, as well as questionnaires inquiring about CSA. One strength of these studies is that the abuse-related measures have tended to include much more detail than was the case in studies discussed in the previous section. However, numbers of participants in these reports on undergraduate populations are much smaller. Of the studies to date, nine were suitable for inclusion in this review based on adequacy of research design and the age range of participants; several studies using some undergraduate participants were excluded because they used overly broad measures of abuse, mixed clinical and nonclinical groups, or included adult participants. Results are somewhat mixed; of the nine studies, five found an association between CSA and eating disturbance and four did not.

Calam and Slade (1989) found that CSA corresponded with higher scores on a measure of eating disturbance. Smolak, Levine, and Sullins (1990) also found that their abused group had higher scores on an eating disorders measure, although this was true only for the total score rather than for any subscales. Beckman and Burns (1990) reported that more students scoring in a bulimic range had extrafamilial abuse after age 12, and Miller, McCluskey-Fawcett, and Irving (1993) found that incest after age 12 was more likely in their bulimic scoring group. Hastings and Kern (1994) found that 14% of individuals scoring in a subclinical bulimic range and 43% of individuals scoring in a bulimic range reported CSA, whereas only 6% of the control group free of eating symptomatology reported abuse.

However, Bailey and Gibbons (1989) reported that physical abuse but not sexual abuse was associated with a BN diagnosis. Schaaf and McCann (1994) found no association between CSA and degree of body size overestimation or body dissatisfaction. Kinzl, Traweger, Guenther, and Biebl (1994) reported no significant differences in total score or subscale scores on an eating disorders measure for Austrian students reporting no, one, or repeated incidents of abuse. Finally, Korte, Horton, and Graybill (1998) found no significant differences in reported bulimic behaviors between a CSA group and nonabused peers.

These mixed findings have also characterized literature exploring CSA and eating disorders in adults, and might best be understood with reference to this research. Following this, I will broaden the discussion beyond a simple CSA–eating disturbance link to an exploration of other factors that may moderate this association.

A number of research designs have been used in examining any CSA–eating disorder associations, including the correlational analyses in nonclinical populations used in the studies on undergraduates. Other reports have investigated clinical groups; for instance, women in inpatient or outpatient treatment for eating disorders have been asked about CSA (e.g., Steiger & Zanko, 1990), and women in treatment for sexual abuse have been assessed for eating disturbance (e.g., Mallinckrodt, McCreary, & Robertson, 1995). Women in clinical groups have tended to show higher rates of the variable under investigation than nonclinical groups. For example, Mallinckrodt et al. (1995) found that incest survivors in treatment had a 47% eating disorder rate, whereas student incest survivors reported a 24% rate. Neumann, Houskamp, Pollock, and Briere (1996), in a meta-analysis of the impact of CSA, reported that sexually abused women in treatment tended to have more severe psychological difficulties than abused women in nonclinical samples. Fairburn, Welch, Doll, Davies, and O'Connor (1997) have suggested that because many individuals with eating disorders never seek treatment, sampling bias in studies on clinical groups may affect results significantly.

For this reason, the most useful literature on adults consists of large-scale community studies and case-control designs. These clearly show a significant association between CSA and bulimia nervosa (Dansky, Brewerton, Kilpatrick, & O'Neil, 1997; Fairburn et al., 1997; Garfinkel et al., 1995), and between CSA and binge eating disorder (Fairburn et al., 1998). Smaller scale studies may not have sufficient power to reveal this relationship, which, as noted previously, is not specific. Numerous risk factors for the development of an eating disorder other than CSA have been delineated (e.g., Connors, 1996; Fairburn et al., 1997; Johnson & Connors, 1987; see also chapter 4, this volume). Furthermore, CSA has been identified as a general risk factor for the development of psychological disturbance in adult women, with significant associations to depression, anxiety, anger, substance abuse, revictimization, suicidality, self-mutilation, impaired self-concept, dissociation, somatization, interpersonal difficulties, and obsessional behavior (Neumann et al., 1996), in addition to eating disorders.

Studies of clinical groups can supplement our understanding of the CSA–eating disturbance link. CSA seems to show a stronger association with BN than with restricting AN (Bushnell, Wells, & Oakley-Browne, 1992; Fullerton, Wonderlich, & Gosnell, 1995; Pribor & Dinwiddie, 1992; Steiger & Zanko, 1990; Waller, 1991). There is considerable evidence that CSA in patients with eating disorders is associated with greater psychiatric comorbidity (Bushnell et al., 1992; Wonderlich et al., 1997). Studies comparing abused and nonabused eating disorder individuals on measures of binge frequency and body dissatisfaction have shown negative findings, suggesting that CSA does not seem to be associated with greater severity of eating disorder symptoms within an eating disordered population (Bushnell et al., 1992; Wonderlich et al., 1997).

MODERATORS OF ABUSE AND OUTCOME RELATIONSHIPS

There is much to be understood about ways in which CSA might operate as a risk factor for disturbances in eating-related attitudes and behaviors. It should be noted that CSA is not invariably associated with diagnosable pathology; for instance, Finkelhor (1990) reported that a substantial proportion of victims (around one quarter to one third) show little or no symptomatology, probably because of less serious abuse and the presence of adequate resources such as social support. Abusive experiences differ greatly in variables such as age of onset, duration, severity, and relationship to the perpetrator, and some of these factors may affect the probability of developing an eating disorder. A few reports have explored this issue in an undergraduate population. Smolak et al. (1990), using a detailed measure of dimensions of abuse, found that severity of abuse (including type, frequency, and level of physical contact) and familiarity with the perpetrator were not related to eating disturbance. Reported reactions at the time of abuse were somewhat related, with women recalling positive reactions tending to have lower total scores on a measure of eating pathology.

Byram, Wagner, and Waller (1995) found that use of physical force and the identity of the abuser were not related to body size overestimation. Age at abuse (before or after age 14) was not related to body perception for the group as a whole, but in the subgroup with the most unhealthy eating attitudes an association was found between reported abuse at an older age and body size overestimation, particularly of the hips.

Abramson and Lucido (1991) found associations between bulimic symptoms and sexual experiences with relatives, greater number of sexual experiences, negative reactions of fear and shock of the abuse, and retrospective negative evaluations of the experience in a combined undergraduate–clinical sample. Negative reaction at the time was the most significant predictor, consistent with the findings of Smolak et al. (1990). Hastings and Kern (1994), using detailed and restrictive criteria for describing abuse, found that overall severity of abuse ratings were related to bulimic classification, although narrower measures of level of physical contact and familiarity of the abuser were not related.

The limited literature shows somewhat discrepant results regarding the relationship between severity of abuse and eating disorder symptoms, with more convergence in a lack of significant association between narrower factors such as familiarity of the perpetrator and level of physical contact with eating disturbance. The two studies that examined the impact of reactions to the abuse (Abramson & Lucido, 1991; Smolak et al., 1990) found an association between reports of more negative reactions and more eating pathology.

Friedrich (1998) commented on the elusive nature of simple, linear connections between CSA and outcomes in general, suggesting that commonly researched issues such as frequency and severity of abuse do not capture the larger context, which includes parent–child relationships as well as child variables. Some research has explored the impact of the family context as a moderator between CSA and eating disturbance. Smolak et al. (1990) reported that parental unreliability was associated with higher levels of eating disturbance for abused undergraduates. Mallinckrodt et al. (1995) found that incest survivors who reported their mothers as less expressive and warm and who described their families as less encouraging of independence were more likely to develop eating disorders than incest survivors depicting more positive family relationships. Hastings and Kern (1994) found that a chaotic family environment seemed to moderate the association between CSA and bulimia nervosa, with a CSA–BN link only in chaotic families. Abramson and Lucido (1991) reported a relationship between disclosure of CSA and bulimic symptoms, with no participants in the bulimic group having discussed their CSA experiences with family or others.

This literature converges in suggesting that perception of negative family interactions and parental characteristics seems to constitute a risk factor for the development of eating disturbances in abused young women. A finding by Weiner and Thompson (1997) may also be related; these authors found that covert sexual abuse was significantly associated with body image and eating disturbances. Covert sexual abuse included sexually charged interactions such as an adult staring at an adolescent's breasts, teasing or harassment about sexual development, and inappropriate sharing of information related to parental sexual issues, all of which are probably associated with poorly boundaried family interactions. These reports are consistent with other findings on the impact of CSA, suggesting that factors such as level of maternal support and intensity of parental reaction to the abuse are related to symptomatic outcomes in girls more generally (Friedrich, 1998; Mannarino & Cohen, 1996). These data on children (e.g., Mannarino and Cohen's participants were between ages 7 and 12), who have not been studied in this manner for eating pathology, suggest that the findings on undergraduates reporting family–parent variables as moderators between CSA and eating disturbance are in fact describing an important phenomenon.

PATHWAYS FROM ABUSE TO EATING DISTURBANCE

It is still not clear how and why CSA in certain family contexts might result in eating disturbance. Authors have proposed hypotheses focusing on the meaning of the body as the site of the original trauma in CSA, the importance of bodily shame, and the wish to reestablish control and reduce vulnerability via body-related actions (Andrews, 1995; Beckman & Burns, 1990; Kearney-Cooke & Striegel-Moore, 1994). Current research does not permit us to explain the pathway between CSA and eating disturbance definitively as yet, but some literature on the general impact of CSA may provide useful ideas.

There is much evidence that CSA increases psychological distress (Briere, 1992; Briere & Runtz, 1993; Friedrich, 1998; Neumann et al., 1996). Briere (1992) identified what he called "tension-reducing activities" as common sequelae of CSA, suggesting that survivors attempt to reduce their painful posttraumatic affect through activities that provide temporary distraction, restore a sense of control, interrupt dysphoric states, and numb psychological pain. He commented that such behaviors, which include self-mutilation and a variety of compulsive behaviors in addition to binge eating, provide sufficient temporary relief for unresolved abuse-related distress that they are likely to be repeated frequently. Moreover, survivors of CSA often have considerable difficulties with trust and the formation of close interpersonal relationships (Briere, 1992; Gold, 1986), which may lead to additional attempts to regulate affects via nonrelational means. An additional factor of potential importance relates to attributional style. Abused girls (Mannarino & Cohen, 1996) and women (Gold, 1986) have been found to make more personal and internal attributions for negative events than controls, and these self-blaming attributions have been related to greater psychological distress and lower self-esteem (Gold, 1986).

It is likely that CSA, in conjunction with family variables such as parental unreliability (Smolak et al., 1990); low maternal warmth and family support for autonomy (Mallinckrodt et al., 1995); chaotic family environment (Hastings & Kern, 1994); and parental alcoholism, low contact, and high expectations (Fairburn et al., 1997) leads to negative attributions about the self and considerable psychological distress in the absence of adequate supports. (Recall that Abramson and Lucido, 1991, found that not one of their bulimic participants had confided in family members about the abuse.) Negative self-evaluation, found by Fairburn et al. (1997) to differentiate between participants with bulimia nervosa and those with other disorders, generates further distress. Locus of control may be an additional factor: Mannarino and Cohen (1996) found that girls with a history of CSA tended to remain more external in their locus of control over time, whereas nonabused participants became more internal, suggesting that a normal developmental pathway was disrupted (these attributions related to being able to effect outcomes rather than to negative events). Moyer et al. (1997) found that binge eating was associated with a more external locus of control in their sample of abused adolescent girls, and a relevant study of abused adults (Waller, 1998) reported that an external locus of control was associated with greater eating disturbance, especially in women with a more severe history of abuse.

Moyer et al. (1997) reported that depression and low self-esteem were correlated with binge eating in abused adolescents. Casper and Lyubomirsky (1997) conducted regression analyses establishing that psychopathology, specifically depression, suicidality, and impulsive behaviors mediated the relationship between CSA and eating disturbance. The previously cited literature suggests that high distress such as depression, negative self-evaluation, inadequate support, and a more external locus of control may render abused individuals especially vulnerable to reliance on some form of tension-reducing behavior such as binge eating.

Binge eating is only one aspect of eating disturbance; we must also examine correlates of body dissatisfaction and dieting vulnerability as we explore the possible impact of CSA. Sharpe et al. (1998) found that insecure attachment was related to more weight concerns in fourth to eighth graders. Lawrence and Thelen (1995) reported that dieting was associated with lower general self-worth for White third and sixth graders, and Hill and Pallin (1998) found that dieting awareness was related to lower global self-worth in 8-year-old girls. French et al. (1995) found that frequency of dieting in adolescents was inversely related to connectedness with family.

Our consideration of the relationship between CSA and dieting vulnerability may be enlarged by noting that several risk factors for CSA have been identified that implicate family variables in both incest and extrafamilial abuse (Finkelhor & Baron, 1986). Risk factors for CSA include lack of closeness with parents and siblings, parents who are physically or emotionally unavailable, punitive treatment within the family, parental conflict, and maternal sociopathy (Brown, Cohen, Johnson, & Salzinger, 1998; Finkelhor, 1984; Finkelhor & Baron, 1986). Growing up in an unhappy family was identified as the most powerful risk factor for CSA in a large national survey (Finkelhor, Hotaling, Lewis, & Smith, 1990). Finkelhor and Baron (1986) have suggested that children in these families might be more susceptible to abuse both because they lack appropriate supervision and because their emotional neediness might render them especially vulnerable to abusers. Moreover, these children are less likely to experience their families as providing a safe haven in which to disclose any abuse that may be occurring. These data suggest that many abused children might be experiencing psychological distress before abuse because they lack emotional nurturance. Distress is likely to increase with the initiation of sexual abuse while self-esteem decreases (Briere, 1992). Moreover, both CSA (Alexander et al., 1998) and eating disorders (Armstrong & Roth, 1989) have been linked to insecure attachment. It is possible that insecure children with low self-worth that then is exacerabated by CSA would be more vulnerable to dieting. Moyer et al.'s (1997) important finding that abused girls reported less satisfaction with their weight than controls with similar BMIs is further evidence that dieting vulnerability itself may be affected by CSA. The need to reduce shame and restore a sense of control through managing the body (e.g., Kearney-Cooke & Striegel-Moore, 1994), although not confirmed as yet, seems probable.

It is also possible that physiological factors may contribute to the relationship between CSA and eating disturbance. CSA has been related to early puberty for girls (Trickett & Putnam, 1993), which may constitute a risk factor for disordered eating in girls in conjunction with other simultaneous stressors and transitions (Levine, Smolak, Moodey, Shuman, & Hessen, 1994). Fairburn et al. (1997) reported that their bulimic research participants were younger at menarche than controls, and that risk of developing BN increased as age at menarche decreased. Some data suggests that survivors of CSA may have a higher BMI in adulthood (Wenninger & Heiman, 1998), although further research is needed on this issue.

To summarize the complex links between CSA and eating disturbance described previously, it may be useful to note that problematic family environments characterized by a preponderance of negative interactions and a dearth of closeness and support have been implicated in the occurrence of both CSA (e.g., Finkelhor & Baron, 1986) and eating disorders (e.g., Connors, 1996). The inadequacies of such environments in meeting important developmental needs may result in CSA and in eating disorder evolving separately. However, if CSA occurs in the life of an individual who is already vulnerable, that child's distress and requirements for aid with emotional regulation will increase. When the relational environment is unresponsive and unsupportive (e.g., Smolak et al., 1990), dieting, bingeing, and purging in efforts to increase self-esteem, restore a sense of control, and manage affects all become more likely.

IMPLICATIONS FOR PREVENTION AND TREATMENT

It is clear that CSA constitutes a significant risk factor for the development of body image and eating problems in adolescents and young adults. Prevention of CSA could thus lead to considerable risk reduction for subsequent eating disorder. Duration of abuse has been linked to poorer outcome in a number of studies outside the eating disorders area (Browne & Finkelhor, 1986), so it is likely that early and appropriate intervention in situations in which CSA has occurred could reduce later symptomatology (Neumann et al., 1996). Helping the survivor disclose to family members and providing guidance to them so that they may respond supportively could be particularly useful. Because family interaction appears to moderate between CSA and eating disturbance, interventions that provide aid to parents and facilitate family functioning might reduce risk. These could include family therapy, treatment for psychological disturbances or substance abuse in parents, and school- or community-based programs promoting family strengths. Chandy et al. (1996) found that resilience in their adolescent sample was associated with having access to a clinic or nurse at school, perceiving low levels of substance use at school, having a view of self as religious or spiritual, and believing that adults care, which suggests that a focus on the school environment and the provision of access to spiritual traditions and caring adults in a variety of arenas might reduce risk of symptomatic behavior.

Appropriate assessment is a vital component of treatment. Studies of adult women in outpatient treatment for eating disorders suggest that perhaps 30% of them have a CSA history (Connors & Morse, 1993). When adolescents present for treatment because of eating problems, clinicians should be aware that CSA may be a contributing factor; however, it cannot be stressed strongly enough that the clinician should be free of any preconceived ideas about whether CSA did or did not occur in a particular case. Therapeutic errors can be made when clinicians inaccurately assume a one-to-one correspondence between CSA and bulimia nervosa, as well as in situations in which therapists fail to assess for abusive experiences that occurred but are not spontaneously disclosed. Openness to whatever historical factors may have contributed to eating disturbance will facilitate treatment most.

The clinician should inquire about CSA in the context of a thorough diagnostic interview that assesses a variety of family issues and past experiences, including maltreatment. Trauma experts recommend that the term "sexual abuse" not be used (e.g., Cortois, 1988), because some individuals would not label their experiences in this manner. Interviewers might instead inquire about whether clients have had any sexual experiences that were unwanted or upsetting. If this is answered affirmatively, the clinician could ask for more detail about what happened, when, with whom, whether anyone else knew or was later told, and how the client coped with and was affected by the experience. Interviewers should be familiar with mandatory abuse reporting laws and child protective services in their state, so that they may take appropriate action if abuse is disclosed that was not previously reported. Clinicians who wish to supplement interview data with a measure assessing trauma might consider using the Trauma Symptom Checklist (Briere & Runtz, 1989), or the Trauma Symptom Checklist Children (Briere, 1996).

Many authors have stressed the importance of some focus in therapy on the traumatic events themselves, not simply on their symptomatic manifestations (Briere, 1992; Cortois, 1988; Herman, 1992; McCann & Pearlman, 1990). An effective treatment for a CSA survivor with eating difficulties should include some processing of the CSA experiences and their impact, so that affective integration and resolution can occur. Individual treatment is very helpful in this area, but the clinician also may wish to consider some sort of group work or any possible intervention including peers. This might be especially important for CSA survivors who have eating problems; Gold (1986) found that CSA survivors reported fewer friends at age 12, and French et al. (1995) reported low connectedness with adolescent peers in frequent dieters. Abused girls have had deviant experiences that set them apart from peers on a more normative track (Cole & Putnam, 1992) and they may particularly long for acceptance. The importance peers place on weight and eating is strongly associated with weight concerns in girls (Taylor et al., 1998), so that inclusion of peers in treatments that might foster connectedness, model healthy weight standards, and promote confidence (found by Taylor et al. to be a significant protective factor for middle schoolers in terms of weight concerns) might be very useful.

CONCLUSION

Downs (1993) has commented that developmental research on the effects of CSA is in its infancy and that much research to date does not take into account the developmental level of the child; for example, the developmental stage of the abused child may be confounded with duration of the abuse. Moreover, progressive accumulation of abuse-related effects may occur as the survivor passes through different developmental stages, even though the abuse may have ceased earlier. Friedrich (1998) also described the need for greater developmental sensitivity, suggesting that future research should focus on studying smaller age ranges of children, so that some important underlying developmental differences are not masked. The limitations of current studies for understanding abused children and adolescents who develop eating disturbances are very evident; there is a dearth of studies examining body image and eating concerns in abused children. Ideally such studies would use more nuanced measures of abuse (see Friedrich, 1998, for suggestions) than have been used thus far, and would include variables that are potential moderators of outcome such as family functioning. Cross-sectional research incorporating such measures would be very useful, but longitudinal work would be especially illuminating, particularly because we do not completely understand all early precursors of eating disorders. Thelen, Powell, Lawrence, and Kuhnert (1992) found that some weight concerns begin between grades 2 and 4 for nonobese girls, so this transition might be especially fruitful for study of abused and nonabused groups.

CSA has been shown to be a risk factor for weight dissatisfaction, dieting, binge eating, and purging in adolescent males and females. Limited research on younger children does not permit firm conclusions at this time. It is likely that eating disorder outcomes are moderated by variables such

as parental support and family functioning. Clinicians treating eating disturbance in children and adolescents should be alert to the possibility that
CSA has occurred and conduct an appropriate assessment of maltreatment.
In such cases, treatment that focuses on the resolution of abusive experiences,
including reattribution of negative self-evaluation, might have a positive
impact on body image and eating problems. Prevention of CSA, early
intervention when it has occurred, and programs that enhance parental
sensitivity are all likely to reduce risk of eating disorders.

REFERENCES

Abramson, E., & Lucido, G. (1991). Childhood sexual experience and bulimia.
Addictive Behaviors, 16, 529–532.

Alexander, P., Anderson, C., Brand, B., Schaeffer, C., Grelling, B., & Kretz, L.
(1998). Adult attachment and longterm effects in survivors of incest. *Child
Abuse and Neglect*, 22, 45–61.

Andrews, B. (1995). Bodily shame as a mediator between abusive experiences and
depression. *Journal of Abnormal Psychology*, 104, 277–285

Armstrong, J., & Roth, D. (1989). Attachment and separation difficulties in eating
disorders: A preliminary investigation. *International Journal of Eating Disorders*,
8, 141–155.

Bailey, C., & Gibbons, S. (1989). Physical victimization and bulimic-like symptoms:
Is there a relationship? *Deviant Behavior*, 10, 335–352.

Beckman, K., & Burns, G. (1990). Relation of sexual abuse and bulimia in college
women. *International Journal of Eating Disorders*, 9, 487–492.

Briere, J. (1992). *Child abuse trauma: Theory and treatment of the lasting effects*.
Newbury Park, CA: Sage.

Briere, J. (1996). *Manual for the Trauma Symptom Checklist Children*. Odessa, FL:
Psychological Assessment Resources.

Briere, J., & Runtz, M. (1989) The Trauma Symptom Checklist (TSC-33). Early
data on a new scale. *Journal of Interpersonal Violence*, 2, 367–379.

Briere, J., & Runtz, M. (1993). Childhood sexual abuse: Longterm sequelae and
implications for psychological assessment. *Journal of Interpersonal Violence*,
8, 312–330.

Brown, J., Cohen, P., Johnson, J., & Salzinger, S. (1998). A longitudinal analysis
of risk factors for child maltreatment: Findings of a 17-year prospective study
of officially recorded and self-reported child abuse and neglect. *Child Abuse
and Neglect*, 22, 1065–1078.

Browne, A., & Finkelhor, D. (1986). Initial and long-term effects: A review of the
research. In D. Finkelhor (Ed.), *A sourcebook on child sexual abuse* (pp. 143–179).
Newbury Park, CA: Sage.

Bushnell, J., Wells, J., & Oakley-Browne, M. (1992). Long-term effects of intrafamilial sexual abuse in childhood. *Acta Psychiatrica Scandinavica, 85,* 136–142.

Byram, V., Wagner, H., & Waller, G. (1995). Sexual abuse and body image distortion. *Child Abuse and Neglect, 19,* 507–510.

Calam, R., & Slade, P. (1989). Sexual experiences and eating problems in female undergraduates. *International Journal of Eating Disorders, 8,* 391–397.

Calam, R., & Waller, G. (1998) Are eating and psychosocial characteristics in early teenage years useful predictors of eating characteristics in early adulthood? A 7-year longitudinal study. *International Journal of Eating Disorders, 24,* 351–362.

Casper, R., & Lyubomirsky, S. (1997). Individual psychopathology relative to reports of unwanted sexual experiences as predictor of a bulimic eating pattern. *International Journal of Eating Disorders, 21,* 229–236.

Chandy, J., Blum, R., & Resnick, M. (1996). Female adolescents with a history of sexual abuse. *Journal of Interpersonal Violence, 11,* 503–518.

Cole, P., & Putnam, F. (1992). Effect of incest on self and social functioning: A developmental psychopathology perspective. *Journal of Consulting and Clinical Psychology, 60,* 174–184.

Connors, M. (1996). Developmental vulnerabilities for eating disorders. In L. Smolak, M. Levine, & R. Striegel-Moore (Eds.) *The developmental psychopathology of eating disorders* (pp. 285–310). Mahwah, NJ: Erlbaum.

Connors, M., & Morse, W. (1993). Sexual abuse and eating disorders: A review. *International Journal of Eating Disorders, 13,* 1–11.

Cortois, C. (1988). *Healing the incest wound: Adult survivors in therapy.* New York: W.W. Norton.

Dansky, B., Brewerton, T., Kilpatrick, D., & O'Neil, P. (1997). Rape, PTSD, and bulimia in a US sample of women. *International Journal of Eating Disorders, 21,* 213–228.

Downs, W. (1993). Developmental considerations for the effects of childhood sexual abuse. *Journal of Interpersonal Violence, 8,* 331–345.

Fairburn, C., Doll, H., Welch, S., Hay, P., Davies, B., & O'Connor, M. (1998). Risk factors for binge eating disorder. *Archives of General Psychiatry, 55,* 425–532.

Fairburn, C., Welch, S., Doll, H., Davies, B., & O'Connor, M. (1997). Risk factors for bulimia nervosa. *Archives of General Psychiatry, 54,* 509–517.

Finkelhor, D. (1984). *Child sexual abuse.* New York: Free Press.

Finkelhor, D. (1990). Early and long-term effects of child sexual abuse: An update. *Professional Psychology: Research and Practice, 21,* 325–330.

Finkelhor, D., & Baron, L. (1986). Risk factors for child sexual abuse. *Journal of Interpersonal Violence, 1,* 43–71.

Finkelhor, D., Hotaling, G., Lewis, I., & Smith, C. (1990). Sexual abuse in a national survey of adult men and women: Prevalence, characteristics, and risk factors. *Child Abuse and Neglect, 14,* 19–28.

French, S., Story, M., Downes, B., Resnick, M., & Blum, R. (1995). Frequent dieting among adolescents: Psychosocial and health behavior correlates. *American Journal of Public Health, 85*, 695–701.

Friedrich, W. (1998). Behavioral manifestations of child sexual abuse. *Child Abuse and Neglect, 22*, 523–531.

Fullerton, D., Wonderlich, S., & Gosnell, B. (1995). Clinical characteristics of eating disorder patients who report sexual or physical abuse. *International Journal of Eating Disorders, 17*, 243–249.

Garfinkel, P., Lin, E., Goering, P., Spegg, C., Goldbloom, D., Kennedy, S., Kaplan, A., & Woodside, D. (1995). Bulimia nervosa in a Canadian community sample: Prevalence and comparison of subgroups. *American Journal of Psychiatry, 152*, 1052–1058.

Gold, E. (1986). Long-term effects of sexual victimization in childhood: An attributional approach. *Journal of Consulting and Clinical Psychology, 54*, 471–475.

Hastings, T., & Kern, J. (1994). Relationships between bulimia, childhood sexual abuse, and family environment. *International Journal of Eating Disorders, 15*, 103–111.

Herman, J. (1992). *Trauma and recovery.* New York: Basic Books.

Hernandez, J. (1995). The concurrence of eating disorders with histories of child abuse among adolescents. *Journal of Child Sexual Abuse, 4*, 73–85.

Hill, A, & Pallin, V. (1998). Dieting awareness and low self-worth: Related issues in 8-year-old girls. *International Journal of Eating Disorders, 24*, 405–413.

Johnson, C., & Connors, M. (1987). *The etiology and treatment of bulimia nervosa: A biopsychosocial perspective.* New York: Basic.

Kearney-Cooke, A., & Striegel-Moore, R. (1994). Treatment of childhood sexual abuse in anorexia nervosa and bulimia nervosa: A feminist psychodynamic approach. *International Journal of Eating Disorders, 15*, 305–319.

Kinzl, J., Traweger, C., Guenther, V., & Biebl, W. (1994). Family background and sexual abuse associated with eating disorders. *American Journal of Psychiatry, 151*, 1127–1131.

Korte, K., Horton, C., & Graybill, D. (1998). Child sexual abuse and bulimic behaviors: An exploratory investigation of the frequency and nature of a relationship. *Journal of Child Sexual Abuse, 7*, 53–64.

Lawrence, C., & Thelan, M. (1995). Body image, dieting, and self-concept: Their relation in African-American and Caucasian children. *Journal of Clinical Child Psychology, 24*, 41–48.

Levine, M., Smolak, L., Moodey, A., Shuman, M., & Hessen, L. (1994). Normative developmental challenges and dieting and eating disturbances in middle school girls. *International Journal of Eating Disorders, 15*, 11–20.

Mallinckrodt, B., McCreary, B., & Robertson, A. (1995). Co-occurrence of eating disorders and incest: The role of attachment, family environment, and social competencies. *Journal of Counseling Psychology, 42*, 178–186.

Mannarino, A., & Cohen, J. (1996). A follow-up study of factors that mediate the development of psychological symptomatology in sexually abused girls. *Child Maltreatment, 1,* 246–260.

McCann, I., & Pearlman, L. (1990). *Psychological trauma and the adult survivor.* New York: Brunner/Mazel.

Miller, D., McCluskey-Fawcett, K, & Irving, L. (1993). The relationship between childhood sexual abuse and subsequent onset of bulimia nervosa. *Child Abuse and Neglect, 17,* 305–314.

Moyer, D., DiPietro, L., Berkowitz, R., & Stunkard, A. (1997). Childhood sexual abuse and precursors of binge eating in an adolescent female population. *International Journal of Eating Disorders, 21,* 23–30.

Neumann, D., Houskamp, B., Pollock, V., & Briere, J. (1996). The long-term sequelae of childhood sexual abuse in women: A meta-analytic review. *Child Maltreatment, 1,* 6–16.

Pope, H., & Hudson, J. (1992). Is childhood sexual abuse a risk factor for bulimia nervosa? *American Journal of Psychiatry, 149,* 455–463.

Pope, H., Mangweth, B., Negrao, A., Hudson, J., & Cordas, T. (1994). Childhood sexual abuse and bulimia nervosa: A comparison of American, Austrian, and Brazilian women. *American Journal of Psychiatry, 151,* 732–737.

Pribor, E., & Dinwiddie, S. (1992). Psychiatric correlates of incest in childhood. *American Journal of Psychiatry, 149,* 52–56.

Rosen, K. (1996). The principles of developmental psychopathology: Illustration from the study of eating disorders. In L. Smolak, M. Levine, & R. Striegel-Moore (Eds.) *The developmental psychopathology of eating disorders* (pp. 3–29). Mahwah, NJ: Erlbaum.

Schaaf, K., & McCanne, T. (1994). Childhood abuse, body image disturbance, and eating disorders. *Child Abuse and Neglect, 18,* 607–615.

Sharpe, T., Killen, J., Bryson, S., Shisslak, C., Estes, L., Gray, N., Crago, M., & Taylor, C. (1998). Attachment style and weight concerns in preadolescent and adolescent girls. *International Journal of Eating Disorders, 23,* 39–44.

Smolak, L., Levine, M., & Sullins, E. (1990). Are child sexual experiences related to eating-disordered attitudes and behaviors in a college sample? *International Journal of Eating Disorders, 9,* 167–178.

Steiger, H., & Zanko, M. (1990). Sexual traumata among eating-disordered, psychiatric, and normal female groups. *Journal of Interpersonal Violence, 5,* 74–86.

Taylor, C., Sharpe, T., Shisslak, C., Bryson, S., Estes, L., Gray, N., McKnight, K., Crago, M., Kraemer, H., & Killen, J. (1998). Factors associated with weight concerns in adolescent girls. *International Journal of Eating Disorders, 24,* 31–42.

Thelen, M., Powell, A., Lawrence, C., & Kuhnert, M. (1992). Eating and body image concerns among children. *Journal of Clinical Child Psychology, 21,* 41–46.

Thompson, R., Authier, K., & Ruma, P. (1994). Behavior problems of sexually abused children in foster care: A preliminary study. *Journal of Child Sexual Abuse, 3,* 79–91.

Trickett, P., & Putnam, F. (1993). Impact of child sexual abuse on females: Toward a developmental psychobiological integration. *Psychological Science, 4*, 81–87.

Waller, G. (1991). Sexual abuse as a factor in eating disorders. *British Journal of Psychiatry, 159*, 664–671.

Waller, G. (1998). Perceived control in eating disorders: Relationship with reported sexual abuse. *International Journal of Eating Disorders, 23*, 213–221.

Weiner, K., & Thompson, K. (1997). Overt and covert sexual abuse: Relationship to body image and eating disturbance. *International Journal of Eating Disorders, 22*, 273–284.

Wells., R., McCann, J., Adams, J., Voris, J., & Ensign, J. (1995). Emotional, behavioral, and physical symptoms reported by parents of sexually abused, nonabused, and allegedly abused prepubescent females. *Child Abuse and Neglect, 19*, 155–163.

Wenninger, K., & Heiman, J. (1998). Relating body image to psychological and sexual functioning in child sexual abuse survivors. *Journal of Traumatic Stress, 11*, 432–562.

Wonderlich, S., Brewerton, T., Jocic, Z., Dansky, B., & Abbott, D. (1997). Relationship of childhood sexual abuse and eating disorders. *Journal of the American Academy of Child and Adolescent Psychiatry, 36*, 1107–1115.

III

ASSESSMENT

It is self-evident that good assessment tools are a prerequisite for meaningful research. It is also clear that the development of good assessment instruments is difficult, tedious, and time-consuming. This already daunting task is made more challenging when children and adolescents will be the respondents. Children's actual development, as well as their ability to comprehend certain constructs and questions, typically requires assessments that are specially designed for them. Children may, for example, have less distinct components of depression than do adolescents (Leadbetter, Kupermind, Blatt, & Hertzog, 1999) and less consolidated eating and body image schemas (Smolak, Levine, & Schermer, 1998). This means that scales based on adult (or even adolescent) constructs may not be appropriate for use with children (Smolak, 1996).

Given these challenges, this section explores assessment in three different areas. Kelly Hill and Claire Pomeroy first discuss the physical evaluation of children and adolescents suspected to suffer from eating disorders or obesity. This is a critically important topic because pediatricians and family practitioners are often the first to see and assess these children. Furthermore, treatment of eating problems in children and adolescents is probably best accomplished by a team that includes a physician. Counselors and psychologists may find that reading through this information gives them a fuller understanding of the physician's role as well as ideas for educating physicians concerning eating disorders.

Rick Gardner provides a careful review of measures available to assess body image disturbance in children and adolescents. This is a particularly tricky area because there are so many definitions of body image operating in the field. Gardner reviews both figural and questionnaire formats and considers the limitations of trying to assess body image in children. He also offers a comprehensive methodological analysis of the issues involved in the measurement of the "perceptual" and attitudinal components of body image. His examination of these important assessment issues serves as a critical guide for the clinician and researcher.

Susan Netemeyer and Donald Williamson remind us first that the *DSM-IV* diagnostic categories for eating disorders were not designed with children in mind. That fact, combined with the limited research available on eating disordered or subthreshold children, makes it extremely difficult to identify good measures of eating disturbance in children. But Netemeyer and Williamson are able to provide guidance as to the variety of potentially useful, psychometrically valid measures that are available.

The most crucial component of a good research project is, of course, a good idea rooted in a strong theoretical model. But without good operationalization of the constructs and valid assessments, the idea's promise cannot be realized. These chapters provide information that should be extremely helpful in designing studies that do our ideas justice.

In addition, from a clinical perspective the chapters offer concrete suggestions, laced with caveats, for the appropriate use of specific assessment strategies with children and adolescents. Clearly, this emerging field will evolve in future years to rival the sophistication found in measurement options currently available for adult samples. These chapters offer an excellent review of these methods for the clinical assessment of eating disorders and obesity, while also providing information central to the formation of future investigations.

REFERENCES

Leadbeater, B., Kuperminc, G., Blatt, S., & Hertzog, C. (1999). A multivariate model of gender differences in adolescents' internalizing and externalizing problems. *Developmental Psychology, 35,* 1268–1282.

Smolak, L. (1996). Methodological implications of a developmental psychopathology approach to the study of eating problem. In L. Smolak, M. Levine, & R. Striegel-Moore (Eds.), *The developmental psychopathology of eating disorders* (pp. 31–56). Mahwah, NJ: Erlbaum.

Smolak, L., Levine, M. P., & Schermer, F. (1998). Lessons from lessons: An evaluation of an elementary school prevention program. In W. Vandereycken & G. Noordenbos (Eds.), *The prevention of eating disorders* (pp. 137–172). London: Athlone Press.

7

ASSESSMENT OF PHYSICAL STATUS OF CHILDREN AND ADOLESCENTS WITH EATING DISORDERS AND OBESITY

KELLY HILL AND CLAIRE POMEROY

Disordered eating results in a wide spectrum of diseases. Eating disorders such as anorexia nervosa (AN) and bulimia may be glamorized in the media and other conditions, such as obesity, are often associated with shame or disgust. Regardless, the eating disorders and obesity represent a major public health problem in the United States and other industrialized countries (Mitchell & Eckert, 1987). Eating disorders affect large numbers of persons, and in particular target adolescent and young adult women (Yager, Anderson, Duelin, Mitchell, & Pavers, 1993). Unfortunately, these disorders carry high morbidity rates and the highest mortality rates of any category of psychiatric illness (Hoffman & Halmi, 1993; Herzog & Bradburn, 1992). Focusing exclusively on psychological aspects of care can result in devastating consequences (Colling & King, 1994; Crisp, Callender, Halek, & Higbee, 1992; Ratnasuriya, Eisler, Szmukler, & Russell, 1991). Optimal treatment involves a multidisciplinary approach that incorporates medical management as an integral part of the overall care of eating-disordered and obese patients (Harris, 1986).

AN is characterized by self-imposed starvation. Patients with AN refuse to eat, lose at least 15% of their body weight, are amenorrheic, have an intense fear of becoming fat, and have a distorted body image (American Psychiatric Association, 1994). In children and prepubescent adolescents AN may be manifested by weight loss or by a failure to grow (Baran, Weltzin, & Kay, 1995). Bulimia nervosa (BN) is characterized by recurrent episodes of binge eating. Bulimics engage in behaviors to prevent weight gain, such as purging and excessive exercise. To meet strict criteria for BN, the bingeing and compensatory activities must occur at least twice a week for three months (American Psychiatric Association, 1994). Binge eating disorder is defined as uncontrollable overeating without compensatory purging or excessive exercise characteristic of BN, and therefore is associated with obesity (American Psychiatric Association 1994; deZwaan & Mitchell, 1992). Morbid obesity, usually defined as greater than 170% of ideal body weight, affects 3 to 5% of the population. Obese adolescents achieve lower socioeconomic status as adults and are less likely to marry normal-weight individuals (Gortmaker, Must, Perrin, Sobal, & Dietz, 1993).

The purpose of this chapter is to review the medical complications of eating disorders and obesity and to offer practical suggestions for assessment and management of patients with these conditions.

PHYSICAL ASSESSMENT

The psychological management of eating disorders is continually challenging because of the serious medical complications that can result from the pathological eating behavior, purging, taxing exercise regimens, or obesity. Treatment of the child and adolescent with aberrant eating must include a thorough assessment of the patient's physical status. A 33-year study by Theander reported an 18% mortality rate in patients with AN (Theander, 1985). Bulimics are also at significant risk for serious medical complications that can be deadly, such as hypokalemia. Conversely, excessive weight and obesity in childhood has important health consequences (Nieto, Szklod, & Cemstock, 1992). A study following children, initially 5 to 18 years of age, for 30 to 52 years, reported that mortality was linked to relative weight. Obese children have higher mortality rates than their normal weight counterparts (Mossberg, 1989). In adults, obesity has been linked to an increased propensity for type II diabetes, hypertension, hyperlipidemia, hyperuricemia, cardiovascular disease, cancers, and subsequent higher total mortality.

Historical Clues

Many adolescents are preoccupied with and critical of their appearance (Harlan, 1993). However, only a small percentage of adolescents go on to develop a true eating disorder. The initial presentation of an eating disorder in children varies depending on the child's age. In some cases, the eating and weight history may be unremarkable or leave no clue that the child was at risk for developing an eating disorder. For children with AN and BN, parents frequently describe the patient as a "perfect child" who had no discipline difficulties and who excelled at school and sports. Perfectionism is commonly found in the premorbid history of AN patients. Often, in both AN and BN, there is a history of finicky eating and weight fluctuations.

There can be a history of being overweight as a young child, and then as an adolescent becoming more preoccupied with their weight, fad diets, and exercise regimens.

A weight history and diet history will provide clues to the severity and chronicity of the eating disorder. A menstrual history is essential to help interpret the extent of hypothalamic pituitary axis dysfunction. Given the high frequency of psychiatric comorbidity, especially depression and chemical dependence (in BN), a psychiatric and substance use history is essential.

The child or adolescent with an eating disorder will typically present in denial that there is a problem. Parents and other members of the child's social systems may be the only ones to provide the history of food restriction, weight preoccupation, distorted body image, fear of fatness, eating patterns, and purging activities. The bulimic client, although usually very ashamed of her bingeing and purging activities, is often more open to receiving help initially. The prepubertal child who develops AN may not initially present with distorted body image but with complaints of stomachache and poor appetite. Only over time and in the treatment process will the body image distortions and fear of fatness come to the surface. Any young female adolescent with a history of weight loss and abdominal complaints should be assessed for an eating disorder.

Most patients with binge eating disorder are overweight but usually appear healthy. They frequently visit physicians for diet advice rather than seeking help for disordered eating. Such requests should prompt a careful evaluation of eating patterns, including bingeing. They may present with depression or fatigue, probably related to feelings relating to self-esteem about body image or other life events. The obese child may present because of personal and parental concerns about overweight or on referral from the schools. (See Table 7-1.)

Physical Exam

All patients evaluated for an eating disorder should receive a complete physical examination (Table 7-2). The exam may reveal abnormalities in one of many of the major systems of the body, including the cardiovascular, hematologic, gastrointestinal, renal, endocrine, and skeletal systems (Hill et al, 1995; McClain et al., 1993). This is a vital opportunity for the physician to exclude other underlying medical illnesses that may present with disordered eating and abnormal weight and confirm the diagnosis of an eating disorder or obesity. Early detection of medical complications and coexisting medical conditions can be done. Other health care professionals can be informed of medical conditions that might alter the psychologic treatment approach. For example, it may be necessary to avoid tricyclic

TABLE 7-1
Major Symptoms and Signs in Eating Disorders

Anorexia Nervosa	Bulimia Nervosa	Binge Eating Disorder
Symptoms		
Denial of illness	Secretive about binge–	Request for diet advice
Amenorrhea	purge behaviors	Eating binges
Agitation (hyperactivity)	Irregular menses	Weight concerns
Irritability, withdrawal	Abdominal pain	Depression
Sleep disturbances,	Abdominal bloating	Symptoms as a result of
lethargy	Lethargy	complications of
Fatigue, headaches	Constipation	obesity
Constipation	Swelling of hands/feet	
Abdominal pain	Depression	
Cold intolerance		
Signs		
Inanition	Often appear well	Often overweight
Low body temperature	Russell's sign	Otherwise usually appear
Bradycardia, hypotension	Parotid gland swelling	well
Dry skin, brittle hair,	Erosion of dental	Signs a result of
brittle nails	enamel	complications of
"Yellow" skin, especially	Edema	obesity
palms		
Lanugo		
Hair loss on scalp		
Edema		

TABLE 7-2
Initial Medical Evaluation of Patients With Eating Disorders

History, with special emphasis on
- Weight history
- Diet history
- Menstrual history (women)/sexual history
- Psychiatric history
- Chemical abuse/dependency history
- Use of diuretics/laxatives/diet pills/ipecac

Physical examination, with special emphasis on
- Weight, degree of inanition
- State of hydration
- Dental examination
- Cardiac, abdominal, and neurologic examinations
- Gynecologic examination

antidepressants in patients with serious cardiac conduction disturbances or to counsel sport coaches of the importance of limiting training regiments. Finally, the initial medical assessment is an opportunity to develop a strong physician–patient alliance, serving as a basis for optimal management of medical complications that may arise during treatment. Development of a therapeutic alliance is essential as many patients with eating disorders or obesity are resistant to the treatment process. AN patients are usually frightened and overwhelmed by the doctor's prescription for "weight gain," whereas patients with bulimia are ashamed of being caught in the binge–purge cycle. Obese patients also commonly feel ashamed and overwhelmed with their eating patterns.

General Appearance

The typical AN patient looks younger than her actual age, having breast atrophy and being "petite" if not yet cachectic. Puberty is arrested. Depending on the severity of malnutrition, secondary sexual characteristics can be lost and the patient may present as a preadolescent (loss of breast development and pubic hair). Lanugo (soft downy hair), hair thinning, and carotenemia (carotene—yellow–red pigments in the blood which may cause a pale yellow–red pigmentation of skin) are common. This is in contrast to the bulimic patient who superficially may look the picture of health, being normal weight and physically in shape. Because in both of these disorders there is an extreme focus on physical appearance, usually these adolescents are extremely meticulous in their makeup and apparel (Hill & Maloney, 1998).

ASSESSMENT OF MEDICAL COMPLICATIONS

Cardiovascular Assessment

Some of the most severe medical complications of eating disorders and obesity involve the cardiovascular system. Many patients with AN suffer from cardiac abnormalities. Tachycardia, hypotension, ventricular arrhythmias, and cardiac failure can occur (Maloney, 1995). The most lethal findings are arrhythmias ranging from superventricular premature contractions to ventricular tachycardia. Prolonged QT intervals are not common but are thought to be a possible etiology of sudden death (Herzog & Bradburn, 1992). Bulimia patients also can have rhythm disturbances. Electrolyte abnormalities are the most common cause of serious rhythm disturbance and cardiac deaths. Hypokalemia, hypocalcemia, hypophosphatemia, or hypomagnesemia predispose patients to potentially fatal arrhythmias. Brady-cardia of less than 60 beats per minute is found in up to 87% of patients with AN. Blood pressure less than 90/60 mmHG is observed in up to 85% of patients with AN. These vital sign aberrations are probably attributable to chronic volume depletion, which can cause dizziness and syncope. When refeeding the low-weight anorexic patient, it is important to carefully moni-tor cardiac function as increased workload on the compromised cardiac reserve can lead to congestive heart failure.

Bulimia patients are also at risk for cardiac complications related to dehydration, orthostatic blood pressure changes, and hypotension. Self-induced vomiting and abuse of laxatives and diuretics are usually implicated. Ipecac abuse, frequently used in bulimia and some patients with anorexia to induce vomiting, is cardiotoxic. When used excessively, ipecac can cause irreversible myocardial damage.

Obesity has been linked to hypertension and vascular disease in adults. So although the adolescent may not be in imminent danger from cardiac complications, the long-term consequences are unclear. Therefore, when evaluating the adolescent with disordered eating or abnormal body weight, it is vital to do a careful cardiac exam. This should include orthostatic vital signs and a baseline electrocardiogram.

Assessment of orthostatic vital signs can be done quickly and easily in the office and gives the clinician a sense of the physical stability of the patient. To most accurately assess for orthostasis, keep the patient supine for 10 minutes before measuring pulse and blood pressure, and then have the patient stand for 2 minutes before repeating the measurements. A change of systolic and diastolic pressures of more than 20 mmHg and more than 10 mmHg, respectively, should alert the physician that the patient may be significantly dehydrated and need immediate attention.

Dermatological and Dental Assessment

The skin is affected in several ways in AN. Nutritional factors are linked to the development of lanugo in the extremities, back, and face as observed in one third of AN patients. The skin can also become dry, thin, and scaly. Carotenodermia (carotene in the skin causing yellow–red coloration) is seen in up to 80% of AN patients.

An important diagnostic sign of BN is skin changes over the dorsum of the hand caused by trauma when the hand is used to induce vomiting, termed Russell's sign. Lesions vary from elongated superficial lacerations to hyperpigmented calluses or scaring (Herzog & Bradburn, 1992). Self-induced vomiting may lead to purpura because of increased intrathoracic pressure associated with vomiting (Mitchell, Pyle, Eckert, Hatsukami, & lantz, 1983).

Dental erosions can be a helpful diagnostic indicator of bulimic behaviors. Decalcification of the lingual, palatal, and posterior occlusal surfaces of the teeth may occur because of frequent vomiting, with the acid bathing the back of the mouth (Herzog & Bradburn, 1992). Often BN is first identified in the dental clinic with subsequent psychiatric referral.

Gastrointestinal Assessment

Any clinician who treats eating disorder patients will inevitably hear complaints of abdominal bloating and uncomfortable stomach fullness. The entire gastrointestinal system can be affected and can complicate the refeeding process.

Esophagus

It has been suggested that primary esophageal motility disorders occur commonly in eating disorder patients and esophageal dismotility may contribute to the pathogenesis of the disease process. They have been reported in up to half the patients with AN and one third of patients with BN (Sharp & Freeman, 1993; Stacher et al., 1986). Stacher reported that 7 of 30 patients with AN had achalasia and other important motility disorders, including diffuse spasm (Sharp & Freeman, 1993).

Decreased stomach motility occurs in patients with AN and BN but usually ceases once a patient resumes normal eating behavior. However, during refeeding patients may complain of abdominal pain and fullness related to delayed gastric emptying. Patients should be forewarned of this side effect. Small intestine function has not been thoroughly studied in these patients, but several studies have reported delayed transient time (Haller, Slovis, Baker, Berdon, & Silverman, 1977; Kiss et al., 1990). Possible mechanisms for abnormal motility in eating disorders include abnormalities in hypothalamic pituitary function and thyroid function as a result of the emaciated state, disturbed sensitivity of colon urgent receptors, or impaired autonomic function. When evaluating stomach complaints, it is very important to ask about laxative abuse. Patients may suffer from alternating diarrhea and constipation. Rectal impaction has been reported in patients who have very little oral intake (Hirakawa et al., 1990).

Pancreas

Pancreatic abnormalities may be associated with eating disorders (Gilinsky, Humphries, Fried, & McClain, 1988; Keane, Fennell, & Tomkin, 1978; McClain, Humphries, Hill, & Nickl, 1993). Acute pancreatitis (inflamation of the pancreas) has been reported sometimes in relation to the refeeding process of anorexic patients. Possible etiologies for the pancreatic abnormalities includes severe protein calorie malnutrition, reflux into the pancreatic ducts from the duodenum as a result of vomiting, and inspissated secretions. In refeeding these patients, pancreatitis may develop if there is rapid increase in caloric intake associated with a dehydrated malnourished state. However, these complications are rare.

Hyperamylasemia (increased amylase in the blood) may be found on laboratory evaluation of patients who engage in restrictive or bulimic behaviors. Elevated serum amylase levels can be used to help differentiate between patients with restricting anorexia and those with bulimic anorexia (Humphries, Adams, Eckfeldt, Levitt, & McClain, 1987; Mitchell et al., 1983). In a control setting such as during hospitalization, amylase activity normalizes. Serum amylase can be useful in monitoring outpatient progress. Modest increases may indicate increased bingeing and purging activity (Gwirtsman et al., 1989).

In BN, parotid (salivary gland beside the ear) enlargement is common. Bilateral painless hypertrophy (general increase in bulk of a part or organ that is not a result of tumor formation) at the parotid gland can be very striking when evaluating the adolescent, and often it is a clue to occult purging activity. It is thought to be secondary to alkalosis, high carbohydrate intake, malnutrition, and the frequency of bingeing and purging. The swelling usually normalizes with nutritional stabilization and the resumption of normal eating behaviors.

Obesity has been associated with a variety of gastrointestinal difficulties. Gallstones occur in approximately one third of morbidly obese patients. In addition, gallstone formation can accompany rapid weight loss secondary to very-low-caloric diets or gastric bypass surgery (Gwirtsman et al., 1989; Shiffman, Sugarman, Kelleem, Brever, & Moore, 1991). Fifty percent of such patients require cholecystectomy. Abnormal liver enzymes (LDH and serum transaminases) usually reflect fatty infiltration of the liver (Worobetz, Inglis, & Shaffer, 1993). In severely obese individuals, portal inflammation and fibrosis called "nonalcoholic steatohepatitis" can develop.

Skeletal Assessment

Osteopenia (decreased calcification or density of bone) frequently develops in patients with AN and malnourished BN. Because bone accretion peaks in late adolescence, the impact on bone mineral density may be greatest if the disease develops during this time. If puberty is interrupted, bone mass may remain persistently low. The decrease in bone density can result in pathological fractures of hip, spine, and long bones. Postulated mechanisms include estrogen deficiency, glucocorticoid excess, malnutrition, and low calcium intake (Gwirtsman et al., 1989). It is important for the clinician to be aware of the risk for developing osteopenia. For now, however, routine studies of bone density are not being recommended. Hormonal replacement (estrogen–progesterone) is under investigation, but preliminary studies have demonstrated no significant effect (Shiffman et al., 1991; Worobetz et al., 1993).

Obesity is associated with degenerative osteoarthritis. Stress on joints, such as knees, is probably related to the increased weight.

Growth

Because eating disorders such as AN and BN are by definition associated with pathological eating and at times severe malnutrition, growth and overall development of children can be affected. In severe cases of caloric restriction, growth can be arrested.

In patients with severe caloric restriction and malnutrition, the physical assessment should include examination of the growth chart. Children who persistently are not following the growth curve should be considered for an eating disorder or other cause of abnormal development. Tanner staging should also be performed. In AN, there can be loss of secondary sexual characteristics, and Tanner staging can be one source of assessing if the patient is progressing in treatment.

Pulmonary

Obesity can be associated with impaired air flow and decreased lung capacities (Klibanski, Biller, Schoenfeld, Herzog, & Saxe, 1995; Rubenstein, Zamel, DuBarry, & Hoffstein, 1991). In the most severe cases, respiratory insufficiency may develop. In addition, obese patients may develop obstructive sleep apnea or the obesity hypoventilation syndrome. In sleep apnea the patient experiences intermittent pauses in breathing, especially while sleeping, resulting in hypoxia, disruptive sleep, and daytime somnolence. In contrast, obesity hypoventilation syndrome results in hypoxia at any time and is a result of decreased lung volumes. Long-term complications of these include pulmonary hypertension, arrhythmias, cardiac failure, and increased risk of sudden death (Najala et al., 1991; Sugarman et al., 1992).

Obesity

Other medical complications of obesity include an increased risk of cancer, particularly the breast, uterus, colon, and prostrate; increased surgical risks and complications, and increased mortality. Decreased fertility is common in the obese with abnormal menstrual function in women and abnormal sperm production in men. An increased risk of adverse perinatal outcomes has been reported for obese women (Rossner, Lagerstrand, Persson, & Saeks, 1991).

LABORATORY EVALUATION

Endocrine and Metabolic

Alterations of endocrine function are characteristic of patients with eating disorders or obesity (Fichter & Pirke, 1990; Perlow, Morgan, Montgomery, Towes, & Porto, 1992). Abnormalities of the hypothalamic pituitary gonadotropin (hormones capable of promoting gonadal growth and function) axis and menstrual abnormalities are observed in both AN and BN (Thomas & Rebar, 1990). By definition, AN patients are amenorrheic (absence or abnormal cessation of the menses). Some authorities have suggested primary central nervous system dysfunction. However, amenorrhea is common in other starvation states and may therefore be attributable to caloric restriction per se. Some studies have reported that 90% of anorexic women will begin menstruating when their body fat increases to 22% of total body weight. However, in 16% of anorexic patients the amenorrhea develops before weight loss and may continue after weight restoration. Again, this implicates a disturbance of hypothalamic function, possibly secondary to psychological stress (Sharp & Freeman, 1993). Therefore, restoration of weight as well as improvement in psychological functioning in some patients is necessary before menses resumes. In patients with AN, hypoestrogenemia (decreased circulating estrogen) with low luteinizing hormone and follicle stimulating hormone levels is frequent. An immature pattern of the response of these hormones to gonadotropin-releasing hormones is characteristic. The uterus may be small and again normalizes with weight gain. In the male AN patient, serum testosterone levels are decreased (Sharp & Freeman, 1993). This is also seen in other starvation states. Abnormal menstrual cycles occur in a subset of patients with BN and also have been associated with abnormal gonadotropin hormone production (Pirke, Fichter, Chlond, & Doevr, 1987).

Cortisol levels are elevated in AN and some BN patients. This reflects a persistent activation of the hypothalamic pituitary adrenal axis (Gold et al., 1986; Gwirtsman et al., 1989). Subsequently, nonsuppression is expected on the dexamethasone suppression test in AN patients. The etiology of hypothalamic pituitary adrenal axis stimulation is not well-defined. The elevated cortisol levels are generally a result of decreased clearance and prolonged half-life, and the secretion rate usually is not significantly altered. Possible etiologies include a primary central nervous system defect, effect secondary to starvation, or stress-induced effect. Abnormal dexamethasone suppression tests have been reported in bulimic patients (Mitchell, Pyle,

Hatsukani, & Boutacoff, 1984). It is unclear if this is a result of hypercortisol-ism or merely represents a failure to absorb dexamethasone from the gastroin-testinal tract (Martola, Rasmussen, & Yen, 1989). In obesity, as observed in binge eaters, abnormal dexamethasone suppression tests result. This could be due because of a higher requirement for the dose of dexamethasone in obese patients who have a large volume of distribution. Therefore, in testing obese patients a repeat test should be performed with a double dose of dexamethasone before the test is interpreted definitively as abnormal.

New disturbances in thyroid function also characterize eating disorders. In AN, Thyroxin levels (T4) may be mildly depressed. This is usually not clinically relevant. Triiodothyronine (T3) levels may be 50% of those found in nonanorexic populations. This is similar to the euthyroid sick pattern, with low total T3 but relatively normal total T4 and thyroid-stimulating hormone. This represents a physiologic down regulation probably secondary to starvation and should therefore not be treated with thyroid hormone replacement. However, because the signs and symptoms of hypo- and hyper-thyroidism can mimic findings in eating disorders, all patients should have thyroid function screening tests as part of their initial evaluation (Curran-Celentano et al., 1985; Spalter, Gwirtsman, Demitrade, & Gold, 1993).

Other endocrine and metabolic abnormalities are also reported in eating disorders. Vasopressin release may be abnormal in AN. Up to 40% may develop a partial neurogenic diabetes insipidus and increased urine output. This is also seen in other starvation states. An elevated cholesterol level (hypercholesterolemia) is a frequent finding in anorexic patients. In contrast to other forms of starvation in which low serum cholesterol values are expected, this can be a useful clinical pearl in aiding in the differential diagnosis of weight loss in young women—for example, distinguishing an eating disorder from inflammatory bowel disease. Elevated serum carotene levels are frequent in AN and may result in orange discoloration of the skin (carotenodermia), as mentioned previously. Additional metabolic ab-normalities associated with obesity include hyperlipidemia, diabetes mellitus, and gout.

Renal, Fluid, and Electrolytes

Abnormal eating patterns can result in a myriad of electrolyte abnor-malities. Restricted caloric intake, frequent vomiting, and diuretic and laxa-tive abuse can all result in serious fluid imbalance. Renal complications seen in AN patients include a decreased glomerular filtration rate and concentrating ability, increased blood urea nitrogen, pitting edema, and hypokalemic nephropathy (Brotman, Stern, & Brotman, 1986). It is interest-ing to note that abnormal or elevated blood urea nitrogen levels are usually observed in AN. This is different from other starvation syndromes.

In cases with chronic dehydration, renal stones may develop (Silber & Kass, 1984). Patients who have a relatively high oxalate intake are at increased risks to develop kidney stones, chronic dehydration, low urine output, and vomiting. Although rare, renal abnormalities involving prolonged low serum potassium levels cause polyuria (excessive excretion of urine), polydipsia (frequent drinking because of extreme thirst), and can result in chronic renal failure.

Electrolyte abnormalities are a common and major problem in many eating disorder patients. Those who abuse laxatives or diuretics and who chronically engage in self-induced vomiting are more at risk. Hypokalemia in an outpatient with an eating disorder suggests persistent purging even if the patient strongly denies that she is vomiting (Greenfield, Mickley, Quinlan, & Roloff, 1995). Dehydration is signaled by a disproportionate increase in the blood urea nitrogen to creatinine ratio (Sheinin, 1986).

Hyponatremia, hypocalcemia, and hypomagnesemia can also occur in AN and BN. The low calcium and potassium may not improve unless magnesium is given simultaneously. Hypomagnesemia may lead to renal calculi production, because there may be increased urinary concentration of calcium (Hall & Beresford, 1989).

Edema may occur during the refeeding process of AN (Silverman, 1983). One form associated with normal plasma protein and albumin levels is of unclear etiology and usually is clinically insignificant. A more ominous form can follow chronic laxative abuse and vigorous purging. This can lead to hypoproteinemia (abnormally small amounts of total protein in the circulating blood plasma) with subsequent hypovolemia and fluid shifts. These patients are at risk for developing shock, renal failure, and cardiovascular collapse (Howard, Leggat, & Chaudry, 1992).

Hematologic and Immunologic

One third of patients with AN develop a mild anemia and thrombocytopenia. Leukopenia occurs in approximately two thirds of patients. The anemia is usually multifactorial (Mira, Stewart, & Abraham, 1989). Starvation-induced bone marrow suppression is most commonly thought to be the cause, but blood lost from the gastrointestinal tract, iron deficiency, and nutritional abnormalities, such as vitamin B12 or folate deficiency, could all potentially contribute. Rarely is the anemia of clinical significance, and transfusion should be used only for the rare patient who has serious medical consequences of the anemia, such as high output congestive heart failure. Leukopenia with a relative lympho-cytosis is common in AN. Thrombocytopenia is rarely clinically significant. In severe cases, there may be significant pancytopenia. Refeeding generally normalizes these abnormalities.

DIFFERENTIAL DIAGNOSIS

From Other Medical–Physical Illnesses

The initial medical assessment must rule out other causes of weight loss or overweight, weight fluctuations, and pathological eating patterns. A variety of medical illnesses can present in similar ways to the eating disorders. These include gastrointestinal disorders, endocrine disorders, chronic infections, malignancies, and hypothalamic lesions. Some rare syndromes may also mimic binge eating and obesity. Usually the diagnosis can be established through a comprehensive history, physical examination, and laboratory screenings. An eating disorder should always be considered in the differential diagnosis for any female adolescent presenting with abdominal complaints or weight fluctuations. The patient should be screened for hypokalemia. When finding hypokalemia in such a youngster, an eating disorder should be high on the differential. Serum albumin is a useful lab when trying to distinguish an eating disorder from inflammatory bowel disease, because hypoalbuminemia is associated with diseases such as Crohn's, whereas in the eating disorders the visceral proteins are preserved.

The presence of other psychiatric comorbidity should be assessed, because it readily can be found and associated with eating disorders or obesity. In particular, these patients need to be assessed for depression (Hill & Maloney, 1998). Major depression with loss of appetite can lead to significant weight loss. Also, atypical depressions with hyperphagia can lead to weight gain. Other psychiatric diagnoses to be evaluated in these patients include anxiety disorders, obsessive–compulsive disorders, and addictive illnesses.

Any coexisting medical illnesses can complicate the treatment process. For example, managing eating disordered patients with diabetes mellitus can be difficult. The typical adolescent struggles with control and body image are magnified. Erratic caloric intake, including restriction or bingeing, can significantly complicate treatment with insulin. In these situations, the psychiatrist must work closely with the medical physician. (See Table 7-3.)

ONGOING MEDICAL MANAGEMENT

The first treatment objective in AN is to renourish the patient to a medically safe weight and restore normal eating patterns to correct the biologic and psychologic sequella of malnutrition. Morbidity and mortality of patients increase with the amount of time the patient remains untreated.

TABLE 7-3
Differential Diagnosis of Eating Disorders

Anorexia Nervosa	Bulimia Nervosa	Binge Eating Disorder
• Gastrointestinal diseases (i.e., inflammatory bowel disease, malabsorption syndrome) • Endocrine Diseases (i.e., thyroid disorders, diabetes mellitus) • Chronic infections • Malignancies • Hypothalamic lesions, tumors • Cystic fibrosis • Zinc deficiency • Superior mesenteric artery syndrome	• Gastrointestinal disease • Hypothalamic lesions, tumors • Connective tissue diseases	• Klein–Levin syndrome • Prader–Willi syndrome • Temporal lobe or linibic seizure • Hypothalamic, frontal lobe, or temporal lobe lesions

In addition, meaningful psychotherapy is difficult until the patient is nutritionally stabilized. However, gaining a treatment alliance with the eating disordered patient can be extremely difficult. In AN, by prescribing weight gain, the physician is asking the patient to engage in a frightening process. It is therefore essential to explain the medical and psychiatric aspects of the disorder to the family and patient. Enlisting the support of the family can be crucial in beginning and sustaining treatment, because these patients are initially very reluctant to engage in the process.

The treatment plan for the patient with AN should include regular weight monitoring and medical and psychiatric care. Patients are frequently referred to the psychiatrist by a pediatrician or family physician who will be able to follow medical complications. If not already in place, the psychiatrist should enlist a primary health care physician to be part of the treatment team. A thorough history must be taken and a review of systems previously discussed in this chapter must be done. When beginning treatment with an AN patient it is essential that the patient initially be weighed every week until weight gain has been clearly established. The first goal is to get the AN patient to quit losing weight. Ultimately, the patient should achieve a healthy weight in which menses resume and bone demineralization does not occur. This weight is initially overwhelming to the patient, and therefore, the first weight goal with an outpatient anorexic patient is to *stop losing weight*.

Approximately one half of patients with AN are able to be treated as outpatients. The remaining AN patients require hospitalization. However, if medically stable, the patient should be allowed an opportunity to eat on his or her own. Criteria for hospitalization include a body weight of less than 25%, syncopal episodes, severe fluid and electrolyte imbalances, cardiac arrhythmias, and severe dehydration (Gortmaker et al., 1993). If weight loss continues, hospitalization needs to be considered. Also, if a patient with AN complains of fatigue, this indicates a serious condition because this symptom occurs late in the disease process, and hospitalization is probably indicated.

Many AN patients who fail to stabilize their weight on an outpatient basis require nasogastric tube feedings. The first hospital day should be used to observe feeding behavior, however. If the patient is unable to eat enough on her own to gain a half a pound every other day, nasogastric tube feedings with a liquid dietary supplement should begin. Usually the patient can tolerate two feedings of 1000 kilocalories per day with increases of 300 kilocalories every other day. It is important, however, to ensure that the AN patient has a chance to refeed herself. If she fails, she will more readily accept tube feedings than if these tube feedings have been used initially. Also, when refeeding a patient, emphasize to her that the weight gain will be carefully monitored so that she will not gain "too fast." Phosphorus levels should be measured during aggressive refeeding. These patients are at risk of developing the refeeding syndrome in which hypophosphatemia, pancreatitis, or cardio-myopathy may occur. Once the patient has achieved a medically safe weight as determined by the treatment team, a family conference should be held to discuss transition to outpatient status. Initially, outpatient visits should be frequent because these patients are at risk of rapidly losing weight and require a second hospitalization.

Patients with BN need hospitalization only if there is increasing and intractable bingeing, purging, and electrolyte disturbances. Otherwise, most patients with BN can be treated on an outpatient basis. To structure a comprehensive nutritional rehabilitation program, an understanding of the bulimia patient's eating patterns and her attitude, mood, and body perception is necessary. In an early report of BN, Russell pointed out that these patients could consume huge amounts of calories, up to 20,000 kilocalories in less than one day (Russell, 1979). Since then, it is clear that highly chaotic and variable eating patterns characterize bulimic individuals. Bulimic individuals may consume as many as 10,000 calories per day compared to 1900 calories for normal control individuals. Marked variability in food intake from day to day and from individual to individual was observed (Hetherington, Altemus, Nelson, Bern, & Gold, 1994). Less energy intake from protein and more energy intake from fat is observed in bulimia patients compared to controls. One of the roles of the treatment team is to lay a firm foundation for nutritional education for the patient, to reinforce structured eating behavior, to help prevent periods of starvation and hunger with subsequent overeating, and to address the fears of weight gain and distorted body image.

TABLE 7-4
Medical Criteria for Admission for Eating Disorders

- significant weight loss
- fainting spells
- dehydration
- electrolyte abnormalities
- fatigue
- cardiac complications
- failure of outpatient treatment to stop weight loss

Tables 7-4 and 7-5 summarize indications for hospitalization for AN and BN.

Treatment of obesity targeting weight loss and maintenance remain incompletely studied and controversial. Liquid protein diets are associated with a variety of untoward consequences, especially electrolyte disturbances, cardiac arrhythmias, and sudden death. More recent formulations of very low-calorie diets can be used safely if used as directed and with careful medical supervision (Andersen, 1992; Pi-Sunyer, 1992; Seim, Mitchell, Pomeroy, & deZwaan, 1995). Nevertheless, patients must be closely monitored, especially for complications such as gallstone formation. The best methods for voluntary weight loss and control remain incompletely studied and controversial (NIH Technology Assessment Conference Panel, 1992). Surgical approaches to weight reduction have been associated with significant medical risks. After jejunoileal bypass (a surgical procedure that bypasses the small intestine to encourage weight loss), up to 6% of patients develop gallstones and, more important, liver injury occurs in about 3% of patients, with a 20% long-term fatality rate as a direct result of the surgery. As a result, this procedure has been largely supplanted by gastric bypass or gastroplasty. Liver injury and gallstones are complications of these newer procedures as well, although they are seen at a lower rate. Thus surgical approaches should be limited to those patients with potentially life-threatening complications of obesity (such as sleep apnea) who have failed nonsurgical therapies. The best recommendation is a gradual weight loss program that includes a balanced diet. This is particularly important for the obese child and adolescent who still need good nutrition because they are

TABLE 7-5
Psychiatric Criteria for Admission

- suicidal ideation
- psychiatric comorbidity
- unable to eat on own, existing only on nasogastric tube feedings

at critical points in their overall growth and development. Weight-loss medications are not recommended because of potential serious drug reactions.

A committee with constituents from the Maternal and Child Health Bureau, Health Resources and Services Administration, and the Department of Health and Human Services developed the following recommendations for obese children (Barlow & Dietz, 1998): Children with a body mass index (BMI) greater than or equal to the 85th percentile with medical complications or greater than or equal to the 95th percentile should undergo evaluation and treatment. A key element in the evaluation is assessment of family and child commitment to a weight management program with the goal of establishing healthy eating patterns and physical activity. Parents must be able to help their children gradually increase in physical activity and reduce intake in high-fat, high-calorie foods.

Successful treatment of eating disorder patients frequently requires a team approach involving psychiatrists and their medical colleagues. Families must be encouraged to keep resistant patients involved in treatment. Long-term follow-up studies indicate the importance to the patient and family of consistent medical and psychiatric support for a complete recovery. It is important to keep in mind that many patients with eating disorders can recover with comprehensive treatment.

CONCLUSION

The pathophysiologies of eating disorders remain unelucidated. Many eating disorder patients are resistant to treatment and relapse. Additional studies are needed to improve the management of these patients. Pharmacological trials with agents that enhance weight gain and anabolism in an acute setting deserve consideration. In contrast to the immediate treatment of severe and malnourished eating disorder patients, the long-term treatment of chronic patients is less obvious. These patients are truly difficult and complex to manage with multiple biopsychosocial problems. There is increasing acknowledgment that concentrating on the eating behavior per se misses a significant central problem such as interpersonal relations. Thus studies to determine if a focus of interpersonal relations might not be more effective than a focus on the disordered eating behaviors are needed. Similarly, the use of medications may inappropriately displace needed interpersonal therapy. For most eating disorder patients, restoring ideal body weight is the first step in improving long-term outcome. This includes a comprehensive physical assessment involving all the major systems of the body.

REFERENCES

American Psychiatric Association. (1994). *Diagnostic and statistical manual of mental disorders* (4th ed.). Washington, DC: Author.

Andersen, T. (1992). Liver and gallbladder disease before and after very-low-calorie diets. *American Journal of Clinical Nutrition, 56,* 235–239.

Barlow, S. E., & Dietz, W. H. (1998). Obesity evaluation and treatment: expert committee recommendations. *Pediatrics, 102*(3), e29.

Baran, S. A., Weltzin, T. E., & Kaye, W. H. (1995). Low discharge weight and outcome in anorexia nervosa. *American Journal of Psychiatry, 152,* 1070–1072.

Brotman, A. W., Stern, T. A., & Brotman, D. L. (1986). Renal disease and dysfunctions in two patients with anorexia nervosa. *Journal of Clinical Psychiatry, 47*(8), 433–434.

Colling, S., & King, M. (1994). Ten-year follow-up - 50 patients with bulimia nervosa. *British Journal of Psychology, 164,* 80–87.

Crisp, A. M., Callender, J. S., Halek, C., & Higbee, L. K. G. (1992). Long-term mortality in anorexia nervosa. *British Journal of Psychiatry, 161,* 104–107.

Curran-Celentano, J., Erdman, J. W., Nelson, R. A., & Grater, S. J. (1985). Alterations in vitamin A and thyroid hormone status in anorexia nervosa and associated disorders. *American Journal of Clinical Nutrition, 42*(6), 1183–1191.

deZwaan, M. S., & Mitchell, J. E. (1992). Binge eating in the obese. *Annals of Medicine, 24,* 303–308.

Fichter, M. M., & Pirke, K. M. (1990). Endocrine dysfunction in bulimia nervosa. In M. M. Fichter, *Bulimia Nervosa: Basic Research, Diagnosis, and Therapy* (pp. 235–257). Chichester, UK: John Wiley & Sons.

Gilinsky, N. H., Humphries, L. L., Fried, M. F., & McClain, C. J. (1988). Computed tomographic abnormalities of the pancreas in eating disorders: A report of two cases with normal laparotomy. *International Journal of Eating Disorders, 7*(4), 567–572.

Gold, P. W., Gwirtsman, H., Avergerinos, P. C., Nieman, L. K., Gallucci, W. T., Kaye, W., Jimerson, D., Ebert, M., Rittmaster, R., Loriaux, D. L., & Chrousos, G. P. (1986). Abnormal hypothalamic-pituitary-adrenal function in anorexia nervosa. *New England Journal of Medicine, 314,* 1334–1342.

Gortmaker,S. L., Must, A., Perrin, J. M., Sobol, A. M., & Dietz, W. H. (1993). Social and economic consequences of overweight in adolescence and young adulthood. *New England Journal of Medicine, 329,* 1008–1012.

Greenfield, D., Mickley, D., Quinlan, D. M., & Roloff, P. (1995). Hypokalemia in outpatients with eating disorders. *American Journal of Psychiatry, 152*(1), 60–63.

Gwirtsman, H. E., Kaye, W. H., George, D. T., Carosella, N. W., Greene, R. C., & Jimerson, D. C. (1989). Hyperamylasemia and its relationship to binge-purge episodes: development of a clinically relevant laboratory test. *Journal of Clinical Psychiatry, 50*(6), 196–204.

Gwirtsman, H. E., Kaye, W. H., George, D. T., Jimerson, D. C., Ebert, M. H., & Gold, P. W. (1989). Central and peripheral ACT4 and cortisol levels in anorexia nervosa and bulimia. *Archives of General Psychiatry, 46,* 61–69.

Hall, R. C., & Beresford, T. P. (1989). Medical complications of anorexia and bulimia. *Psychiatric Medicine, 7*(4), 165–192.

Haller, J. O., Slovis, T. L., Baker, D. H., Berdon, W. E., & Silverman, J. A. (1977). Anorexia nervosa: The paucity of radiologic findings in more than fifty patients. *Pediatric Radiology, 5*(3), 145–147.

Harlan, W. R. (1993). Epidemiology of childhood obesity. A national perspective. *Annals of New York Academy of Science, 699,* 1–5.

Harris, R. T. (1986). Eating disorders: Diagnosis and management by the internist. *Southern Medical Journal, 79,* 871–878.

Herzog, D., & Bradburn, I. (1992). The nature of anorexia nervosa and bulimia nervosa in adolescents in P. J. Cooper & A. Stein (Eds.), *Feeding problems & eating disorders in children and adolescents* (pp. 126–135). Chur, Switzerland: Harwood Academic

Hetherington, M. M., Altemus, M., Nelson, M. L., Bernat, A. S., & Gold, P. W. (1994). Eating behavior in bulimia nervosa: Multiple meal analyses. *American Journal of Clinical Nutrition, 60*(6), 864–873.

Hill, K. K., & Maloney, M. J. (1997). Treating anorexia nervosa patients in the era of managed care. *Journal of the American Academy of Child and Adolescent Psychiatry, 36*(11), 1632–1633.

Hill, K. K., & Maloney, M. J. (1998). Anorexia nervosa and bulimia. In W. Klykylo (Ed.), *Clinical child psychiatry.* Philadelphia: Saunders.

Hill, K. K., McClain, C. J., Gaetke, L., & Saddler, A. (1995). *Eating disorders in women. Nutritional concerns of women.* Boca Raton, FL: CRC Press.

Hirakawa, M., Okada, T., Iida, M., Tamai, H., Kobayashi, N., Nakagawa, T., & Fujishima, M. . J. (1990). Small bowel transit time measured by hydrogen breath test in patients with anorexia nervosa. *Digestive Diseases and Sciences, 35*(6), 733–736.

Hoffman, L., Halmi, K. (1993). Comorbodity and course of anorexia nervosa. *Child and Adolescent Clinics of North America, 2,* 129–144.

Howard, M. R., Leggat, H. M., & Chaudhry, S. (1992). Dermatological and immunological abnormalities in eating disorders. *British Journal of Hospital Medicine, 48,* 234–239.

Humphries, L. L., Adams, L. J., Eckfeldt, J. H., Levitt, M. D., & McClain, C. J. (1987). Hyperamylasemia in patients with eating disorders. *Annals of Internal Medicine, 106*(1), 50–52.

Keane, F. B., Fennell, J. S., & Tomkin, G. H. (1978). Acute pancreatitis, acute gastric dilatation and duodenal ileus following refeeding in anorexia nervosa. *Irish Journal of Medical Science, 147*(5), 191–192.

Kiss, A., Bergmann, H., Abatzi, T. A., Schneider, C., Wiesnagrotzki, S., Hobart, J., Steiner-Mittelbach, G., Gaupmann, G., Kugi, A., Stacher-Janotta, G., et al. (1990). Oesophageal and gastric motor activity in patients with bulimia nervosa. *Gut, 31*(3), 259–265.

Klibanski, A., Biller, B. M., Schoenfeld, D. A., Herzog, D. B., & Saxe, V. C. (1995). The effects of estrogen administration on trabecular bone loss in young women with anorexia nervosa. *Journal of Clinical Endocrinology and Metabolism, 80*(3), 898–904.

Maloney, M. J. (1995). Eating disorders during adolescence. *Anneles Nestle, 53,* 101.

Martola, J. F., Rasmussen, D. O., & Yen, S. S. C. (1989). Alternatives of the adreno cortico tropin-cortisol axis in normal weight bulimic women: evidence for a central mechanism. *Journal of Clinical Endocrinology and Metabolism, 68,* 517–522.

McClain, C. J., Humphries, L. L., Hill, K. K., & Nickl, N. J. (1993). Gastrointestinal and nutritional aspects of eating disorders. *Journal of the American College of Nutrition, 12*(4), 466–474.

Mira, M., Stewart, P. M., & Abraham, S. F. (1989). Vitamin and trace element status of women with disordered eating. *American Journal of Clinical Nutrition, 50*(5), 940–944.

Mitchell, J. E., & Eckert, E. D. (1987). Scope and significance of eating disorders. *Journal of Consulting Clinical Psychology, 55*(5), 628–634.

Mitchell, J. E., Pyle, R. L., Eckert, E. D., Hatsukami, D., & Lentz, R. (1983). Electrolyte and other physiological abnormalities in patients with bulimia. *Psychological Medicine, 13*(2), 273–278.

Mitchell, J. E., Pyle, R. L., Hatsukani, K., & Boutacoff, L. I. (1984). The dexametnasone suppression test in patients with bulimia. *Journal of Clinical Psychiatry, 45,* 508–511.

Mossberg, H. O. (1989). 40-year follow-up of overweight children. *Lancet, 2*(8661), 491–493.

Najala, R., Partinen, M., Sane, T., Pelkonen, R., Huikur, K., & Seppalainen, A. M. (1991). Obstructive sleep apnea syndrome in morbidly obese patients. *Journal of Internal Medicine, 230,* 125–129.

Nieto, F. J. M., Szklod, G. W., & Cemstock. (1992). Childhood weight and growth rate as predictors of adult mortality. *American Journal of Epidemiology, 136,* 201–213.

NIH Technology Assessment Conference Panel. (1992). Methods for voluntary weight loss and control. *Annals of Internal Medicine, 116,* 942–949.

Perlow, J. H., Morgan, M. A., Montgomery, D., Towes, C. V., & Porto, M. (1992). Perinatal outcome in pregnancy complicated by massive obesity. *American Journal of Obstetrics and Gynecology, 167,* 958–962.

Pi-Sunyer, F. X. (1992). The role of very-low-calorie diets in obesity. *American Journal of Clinical Nutrition, 56,* 240–243.

Pirke, K. M., Fichter, M. M., Chlond, C., & Doevr, P. (1987). Disturbances of the menstrual cycle in bulimia nervosa. *Clinical Endocrinology, 27,* 245–251.

Ratnasuriya, R. M., Eisler, I., Szmukler, G. I., & Russell, G. F. M. (1991). Anorexia nervosa: Outcome and prognostic factors after 20 years. *British Journal of Psychiatry, 158*, 495–502.

Rossner, S., Lagerstrand, L., Persson, H. E., & Sachs, C. (1991). The sleep apnea syndrome in obesity: Risk of sudden death. *Journal of Internal Medicine, 230*, 135–141.

Rubenstein, I., Zamel, N., DuBarry, L., & Hoffstein, V. (1991). Airflow limitation in morbidly obese, nonsmoking men. *Annals of Internal Medicine, 112*, 828–832.

Russell, G. (1979). Bulimia nervosa: An ominous variant of anorexia nervosa. *Psychological Medicine, 9*(3), 429–448.

Seim, H. C., Mitchell, J. E., Pomeroy, C., & deZwaan, M. (1995). Electrocardiographic finds associated with very low calorie dieting. *International Journal of Obesity, 19*, 817–819.

Sharp, C. W., & Freeman, C. P. (1993). The medical complications of anorexia nervosa. *British Journal of Psychiatry, 162*, 452–462.

Sheinin, J. C. (1986). Medical aspects of eating disorders. *Adolescent Psychiatry, 13*, 405–421.

Shiffman, M. L., Sugarman, H. J., Kelleem, J. M., Brewer, W. H., & Moore, E. W. (1991). Gallstone formation after rapid weight loss: A prospective study in patients undergoing gastric bypass surgery for treatment of morbid obesity. *American Journal of Gastroenterology, 86*, 1000–1005.

Silber, T. J., & Kass, E. J. (1984). Anorexia nervosa and nephrolithiasis. *Journal of Adolescent Health Care, 5*(1), 50–52.

Silverman, J. A. (1983). Anorexia nervosa: Clinical and metabolic observations. *International Journal of Eating Disorders, 2*(4), 159–166.

Spalter, A. R., Gwirtsman, H. E., Demitrack, M. A., & Gold, P. W. (1993). Thyroid function in bulimia nervosa. *Biological Psychiatry, 33*, 408–414.

Stacher, G., Kiss, A., Wiesnagrotzki, S., Bergmann, H., Hobart, J., & Schneider, C. (1986). Oesophageal and gastric motility disorders in patients categorized as having primary anorexia nervosa. *Gut, 27*(10), 1120–1126.

Sugarman, H. J., Fairman, R. P., Sood, R. K., Engle, K., Wolfe, L., Kellun, J. M. (1992). Long-term effects of gastric surgery for treating respiratory insufficiency of obesity. *American Journal of Clinical Nutrition, 55*, 597–601.

Theander, S. (1985). Outcome and prognosis in anorexia nervosa and bulimia: Some results of previous investigations, compared with those of a Swedish long-term study. *Journal of Psychiatric Research., 19*(2–3), 493–508.

Thomas, M. A., & Rebar, R. W. (1990). The endocrinology of anorexia nervosa. *Current Opinion in Obstetrics and Gynecology, 2*, 831–836.

Worobetz, L. J., Inglis, F. G., & Shaffer, E. A. (1993). The effect of isodeoxydolic acid therapy on gallstone formation in the morbidly obese during rapid weight loss. *American Journal of Gastroenterology, 88*, 1705–1710.

Yager, J., Andersen, A., Deulin, M., Mitchell, J., Pavers, P., Yates, A. (1993). Practice guidelines for eating disorders. *American Journal of Psychiatry, 150*(2), 212–228.

8

ASSESSMENT OF BODY IMAGE DISTURBANCE IN CHILDREN AND ADOLESCENTS

RICK M. GARDNER

The increasing prevalence of body image disturbance (BID) in both young adults and children and its relationship to various clinical disorders has generated considerable interest in the issue of body image. Dozens of studies have linked BID to low self-esteem, neuroticism, depression, eating disorders, and general psychological distress (e.g., Brodie, Bagley, & Slade, 1994; Cash & Brown, 1987; Garner & Garfinkel, 1981; Slade & Russell, 1973; Thompson, Penner, & Altabe, 1990). The relationship between body image disturbance and the resultant dissatisfaction with one's body image has been linked strongly to eating disorders, including both anorexia nervosa and bulimia nervosa. Therefore, the ability to assess BID has become an important issue because of its known association to these disorders.

Most researchers distinguish between two components of BID—namely, perceptual body-size distortion and the attitudinal or affective element. Perceptual distortion consists of inaccurate judgments of one's body size. Individuals with eating disorders frequently overestimate their actual body size. The attitudinal component consists of dissatisfaction with one's body size, shape, or some other aspect of body appearance. However, because research in eating disorders predominantly used the perceptual assessment methods (Cash & Brown, 1987), significantly fewer studies have examined the attitudinal component (Cash & Deagle, 1997). Cash and Brown (1987) concluded that studies using perceptual size-estimation measures of BID alone were largely responsible for the inconsistent findings in the eating disorder literature. Greater consistency of findings has been obtained with attitudinal measures. Furthermore, these two components of BID appear to function largely independently of one another (Garner & Garfinkel, 1981). Research findings increasingly have concluded that body image is a multidimensional construct, and the assessment of BID requires multimethod and multimodal measurement techniques (Keeton, Cash, & Brown, 1990).

Researchers have investigated whether age is a critical factor in the development of BID. Several studies have demonstrated greater perceptual distortion during adolescence as compared to adulthood (Button, Fransella, & Slade, 1977; Halmi, Goldberg, & Cunningham, 1977; Slade, 1985). These findings have led some researchers to hypothesize that the ability to report body size accurately involves perceptual maturation. However, other researchers have reported that children in the age range of 6 through 14 have relatively accurate perceptions of body size (Gardner, Friedman, Jackson, & Stark, 1999; Gardner, Sorter, & Freidman, 1997).

Age also pertains to the development of body image ideals. In general, as age increases, the definition of an ideal body size becomes increasingly thinner (Cohn, Adler, Irwin, Millstein, Kegeles, & Stone, 1987). Gardner, Stark, Jackson, and Friedman (1999) have reported dissatisfaction with body size in girls that begins as early as age 7 and increases through age 14.

This chapter will discuss the application and limitations of various methodologies and techniques that have been used to assess both the perceptual and attitudinal components of BID.

FIGURAL STIMULI TO MEASURE BODY DISSATISFACTION

In recent years there has been an increasing trend to use schematic drawings or figural scales to measure body size dissatisfaction. These scales, sometimes referred to as contour drawings or silhouettes, consist of a set of line drawings of the human body that range in size from very underweight to very overweight. Thompson (1996) has described several sets of these figural stimuli and has provided the reliability, validity, and standardization measurements for each scale.

Each scale presents a discrete number of figures, typically between 5 and 12. Research participants are asked to select the figures that represent their current size and the size they would like to be ideally. The difference between the two ratings is the discrepancy index and represents body dissatisfaction. Table 8-1 briefly describes and summarizes several figural scales that have been developed specifically for children and adolescents.

METHODOLOGICAL ISSUES WHEN USING FIGURAL STIMULI

Figural stimuli have been used extensively with children and adolescents to measure their body size satisfaction. In the case of older adolescents,

TABLE 8-1
Figural Stimuli Used for Assessing Elements of Body Image in Children and Adolescents

Author(s)	Test name	Description of figures	Test–retest reliability	Standardization sample
Dwyer, Feldman, Seltzer, & Mayer (1969)	None given	6 male and 6 female figure drawings	Not given	446 female and 145 male high school students
Brennan & Kevany (1985)	None given	6 female figure drawings	Not given	218 females, ages 14 to 17
Carroll, Gleeson, Risby, & Dugdale (1986)	None given	6 male and 6 female figure drawings	Not given	296 females, ages 11 to 19, 252 males ages 11 to 18
Collins (1991)	None given	7 male and 7 female figure drawings	3 days: self = .71; ideal/ self = .59; ideal/other child = .38	1118 preadolescent children
Childress, Brewerton, Hodges, & Jarrell (1993)	Kid's Eating Disorder Survey	8 male and 8 female figure drawings	4 months, .83 for entire survey; not given for figures only	3178 children, grades 5–8
Sherman, Iacono, & Donnelly (1995)	Body Rating Scale	2 scales; 9 female figures representing a preadolescent (BRS 11) and adolescent (BRS 17) female	Test–retest not given, see article for other reliability measures	108 females age 11, 102 females age 17
Veron-Guidry & Williamson (1996)	Body Image Assessment— Children	2 scales; 9 silhouettes of male and female children and preadolescents	Immediate: (current = .94; ideal = .93), 1 week: (current = .79; current/ ideal = .67)	22 males and females, ages 8–10 40 males and females, ages 8–10
Sands, Tricker, Sherman, Armatas, & Maschette (1997)	Body Image Scale	7 side profiles of pre-pubescent boys and girls	3 months: current = .56 6 months: current = .40	26 females and 35 males, ages 10–12
Tiggemann & Pennington (1990)	None given	9 figure drawings of children and adolescents	Not given	34 females and 37 males; ages 9–10; 40 females and 38 males, ages 15–16

figural stimuli standardized with adult participants sometimes have been used in lieu of more age-appropriate measurements.

One limitation of the use of figural stimuli occurs because most scales do not readily allow for measurement of body size estimation or the amount of distortion that is present in judgments, both important issues in the study of eating disorders. Three studies have addressed this limitation. Williamson, Davis, Bennett, Goreczny, and Gleaves (1989) converted adults' "current self" silhouette selections to T scores based on height–weight normative tables in order to produce an index of whole-body size-estimation accuracy. Keeton et al. (1990) photographed adults in a standard frontal pose. Participants rated their perceived body size and ideal body size, using the silhouette drawings developed by Williamson et al. (1989). In addition, independent judges (two men, two women) matched participants' photos to the silhouette drawings to provide an additional objective rating of actual body size. The discrepancy between the perceived self-rating and the judges' ratings then was used as a measure of perceptual accuracy. Gardner et al. (1999) developed two new contour scales, a 2-figure analogue scale and a 13-figure scale, both using the dimensions from a frontal view photograph of an adult male and female with height and weight of the median American. Participants' ratings on these scales can be converted to reflect perceived size distortion.

Aside from these approaches, none of which have been used with children, figural scales generally limit body image measurements to body dissatisfaction (i.e., the discrepancy between the perceived and ideal body size) and do not address distortions in body size judgments. Typically, investigators interested in this aspect of body image in younger individuals will need to use a perceptual measure of size estimation, several of which are described later in this chapter.

Another limitation with figural scales for children are that they are age-specific. The shape of children's bodies changes so much during early childhood and into adolescence that no single figural scale would be appropriate for all age ranges. None of the existing scales have been standardized for children under the age of 8 even though perceptual body image studies with children have used children as young as 5 years of age (Gardner, Urrutia, Morrell, Watson, & Sandoval, 1990). Investigators who want to use these figural scales with children should closely attend to the standardization sample for which they were designed, as indicated in Table 8-1.

Some of the figural scales described in Table 8-1 have reliability coefficients reflecting stability of assessment that fall near or below Nunnally's (1970) criterion of .70 as the minimally acceptable coefficient for a psychometrically sound measurement instrument. For most of the scales, reliability coefficients fall well below this criterion when test–retest intervals exceed more than one week. Thompson (1996) cautioned against the use of scales with reliability coefficients below this criterion.

Thompson (1996) also noted in his review that the standardization sample for many of these scales was constructed on Caucasian individuals. For instance, all of the figural stimuli in Table 8-1 were constructed with obvious Caucasian characteristics, particularly with respect to facial features. The ability to generalize to ethnic groups that have different physical features is largely unknown. Altabe (1996) discussed these limitations and made suggestions for the investigation of body image in diverse populations.

Gardner, Friedman, and Jackson (1998) have discussed several concerns pertaining to methodological procedures when using figural stimuli. Their concerns refer to figural stimuli designed for adults but are similarly applicable to scales used with children and adolescents. The authors specifically address the following issues that arise from (a) scale coarseness, (b) restriction of scale range, (c) measurement assumptions, and (d) administration of stimuli.

Scale Coarseness

Figural scales require participants to select one illustration from a finite number of drawings. The authors cite research that shows how information is lost when a "coarse" response scale that has a small, finite number of alternatives is used to represent a near continuous or "fine" variable.

Restriction of Scale Range

These authors also remarked that a restriction of range phenomena exists when using figural stimuli. Brodie et al. (1994) and Gardner, Friedman, and Jackson (1998) have shown that preadolescent and adolescent individuals will select from among only three of the presented figures between 85% and 90% of the time. Therefore, investigators who use scales with a nominally large number of figures functionally use scales with only three or four figures for most of their participants. The authors speculated that this phenomenon occurs when the relatively large amount of distortion that is usually incorporated between the adjacent figural stimuli couples with the small amount of perceived distortion typically reported by most participants.

Measurement Assumptions

Another issue raised by Gardner et al. (1998) is the scale of measurement presumed to underlie figural scales. They present evidence to show that the commonly used scale developed by Stunkard, Sorenson, and Schlusinger (1983) represents an ordinal scale. Gardner et al. measured body widths of the chest and waist regions for each of the figures in the Stunkard et al. scale and found inconsistent differences in size between successive figures.

Even though nonparametric statistics are the most appropriate for ordinal data, their review of 15 studies using figural stimuli revealed such statistics were never used. M. Thompson and Gray (1995) and Gardner et al. (1999) have developed figural scales for adults that present consistent differences in size between successive figures.

Administration of Stimuli

Finally, Gardner et al. (1998) noted that the method of presentation of figural stimuli is important. Typically, all figures are presented on a single sheet of paper with the figures arranged in ascending size from left to right. Participants select the figures that represent their actual size and their ideal size. However, this testing procedure is likely to produce spuriously high test–retest reliability coefficients because participants would have little difficulty remembering which figure they selected previously. An alternative procedure used by a few researchers (see, for example, Veron-Guidry & Williamson, 1996) involves the placement of each figure on a separate card and the random arrangement of cards for each testing session.

SUBJECTIVE AND ATTITUDINAL MEASURES OF APPEARANCE DISSATISFACTION

Several scales have been developed to measure appearance dissatisfaction in children and adolescents. The most commonly used instruments are described in Table 8-2. In some instances, instruments that initially were developed for use with adults have been revised and standardized for younger individuals (see references in Table 8-2 under standardization sample). Some of the scales provide a global, comprehensive assessment of body satisfaction and others focus on satisfaction with specific body areas. Two of the scales are subscales of larger tests designed to measure eating disorder tendencies. These include (a) the Eating Disorder Inventory, Versions 1 and 2 (Garner, 1990; Garner & Olmsted, 1984) that contains a 9-item subscale to measure feelings about body size satisfaction; and (b) the McKnight Risk Factor Survey III (MFRS-III; Shisslak et al., 1999) that contains a 5-item subscale to measure concerns with body weight and shape. Most of the instruments described have acceptable psychometric properties. One instrument is not published (Merbaum, Marwit, & Hermann, 1986) and is only available from the authors.

One of the most widely adopted measures of body size dissatisfaction is the discrepancy obtained by measuring how individuals perceive their current body size compared to their idealized body size. This discrepancy can be measured in younger individuals by using the figural stimuli described previously or by using one of the perceptual measures of body size estimation described in the next section.

MEASURES OF BODY SIZE ESTIMATION: THE PERCEPTUAL COMPONENT

Some of the earliest research on body image focused on the question of how accurately individuals are able to estimate their body size. This research followed the seminal work of Slade and Russell (1973), who first reported that individuals with eating disorders overestimate their body size. A variety of innovative techniques subsequently have been developed to measure the accuracy of size estimations.

SITE VERSUS WHOLE BODY SIZE ESTIMATION TECHNIQUES

Some measurement techniques involve whole-image procedures that adjust the body size smaller or larger via modification of a photograph or video image. Other techniques allow for single-site assessment, which is a useful tool for investigators interested in measuring estimation errors for specific body regions. Both methods derive a body perception index of the direction and degree of size distortion relative to actual body size (Cash & Deagle, 1997). Thompson (1996) described many of these measures, including their reliability and the standardization samples that were used in their development.

Body Site Estimation Techniques

Several of the size estimation techniques described by Thompson (1996) have been used in studies with children and adolescents. One site estimation technique that uses the Adjustable Light Beam Apparatus developed by Thompson and Spana (1988) has individuals adjust the width of four light beams that are projected on a wall to match the perceived size of their cheeks, waist, hips, and thighs. Fabian and Thompson (1989) used this technique with females between the ages of 10 and 15. In earlier research, Slade and Russell (1973) used a similar device called the Movable Caliper Technique that allowed anorexic females to adjust the distances between two lights to match their perceived body sizes. Although this device has not been used with children, it should prove to be a useful technique for younger participants.

Koff and Kiekhofer (1978) measured body-part size estimations in children in grades 1, 3, and 5. Children were seated in front of a 4-foot-

TABLE 8-2
Measures for Assessing Body Appearance Dissatisfaction in Children and Adolescents

Author(s)	Test Name	Description of Test	Reliability IC: Internal Consistency TR: Test–retest	Standardization Sample
Garner & Olmstead (1984); Garner (1991b)	Eating Disorder Inventory (EDI and EDI-2). Body Dissatisfaction Scale	9-item subscale assesses feelings about satisfaction with body size; items are 6-point, forced choice; reading level is 5th grade	IC: Adolescents (11–18) Females: .91 Males: .86 Children (8–10) Females = .84	610 males and females ages 11–18 (Shore & Porter, 1990) 109 males and females ages 8–10 (Wood et al., 1996)
Garner (1991)	Eating Disorders Inventory for Children (EDI-C) Body Dissatisfaction Scale	Same 9-item subscale as EDI. Wording was rephrased for grades 1–2 reading level	No data	None
Mendelson & White (1982)	Body Esteem Scale	Participants report their degree of agreement with various statements about their bodies	IC: split-half reliability = .85	97 males and females, ages 8.5–17.4
Peterson, Schulenberg, Abramowitz, Offer, & Jarcho (1984)	Self-Image Questionnaire for Young Adolescents (SIQYA) - Body Image Subscale	11-item body image subscale assesses positive feelings toward the body; designed for ages 10–15	IC: Males = .81, Females = .77 TR: 1 year = .60, 2 years = .44	335 6th grade students
Merbaum, Martwit, & Hermann (1986)	Body Concept Scale	Participants evaluate 27 external body parts using a five-color code system, with ratings from extremely favorable to extremely unfavorable	No data	148 children, ages 8–14

Reference	Measure	Description	Reliability	Sample
Cooper, Taylor, Cooper, & Fairburn (1987)	Body Shape Questionnaire (BSQ)	34-item self-report questionnaire about the phenomenal experience of "feeling fat"	No data	81 eating disordered patients age 18 and under (Bunnell, Cooper, Hertz, & Shenker, 1992)
Thelen, Powell, Lawrence, & Kuhnert (1992)	Body Image and Eating Questionnaire	14 items focusing on overweight concerns, dieting, and restraint. Items assessed by 4- or 5-point Likert scale or yes–no format	IC: all values ≥ .68	191 children, ages 7.8–13.6
Mintz & Betz (1986)	Body-Cathexis Scale	Participants rate satisfaction with 15 body characteristics or parts, using response scale ranging from 1 (extremely satisfied) to 7 (extremely dissatisfied)	No data	170 females, ages 8.1–15.5 (Hill, Oliver, & Rogers, 1992)
Shisslak et al. (1999)	McKnight Risk Factor Survey III (MFRS-III)	5-item subscale assesses concern with body weight and shape	IC: Elementary = .82 Middle school = .86 High school = .87 TR: Elementary = .79 Middle school = .84 High school = .90	103 females, 4th–5th grade; 420 females, 6–8th grade; 66 females, 9–12th grade
Siegel, Yancey, Aneshensel, & Schuler (1999)	Body Satisfaction Scale	Participants rated satisfaction with four aspects of pubertal development, using response scale ranging from 1 (very dissatisfied) to 4 (very satisfied)	IC: .73 to .80	469 males and 407 females, ages 12 to 17

long wooden rod mounted horizontally at eye level and were told that they would be asked to estimate or guess the size of some of their body parts. Both ends of the wooden rod were fitted with cloth "sleeves" that ended in stiff cardboard collars. When in a closed position, the sleeves met at the center and covered the entire rod. The experimenter manipulated the sleeves by their collars and exposed lengths of the rod to correspond to the child's size estimate of a particular body part. Body parts measured by this technique included head width, lips, arm, hand, leg, foot, and waist. The authors concluded that children are capable of relatively accurate body-part size estimation and that the skill necessary to perform this task appears to be established by age 6.

Krietler and Krietler (1970) developed a similar procedure. Participants, including young children, were asked to estimate size aspects of their body by using only their hands and fingers. Participants were instructed to indicate the size of things by bringing their hands (or fingers, for smaller objects) nearer or farther apart. Children made these estimations while standing and with their eyes closed. Children as young as 4 years were able to estimate their body height; the width of their mouths, shoulders, waists, and hips; the length of their hands, faces, and noses; and the height of their foreheads (Krietler & Krietler, 1986). Gleghorn, Penner, Powers, and Schulman (1987) cited a similar procedure in which blindfolded participants adjusted the distance between two calipers to match their perceived body size. This procedure was not tested on individuals younger than 17.

Whole Body Size Estimation Techniques

Dillon (1962) developed one of the earliest approaches to whole body size estimation by constructing a wooden doorway whose size was adjustable both horizontally and vertically. Participants were told to estimate their own dimensions of height and width and to instruct the experimenter to adjust the doorway frame so that they could barely squeeze through it. The individuals tested with this procedure ranged in age from 21 to 50 years of age. As a consequence, it is not known whether young children would be able to perform the required judgments.

Glucksman and Hirsch (1969) developed a whole body size estimation technique called the Distorting Photograph Technique. This technique used a variable anamorphic lens apparatus capable of distorting the width of a photographic image while keeping the height constant. The width could be adjusted from 20% under to 20% over actual body size. Speaker, Schultz, Grinker, and Stern (1983) have successfully used this technique with obese boys ages 12 to 14.

Several investigators, beginning with Allebeck, Hallberg, and Espmark (1976), have used video techniques to distort images of the whole body.

Thompson (1996) has described several variants of this procedure. In all cases, a video image of a participant's body is presented to the participant. The participant then adjusts the width of image while the height remains constant. In some of the early research with this procedure, the video images were presented on a television screen (e.g., Gardner, Martinez, & Sandoval, 1987). More recently, however, investigators have used video projection techniques that can project a life size image of the participant (e.g., Gardner et al., 1997; Gardner et al., 1999; Probst, Vandereycken, Van Coppenolle, & Pieters, 1995). Although typically used to distort whole images, these video techniques have also been used to estimate the size of specific body sites (Gardner & Bokenkamp, 1995).

These video techniques have been used only infrequently to measure body size estimation in young children. Gardner et al. (1990) used a distorting television–video method to measure children's judgments of their body size. The children in this study ranged in age from 5 to 13. Gardner, Gardner, and Morrell (1990) also used this technique to measure body size distortion in sexually and physically abused children ages 6 to 10. More recently, Gardner and his colleagues (Gardner et al., 1997; Gardner et al., 1999) used life-size video projections to measure body size estimations in children 6 through 14 years old.

One useful psychophysical procedure for younger children, used in conjunction with the video technique, is the staircase method (Cornsweet, 1962). Children are initially presented with a video image of themselves that is distorted either too wide or too thin. Immediately after it appears, the image is sequentially distorted in size, either wider or thinner, at a constant rate of change. Children indicate when the changing body size is the same as their perceived size. The direction of distortion then reverses and the child indicates when the image, now being sequentially distorted in the opposite direction, becomes equal to their perceived size. Several such data sequences are completed, after which perceived body size is taken as the average of the transition points. Advantages of this method are that it is fast moving and captures the attention of even the youngest children and that it allows a large number of data trials to be collected in a relatively short period of time (Gardner et al., 1990; Gardner et al., 1999).

Another whole-body technique has involved the use of a distorting mirror (Brodie, Slade, & Rose, 1989; Traub & Orback, 1964). A pliable mylar sheet is flexed to adjust the participant's body size. Readings are then made of the amount of distortion present in the perceived and ideal sizes. Although this methodology has not been used with young children, it should prove as effective as the video methodologies that it closely mimics.

The Body Image Distortion Evaluation uses a computer-based analysis of redrawn images of standardized human figures (Gustavson et al., 1990). Participants are presented a sex-appropriate line drawing of a person that includes both a frontal and a side view. Participants alter the drawings so that the figures look like themselves, and a custom computer program measures the amount of body image distortion. This procedure has been successfully used with participants as young as 14 years.

Methodological Issues With Perceptual Measures

Several articles have reviewed the methodological problems that exist in the research on the perceptual aspects of body image (e.g., Cash & Pruzinsky, 1990; Gardner, 1996; Polivy, Herman, & Pliner, 1990; Smeets, Smit, Panhuysen, & Ingleby, 1997; Thompson, 1996). These authors often have characterized the research as poorly conceived and conducted. As Gardner (1996) concluded, a variety of methodologies used to measure the perceptual aspects of body image are of questionable or unknown reliability and validity. Smeets et al. (1997) also stated that "the diversity of research procedures of assessing body image and their related weaknesses has obscured our understanding of the [body image] disturbance" (pp. 263–264).

A detailed listing of all the methodological concerns is well beyond the scope of this chapter. Researchers planning studies in this area are encouraged to review the aforementioned articles detailing those concerns. Very few studies have used prospective designs that allow for the assessment of the long-term stability of perceptual measures. Although high test–retest reliability of various perceptual measures has been shown over short intervals of time, Gardner et al. (1999) found test–retest judgments of perceived size in children to be very low over intervals of one year ($r = .19$) and two years ($r = .009$). Flanery (1990) has observed that nearly all children's self-report measures show reliability coefficients of .80 for short time intervals but that significantly lower values are obtained as time intervals increase.

Cash and Deagle (1997) conducted a meta-analysis of 66 studies of perceptual measures of body image among anorexic and bulimic patients. They found that a greater overestimation of body size occurred when studies used whole-body rather than body-part size estimates. It is likely that similar results would occur when studying nonclinical populations, including studies with children and adolescents.

Gardner (1996) has criticized the psychophysical procedures most often used in measuring size estimation accuracy when multiple measures are taken. Almost all of the experimental procedures require participants to make their judgments of body size on ascending and descending trials using the psychophysical method of limits. Participants see an initial stimulus, such as a video image, light beam, two separated lights, and so forth, that is either too small or too large and make adjustments until the stimulus represents their perceived body size. Several investigators have found that individuals who are decreasing an initial image that is too large will reach a final judgment of his or her body size that is still too large. Conversely, participants increasing a too-small image will reach a final judgment that is still too small. Furthermore, the magnitude of the error is not the same for ascending and descending trials, in that larger errors occur on descending trials (Gardner, 1996). This finding is consistent in adults as well as children. Therefore, the common practice of averaging results from ascending and descending trials to determine an individual's body size estimate may be questionable.

Gardner (1996) has also observed that the use of traditional psychophysical procedures may confound the perceptual and attitudinal components of body image distortion. He has advocated the use of more sophisticated psychophysical techniques that would allow for a separation of the attitudinal and perceptual components. Specifically, he recommends the use of the signal detection approach as well as the more sophisticated adaptive probit estimation technique (Fonagy, Benster, & Higgitt, 1990). Adaptive probit estimation is a derivative of the psychophysical method of limits, and permits the calculation of point of subjective equality (PSE) and difference threshold values. This technique permits a precise measurement of a participant's subjective judgment of his or her body size, as well as a determination of how much change in size must occur for that change to be detected. Investigators have used these techniques with increasing frequency in recent years (e.g., Altabe & Thompson, 1995; Strauman & Glenberg, 1994; Szymanski & Seime, 1997) and have shown them to be beneficial in measuring body size estimation in children and young adolescents (Gardner et al., 1990, 1997). Thompson, Heinberg, Altabe, and Tantleff-Dunn (1999) reviewed the theoretical underpinnings and advantages of these psychophysical approaches (pp. 290–293, 307–310).

Thompson (1996) briefly reviewed several other methodological issues that should be considered when measuring body size estimation. Although these issues have been examined primarily with older participants, many of them are applicable to younger individuals as well. Factors that affect size estimates include practice effects, type of clothing worn, illumination levels, degree of hunger, menstrual cycle, recent media exposures, exercise, and visuospatial abilities. Instructional protocols are also important. Affective instructions have been shown to result in different size estimations than cognitive instructions (Thompson, 1991). In addition, several investigators have reported that the actual size of the participant affects perceptual size estimations (Coovert, Thompson, & Kinder, 1988; Penner, Thompson, & Coovert, 1991; Thompson, 1987; Williamson, Cubic, & Gleaves, 1993). In general, smaller size participants overestimate their body size to a greater extent than larger size participants, a factor that could be particularly important in the comparison of size estimations across younger age groups.

DEVELOPMENTAL FACTORS IN BODY IMAGE

Special considerations need to be made when attempting to measure body image in younger children. These considerations apply to both the measures of size, weight, and appearance satisfaction as well as the perceptual measures of size estimation.

Perceptual and Attentional Capabilities

Perceptual and attentional capabilities are particularly critical with younger children. Gardner and his colleagues have measured body size estimations in children as young as 5 (Gardner et al., 1990). However, children under the age of 7 years have limited attentional capabilities, which can make measurements that require a large number of trials problematic (Gardner et al., 1998). Wohlwill (1960) has discussed the developmental changes that occur in perception, including the limitations that arise with younger children.

Cognitive Demands

Complex psychophysical tasks also may make unreasonable cognitive demands on younger children. Stone and Lemanek (1990) have reviewed a number of developmental issues that affect the use of self-report techniques with children. They outline specific cognitive and social–cognitive skills believed to underlie children's ability to produce accurate reports about themselves.

CONCLUSION

Clearly there is a need for additional studies on BID in younger children, particularly those using a prospective design. The vast majority of studies already conducted have been cross-sectional designs with college students or, less frequently, high school students. There is increasing evidence that BID often precedes eating disorders and that the antecedent disturbance in BID may occur in childhood, often well before adolescence (Gardner, Stark, Friedman, & Jackson, 2000). As mentioned earlier, girls' dissatisfaction with their body size begins to manifest itself as early as age 7. In measuring BID, it is important that both the perceptual and attitudinal components be appraised because both can serve as independent measures that predict eating disorders. Cash and Brown (1987) and Keeton et al. (1990) have concluded that attitudinal measures of body image may have more clinical relevance than perceptual parameters, particularly size estimation accuracy. Although these conclusions were based on reviews of studies conducted mainly with adults, it seems likely that a similar conclusion would apply to studies with children.

Investigators interested in measures of size, shape, weight, and appearance satisfaction may wish to use one of the figural scales described in Table 8-1. The discrepancy between the perceived size and ideal size is widely accepted as a valid measure of body size dissatisfaction. A scale with test–retest reliability of at least .70 should be used. Investigators must be aware of the methodological shortcomings of these scales. They should select a scale that is age appropriate for the population that they are investigating and, whenever possible, use a scale with the smallest degree of change between adjacent figures. Particular care should be taken when presenting the stimuli, because they should not be arranged in any ascending or descending sequence of size. Instructional protocols are important also because any emphasis on affective and cognitive directions will result in different size estimates.

Several good questionnaires exist for measures of body satisfaction. Many of these have been widely used in studies with children, and most have good psychometric properties. These scales, used in conjunction with the figural scales mentioned previously, should give stable measures of body satisfaction.

For perceptual measures of size estimation, researchers are encouraged to investigate one of the video distortion methods because these have been used successfully in studies with children as young as 5 and 6 years of age. Among the traditional psychophysical techniques, the staircase method (Cornsweet, 1962) may be used in conjunction with the video distortion techniques and has proven very successful with younger children (Gardner et al., 1990, 1997). Researchers using this methodology are cautioned that greater size estimation errors may occur on descending as compared to ascending trials.

Researchers are also encouraged to investigate some of the recent technical innovations in measuring body size estimations. For example, Gardner and his colleagues have developed custom computer software for projecting life size images of children. This software allows for the use of a variety of psychophysical procedures, including the method of limits, the staircase method, a signal detection methodology, and adaptive probit estimation procedures. The latter two procedures are particularly beneficial in allowing the investigator to derive a perceptual index of body size distortion independent of attitudinal factors.

REFERENCES

Allebeck, P., Hallberg, D., & Espmark, S. (1976). Body image—An apparatus for measuring disturbances in estimation of size and shape. *Journal of Psychosomatic Research, 20,* 583–589.

Altabe, M. (1996). Issues in the assessment and treatment of body image disturbance in culturally diverse populations. In J. K. Thompson (Ed.), *Body image, eating disorders, and obesity* (pp. 129–148). Washington, DC: American Psychological Association.

Altabe, M., & Thompson, J. K. (1995). Body image disturbance: Advances in assessment and treatment. In VandeCreek, L. & Knapp, S. (Eds.), *Innovations in clinical practice: A source book, Volume 14* (pp. 89–110). Sarasota, FL: Professional Resource Press/Professional Resource Exchange.

Brennan, N., & Kevany, J. (1985). Anthropometry and body image in a selected sample of adolescent girls. *Irish Journal of Medical Science, 154,* 220–227.

Brodie, D., Bagley, K., & Slade, P. (1994). Body-image perception in pre- and post-adolescent females. *Perceptual and Motor Skills, 78,* 147–154.

Brodie, D., Slade, P., & Rose, H. (1989). Reliability measures in disturbing body image. *Perceptual and Motor Skills, 69,* 723–732.

Bunnell, D., Cooper, P., Hertz, S., & Shenker, I. (1992). Body shape concerns among adolescents. *International Journal of Eating Disorders, 11,* 79–83.

Button, E. J., Fransella, F., & Slade, P. D. (1977). A reappraisal of body perception disturbance in anorexia nervosa. *Psychological Medicine, 7,* 235–243.

Carroll, D., Gleeson, C., Risby, B., & Dugdale, A. (1986). Body build and the desire for slenderness in young people. *Australian Pediatric Journal, 22,* 121–125.

Cash, T. F., & Brown, T. A. (1987). Body image in anorexia nervosa and bulimia nervosa: a review of the literature. *Behavioral Modification, 11,* 487–521.

Cash, T. F., & Deagle, E. (1997). The nature and extent of body-image disturbances in anorexia nervosa and bulimia nervosa: A meta-analysis. *International Journal of Eating Disorders, 22,* 107–125.

Cash, T. F., & Pruzinsky, T. (1990). *Body images: Development, deviance, and change.* New York: Guilford Press.

Childress, A., Brewerton, T., Hodges, E., & Jarrell, M. (1993). The kids' eating disorders survey (KEDS): A study of middle school students. *Journal of the American Academy of Child and Adolescent Psychiatry, 32,* 843–850.

Cohn, L., Adler, N., Irwin, C., Millstein, S., Kegeles, S., & Stone, G. (1987). Body-figure preferences in male and female adolescents. *Journal of Abnormal Psychology, 96,* 276–279.

Collins, M. (1991). Body figure perceptions and preferences among preadolescent children. *International Journal of Eating Disorders, 10,* 199–208.

Cooper, P., Taylor, M., Cooper, Z., & Fairburn, C. (1987). The development and validation of the Body Shape Questionnaire. *International Journal of Eating Disorders, 6,* 485–494.

Coovert, D. L., Thompson, J. K., & Kinder, B. N. (1988). Interrelationships among multiple aspects of body image and eating disturbance. *International Journal of Eating Disorders, 7,* 495–502.

Cornsweet, T. N. (1962). The staircase method in psychophysics. *American Journal of Psychology, 75,* 485–568.

Dillon, D. J. (1962). Measurement of perceived body size. *Perceptual and Motor Skills, 14*, 191–196.

Dwyer, J., Feldman, J., Seltzer, C., & Mayer, J. (1969). Adolescent attitudes toward weight and appearance. *Journal of Nutrition Education, 1*, 14–19.

Fabian, L., & Thompson, J. K. (1989). Body image and eating disturbance in young females. *International Journal of Eating Disorders, 8*, 63–74.

Flanery, R. C. (1990). Methodological and psychometric considerations in child reports. In A. M. La Greca (Ed.), *Through the eyes of the child: Obtaining self-reports from children and adolescents* (pp. 57–82). Boston: Allyn and Bacon.

Fonagy, P., Benster, R., & Higgitt, A. (1990). Adaptive probit estimation and body size: The evaluation of a new psychophysical technique. *British Journal of Psychology, 81*, 159–171.

Gardner, R. M. (1996). Methodological issues in assessment of the perceptual component of body image disturbance. *British Journal of Psychology, 87*, 327–337.

Gardner, R. M. & Bokenkamp, E. D. (1995). The role of sensory and non-sensory factors in body estimations of eating disorder subjects. *Journal of Clinical Psychology, 52*(1), 3–15.

Gardner, R., Friedman, B., & Jackson, N. (1998). Methodological concerns when using silhouettes to measure body image. *Perceptual and Motor Skills, 86*, 387–395.

Gardner, R., Friedman, B., Jackson, N., & Stark, K. (1998, April). *Predictors of eating disorder tendencies in children ages six through fourteen.* Paper presented at the Eighth New York International Conference on Eating Disorders, New York City.

Gardner, R. M., Friedman, B. N., Jackson, N. A., & Stark, K. (1999). Body size estimations in children six through fourteen: A longitudinal study. *Perceptual and Motor Skills, 88*, 541–555.

Gardner, R. M., Gardner, E. A., & Morrell, J. A. (1990). Body image of sexually and physically abused children. *Journal of Psychiatric Research, 24*, 313–321.

Gardner, R. M., Martinez, R., & Sandoval, Y. (1987). Obesity and body image: An evaluation of sensory and non-sensory components. *Psychological Medicine, 17*, 927–932.

Gardner, R. M., Sorter, R. G. & Friedman, B. N. (1997). Developmental changes in children's body image. *Journal of Social Behavior and Personality, 12*, 1019–1036.

Gardner, R. M., Stark, K., Friedman, B. N., & Jackson, N. A. (2000). Predictors of eating disorder scores in children ages six through fourteen: A longitudinal study. *Journal of Psychosomatic Research, 49*, 1–7.

Gardner, R., Stark, K., Jackson, N., & Friedman, B. (1999). Development and validation of two new body-image assessment scales. *Perceptual and Motor Skills, 89*, 981–993.

Gardner, R., Urrutia, R., Morrell, J., Watson, D., & Sandoval, S. (1990). Children's judgments of body size and distortion. *Cognitive Development, 5*, 385–394.

Garner, D. M. (1991a). *Eating Disorder Inventory for Children* (EDI-C). Odessa, FL: Psychological Assessment Resources.

Garner, D. (1991b). *Manual for the eating disorder inventory—2 (EDI-2)*. Odessa, FL: Psychological Assessment Resources.

Garner, D. M., & Garfinkel, P. E. (1981). Body image in anorexia nervosa: Measurement, theory and clinical implications. *International Journal of Psychiatric Medicine, 11*, 263–284.

Garner, D., & Olmsted, M. (1984). *Manual for the eating disorder inventory (EDI)*. Odessa, FL: Psychological Assessment Resources.

Gleghorn, A. A., Penner, L. A., Powers, P. S., & Schulman, R. (1987). The psychometric properties of several measures of body image. *Journal of Psychopathology and Behavioral Assessment, 9*, 203–218.

Glucksman, M. L., & Hirsch, J. (1969). The response of obese patients to weight reduction: III. The perception of body size. *Psychosomatic Medicine, 131*, 1–7.

Gustavson, C. R., Gustavson, J. C., Pumariega, A. J., Reinarz, D. E., Dameron, R., Gustavson, A. R., Pappas, T., & McCaul, K. (1990). Body-image distortion among male and female college and high school students and eating-disordered patients. *Perceptual and Motor Skills, 71*, 1003–1010.

Halmi, K., Goldberg, S., Cunningham, S. (1977). Perceptual distortion of body image in adolescent girls: Distortion of body image in adolescence. *Psychological Medicine, 7*, 253–257.

Hill, A., Oliver, S., & Rogers, P. (1992). Eating in the adult world: The rise of dieting in childhood and adolescence. *British Journal of Clinical Psychology, 31*, 95–105.

Keeton, W. P., Cash, T. F., & Brown, T. A. (1990). Body image or body images?: Comparative, multidimensional assessment among college students. *Journal of Personality Assessment, 54*, 213–230.

Koff, E. & Kiekhofer, M. (1978). Body-part size estimation in children. *Perceptual and Motor Skills, 47*, 1047–1050.

Krietler, H., & Krietler, S. (1970). Movement and aging: A psychological approach. In D. Brunner & E. Jokl (Eds.), *Physical activity and aging* (pp. 302–306). Basel, Switzerland: Karger.

Krietler, S., & Krietler, H. (1986). Body Image: The dimension of size. *Genetic, Social, and General Psychology Monographs, 114*, 7–32.

Mendelson, B. K., & White, D. R. (1982). Relation between body-esteem and self-esteem of obese and normal children. *Perceptual and Motor Skills, 54*, 899–905.

Merbaum, M., Marwit, S., & Hermann, J. (1986). *Children's and adolescent's perception of body parts: appearance, effectiveness, and vulnerability*. Unpublished manuscript.

Mintz, L., & Betz, N. (1986). Sex differences in the nature, realism, and correlates of body image. *Sex Roles, 15*, 185–195.

Nunnally, J. (1970). *Psychometric theory*. New York: McGraw-Hill.

Penner, L. A., Thompson, J. K., & Coovert, D. L. (1991). Size estimation among anorexics: Much ado about very little? *Journal of Abnormal Psychology, 100*, 90–93.

Petersen, A. C., Schulenberg, J. E., Abramowitz, R. H., Offer, D., & Jarcho, H. D. (1984). A self-image questionnaire for young adolescents (SIQYA): Reliability and validity studies. *Journal of Youth and Adolescence, 13*(2), 93–111.

Polivy, J., Herman, C. P., & Pliner, P. (1990). Perception and evaluation of body image: The meaning of body shape and size. In J. M. Olson & M. P. Zanna (Eds.), *Self-inference processes: The Ontario symposium, vol. 6: Ontario symposium on personality and social psychology* (pp. 87–114). Hillsdale, NJ: Erlbaum.

Probst, M., Vandereycken, W., Van Coppenolle, H., & Pieters, G. (1995). Body size estimation in eating disorder patients: Testing the video distortion method on a life-size screen. *Behavioral Research Therapy, 33*, 985–990.

Sands, R., Tricker, J., Sherman, C., Armatas, C., & Maschette, W. (1997). Disordered eating patterns, body image, self-esteem, and physical activity in preadolescent school children. *International Journal of Eating Disorders, 21*, 159–166.

Sherman, D., Iacono, W., & Donnelly, J. (1995). Development and validation of body rating scales for adolescent females. *International Journal of Eating Disorders, 18*, 327–333.

Shisslak, C. M., Renger, R., Sharpe, T., Crago, M., McKnight, K. M., Gray, N., Bryson, S., Estes, L. S., Parnaby, O. G., Killen, J., & Taylor, C. B. (1999). Development and evaluation of the McKnight Risk Factor Survey for assessing potential risk and protective factors for disordered eating in preadolescent and adolescent girls. *International Journal of Eating Disorders, 25*, 195–214.

Shore, R. A., & Porter, J. E. (1990). Normative and reliability data for 11 to 18 year olds on the Eating Disorder Inventory. *International Journal of Eating Disorders, 9*, 201–207.

Siegel, J. M., Yancey, A. K., Aneshensel, C. S., & Schuler, R. (1999). Body image, perceived pubertal timing, and adolescent mental health. *Journal of Adolescent Health, 25*, 155–165.

Slade, P. (1985). A review of body-image studies in anorexia nervosa. *Journal of Psychiatric Research, 19*, 255–266.

Slade, P. D., & Russell, G. F. M. (1973). Awareness of body dimensions in anorexia nervosa: Cross-sectional and longitudinal studies. *Psychological Medicine, 3*, 188–199.

Smeets, M. A. M., Smit, F., Panhuysen, G. E. M., & Ingleby, J. D. (1997). The influence of methodological differences on the outcome of body size estimation studies in anorexia nervosa. *British Journal of Clinical Psychology, 36*, 263–277.

Speaker, J. G., Schultz, C., Grinker, J. A., & Stern, J. S. (1983). Body size estimation and locus of control in obese adolescent boys undergoing weight reduction. *International Journal of Obesity, 7*, 73–83.

Stone, W. L., & Lemanek, K. L. (1990). Developmental issues in children's self-reports. In A. M. La Greca (Ed.), *Through the eyes of the child: Obtaining self-reports from children and adolescents* (pp. 18–56). Boston: Allyn and Bacon.

Strauman, T. J., & Glenberg, A. M. (1994). Self-concept and body-image disturbance: Which self-beliefs predict body size overestimation? *Cognitive Therapy
and Research, 18*(2), 105–125.

Stunkard, A., Sorenson, T., & Schlusinger, F. (1983). Use of the Danish Adoption
Register for the study of obesity and thinness. . In S. Kety, L. P. Rowland, R.
L. Sidman, & S. W. Matthysse (Eds.), *The genetics of neurological and psychiatric
disorders* (pp. 115–120). New York: Raven.

Szymanski, L. A., & Seime, R. J. (1997). A re-examination of body image distortion:
Evidence against a sensory explanation. *International Journal of Eating Disorders,
21*, 175–180.

Thelen, M., Powell, A., Lawrence, C., & Kuhnert, M. (1992). Eating and body
image concerns among children. *Journal of Clinical Child Psychology, 21*, 41–46.

Thompson, J. K. (1987). Body size distortion in anorexia nervosa: Reanalysis and
reconceptualization. *Internal Journal of Eating Disorders, 6*, 379–384.

Thompson, J. K. (1991). Body shape preferences: Effects of instructional protocol
and level of eating disturbance. *International Journal of Eating Disorders, 10*, 193–
198.

Thompson, J. K. (1996). Assessing body image disturbance: Measures, methodology,
and implementation. In J. K. Thompson (Ed.), *Body image, eating disorders, and
obesity* (pp. 49–81). Washington, DC: American Psychological Association.

Thompson, J. K., Heinberg, L. J., Altabe, M., & Tantleff-Dunn, S. (1999). *Exacting
beauty: Theory, assessment, and treatment of body image disturbance*. Washington,
DC: American Psychological Association.

Thompson, J. K., Penner, L., & Altabe, M. (1990). Procedures, problems, and
progress in the assessment of body images. In T. F. Cash & T. Pruzinsky (Eds.),
Body images: Development, deviance, and change. New York: Guilford Press.

Thompson, J. K., & Spana, R. (1988). The adjustable light beam method for
the assessment of size estimation accuracy: Description, psychometrics, and
normative data. *International Journal of Eating Disorders, 5*, 1061–1068.

Thompson, M., & Gray, J. (1995). Development and validation of a new body-
image assessment scale. *Journal of Personality Assessment, 64*, 258–269.

Tiggemann, M., & Pennington, B. (1990). The development of gender differences
in body-size dissatisfaction. *Australian Psychologist, 25*, 306–311.

Traub, A. C., & Orbach, J. (1964). Psychophysical studies of body image. 1. The
adjusting body-distorting mirror. *Archives of General Psychiatry, 11*, 53–66.

Veron-Guidry, S., & Williamson, D. (1996). Development of a body image assessment procedure for children and preadolescents. *International Journal of Eating
Disorders, 20*, 287–293.

Williamson, D. A., Cubic, B. A., & Gleaves, D. H. (1993). Equivalence of body
image disturbances in anorexia and bulimia nervosa. *Journal of Abnormal Psychology, 102*, 177–180.

Williamson, D. A., Davis, C. J., Bennett, S. M., Goreczny, A. J., & Gleaves, D. H. (1989). Development of a simple procedure for assessing body image disturbances. *Behavioral Assessment, 11*, 433–446.

Wohlwill, J. F. (1960). Developmental studies of perception. *Psychological Bulletin, 57*, 249–288.

Wood, K. C., Becker, J. A., & Thompson, J. K. (1996). Body image dissatisfaction in preadolescent children. *Journal of Applied Developmental Psychology, 17*, 85–100.

9

ASSESSMENT OF EATING DISTURBANCE IN CHILDREN AND ADOLESCENTS WITH EATING DISORDERS AND OBESITY

SUSAN B. NETEMEYER AND DONALD A. WILLIAMSON

This chapter summarizes methods for evaluating the psychological and behavioral characteristics of anorexia nervosa and bulimia nervosa in children and young adolescents. Although knowledge about assessment of eating disorders in older adolescents and adults has increased dramatically in the past two decades, relatively little attention has been devoted to assessing these disorders in younger individuals. There has been considerable recent interest and research in childhood anorexia nervosa; however, early-onset bulimia nervosa remains very poorly understood, except that there is a general consensus that it is very rare (Stein, Chalhoub, & Hodes, 1998). This chapter reviews interview procedures, self-report measures, and behavioral assessment procedures that have been tested in children and adolescents or that show promise for future use. First, basic psychometric issues by which these procedures are evaluated are reviewed and special problems that complicate the assessment of eating disturbance in children are discussed. The next four sections describe the assessment procedures and instruments that have been developed, along with psychometric research that evaluates them. Finally, suggestions for future research and conclusions are presented.

PSYCHOMETRIC ISSUES IN ASSESSMENT

Because psychological assessment usually involves an attempt to measure or quantify abstract constructs, a chapter on assessment should include a discussion of the psychometric issues that determine the strength or weakness of inferences made from these measurements. The *reliability* of an assessment technique is the degree to which an observed score is free from measurement error and produces consistent results. *Test–retest* reliability is concerned with the stability of test scores over time. *Internal consistency* reliability is the degree of consistency of the items of a test. It is measured by examining the intercorrelations among the test items. Two common methods for measuring internal consistency are Cronbach's (1951) coefficient alpha, which is used with multiple-choice tests, and the Kuder–Richardson Formula 20 (Kuder & Richardson, 1937), which is used for tests with dichotomous items. It is important to note that the items of a test may be highly intercorrelated (i.e., highly internally consistent) but not unidimensional in that all the items do not necessarily tap the same construct (Clark & Watson, 1995). If two different forms of the same assessment instrument are to be used, there should be evidence of the equivalence of those forms (called *alternate forms* reliability). Finally, *interrater* reliability is concerned with the degree of consistency between or among separate ratings or observations of behavior.

An assessment instrument is *valid* if there is evidence to support the appropriateness of inferences that one makes from it. Therefore, an instrument may be valid for one purpose and invalid for another. Validity evidence is usually summarized along four dimensions: content validity, criterion validity, construct validity, and incremental validity. *Content* validity is typically rated by expert judges and pertains to the relevance and representativeness of a test's items to the domain of interest. *Criterion* validity is determined by comparing scores with some sort of performance on an outside (criterion) measure. There are two main types: *Predictive* validity is concerned with making predictions about some future performance on a criterion measure, whereas in *concurrent* validity the predictor and criterion measures are assessed at about the same time. *Construct* validity is generally considered to be the most important type of validity evidence, and it should be collected through numerous sources. Evidence supporting construct validity is that which suggests the instrument is actually measuring what it is supposed to measure. Finally, *incremental* validity refers to the usefulness and cost-effectiveness of an assessment technique. To be incrementally valid, a test must produce accurate results above and beyond those that could be obtained without it.

SPECIAL PROBLEMS IN ASSESSING CHILDREN AND ADOLESCENTS

Diagnostic Issues

There are several problems associated with applying traditional diagnostic systems to children that can result in missed cases of clinically significant disorders. First, the diagnostic criterion for anorexia nervosa specified by the fourth edition of the *Diagnostic and Statistical Manual of Mental Disorders* (*DSM-IV*; American Psychiatric Association, 1994), which requires amenorrhea for at least three months when menstrual cycles "would otherwise be expected to occur," clearly does not apply to premenarcheal females. In addition, *DSM-IV* criteria specify that the individual must attain or maintain a body weight of at least 15% below what is expected for age and height. This criterion does not take into consideration the effect poor nutrition can have on growth retardation and on delayed maturation. Therefore, it is very difficult to determine when menstrual cycles would be expected to occur or to predict expected height (and therefore weight) in an individual who has engaged in a pattern of restrictive eating. It is also important to remember that some children and young adolescents will not present with weight loss; however, failure to gain weight during a time of expected growth may be seen as equivalent to weight loss in older adolescents and adults. It has been suggested that changes in a child's weight curve be used to assess disturbances rather than the child's weight per se (Bryant-Waugh & Kaminski, 1993). The *DSM-IV* criteria for anorexia nervosa also require that the individual experience extreme fears of gaining weight and disturbances in body image. This criterion may be problematic in that it is unclear whether children have the cognitive ability to perceive and verbalize such abstract fears or whether they can express them only in more concrete terms such as reporting feelings of fullness or nausea, abdominal pain, or appetite loss (Robin, Gilroy, & Dennis, 1998).

Because of these problems with *DSM-IV* diagnostic criteria, Bryant-Waugh and Kaminski (1993) proposed that a diagnostic checklist designed specifically for children be used instead. This checklist includes (a) determined food avoidance, (b) weight loss or failure to maintain weight gain expected for age, and (c) overconcern with weight and shape as evidenced by at least two of the following: preoccupation with weight or caloric intake, distorted body image, fear of fatness, or self-induced vomiting, extensive exercise, or laxative abuse.

Variations in Childhood Eating Disturbance

Children presenting with disturbed eating patterns for which no organic cause can be found may be experiencing any of a number of problems. Bryant-Waugh and Kaminski (1993) suggested that in addition to anorexia and bulimia nervosa, childhood eating disturbance might suggest the following conditions: (a) food avoidance emotional disorder, (b) food refusal, (c) selective eating, (d) pervasive refusal, or (e) appetite loss as a result of depression.

Food avoidance emotional disorder (FAED; Higgs, Goodyer, & Birch, 1989) is used to describe children who avoid food but do not display the other symptoms of anorexia nervosa and who have signs of other emotional problems such as depression, school avoidance, and obsessive thoughts. Because individuals with anorexia nervosa often have problems with anxiety and depression as well, it is unclear whether FAED is a distinct syndrome or is merely anorexia nervosa at a subclinical level. Food refusal (eating only certain types of foods or food "fads") and selective eating (food refusal for a longer period of time) are common problems in childhood and are relatively easy to distinguish from anorexia nervosa because although these children will eat only certain foods, preoccupation with weight and shape is usually absent and the types of foods that the child prefers are typically high in carbohydrates and calories (e.g., potatoes, bread, macaroni). In addition, children who present with food refusal and selective eating are frequently within the normal height and weight range (Bryant-Waugh & Lask, 1995).

Pervasive refusal syndrome (Lask, Britten, Kroll, Magagna, & Tranter, 1991) is characterized by a refusal not only to eat and drink but also to walk, talk, or to engage in self-care. Lask et al. (1991) suggested that this syndrome may be a variant of posttraumatic stress disorder. Appetite loss secondary to depression may be confused with anorexia nervosa because of the child's decrease in eating and weight. However, in cases of depression, deliberate avoidance of high-calorie foods and overconcern with weight and shape are usually absent. Cases in which depression accompanies anorexia nervosa are more complex, however, and appear to be relatively common (Fosson, Knibbs, Bryant-Waugh, & Lask, 1987).

We have found that some children and young adolescents who present with food refusal and avoidance are best diagnosed with an oppositional disorder, in that the avoidance of food represents an attempt to rebel against and gain control over the parents or over some situation in the home. In the early stages of the disorder, these children frequently avoid foods that their parents want them to eat, such as meat and vegetables, and prefer to eat high-calorie sweets and snack foods instead, and they are not overly concerned with their weight. However, if the child discovers that food avoidance and weight loss are effective ways to gain control within the family and if he or she receives positive reinforcement for weight loss (e.g., from peers), a syndrome more like anorexia nervosa can develop.

Other Problems in Assessment

Children and young adolescents may provide invalid information during evaluation for several reasons. First, as mentioned earlier, it is unclear whether young children have the ability to provide accurate and reliable information regarding their cognitive–emotional state and they may misunderstand terms such as dieting and binge eating unless they are clearly explained (Babbitt, Edlen-Nezin, Manikam, Summers, & Murphy, 1995). Second, they may be motivated to provide misleading information during assessment because of limits on confidentiality for minors and fears of censure from parents or others. The evaluator must be skilled in eliciting information and must avoid being perceived by the child as taking the family's "side" against him or her. Giving invalid information is also a problem in research with children and adolescents. Because ethical guidelines require that both the child and parent must provide informed assent–consent before the child's participation, it is likely that children who have problems with eating either give false information or avoid participation in these studies. Finally, the child's lack of control over his or her own eating may be problematic as well, especially in the diagnosis of bulimia nervosa. It has been suggested that the very low rate of diagnosis of bulimia nervosa in children may be partially a result of the fact that young children do not have access to binge foods or the money to obtain them, nor do they have the level of privacy required to secretly engage in binging and purging behaviors (Thelen, Lawrence, & Powell, 1992).

ASSESSMENT PROCEDURES

A thorough assessment of eating disturbance in children and adolescents includes (a) findings from a physical examination and laboratory testing, (b) nutritional assessment, (c) interviews with the child and parents or guardians, (d) results of self-report questionnaires, and (e) behavioral assessment findings. A physical exam is essential to rule out a physical etiology for the eating disturbance and can be provided by the referring physician or the child's pediatrician, with whom the assessment team should be in fairly close contact. The nutritional assessment is best conducted by a registered dietitian and should include not only an account of the child's current eating patterns but also his or her developmental history, including weight history, food likes and dislikes, early food fads, and "picky" eating, because it has been shown that these behaviors are related to the development of eating disorders (Marchi & Cohen, 1990).

It is essential to gather information from parents or guardians as well as from the child or adolescent during the assessment process. Ideally, interviews will be conducted with the child and parents together and then with the child alone. The interviewer should attempt to determine (a) the family context around the time of the onset of symptoms, including stresses such as marital and financial problems or school problems; (b) the history of the disturbance, including times of improvement or deterioration in symptoms and the factors associated with each; (c) the parents' and siblings' perception of the problem and history of reactions and attempts to manage it; and

(d) any family history of eating disorders or other psychiatric problems. In addition, family interactions should be assessed, either through questioning or direct observations. These interactions include alliances and hostilities among family members, interpersonal boundaries, and the marital relationship between the parents as well as the child's involvement in parental problems (Tranter, 1993). The interviewer should also question the parents and child regarding the child's personality traits, because individuals with eating disorders tend to be high achievers, obsessional, perfectionistic, anxious, and depressed (Vitousek & Manke, 1994).

STRUCTURED INTERVIEWS

Research on the diagnosis of eating disorders has found that reliable diagnosis of eating disorders is best accomplished using structured interviews. Three structured interview procedures have been developed for the purpose of diagnosing or assessing eating disorders: (a) Eating Disorder Examination, (b) Structured Interview for Anorexia and Bulimia Nervosa, and (c) Interview for Diagnosis of Eating Disorders. The research samples for each of these methods included eating disordered persons of varied ages, including children and adolescents. A fourth interview procedure, the Clinical Eating Disorder Rating Instrument (Palmer, Christie, Cordle, Davies, & Kendrick, 1987) is not well-developed and will not be reviewed.

Eating Disorder Examination (EDE)

The EDE is the most widely used interview method for eating disorders. This interview was developed to measure the symptoms of anorexia and bulimia nervosa (Fairburn & Cooper, 1993). The EDE has been revised 12 times since it was first described by Cooper and Fairburn (1987) and has four subscales: (a) restraint, (b) eating concern, (c) shape concern, and (d) weight concern (Fairburn & Cooper, 1993). Studies of interrater reliability and internal consistency for these four scales have found them to be very reliable (Fairburn & Cooper, 1993). Also, tests of the validity of the EDE subscales have found them to measure the symptoms of anorexia and bulimia nervosa and to be correlated with other measures of disturbed patterns of eating (Fairburn & Cooper, 1993). Norms for the four subscales have been developed in a number of studies, and they have been summarized by Fairburn and Cooper (1993).

The EDE was originally designed to assess the psychopathology of eating disorders (Cooper & Fairburn, 1987) and it has been used as a measure of treatment outcome in a number of treatment studies (Williamson, Anderson, & Gleaves, 1996). The EDE was not developed specifically for diagnosing eating disorders, but has been adapted (see Fairburn & Cooper,

1993) for the purpose of diagnosing anorexia and bulimia nervosa using *DSM-IV* diagnostic criteria (American Psychiatric Association, 1994). Bryant-Waugh, Cooper, Taylor, and Lask (1996) examined a slightly modified version of the EDE in a small study of eating-disturbed children and found that it produced scores consistent with adult norms for females with eating disorders.

Structured Interview for Anorexia and Bulimic Disorders (SIAB-EX)

The SIAB was originally described by Fichter et al. (1990). It was revised for a third version, which is called SIAB-EX (expert rating), and the psychometric research on this version has been reported by Fichter, Herpertz, Quadflieg, and Herpertz-Dahlmann (1998). The SIAB-EX was developed to measure the specific and general psychopathology of eating disorders. This structured interview has 87 ratings pertaining to a wide variety of problems commonly observed in eating disorders. Factor analysis of 61 of the 87 ratings yielded six factors, which form the six subscales of the SIAB-EX: (a) body image; (b) general psychopathology; (c) measures to counteract weight gain, fasting, and substance abuse; (d) sexuality and social integration; (e) bulimic symptoms; and (f) atypical binges. Interrater reliability and internal consistency estimates for the six scales were found to be satisfactory. The SIAB-EX can be used for the purpose of establishing an eating disorder diagnosis, but there have been no formal tests of the validity of this interview for diagnosing eating disorders. The SIAB-EX has been translated into English, German, Spanish, and Italian.

Interview for Diagnosis of Eating Disorders (IDED)

The IDED was originally described by Williamson (1990). The IDED has undergone three revisions, and the fourth version is called IDED-IV (Kutlesic, Williamson, Gleaves, Barbin, & Murphy-Eberenz, 1998). The IDED was designed specifically for establishing an eating disorder diagnosis. The IDED-IV has questions and symptom rating scales that specifically measure the *DSM-IV* (American Psychiatric Association, 1994) diagnostic criteria for anorexia nervosa, bulimia nervosa, and binge eating disorder. Also, many different symptom patterns of eating disorder not otherwise specified are measured by the IDED-IV. Tests of the interrater reliability and internal consistency of the IDED-IV have found it to be very reliable for establishing an eating disorder diagnosis (Kutlesic et al., 1998). Also, concurrent validity of the IDED-IV has been established (Kutlesic et al., 1998). The IDED-IV has been used to establish eating disorder diagnoses in many studies and is a relatively quick method for screening of eating disorders. The IDED has been translated into Spanish.

SELF-REPORT MEASURES

Some of the psychological tests that were developed primarily for young adults have been tested in studies of children and adolescents. These include the Eating Attitudes Test, the Dutch Eating Behavior Questionnaire Restraint Scale, and the Eating Disorder Inventory. Other self-report measures were developed specifically for use with children, including the Children's Eating Attitudes Test, Kid's Eating Disorder Survey, McKnight Risk Factor Survey III, Dieting and Body Image Questionnaire, and the Dietary Intent Scale. One scale, the Children's Eating Behavior Inventory, was designed to assess parental reports of eating problems in children.

Eating Attitudes Test (EAT)

The EAT was developed by Garner and Garfinkel (1979) to measure the attitudes, thoughts, and behaviors associated with anorexia nervosa. The original 40-item test was shortened to 26 items, and this version is called the EAT-26 (Garner, Olmsted, Bohr, & Garfinkel, 1982). The EAT has been used extensively with adults. It has been found to be reliable and valid in a number of studies (Williamson et al., 1996). The EAT differentiates anorexia and bulimia nervosa patients from controls, but bulimic and anorexic patients generally score in the same range on the EAT (Williamson, Prather, McKenzie, & Blouin, 1990). Thus the EAT is a very good screening measure for eating disorders. The EAT has been used for this purpose in a number of studies of children and adolescents (e.g., Calam & Waller, 1998; Gralen, Levine, Smolak, & Murnen, 1990). The EAT has been adapted for children as young as 10 years old (Hill, Weaver, & Blundell, 1990). Norms for adolescents have been published by Wood, Waller, Miller, and Slade (1992). The reading level for the EAT is fifth grade, and one adaptation of the EAT has a third-grade reading level (Williamson, Anderson, Jackman, & Jackson, 1995).

Dutch Eating Behavior Questionnaire—Restraint Scale (DEBQ—Restraint Scale)

The DEBQ—Restraint Scale is a very good measure of dieting or "pure" dietary restraint (Gorman & Allison, 1995). The DEBQ was developed by Van Strien, Fritjers, Bergers, and Defares (1986) to measure three aspects of eating behavior: restrained eating, emotional eating, and external eating. The Restraint Scale of the DEBQ has received the most attention from researchers and has been found to be reliable and valid in a number of studies (Gorman & Allison, 1995). The reading level of this scale has been found to be between the fifth and eighth grades (Allison & Franklin, 1993).

It has been used in a number of studies with children and adolescents as a measure of dieting behavior (e.g., Hill, Oliver, & Rogers, 1992; Wardle & Beales, 1986; Wardle & Marsland, 1990).

Eating Disorder Inventory-2 (EDI-2)

The EDI-2 is a 91-item self-report inventory (Garner, 1991), expanded from the original 64-item EDI (Garner, Olmsted, & Polivy, 1983). The EDI-2 has 11 scales: (a) drive for thinness, (b) bulimia, (c) body dissatisfaction, (d) ineffectiveness, (e) perfectionism, (f) interpersonal distrust, (g) interoceptive awareness, (h) maturity fears, (i) asceticism, (j) impulse regulation, and (k) social insecurity. Many studies have supported the reliability and validity of the EDI and EDI-2, and the reading level of this test is fifth grade (Williamson et al., 1995). Adolescent norms for the EDI have been published by Rosen, Silberg, and Gross (1988) and Shore and Porter (1990). The EDI-2 continues to be used in studies of adolescents (Keel, Klump, Leon, & Fulkerson, 1998).

Children's Eating Attitudes Test (ChEAT)

Maloney, McGuire, and Daniels (1988) developed the ChEAT as a child's version of the EAT and found it to be a reliable measure with children. Two factor analytic studies of the ChEAT have been conducted. Williamson et al. (1997) found three factors: (a) dieting, (b) concern with eating, and (c) social pressure to gain weight. The dieting factor was found to be negatively correlated with measures of adiposity and social pressure to gain weight was positively correlated with adiposity. These data were supportive of the validity of these two factors. Another study of the factor structure of the ChEAT produced the same three factors as in the previous study, along with another factor called restricting and purging (Kelly, Ricci-ardelli, & Clarke, 1999). Further research on the reliability and validity of the ChEAT is needed.

Kid's Eating Disorder Survey (KEDS)

The KEDS was developed by Childress, Brewerton, Hodges, and Jarrell (1993) as a measure of eating disorder symptoms in children. The 12 questions of the KEDS ask about weight dissatisfaction, restrictive eating, and purging. The KEDS was found to be sensitive to identifying children with eating disorder symptoms and proved to be a good survey method for assessing specific eating and purging habits. A recent study found that the body image silhouettes (BIS) of the KEDS have adequate to good test–retest reliability and that BIS scores correlated with eating disturbance, adiposity, and age

(Candy & Fee, 1998). The KEDS questionnaire must be considered to be in the early stages of psychometric development.

McKnight Risk Factor Survey III (MRFS-III)

The MFRS-III was developed to measure risk and protective factors for eating disorders in preadolescent and adolescent girls (Shisslak et al., 1999). This questionnaire has either 75 (elementary school version) or 79 (middle and high school versions) items that assess:

1. Reactions to body changes,
2. Weight control behaviors,
3. Concern with body weight and shape,
4. Binge eating and purging,
5. Weight teasing,
6. Parental concern with appearance,
7. Peer concerns with appearance,
8. Dating,
9. Life events,
10. Demographic information,
11. Media modeling for thinness,
12. Confidence,
13. Social support,
14. Substance abuse,
15. Attempts to gain weight,
16. School performance,
17. Safety,
18. Depression,
19. Social activity,
20. Perfectionism,
21. Emotional eating,
22. Physical appearance,
23. Sports pressure to be thin,
24. Physical health,
25. Healthy behaviors,
26. Parental involvement in school,
27. Watching eating behavior for health reasons,
28. Sexual touches, and
29. Parental body size.

The reliability and validity of these scales were tested by Shisslak et al. (1999). The scales that met the customary criterion for acceptable reliability (test–retest reliability and internal consistency estimates < 0.70) were weight control behaviors, concern with body weight and shape, and weight teasing scales. Thus most of the scales of the MRFS-III will require further psycho-metric development. The MRFS-III appears to be a very good initial effort to measure risk and protective factors related to eating disorders, but consid-erable psychometric research on this measure is needed before widespread use is warranted.

Dieting and Body Image Questionnaire (DBIQ)

The DBIQ was developed by Thelen, Powell, Lawrence, and Kuhnert (1992) as a measure of eating and body image concerns among children. The DBIQ has two scales, "dieting" and "overweight," which measures concerns about being or becoming overweight. The two scales were found to be internally consistent. A second study (Lawrence & Thelen, 1995) found that Caucasian girls reported dieting much more frequently than boys and African American girls. This measure is also in the developmental stages and further research on its psychometric properties is needed.

Dietary Intent Scale (DIS)

The DIS was developed by Stice (1998a, 1998b) to measure dietary restraint in adolescent girls. The DIS has nine questions about intentional efforts to restrict food intake to control body weight. The scale was found to be internally consistent and to have good test–retest reliability. The DIS was found to be highly correlated with the DEBQ-Restraint Scale and with the Restraint Scale (Herman & Polivy, 1980), which supports the validity of the DIS as a measure of dietary restraint. The DIS was used in a longitudi-nal study of bulimic symptoms and it loaded on the dietary restraint construct of the structural model that was tested in the study. These preliminary findings suggest that the DIS may be a good measure of dietary restraint in adolescent girls.

Children's Eating Behavior Inventory (CEBI)

The CEBI is a parent-report instrument designed to measure eating and mealtime problems in children (Archer, Rosenbaum, & Streiner, 1991). It contains 40 questions that are used to gather information about the child's food preferences and dislikes, compliance during mealtimes and self-feeding skills, and family members' perception of stresses during mealtime. The CEBI yields a total eating problem score, as well as the percentage of items perceived to be a problem. It was standardized on children (2 to 12 years old) who had been referred for eating problems or had developmental or other disabilities that put them at risk for eating problems and a control group of children with normal eating behaviors. The CEBI was found to have adequate internal consistency and test–retest reliability. Construct validity was demonstrated by its ability to differentiate the clinical sample of children from the nonclinical sample and its ability to reflect improvement in eating problems after treatment. Archer et al. (1991) reported that it can be completed in about 15 minutes and suggested that it be used as a companion to the child-report Children's Eating Attitudes Test (Maloney et al., 1988), because many of the items on the CEBI are similar or identical to those on the ChEAT. However, it is important to note that none of the children on which the CEBI was validated were diagnosed with either anorexia or bulimia nervosa, and its applicability to these disorders is only hypothetical.

BEHAVIORAL ASSESSMENT

Behavioral assessment procedures can provide more direct information than that gained from traditional interview or questionnaire measures. These procedures are designed to be idiosyncratic measures of eating disorder symptoms and are quite useful in establishing an individual's baseline level of eating disturbance and to assess progress over the course of treatment.

Food Monitoring Procedures

Self-monitoring is one of the most widely used procedures in the behavioral assessment of eating disturbance (Williamson, 1990). Ideally, self-monitoring records should include time of day, type and quantity of food consumed, and the context in which the food was eaten. Also, the person should report whether he or she felt in control while eating and whether the eating episode was identified as a binge. Data from self-monitoring records can be used for diagnosis and treatment planning and for evaluating treatment outcome. Self-monitoring requires skills such as reading, writing, measurement skills, adequate short-term and long-term memory, and motivation to keep accurate records. Children between the ages of 10 and 12 have been found to keep more reliable records than either younger children, who may lack the requisite skills, or adolescents who possess these skills but lack sustained motivation (Babbitt et al., 1995).

Test Meals

The use of test meals, in which the person is asked to consume a standard amount of food, can be particularly useful for evaluating patients who minimize problems associated with eating to avoid treatment (Williamson, 1990). Parameters that can be measured include amount and caloric density of food consumed, avoidance tactics used, speed of eating, and subjective or objective indices of anxiety before, during, and after eating. In an attempt to establish the validity of test meals, Rosen, Leitenberg, Fondacaro, Gross, and Willmuth (1985) found that bulimic eaters who were prevented from vomiting after eating consumed less than normal eaters, experienced more anxiety, and reported more negative food- and weight-related thoughts. However, the validity of test meals in the assessment of children diagnosed with eating disorders has not been established.

Behavioral Eating Test (BET)

A standardized version of a test meal that was designed to assess food and beverage consumption in children is the BET (Jeffrey et al., 1980). Studies using the BET have focused on children's consumption of high-nutrition foods and low-nutrition foods in response to television advertisements (Jeffrey, McLellarn, & Fox, 1982). The test consists of an equal number of standard servings of nutrient-dense foods (e.g., cheese, carrots, milk) and foods that are poor in nutrition (e.g., candy bar, sugary cereal, soda pop). Children are instructed to taste each of the foods they like, and to eat as much of them as desired. They are then unobtrusively observed for eight minutes and the amount of food not consumed is weighed and converted to caloric equivalents. The BET procedure has moderate test–retest reliability, and children who eat a larger proportion of high-nutrition foods in the test meal eat fewer low-nutrition foods at home (Jeffrey et al., 1982). The BET has been recommended as a behavioral measure of food consumption in normal weight and overweight children. It could also be used with children suspected of eating disturbances by tailoring the foods presented to the child's food avoidance (e.g., high-calorie foods versus low-calorie foods). Subsequent administrations of the BET procedure could be used to measure treatment effects. However, as with test meals in general, these uses have not been empirically validated for children.

Bob and Tom's Method of Assessing Nutrition (BATMAN)

The goal of the BATMAN procedure is to measure mealtime behavior and parental variables that influence the child's eating. It uses a time sampling procedure to observe and record the child's behavior during mealtime (e.g., playing with food, crying, time away from table), the parent's response to the behavior (e.g., physical or verbal discouragement or encouragement), and the child's response to the interaction (Klesges et al., 1983). It has been used to identify psychosocial variables associated with childhood obesity in very young children. The BATMAN has high levels of interrater and test–retest reliability. Parental behaviors have been shown to significantly correlate with the relative weight of the child (e.g., prompts to eat, food offers are associated with higher weight). The BATMAN procedure has not been validated for use in eating disordered children; however, it might be helpful in establishing a functional analysis of parental behavior leading to increased and decreased eating.

CONCLUSION

Effective assessment and treatment of eating disturbance in children and adolescents is limited by the amount of information currently available. Although much is known about eating disorders in older adolescents and young adults, it is unclear whether this knowledge can be extended to individuals who experience eating disturbance at younger ages. Several assessment issues require further research. First, it is important to accurately estimate prevalence rates of eating disorders in children and young adolescents to determine the scope of the problem in this population. However, accurate prevalence rates cannot be determined without first having standard diagnostic criteria by which to define the occurrence of the disorders. Therefore, research is needed to differentiate eating disturbance related to anorexia and bulimia nervosa from that related to other eating problems and to more clearly define the syndromes of anorexia and bulimia nervosa in young individuals. It is also important to continue efforts to develop assessment measures designed and validated specifically for use with children, because many of the structured interviews and self-report measures described previously were originally designed for older respondents. Research should also focus on developing more evidence to support the validity of using adult measures with children, as well as to extend the use of measures designed for other populations (e.g., overweight children, developmentally disabled children) with young anorexic and bulimic individuals. Finally, early identification of risk factors associated with the development of eating disorders and early intervention may help to prevent the disorders or to ameliorate their effects. Therefore, assessment measures of risk factors such as overconcern with shape and weight and perceived social pressure for thinness (Shisslak et al., 1999) are needed. The McKnight Risk Factor Survey-III described earlier, which is in the early stages of development, appears to be a promising way to begin.

Research on assessment of eating disturbance should be developed along two different paths. Reliable and valid diagnoses of eating disorders depend on the accurate and sensitive use of assessment instruments. Therefore, clinical assessment must focus on the development and validation of techniques that can identify true cases of eating disorders and distinguish them from "normal" dieting and body dissatisfaction, which is becoming common at younger ages (Maloney et al., 1988). Also, clinical instruments that measure treatment outcome in children and adolescents are needed. The second line of assessment research should extend the work that has already begun on preventing eating disorders. Prevention research should be directed toward identifying individuals with early signs of eating disturbance and toward measuring the effectiveness of prevention efforts.

REFERENCES

Allison, D. B., & Franklin, R. D. (1993). The readability of three measures of dietary restraint. *Psychotherapy in Private Practice, 12,* 53–57.

American Psychiatric Association. (1994). *Diagnostic and statistical manual of mental disorders* (4th ed.). Washington, DC: Author.

Archer, L. A., Rosenbaum, P. L., & Streiner, D. L. (1991). The Children's Eating Behavior Inventory: Reliability and validity results. *Journal of Pediatric Psychology, 16,* 629–642.

Babbitt, R. L., Edlen-Nezin, L., Manikam, R., Summers, J. A., & Murphy, C. M. (1995). Assessment of eating and weight-related problems in children and special populations. In D. B. Allison (Ed.), *Handbook of assessment methods for eating behavioral and weight-related problems: Measures, theory, and research* (pp. 431–485). Thousand Oaks, CA: Sage.

Bryant-Waugh, R., Cooper, P. J., Taylor, C. L., & Lask, B. D. (1996). The use of the Eating Disorder Examination with children: A pilot study. *International Journal of Eating Disorders, 19,* 391–397.

Bryant-Waugh, R., & Kaminski, Z. (1993). Eating disorders in children: An overview. In B. Lask & R. Bryant-Waugh (Eds.), *Childhood-onset anorexia nervosa and related eating disorders* (pp. 17–29). East Sussex, UK: Erlbaum.

Bryant-Waugh, R., & Lask, B. (1995). Annotation: Eating disorders in children. *Journal of Child Psychology and Psychiatry, 36,* 191–202.

Calam, R., & Waller, G. (1998). Are eating and psychosocial characteristics in early teenage years useful predictors of eating characteristics in early adulthood? A 7-year longitudinal study. *International Journal of Eating Disorders, 24,* 339–362.

Candy, C. M., & Fee, V. E. (1998). Reliability and concurrent validity of the Kids' Eating Disorder Survey (KEDS) body image silhouettes with preadolescent girls. *Eating Disorders: The Journal of Treatment and Prevention, 6,* 297–308.

Childress, A. C., Brewerton, T. D., Hodges, E. L., & Jarrell, M. P. (1993). The Kids' Eating Disorders Survey (KEDS): A study of middle school students. *Journal of the American Academy of Child and Adolescent Psychiatry, 32,* 843–850.

Clark, L. A., & Watson, D. (1995). Constructing validity: Basic issues in objective scale development. *Psychological Assessment, 7,* 309–320.

Cooper, Z., & Fairburn, C. G. (1987). The Eating Disorder Examination: A semistructured interview for the assessment of the specific psychopathology of eating disorders. *International Journal of Eating Disorders, 6,* 1–8.

Cronbach, L. J. (1951). Coefficient alpha and the internal structure of tests. *Psychometrika, 16,* 297–334.

Fairburn, C. G., & Cooper, Z. (1993). The Eating Disorder Examination (12th ed.). In C. G. Fairburn & G. T. Wilson (Eds.), *Binge eating: Nature, assessment, and treatment* (pp. 317–332). New York: Guilford Press.

Fichter, M. M., Elton, M., Engel, K., Meyer, A. -E., Poustka, F., & Mall, H. (1990). The Structured Interview for Anorexia and Bulimia Nervosa (SIAB): Development and characteristics of a (semi)-standardized instrument. In M. Fichter (Ed.), *Bulimia nervosa: Basic research, diagnoses and therapy* (pp. 55–70). Chichester, UK: Wiley.

Fichter, M. M., Herpertz, S., Quadflieg, N., & Herpertz-Dahlmann, B. (1998). Structured interview for anorexic and bulimic disorders for DSM-IV and ICD-10: Updated (third) revision. *International Journal of Eating Disorders, 24,* 227–249.

Fosson, A., Knibbs, J., Bryant-Waugh, R., & Lask, B. (1987). Early-onset anorexia nervosa. *Archives of Disease in Childhood, 61,* 114–118.

Garner, D. M. (1991). *Eating Disorder Inventory-2 manual.* Odessa, FL: Psychological Assessment Resources.

Garner, D. M., & Garfinkel, P. E. (1979). The Eating Attitudes Test: An index of the symptoms of anorexia nervosa. *Psychological Medicine, 9,* 273–279.

Garner, D. M., Olmsted, M. P., Bohr, Y., & Garfinkel, P. E. (1982). The Eating Attitudes Test: Psychometric features and clinical correlates. *Psychological Medicine, 12,* 871–878.

Garner, D. M., Olmsted, M. P., & Polivy, J. (1983). Development and validation of a multidimensional eating disorder inventory for anorexia nervosa and bulimia. *International Journal of Eating Disorders, 2,* 15–34.

Gorman, B., & Allison, D. B. (1995). Measurement of dietary restraint. In D. B. Allison (Ed.), *Methods for the assessment of eating behaviors and weight related problems* (pp. 149–184). Newbury Park, CA: Sage.

Gralen, S. J., Levine, M. P., Smolak, L., & Murnen, S. K. (1990). Dieting and disordered eating during early and middle adolescence: Do the influences remain the same? *International Journal of Eating Disorders, 9,* 504–512.

Herman, C. P., & Polivy, J. (1980). Restrained eating. In A. J. Stunkard (Ed.), *Obesity* (pp. 208-225). Philadelphia: Saunders.

Higgs, J., Goodyer, I., & Birch, J. (1989). Anorexia nervosa and food avoidance emotional disorder. *Archives of Disease in Childhood, 64,* 346–351.

Hill, A. J., Oliver, S., & Rogers, P. J. (1992). Eating in the adult world: The rise of dieting in childhood and adolescence. *British Journal of Clinical Psychology, 31,* 95–105.

Hill, A. J., Weaver, C., & Blundell, J. E. (1990). Dieting concerns of 10-year-old girls and their mothers. *British Journal of Clinical Psychology, 29,* 346–348.

Jeffrey, D. B., Lemnitzer, N. B., Hickey, J. S., Hess, M. S., McLellarn, R. W., & Stroud, J. M. (1980). The development of a behavioral eating test and its relationship to a self-report food attitude scale in young children. *Behavioral Assessment, 2,* 87–89.

Jeffrey, D. B., McLellarn, R. W., & Fox, D. J. (1982). The development of children's eating habits: The role of television commercials. *Health Education Quarterly, 9,* 174–189.

Keel, P. K., Klump, K. L., Leon, G. R., & Fulkerson, J. A. (1998). Disordered eating in adolescent males from a school-based sample. *International Journal of Eating Disorders, 23,* 125–132.

Kelly, C., Ricciardelli, L. A., & Clarke, J. D. (1999). Problem eating attitudes and behaviors in young children. *International Journal of Eating Disorders, 25,* 281–286.

Klesges, R. C., Coates, T. J., Brown, G., Sturgeon-Tillisch, J., Moldenhauer-Klesges, L. M., Holzer, B., Woolfrey, J., & Vollmer, J. (1983). Parental influences on children's eating behavior and relative weight. *Journal of Applied Behavior Analysis, 4,* 317–378.

Kuder, G. F., & Richardson, M. W. (1937). The theory of the estimation of reliability. *Psychometrika, 2,* 151–160.

Kutlesic, V., Williamson, D. A., Gleaves, D. H., Barbin, J. M., & Murphy-Eberenz, K. P. (1998). The Interview for Diagnosis of Eating Disorders IV: Application to DSM-IV diagnostic criteria. *Psychological Assessment, 10,* 41–48.

Lask, B., Britten, C., Kroll, L., Magagna, J., & Tranter, M. (1991). Pervasive refusal in children. *Archives of Disease in Childhood, 66,* 866–869.

Lawrence, C. M., & Thelen, M. H. (1995). Body image, dieting, and self-concept: Their relation in African-American and Caucasian children. *Journal of Clinical Child Psychology, 24,* 41–48.

Maloney, M. J., McGuire, J. B., & Daniels, S. R. (1988). Reliability testing of a children's version of the Eating Attitudes Test. *Journal of the American Academy of Child and Adolescent Psychiatry, 27,* 541–543.

Marchi, M., & Cohen, P. (1990). Early childhood eating behaviors and adolescent eating disorders. *Journal of the American Academy of Child and Adolescent Psychiatry, 29,* 112–117.

Palmer, R., Christie, M., Cordle, C., Davies, D., & Kendrick, J. (1987). The Clinical Eating Disorder Instrument (CEDRI): A preliminary description. *International Journal of Eating Disorders, 6,* 9–16.

Robin, A. L., Gilroy, M., & Dennis, A. B. (1998). Treatment of eating disorders in children and adolescents. *Clinical Psychology Review, 18,* 421–446.

Rosen, J. C., Leitenberg, H., Fondacaro, K. M., Gross, J., & Willmuth, M. E. (1985). Standardized test meals in assessment of eating behavior in bulimia nervosa: Consumption of feared foods when vomiting is prevented. *International Journal of Eating Disorders, 4,* 59–70.

Rosen, J. C., Silberg, N. T., & Gross, J. (1988). Eating Attitudes Test and Eating Disorder Inventory: Norms for adolescent girls and boys. *Journal of Consulting and Clinical Psychology, 56,* 305–308.

Shisslak, C. M., Renger, R., Sharpe, T., Crago, M., McKnight, K. M., Gray, N., Bryson, S., Estes, L. S., Parnaby, O. G., Killen, J., & Taylor, C. B. (1999). Development and evaluation of the McKnight Risk Factor Survey for assessing potential risk and protective factors for disordered eating in preadolescent and adolescent girls. *International Journal of Eating Disorders, 25,* 195–214.

Shore, R. A., & Porter, J. E. (1990). Normative and reliability data for 11 to 18 year olds on the Eating Disorder Inventory. *International Journal of Eating Disorders, 9,* 201–207.

Stein, S., Chalhoub, N., & Hodes, M. (1998). Very early-onset bulimia nervosa: Report of two cases. *International Journal of Eating Disorders, 24,* 323–327.

Stice, E. (1998a). Relations of restraint and negative affect to bulimic pathology: A longitudinal test of three competing models. *International Journal of Eating Disorders, 23,* 243–260.

Stice, E. (1998b). Prospective relation of dieting behaviors to weight change in a community sample of adolescents. *Behavior Therapy, 29,* 277–297.

Thelen, M. H., Lawrence, C. M., & Powell, A. L. (1992). Body image, weight control, and eating disorders among children. In J. H. Crowther, D. L. Tennenbaum, S. E. Hobfoll, & M. A. P. Stephens (Eds.), *The etiology of bulimia nervosa: The individual and family context* (pp. 81–101). Washington: Hemisphere.

Thelen, M. H., Powell, A. L., Lawrence, C., & Kuhnert, M. E. (1992). Eating and body image concerns among children. *Journal of Clinical Child Psychology, 21,* 41–46.

Tranter, M. (1993). Assessment. In B. Lask & R. Bryant-Waugh (Eds.), *Childhood-onset anorexia nervosa and related eating disorders* (pp. 109–125). East Sussex, UK: Erlbaum.

Van Strien, T., Frijters, J. E. R., Bergers, G. P. A., & Defares, P. B. (1986). The Dutch Eating Behavior Questionnaire (DEBQ) for assessment of restrained, emotional, and external eating behavior. *International Journal of Eating Disorders, 5,* 295–315.

Vitousek, K. & Manke, F. (1994). Personality variables and disorders in anorexia nervosa and bulimia nervosa. *Journal of Abnormal Psychology, 103,* 137–147.

Wardle, J., & Beales, S. (1986). Restraint, body image, and food attitudes in children from 12–18 years. *Appetite, 7,* 209–217.

Wardle, J., & Marsland, L. (1990). Adolescent concerns about weight and eating: A social-developmental perspective. *Journal of Psychosomatic Research, 34,* 377–391.

Williamson, D. A. (1990). *Assessment of eating disorders: Obesity, anorexia, and bulimia nervosa.* Elmsford, NY: Pergamon Press.

Williamson, D. A., Anderson, D. A., & Gleaves, D. H. (1996). Anorexia nervosa and bulimia nervosa: Structured interview methodologies and psychological assessment. In K. Thompson (Ed.), *Body Image, eating disorders, and obesity: An integrative guide for assessment and treatment* (pp. 205–223). Washington, DC: American Psychological Association.

Williamson, D. A., Anderson, D. A., Jackman, L. P., & Jackson, S. R. (1995). Assessment of eating disordered thoughts, feelings, and behaviors. In D. B. Allison (Ed.), *Methods for the assessment of eating behaviors and weight related problems* (pp. 347–386). Newbury Park, CA: Sage.

Williamson, D. A., DeLany, J. P., Bentz, B. G., Bray, G. A., Champagne, C. M., & Harsha, D. W. (1997). Gender and racial differences in dieting and social pressures to gain weight among children. *Journal of Gender, Culture, and Health, 2*, 231–234.

Williamson, D. A., Prather, R. C., McKenzie, S. J., & Blouin, D. C. (1990). Behavioral assessment procedures can differentiate bulimia nervosa, compulsive overeater, obese, and normal subjects. *Behavioral Assessment, 12*, 239–252.

Wood, A., Waller, G., Miller, J., & Slade, P. (1992). The development of eating attitudes test scores in adolescence. *International Journal of Eating Disorders, 11*, 279–282.

IV

PREVENTION
AND TREATMENT

Prevention and treatment are clearly interrelated entities. One of the strongest arguments for prevention is that our health system will never be able to fully serve all persons suffering with eating and body image problems. Designing good prevention programs is, therefore, an important public health priority. Conversely, we are not likely to be able to prevent all cases of eating problems and obesity; hence the development of effective treatment also remains an important goal. The final section of this volume reviews the literature concerning the prevention and treatment of body image disturbances, eating problems, and obesity in children and adolescents.

Michael Levine and Linda Smolak offer a review of programs aimed at preventing body image and eating problems among children and adolescents. Their review suggests considerable promise among evaluated programs. There is increasing evidence that prevention can affect knowledge, attitudes, and behaviors. At this time, no program has proven to be optimally effective. However, there are elements of programs and information garnered from a decade of research that suggest paths for future program development and research evaluation.

Thomas Robinson and Joel Killen review extant literature on obesity prevention and also present their own ambitious prevention program. This program has the multiple components that seem essential to long-term success. Given the recent increases in obesity prevalence among children and adolescents, this will be a carefully watched project.

Stacy Gore, Jillon Vander Wal, and Mark Thelen review the therapies available for treating eating and body image problems among children and adolescents. In general, treatment programs that are tailored to the developmental needs of children and teenagers are yet to be developed. Nonetheless, there is reason to be optimistic about the potential for successful treatment. These authors offer suggestions for adapting extant therapies for application with youth that will facilitate future research and contemporary treatment options.

Myles Faith, Brian Saelens, Denise Wilfley, and David Allison consider treatment of obesity. The magnitude of the obesity problem among children and adolescents, particularly those from certain ethnic minority groups, has driven a substantial amount of research in this area. There does seem to be moderate success in treating obese children and adolescents, perhaps more so than in adults. As Faith and his colleagues note, children may be more amenable to intervention because their eating behaviors are not as ingrained as those of adults. This point underscores a similarity between prevention and treatment, because Levine and Smolak suggest that children may have less developed schema related to thinness and weight and hence may be more responsive to prevention programs (see also Smolak & Levine, 1994; Smolak, Levine, & Schermer, 1998).

Finally, David Sarwer discusses cosmetic and reconstructive surgery. Sarwer argues that there is a strong relationship between these surgeries and body image issues, though not necessarily body image pathology. As cosmetic surgeries continue to increase among adolescents, it is important for eating disorder specialists to understand the desire for such surgery as both a potential warning sign and as a possible treatment option. Sarwer's chapter provides an analysis that, for many of us, is an introduction to this complex and controversial field.

Given the relationship between prevention and treatment, it is not surprising to note that there are common themes across the chapters. First, there is truly a remarkable shortage of well-designed, controlled studies in all of these areas. Robinson and Killen are particularly thorough in outlining what is involved in careful evaluation of prevention and treatment programs. Second, more attention needs to be given to the developmental levels and ethnic membership of target groups. Third, there is a solid foundation to guide theory development and research in each of these areas. These chapters all underscore important pathways for future efforts.

REFERENCES

Smolak, L., & Levine, M. P. (1994). Toward an empirical basis for primary prevention of eating problems with elementary school children. *Eating Disorders: The Journal of Treatment and Prevention, 2,* 293–307.

Smolak, L., Levine, M. P., & Schermer, F. (1998). Lessons from lessons: An evaluation of an elementary school prevention program. In W. Vandereycken & G. Noordenbos (Eds.), *The prevention of eating disorders* (pp. 137–172). London: Athlone Press.

10

PRIMARY PREVENTION OF BODY IMAGE DISTURBANCES AND DISORDERED EATING IN CHILDHOOD AND EARLY ADOLESCENCE

MICHAEL P. LEVINE AND LINDA SMOLAK

The relatively limited research on prevention of body image problems and eating problems in groups of children, adolescents, and young adults has been the subject of a number of recent reviews (e.g., Austin, 2000; Franko & Orosan-Weine, 1998; Levine & Piran, in press; Piran, Levine, & Steiner-Adair, 1999; Shisslak, Crago, Estes, & Gray, 1996; Vandereycken & Noordenbos, 1998). As a consequence, we first attempt to clarify some important conceptual issues before providing a relatively brief, updated review of current theory and research. The chapter concludes with a consideration of theoretical, practical, and methodological issues that we feel need to be addressed to improve practice and research in prevention.

CONCEPTUAL ISSUES

Prevention

Prevention is derived from the Latin *"praevenire,"* meaning to come before, anticipate, or forestall. Prevention in this context transforms knowledge (theory, data, and conviction) into multidimensional social policies and practices designed to keep large or fairly large groups of children and adolescents from developing body image problems and eating problems in the first place (Albee & Gullotta, 1997).

What used to be known as "primary prevention" is now divided into two subcategories (Mrazek & Haggerty, 1994): (a) "Universal" prevention, sometimes known as "public health prevention," tries to change the population at large, for example, by changing laws that regulate advertising practices of the over-the-counter diet industry; and (b) "selective prevention" refers to programs that focus on *nonsymptomatic* people who are considered high risk because of, for example, low self-esteem or entry into an environment that is competitive, perfectionist, and focused on weight and shape, such as an elite ballet company (Piran, 1999). In terms of research methodology, the ideal demonstration of a "prevention effect" would be a longitudinal study in which the experimental group later developed both a meaningfully low rate of new cases of the index problems (a reduced incidence) and fewer new cases than people in the control condition. Moreover, in an ideal study researchers should be able to demonstrate that the individual and contextual risk factors for the experimental group remain low or have been reduced, and individual and contextual factors known to promote resilience are increased.

"Secondary prevention" (which included elements of selective prevention) is now called "targeted or indicated prevention" (Mrazek & Haggerty, 1994). This refers to efforts to prevent further development of full-blown problems in people who are already displaying either early (prodromal) signs of the disorder (e.g., experimentation with self-induced vomiting as a weight-management technique) or steps along the path to the disorder (e.g., negative body image + weight concerns + skipping lunch). The ideal research demonstration of a targeted prevention "effect" would be similar methodologically to that for universal and selected prevention, except that a salient, significant pretest-to-follow-up *reduction* in psychological and contextual risk factors, and prodromal symptoms for the experimental group would also be needed. These conceptual distinctions are important because classroom-based prevention programs for children and for adolescents have been designed as if universal prevention were the only issue, even though they then test for reductions in dieting, negative body image, and so forth (Smolak, 1999).

Rationale for Prevention

Efforts to prevent negative body image and disordered eating by focusing on the experiences of children and adolescents ages 8 through 14 draw their impetus from four facts. First, full-blown eating disorders are prevalent and debilitating; they are also very difficult to treat, even with multidisciplinary and expert intervention. Even if these were not disorders shrouded in anxiety, secrecy, and shame, there simply are not enough mental health professionals to meet this challenge. This means that prevention is the only reasonable approach to eating disorders as a health care problem. Second, as we have shown elsewhere (Smolak & Levine, 1996; Smolak Levine, & Schermer, 1998b; chapter 2, this volume), a fair number of elementary schoolchildren and many adolescents embrace cultural values about the glories of thinness and the horrors of fat in ways that leave them dissatisfied with their weight, shape, and self, and therefore inclined to engage in unhealthy forms of eating and weight management.

Third, the transition from late childhood to early adolescence is a period of high risk, especially for girls, for the development of body dissatisfaction and dysfunctional weight management practices that may intensify disordered eating (Smolak & Levine, 1996). This strongly suggests that prevention efforts need to concentrate on the cultural contexts for girls before age 13, including the ways in which boys and men are socialized to think about and behave toward the bodies, appetites, and gender roles of girls. Finally, there is substantial evidence that modifiable sociocultural factors, embodied in the mass media, families, schools, and peer interactions, help the normative continuum of negative body image and disordered eating among girls to flourish (Stice, 1994; Thompson, Heinberg, Altabe, & Tantleff-Dunn, 1999). These factors include sexual harassment and other forms of objectification and dehumanization; myths about body fat, obesity, and dieting; and failure to provide frequent and adequate models of female power, competency in multiple roles, and diversity in weight and shape (Levine & Smolak, 1998; Smolak, 1999; Smolak & Levine, 1996; Smolak & Murnen, 2001; chapter 2, this volume). Social changes that have led to, for example, increased female participation in athletics and reductions in the percentage of men who smoke cigarettes demonstrate the viability of massive sociocultural change.

Goals of Prevention

Although many programs fall under the general rubric of "eating disorders prevention," their specific goals are to prevent negative body image and eating problems.

Body Image

Body image is a complex synthesis of psychophysical elements that are perceptual, emotional, cognitive, and kinesthetic (Thompson et al., 1999). In the prevention literature this concept is approximated as "body dissatisfaction" and "negative body image." Technically, the goal of prevention is to help children and adolescents avoid (in the case of universal and selective programs) or eliminate (in the case of targeted programs) a collection of body-related perceptions (e.g., I see myself as being fat), feelings (e.g., I do not like my body because I am fat), and beliefs (e.g., it is very important for me to be thin) that motivate unhealthy behavior, unhealthy levels of anxiety and despair, and social withdrawal (Smolak et al., 1998b).

Eating Problems

The prevention of body image disturbances necessarily shades into the prevention of "eating problems." This is a broad term for the continuum of maladaptive, unhealthy beliefs, attitudes, weight-management practices, and eating habits that runs from "weight preoccupation" through subthreshold eating disorders to full-blown anorexia nervosa, bulimia nervosa, and eating disorders not otherwise specified (Shisslak, Crago, & Estes, 1995). This concept does not reject or ignore the role of potential discontinuities (e.g., personality disorder) in the development of full-blown, chronic eating disorders. Rather, it emphasizes the interconnections among, as well as the negative health and sociocultural implications of, various degrees and combinations of negative body image, intense shame and public self-consciousness about weight and shape, calorie-restrictive dieting, binge-eating, and excessive exercise to compensate for calories eaten.

PARADIGMS FOR PRIMARY PREVENTION

Levine and colleagues (e.g., Levine & Piran, 2001) have described three paradigms in the prevention of eating disorders (see also Piran, 1996). Before exploring their differences, which have significant implications for policies and practices, it is important to note that they share a number of features, such as (a) attention to the clash between the natural diversity of weights and shapes versus the narrow, pernicious cultural values about femininity, beauty, and restraint (Levine & Smolak, 1998); (b) awareness of the sociocultural and developmental rationale for prevention (see above); (c) the value of cultural "literacy" training to raise students' ability to understand, critique, and resist unhealthy messages from the mass media and other "sociocultural influences"; and (d) promotion of problem solving, decision making, assertion, communication, and other "life skills" that appear to strengthen resilience to negative affect, low self-esteem, social insecurity, and other potential contributors to negative body image and eating problems.

Disease-Specific Pathways Model

This model assumes that analysis of the *specific* pathway(s) leading to negative body image and then to eating problems will help eliminate or reduce the specific factors that constitute those pathways (see, e.g., Killen, 1996; Stewart, 1998; Stice, Mazotti, Weibel, & Agras, 2000). A prototypical example is the work of Killen, Taylor, and colleagues in researching and then trying to prevent or reduce "weight concerns" in middle school students (Killen, 1996; Killen et al., 1993). Killen and other proponents of disease-specific pathways (DSP) models use social learning or cognitive–behavioral mechanisms (e.g., self-monitoring, modeling, direct instruction, guided practice) to promote healthy exercise and weight management practices and to "inoculate" students against unhealthy weight and shape concerns and the intention to diet (e.g., Killen, 1996; Smolak et al., 1998b; Stewart, 1998). DSP programs are usually directed from the "top down" by teachers or experts (Piran, 1996).

Nonspecific Vulnerability-Stressor Model

Researchers in community mental health have demonstrated that there is a *nonspecific* relationship between mental disorders and life stress, lack of coping skills, and lack of social support (Albee & Gullotta, 1997; Bloom, 1996). This nonspecific vulnerability-stressor (NVS) model highlights the need to improve the life skills (and thus the resilience) of girls and boys. It also emphasizes the need for responsible adults, working in collaboration with the girls and boys themselves, to improve the contexts of children's lives (and especially girls' lives) in ways that reduce stress and that promote resilience and other forms of health. The NVS model advocates, for example, increasing social support for girls (e.g., mentoring by older women), creating more opportunities for success in ways unrelated to appearance, reducing weight-related teasing and other forms of sexual harassment, and transforming institutions such as schools and the mass media. Smolak and Levine's developmental model, which combines the disease-specific and NVS models, points to a particular need for multidimensional, integrated efforts to help young girls negotiate the normative and often simultaneous stressors they face in making the transition from late childhood to early adolescence (Smolak, 1999; Smolak & Levine, 1996; Smolak et al., 1998b). Prevention from a nonspecific community mental health perspective should help prevent the high levels of anxiety, depression, and substance use that often accompany and sustain serious eating problems (Smolak, 1999).

Empowerment-Relational Model

The Empowerment-Relational model, expressed most clearly in theoretical and empirical work by Piran (1996, 1999), positions girls as the ultimate authorities on their own bodies and attitudes. Therefore, as described in detail later, a major goal for prevention is the creation of opportunities for girls to articulate to each other, and to themselves, contextualized experiences of the body that are often silenced by social conditions that cast girls as natural targets of objectification or as individually responsible for victimization. This helps the girls to transform a strong sense of private insecurity, distress, and shame into a communal sense of injustice and thereby into plans for constructive action. These actions, in turn, often serve simultaneously to transform the contexts (e.g., alter unhealthy environments and build a positive sense of community) and to transform the girls themselves (e.g., enlarge their skills for establishing themselves in terms other than appearance or sexual objectification).

Occasionally, the prevention specialist applying the empowerment-relational model serves as a source of expert knowledge about body image, disordered eating, health, and activism. However, the model is "child- or adolescent-driven" (vs. top-down, expert-driven), so it emphasizes the adult woman's role as an advocate of "encouraging conditions" and systemic change, a facilitator of dialogue, a mentor, and a positive role model (see also Shisslak, Crago, Renger, & Clark-Wagner, 1998).

REVIEW OF THE LITERATURE

As of December 2000, we have obtained 42 published and unpublished studies of the prevention of negative body image or eating problems in elementary, middle, and high school students. These programs have been delivered en masse, and therefore without significant tailoring, to a mixture of individuals in general, nonsymptomatic individuals at risk, and individuals with eating problems. The difficulty of doing prevention research, coupled with the influence of the DSP model's assumption about the necessity to first clarify specific etiological factors, is seen in the fact that the earliest study was published in 1986 (Porter, Morrell, & Moriarty, 1986), and 67% of the studies were published in or after 1996.

Elementary School

There have been 10 studies of children ages 9 through 11. Two recent controlled studies of media literacy programs (Kusel, 1999; Neumark-Sztainer, Sherwood, Coller, & Hannan, 2000) are reviewed in a later section.

Richman (1993) evaluated the effectiveness of six 1- to 2-hour lessons that addressed social pressures to be thin, the nature of healthy and disordered eating, and the relationship between body size and self-esteem. Compared to a nonrandom control group attending a different school, 5th- and 6th-grade students (mean age = 10.4) receiving the curriculum learned more about the topics and had greater body satisfaction. They also had lowered scores on the ChEAT, but this effect was matched by an unanticipated improvement in the control group.

Huon, Roncolato, Ritchie, and Braganza (1997) also evaluated, in an uncontrolled, repeated measures design with six-month follow-up, six weekly lessons designed to help girls (median age = 10.75) understand how peers, media, and physical development influence their body image and dietary practices. The girls worked individually and in discussion groups. The complex patterns of findings is illuminating. There were no significant pre- to postprogram changes in nutritional knowledge, body liking, body dissatisfaction or drive for thinness. However, these stabilities in mean change scores masked tremendous variability; some children benefited and, very unfortunately perhaps, some deteriorated (e.g., their drive for thinness increased). Girls who initially had the most unhealthy attitudes toward eating tended to show the greatest improvement.

Kater, Rohwer, and Levine (2000) reported more positive outcomes in their uncontrolled, pre- to postevaluation of a more extensive, 10-lesson elementary school curriculum. One category of lessons helps children understand what they *cannot and should not try to control*: the developmental changes of puberty, the impact of genetics on size and shape, and the short- and long-term impact of calorie-restrictive dieting. A second category teaches children *what they can control*, namely development of a multifaceted identity, moderation and variety in nutrition and exercise, and selection of realistic, encouraging role models. The final category of lessons focuses on the development of resilience to unhealthy sociocultural messages about thinness and weight management, with a focus on critical thinking about media and about the history of cultural attitudes concerning body image. The participants in this preliminary study were 166 boys and girls ages 9 through 10 and 56 boys and girls ages 11 through 12. There were very positive pre- to postprogram changes in knowledge of curricular material, acceptance of diversity in shape and weight, positive body esteem, and rejection of the glorification of thinness. A controlled evaluation of this program with 390 boys and girls ages 9 through 11 has recently been completed and the results are equally promising (K. Kater, personal communication, September 28, 1999). Relative to controls who showed no changes, children receiving the curriculum reported many improvements in knowledge, body satisfaction, critical thinking about media, intentions to diet, and healthy choices related to nutrition and exercising.

Smolak and colleagues conducted a controlled, quasi-experimental longitudinal evaluation of a 10-lesson curriculum for 4th- and 5th-grade girls and boys (Smolak & Levine, in press; Smolak et al., 1998a, 1998b). Based on the DSP model, the focus was health promotion in the form of, for example, healthy eating and exercising, and tolerance of and appreciation for diversity in weight and shape, including avoidance of teasing. Parents of children in the curriculum condition received nine newsletters that paralleled the children's lessons, as well as a final newsletter pertaining to the nature and identification of eating problems.

This program produced some significant short-term gains in knowledge about nutrition, dieting effects, body fat, and fat people. However, with the exception of a positive change in the tendency of 5th graders to reduce their prejudicial assumptions about fat people, there were no significant pre- to postprogram effects with regard to attitudes and behaviors (Smolak et al., 1998a, 1998b). The two-year longitudinal follow-up compared experimental and control participants (now ages 11 through 13), along with a new control group consisting of young adolescents from schools not included in the original study (Smolak & Levine, in press). Compared to this new control group, experimental participants were more knowledgeable, had higher body esteem, and used fewer unhealthy weight management techniques. The scores of the original control group were intermediate, raising the possibility that the sociocultural impact of the original curriculum may have "spilled over" and influenced control participants within the same elementary schools (see McVey & Davis, 1998, for a similar phenomenon in regard to prevention with middle school students).

Coller, Neumark-Sztainer, Bulfer, and Engebretson (1999) recently conducted an uncontrolled evaluation of a very similar six-lesson program for 22 girls ages 10 through 12 and their parents. Although the girls were engaged by the program's emphasis on activity-based learning concerning body image, media, and healthy eating, the program produced minimal changes in eating attitudes and behaviors.

It is noteworthy that in Smolak et al.'s (1998b) research, body esteem improved over the course of the pre- to postprogram assessment for all conditions except the 4th-grade girls who participated in the program. This troubling finding recalls the work of Huon et al. (1997) in suggesting that program content may have, for at least a significant minority of the girls, intensified or created negative feelings about their bodies.

Middle School

There have been 17 studies of prevention with adolescents in grades 6 to 8—ages 11 to 14. Two (Piran, 1999; C. Steiner-Adair & L. Shostrom, personal communication, February 8, 2000) are reviewed later in our consideration of the feminist-systemic perspective. With the exception of Porter et al.'s (1986) fairly successful pilot study of a one-day program for children attending a summer camp, the remaining 14 studies are evaluations of classroom curricula. This section concentrates on a sample of controlled evaluations with at least three-month follow-up evaluations.

Killen et al. (1993; Killen, 1996) were the first to publish a controlled, long-term evaluation of a well-designed program that is clearly grounded in both the DSP model and extensive experience in prevention research and health promotion using social learning theory. The 18 lessons addressed many important topics via a variety of instructional techniques for improving and reinforcing knowledge, efficacy expectations, cultural literacy and resistance skills, and healthy behaviors. The program produced only modest increases in knowledge and no short- or long-term changes in attitudes or behaviors, but its developers feel that lack of statistical power obscured a positive impact of the program on students with high levels of weight concerns (Killen, 1996; C. Barr Taylor, personal communication, December 15, 1998).

Another controlled evaluation of an intensive cognitive social learning program for adolescents ages 13 through 14 also produced disappointing but intriguing results (Stewart, Carter, Drinkwater, Hainsworth, & Fairburn, in press; see also Stewart, 1998). Six 45-minute lessons addressed sociocultural pressures to be thin, dieting and body weight regulation, the nature and signs of disordered eating, and aspects of the NVS model such as coping with stress, low self-esteem, and developmental tasks of adolescence. This program enhanced the knowledge of the experimental group, and this effect was maintained at six-month follow-up. For the experimental group, but not the control group, there were small but significant pre- to postprogram decreases in dietary restraint, shape concerns, eating concerns, and EDE-Q and EAT scores. However, at the six-month follow-up scores on all these variables reverted to baseline. This pattern of results is very similar to that reported by Richman (1997) in a more intensive, longitudinal evaluation of the six-unit prevention program described earlier (Richman, 1993).

O'Dea and Abraham (2000) evaluated a nine-lesson program titled *Everybody's Different*. Eschewing the information giving by authoritative adults that is associated with the top-down DSP model, this curriculum offers group-oriented, cooperative, "student-centered learning" activities to help young adolescent boys and girls to foster a positive body image and self-esteem, to promote life skills, and to engage positive feedback from significant others. Hence the NVS model, and to some extent the participatory aspects of the empowerment-relational model, are prominent in O'Dea and Abraham's (2000) work (see also O'Dea & Maloney, 2000). At posttest and relative to the control group, body satisfaction increased and weight loss efforts decreased for participants in the program. Moreover, the program was successful in the short- and long-term in decreasing concerns about physical appearance and social acceptance. However, there were no significant changes in EDI-Drive for Thinness, and the relative improvement in body satisfaction dissipated at 12-month follow-up. More troubling, there was a significant pre- to follow-up increase of 9% in the number of girls in the intervention group trying to lose weight, whereas the comparable figure for the control group was 6% (a nonsignificant increase).

Implications

Several prominent reviewers (e.g., O'Dea & Abraham, 2000; Stewart, 1998; Stice et al., 2000) have concluded that universal prevention programs (as opposed to targeted programs) based on the DSP model are thoroughly ineffective in producing positive effects other than modest, transient, and perhaps even dangerous increases in knowledge. This is likely an oversimplification of a very complex state of affairs in a field that is hamstrung by the absence of a critical mass of well-designed studies (Franko & Orosan-Weine, 1998; Levine & Piran, 2001). We have identified 42 published and unpublished studies of prevention programs that (a) worked with children and adolescents ages 8 to 18; (b) were not designed for participants who already had significant body image and eating problems; and (c) assessed short-term attitudinal or behavioral change. Of those studies, 27 (64.3%) reported at least one significant positive change in one of those categories. Studies with elementary and middle schoolchildren indicate that curricular programs emphasizing various combinations of the DSP and NSVS components can have a positive *short-term* effect on knowledge, body esteem, self-acceptance, and eating behaviors. However, it is apparent that achievement of long-term positive effects remains an elusive goal, and most likely will require both booster sessions with the students and more attention to changing the behavior of adults, peers, and the various contexts that shape the students' lives (Levine & Piran, 2001; Neumark-Sztainer, 1996; Smolak & Levine, 1996).

It is also important to note that several researchers have used the DSP model to produce encouraging longer term (6 to 12 months) prevention effects in the eating attitudes and behaviors of high school students in Israel (Neumark-Sztainer, Butler, & Palti, 1995) and Italy (Santonastaso et al., 1999). Clearly, further research is needed to evaluate programs that are carefully designed, intensive, and long-term (Franko & Orosan-Weine, 1998).

MAJOR AREAS FOR FURTHER DEVELOPMENT

In this section we present some key issues that need to be elaborated in programs to prevent eating problems in middle and elementary school children.

Incorporating a Developmental Perspective

Smolak is a leading advocate for inclusion of a developmental perspective in the design and evaluation of prevention programs for people of any age, and especially for children and adolescents ages 6 to 13 (Smolak, 1999; Smolak & Levine, 1994, 1996; Smolak et al., 1998b; see also Shisslak et al., 1996; chapter 2, this volume). Table 10-1 presents a summary of the basic assumptions and principles of this perspective.

Developmental specificity in programming is a particularly important principle for prevention work aimed at elementary school children, their parents, and their teachers. Tailoring lessons to the developmental level of younger children is much more than "making lessons fun" or "translating adolescent lessons, but not using words or text that are too complicated." Certain topics (e.g., purging) might well be avoided entirely because the egocentrism of children (and, possibly, young adolescents) leads them to acquire knowledge about unhealthy behaviors without any concern that short- or long-term harm could befall them personally. Conversely, other topics that are quite consonant with the concrete cognitive operations of children ages 7 through 10 might be emphasized to the point of overlearning. Examples include fat deposition as a fact of healthy pubertal development; nutritional needs of older children and young adolescents who want to be strong in sports and to just have fun playing; the development of competencies, rather than relying on physical attractiveness as the prime measure of self-worth; the unfairness of prejudice on the basis of weight, shape, ethnicity, and gender (Shisslak et al., 1998; Smolak, 1999; Smolak et al., 1998b).

Studies of the development of social cognition and of the self suggest that social comparison is a limited process in middle childhood and that

TABLE 10-1
Basic Principles and Assumptions of a Developmental Approach
to Prevention

- Transactions between personal vulnerabilities and psychosocial stressors shape risk for eating problems
- Periods of transition (e.g., from childhood to adolescence) constitute periods of high risk and periods for the reorganization of people and systems in the direction of resilience
- Parents are important sources of negative influences (risk) and positive influence (resilience) throughout childhood and adolescence, whereas peers become increasingly important in late childhood and adolescence
- Understanding and changing the multisystemic ecology of children and adolescents is a critical element of preventing eating problems
- Etiology and prevention of eating problems needs to be placed in the context of the relationship between gender socialization, ethnicity, and risk for (or resilience to) anxiety, depression, and other emotional issues
- Childhood is particularly important for prevention efforts because the "thinness schema," prejudice toward fat and fat people, and social comparison processes have not been consolidated
- Developmental psychologists can help prevention specialists develop classroom lessons and other educational experiences that are tailored to the cognitive level and interests of the target populations

components of the self are less well organized and more strongly connected to situations (Ewell, Smith, Karmel, & Hart, 1996; Smolak, 1999). This implies that teachers and parents might more easily affect elementary school students' (versus adolescents') acceptance of the natural diversity of weights and shapes while discouraging comparison to manufactured images of slenderness in the mass media. In the same vein, teachers, parents, and other adult mentors of elementary school children should provide, particularly to the girls, multiple and highly salient opportunities to see that (a) children can establish interests and friendships in many ways that have nothing to do with weight or shape and (b) men and women with a variety of body shapes have interesting, happy, and meaningful lives. Thus the child's lower level of organization in self-concept and higher degree of situational flexibility in self-perception provide an opportunity to develop the self, relationships, and other interests in ways that counteract the powerful "thinness schema" present in so many adolescent girls and a minority of adolescent boys (Smolak, 1999; Smolak & Levine, 1996; Smolak et al., 1998b).

Research has also shown that, compared to adolescents, children tend to have a greater sense of perceived control over their personal characteristics and actions—in other words, they are less likely to attribute influence to social contexts (Ewell et al., 1996). This means they are more likely to be assertive and self-confident in pursuing their own interests and in standing up for what they believe in. Assertion of this sort, as a component of developing one's own "attitude," should be encouraged for girls as part of a healthy feminine gender role. This form of resilience is, in general, more common in African American females (Nichter, Vackovic, & Parker, 1999), which may be one reason that this group has lower rates of anorexia nervosa and bulimia nervosa (Striegel-Moore & Smolak, 1996).

An Ecological–Empowerment Perspective

The rationale for prevention reviewed earlier, coupled with the emphases of all three major prevention models, points directly to the importance of constructing multiple, interlocking contexts and systems that reduce risk factors and increase resilience (Levine & Piran, 2001; Neumark-Sztainer, 1996; O'Dea & Maloney, 2000; Piran, 1996, 1999; Smolak & Levine, 1996; Smolak et al., 1998b). That is, there is a need to blend education and skill-building for individual students with careful attention to the attitudes and behaviors of influential adults and with an insistence on "institutional" practices, policies, and traditions that respect and empower girls and women. The Empowerment–Relational model advocates the developmental importance of engaging the children and adolescents themselves in the active process of analyzing, identifying, and transforming their own environments (O'Dea & Maloney, 2000; Piran, 1999).

Piran (1999) has evaluated 10+ years of her efforts to apply her Empowerment–Relational model (described previously) to selective and targeted prevention within a very high risk setting: an elite, residential ballet company. Topics emerging from discussion and clarification of the "lived experience" of the girls included sexual harassment, lack of privacy, sexism, racism, and various forms of disrespect that some adults and some students showed toward the developing female body and its diversity. Piran served as a consultant to the school and was thus well-positioned to help students to demand, create, and support healthy changes in the school policies, norms— and, in a few instances, staff.

Piran's (1999) uncontrolled study used a cross-sectional design with three different waves of students at three different time periods (1987, 1991, and 1996). Nevertheless, two of the key findings are impressive, especially because the ballet company has become even more successful in placing its students in professional dance companies. First, over the past 10 years the prevalence of eating disorders among the girls ages 10 through 18 has dropped from around 10% to just one case of anorexia nervosa and no cases of bulimia nervosa. Second, there have been significant reductions in the percentage of students who binged, vomited, used laxatives, and relied on other unhealthy forms of weight management.

The Empowerment–Relational perspective, as facilitated by advocate–mentors, is a very promising development for prevention of eating disorders. The Full of Ourselves program, developed recently by the Harvard Eating Disorder Center (www.hedc.org), consists of eight units designed to help girls ages 13 through 14 become more assertive and more supportive of each other as they learn about weightism, media literacy, activism, leadership, and the politics of body image. The girls are given the opportunity to work closely with trained adult mentors and to serve as mentors themselves for younger girls. A preliminary controlled evaluation of girls in 24 different groups ($N = 453$) revealed that the program resulted in greater knowledge, self-esteem, body esteem, and public resistance to teasing (C. Steiner-Adair & L. Shostrom, personal communication, February 8, 2000).

We also see a place for ecological approaches that are directed from the "top down" by mental health professionals. Latzer and Shatz (1999) have recently described how psychological and nursing professionals working in an Israeli kibbutz implemented a multidimensional, integrated combination of education for adolescents and their families, training for professionals, and provision of skilled counseling, treatment, and support services. This well-orchestrated plan brought together programs with a wide scope (e.g., raising the community's awareness of how sociocultural factors contribute to many challenges faced by adolescent girls), a moderate scope (e.g., helping families with teenage girls understand the impact of the pubertal transition on body image), and a narrow focus (e.g., the necessity of helping girls evincing the warning signs of disordered eating). Latzer and Shatz are still evaluating the project, but preliminary evidence indicates an increase in public awareness about the nature and causes of eating disorders, an increase in early identification of disordered eating (targeted prevention), and a possible reduction in the incidence of serious eating disorders.

We recently served as volunteer consultants to the Office of Women's Health's (U.S. Public Health Service) BodyWise program, which is designed to motivate, educate, and support middle-school teachers who want to help prevent eating problems; www.health.org/gpower/ adultswhocare2/resources/ Pubs/bodywise.htm). Rather than promoting development of new curricula targeting the knowledge, attitudes, and skills of middle school *students,* we drew on the work of Piran (1996, 1999) and Neumark-Sztainer (1996) to argue strongly that this program should focus on what those *teachers* can do, as personal agents of influence inside and outside the classroom, to promote all three forms of prevention, especially the universal (see also Toledo & Neumark-Sztainer, 1999). Moreover, we strongly believe that any guidance provided to teachers needs to have a constructive effect on males (teachers, administrators, and students), as well as females. The prevention of negative body image and eating problems is not "just a women's issue." Research reviewed by Thompson et al. (1999) clearly shows that the behavior of men (e.g., as fathers and coaches) and boys plays a very significant role in the culture(s) and events that shape and all too often undermine the body image of girls and women.

Teachers and other concerned adults need to be educated about the sociocultural perspective, including the role of media, school personnel, parents, and male and female peers in the modeling and direct promotion of risk factors such as harassment, teasing, criticism, and sexism. As reflected in the success of books such as *Reviving Ophelia* (Pipher, 1994), many adults are already concerned about girls as they make the transition from late childhood to early adolescence. We believe experts can enlist teachers and support them in the process of examining the ways in which their own attitudes and behaviors, their classrooms, their halls, their school policies, and their school "culture" may be inadvertently nurturing body image problems and disordered eating (see Piran, 1999). Rather than constructing more curricula with a disease-specific focus, teachers need to be encouraged to work together and with other influential staff (e.g., school nurse, coaches, principals) to identify and eliminate, via policy and via practice, the following: fat jokes; weight-loss contests and public weigh-ins; sexist posters; sexual harassment in the halls; the absence of women in power from the administration, from textbooks, and from motivational posters on the walls; and selection of only tall, thin girls as cheerleaders or class secretary.

We are convinced that the universal, selective, and targeted prevention of eating problems in children and adolescents requires adults to collaborate to create safe and respectful environments for girls and boys. Taking the personal, professional, and political steps to do so will require courage and commitment on the part of women *and* men, which should help create, and expose children to, new models of gender for everyone, as well as enhanced respect for women (Piran, 1996, 1999; Shisslak et al., 1998).

Literacy, Critique, and Activism

One major goal of the Empowerment–Relational model, and to some extent the NVS model, is to transform the body from being an isolated repository of shame and doubt to a site of action, power, individual expression, *and* connection to self, peers, adults, and the larger community. A very promising vehicle for this developmental process is the set of experiences known as "media literacy" (Berel & Irving, 1998; Levine, Piran, & Stoddard, 1999; Steiner-Adair & Vorenberg, 1999).

When used in the context of prevention and health promotion, media literacy refers to an expanding cycle of the "Five A's" (Thoman, 1998). Participants in a class or other group are first helped to raise their *awareness* of the presence of mass media in their lives. The facilitator and participants then begin to *analyze* the artistic and persuasive content of media, the ways in which media are constructed, and the personal, social, and economic impact of media messages and media use. This leads to a desire for action, that is, to *activism*, often in the form of public protest that the glorification of slenderness, the denigration of fat people, the objectification of passive women, and other pernicious features of mass media are unfair and unhealthy.

Such efforts at personal and collective expression tend to be accompanied by a sense that there are important alternative messages and positions that need to be expressed in the media. This leads to questions about how people with a personal–social cause can use the media as a form of *advocacy*. Further questions arise: Who has and controls *access* to mass media, and how do ordinary citizens, including children in elementary and middle school, "get on TV" or "get in the newspaper"? The answers produce more knowledge and more action, thus extending the cycle of awareness, analysis, and activism in regard to the transformation of this "sociocultural factor" (Levine et al., 1999).

Some very recent evidence suggests that media literacy is a promising way to engage children and adolescents in learning about the relationship between sociocultural factors and body image; increasing "life skills" for critical thinking, decision making, and clear speaking and writing; and fostering a sense of empowerment, as a group and as individuals, to speak out against what is perceived and felt as unfair, such as prejudice against fat people or discrimination against girls and women (see also Berel & Irving, 1998; Irving, DuPen, & Berel, 1998). Kusel (1999) evaluated a brief media literacy program for 4th through 6th graders (mean age = 10.8). The program, which used videos and discussion to dissect deceptive media techniques and to critically evaluate appearance-related messages, produced significant pre- to posttest improvements in eating attitudes and behaviors, body image, self-esteem, and internalization of the slender ideal. Pre- to three-month follow-up changes were not reported, but posttest to follow-up changes indicated that program participants continued to question the media, to be aware of body stereotypes, and to have lower body image distortion.

Two other controlled studies also provide support for the role of media literacy in a more comprehensive education and ecological approach to prevention. Neumark-Sztainer et al. (2000) evaluated the effects of six 90-minute lessons, including an emphasis on activism and advocacy, on 5th- and 6th-grade girls (mean age = 10.6) participating in 12 Girl Scout troops. There were positive effects, evident at three-month follow-up, on internalization of the slender ideal, belief in ability to affect weight-related social norms, and likelihood of reading *Seventeen*, a magazine that glorifies slenderness and concentrates on female identity in terms of clothes, make-up, and boys (Peirce, 1990).There was no effect on dieting behaviors, and the modest posttest improvement in body size acceptance was not maintained at follow-up. Piran, Levine, Irving, and EDAP (2000) found similar results in a quasi-experimental evaluation of the effects of the GO GIRLS!™ media literacy program for girls ages 14 to 18 (Eating Disorders Awareness & Prevention, Inc; www.edap.org).

Race, Gender, and Class

It is common for those interested in prevention to call for greater attention to the ethnic diversity of the audience. Yet with few exceptions (e.g., Nichter et al., 1999) this remains a goal rather than a reality. Further-more, authors are rarely specific about implementing cultural "sensitivity."

Ethnic group membership is related to the development of eating attitudes, problems, and disorders, but ethnic groups are not interchangeable in terms of their cultural risks for eating problems (Smolak & Striegel-Moore, 2001). Body dissatisfaction is somewhat less of a problem among African American girls than Caucasian girls, but Hispanic and Asian American girls may not enjoy such protection (Robinson et al., 1996). On the other hand, obesity, and perhaps binge-eating disorder, are more of an issue in the Black community than in the White.

Thus cultural sensitivity requires awareness of the different ethnic groups being served. This poses a problem because there are few available data concerning risk and protective factors for the development of eating problems within various ethnic groups. If one applies the DSP model to prevention of negative body image and eating problems, then empirical and theoretical guidance is available only for White girls. There are some data indicating that relationships among components of eating problems are similar for girls of various ethnic backgrounds (French et al., 1997), but there is little justification for assuming that models developed with White girls will generalize. For example, ethnic identity development may be an issue among girls from ethnic minority groups, and the ability of African American children to detach self-esteem from racist societal attitudes (Crocker, Luhtanen, Blaine, & Broadnax, 1994) may alter the meaning of weight- and shape- related teasing in this group.

Substantially more research is needed, but some preliminary recommendations for the development of ethnically sensitive programs are warranted. First, use a multiethnic team to model and otherwise teach respect for diversity in ethnicity as well as in weight and shape. Second, create materials and activities that are multiethnic. For example, if advertisements or television images are used as part of a media literacy program, an effort should be made to include pictures of girls and women from all ethnic groups. If this is impossible (because of the predominance of White women in the media), then (under)representation of ethnic minorities in the media should be a specific topic of discussion.

Third, given that many prevention programs include a nutrition education component, it is important to acknowledge ethnic and social class differences in food preferences, eating patterns, and social contexts for meals (Nichter et al., 1999). Including foods from the ethnic groups involved may make the program more appealing and educational to a variety of girls. The same may be true of exercise opportunities and interests. Fourth, there needs to be a sensitivity to the eating problems and attitudes represented in the various ethnic groups. African American girls, for example, may not want to discuss the slender ideal as much as White girls do, unless the African American girls are permitted, and even encouraged, to discuss why they do not subscribe to the ideal (Nichter et al., 1999). Discussions of obesity and its associated health risks, as well as its sociocultural meaning, may seem more pressing to African American, Native American, and Latina girls (Striegel-Moore & Smolak, 1996).

Finally, in recent years prevention specialists have devoted more attention to empowering girls and women to resist sexual harassment, negative images of women, and restricted roles as a component of femininity (e.g., Piran, 1996, 1999; Smolak, 1999). Like sexism, racism limits girls' opportunities to be something other than a body or a subservient role. Racism may also increase girls' risk of sexual harassment and sexual violence. Racism in the form of "model minority" expectations may create difficulties in terms of perfectionism for Asian Americans. Just as there is a discussion of sexism and girls' roles, there needs to be a recognition of racism and support for helping individual girls negotiate the difficulties created by it. As with sexism, there also needs to be substantial institutional responsivity to racial problems and a willingness to support institutional change. Positive adaptations of ethnic minority groups need to be recognized. The attitude and skill with which minority girls and women learn to face and transcend discrimination may well have a positive effect on the documented tendency of many girls to become silent and passive as they make the transition from childhood to adolescence (Nichter et al., 1999). Thus empowerment and resistance in the face of racism also need to be a component of prevention programs for minority and majority girls alike.

Universal Versus Targeted Prevention

A number of researchers have commented on the failure of many curricular- and school-based prevention programs to distinguish between universal and targeted prevention (e.g., Killen, 1996; Smolak et al., 1998b). Mann and colleagues (1997), in a controversial but nevertheless important article, have argued that programs that target high risk and subclinical populations may actually have an unhealthy, iatrogenic effect on girls and young women who are not in those categories. An increasing number of programs have been successful in using a variety of techniques to facilitate prevention (or potentially preventive changes) in adolescents and college students who are at high risk for disordered eating because of strong weight and shape concerns, high levels of body dissatisfaction, or subthreshold eating problems. Examples include Piran's (1999) Empowerment–Relational program and Killen et al.'s (1993; Killen, 1996) social learning program for middle school students. Future research is needed to develop models and strategies for prevention that enable tailoring of individual or small-group programs on the basis of risk or clinical status without somehow stigmatizing those children or adolescents. Perhaps CD-ROM technology or the Internet (see, e.g., Winzelberg et al., 1998) will facilitate this type of ethical tailoring in balance with both a "universal" emphasis on developmental education and multisystemic, ecological support for decreasing risk and increasing resilience.

IMPLICATIONS FOR PREVENTION

A review of the prevention literature reveals the highly variable, often questionable methodology of the studies, many of which are "pilot" projects.

TABLE 10-2
Basic Ingredients of an Ideal Prevention Outcome Study

- Specification of goal as universal prevention and/or behavior change in children or adolescents already showing prodromal problems
- Clear translation of a theoretical model for prevention into specific program components
- Unbiased assignment of samples to experimental and comparison conditions, plus assessment of cross-fertilization of programmatic ideas to the comparison group
- Valid measurement, using quantitative and qualitative data, of outcome variables pertaining to risk (e.g., belief in the importance of thinness), resilience (e.g., definition of self in terms of multiple interests and competencies unrelated to weight and shape), and the continuum of eating problems
- Specification of program ingredients, how program staff were trained and supported in implementing them, and to what extent (e.g., in terms of attendance and completion of assignments) children participated in the program
- Assessment of outcome variables and potential influences (e.g., BMI, gender, ethnicity, depression) before the program (e.g., at age 10), immediately following the program (e.g., three months later), and during at least one follow-up wave that coincides with the period of risk (e.g., middle adolescence)
- Assessment of changes in the ecology of the children's and adult's lives (e.g., in the school system)
- Data analyses that are sensitive to the possibility that some children in the experimental group may be negatively affected by the prevention program as well as to effect sizes

Table 10-2 presents an idealized checklist of the essential ingredients that would enable researchers to draw conclusions about the nature and effects of programs designed to reduce the number of new cases of the continuum of body image and eating problems (see chapter 11, this volume).

Only a couple of projects completed (e.g., Killen et al., 1993; Neumark-Sztainer et al., 1995; Stewart et al., in press) have come close to fulfilling these extensive (and expensive) criteria. Nevertheless, attention to these rigorous details is necessary if we are ever to demonstrate "prevention effects." This type of careful research is also necessary to make good decisions about how scarce human and financial resources are to be allocated across universal, selective, and targeted prevention.

CONCLUSION

Treatment will not substantially reduce the prevalence of disordered eating, because it is clear that treatment is very difficult and that many sufferers do not seek help because they are secretive, ashamed, and depressed. Moreover, there is overwhelming evidence that sociocultural factors contribute to eating disorders and related conditions such as depression (Thompson et al., 1999). These are only two of the many reasons a number of theorists have come to acknowledge that prevention is not a professional luxury awaiting the ascension of a particularly compelling DSP model. With that said, there is no escaping the fact that the prevention of body dissatisfaction and eating problems is a very complex challenge (Carter, Stewart, Dunn, & Fairburn, 1997). This should not produce despair or cynicism about prevention. All it means is that mental health professionals, dedicated researchers, activists, parents, and a variety of professionals (e.g., school administrators, athletic directors, and teachers) must work together to extend, integrate, apply, and carefully evaluate all the three major models of prevention. Social learning theory continues to offer many useful tools for education and behavioral change, but it needs to be informed and transformed by a feminist developmental perspective, by an ecological sensibility, and by the willingness of adults to change in the ways we are asking youth to change.

REFERENCES

Albee, G. W., & Gullotta, T. P. (1997). Primary prevention's evolution. In G. W. Albee & T. P. Gullotta (Eds.), *Primary prevention works* (pp. 3–22). Thousand Oaks, CA: Sage.

Austin, S. B. (2000). Prevention research in eating disorders: Theory and new directions. *Psychological Medicine, 30,* 1249–1260.

Berel, S., & Irving, L. (1998). Media and disturbed eating: An analysis of media influence and implications for prevention. *Journal of Primary Prevention, 18,* 415–430.

Bloom, M. (1996). *Primary prevention practices.* Thousand Oaks CA: Sage.

Carter, J., Stewart, D., Dunn, V., & Fairburn, C. (1997). Primary prevention of eating disorders: Might it do more harm than good? *International Journal of Eating Disorders, 22,* 167–173.

Coller, T. G., Neumark-Sztainer, D., Bulfer, J., & Engebretson, J. (1999). Taste of Food, Fun, and Fitness: A community-based program that teaches young girls to feel better about their bodies. *Journal of Nutrition Education, 31,* 283E.

Crocker, J., Luhtanen, R., Blaine, B., & Broadnax, S. (1994). Collective self-esteem and psychological well-being among white, black, and Asian college students. *Personality and Social Psychology Bulletin, 20,* 503–513.

Ewell, F., Smith, S., Karmel, M. P., & Hart, D. (1996). The sense of self and its development: A framework for understanding eating disorders. In L. Smolak, M. P. Levine, & R. Striegel-Moore (Eds.), *The developmental psychopathology of eating disorders: Implications for research, prevention, and treatment* (pp. 107–133). Mahwah, NJ: Erlbaum.

Franko, D. L., & Orosan-Weine, P. (1998). The prevention of eating disorders: Empirical, methodological and conceptual considerations. *Clinical Psychology: Science and Practice, 5,* 459–477.

French, S. A., Story, M., Neumark-Sztainer, D., Downes, B., Resnick, M., & Blum, R. (1997). Ethnic differences in psychosocial and health behavior correlates of dieting, purging, and binge eating in a population-based sample of adolescent females. *International Journal of Eating Disorders, 22*, 315–322.

Huon, G. F., Roncolato, W. G., Ritchie, J. E., & Braganza, C. (1997). Prevention of diet-induced disorders: Findings and implications of a pilot study. *Eating Disorders: The Journal of Treatment & Prevention, 5*, 280–293.

Irving, L., DuPen, J., & Berel, S. (1998). A media literacy program for high school females. *Eating Disorders: The Journal of Treatment & Prevention, 6*, 119–131.

Kater, K. J., Rohwer, J., & Levine, M. P. (2000). An elementary school project for developing healthy body image and reducing risk factors for unhealthy and disordered eating. *Eating Disorders: The Journal of Treatment & Prevention, 8*, 3–16.

Killen, J. D. (1996). Development and evaluation of a school-based eating disorder symptoms prevention program. In L. Smolak, M. P. Levine, & R. Striegel-Moore (Eds.), *The developmental psychopathology of eating disorders: Implications for research, prevention, and treatment* (pp. 313–339). Mahwah, NJ: Erlbaum.

Killen, J. D., Taylor, C. B., Hammer, L., Litt, I., Wilson, D. M., Rich, T., Simmonds, B., Kraemer, H., & Varady, A. (1993). An attempt to modify unhealthful eating attitudes and weight regulation practices of young adolescent girls. *International Journal of Eating Disorders, 13*, 369–384.

Kusel, A. (1999). *Primary prevention of eating disorders through media literacy training of girls.* Unpublished doctoral dissertation, California School of Professional Psychology, San Diego.

Latzer, Y., & Shatz, S. (1999). Comprehensive community prevention of disturbed attitudes to weight control: A three-level intervention program. *Eating Disorders: The Journal of Treatment & Prevention, 7*, 3–31.

Levine, M. P., & Piran, N. (2001). The prevention of eating disorders: Towards a participatory ecology of knowledge, action, and advocacy. In R. Striegel-Moore & L. Smolak (Eds.), *Eating disorders: Innovative directions for research and practice* (pp. 233–253). Washington, DC: American Psychological Association.

Levine, M. P., Piran, N., & Stoddard, C. (1999). Mission more probable: Media literacy, activism, and advocacy as primary prevention. In N. Piran, M. P. Levine, & C. Steiner-Adair (Eds.), *Preventing eating disorders: A handbook of interventions and special challenges* (pp. 3–25). Philadelphia: Brunner/Mazel.

Levine, M. P., & Smolak, L. (1998). The mass media and disordered eating: Implications for primary prevention. In W. Vandereycken & G. Noordenbos (Eds.), *The prevention of eating disorders* (pp. 23–56). London: Athlone.

Mann, T., Nolen-Hoeksema, S., Huang, K., Burgard, D., Wright, A., & Hanson, K. (1997). Are two interventions worse than none? Joint primary and secondary prevention of eating disorders in college females. *Health Psychology, 16*, 215–225.

McVey, G., & Davis, R. (1998). *A long-term controlled evaluation of an elementary school prevention program for eating problems.* Unpublished manuscript, Department of Psychology, Hospital for Sick Children, Toronto.

Mrazek, P. J., & Haggerty, R. J. (Eds.). (1994). *Reducing risks for mental disorders: Frontiers for preventive intervention research.* Washington, DC: National Academy Press.

Neumark-Sztainer, D. (1996). School-based programs for preventing eating disturbances. *Journal of School Health, 66,* 64–71.

Neumark-Sztainer, D., Butler, R., & Palti, H. (1995). Eating disturbances among adolescent girls: Evaluation of a school-based primary prevention program. *Journal of Nutrition Education, 27,* 24–30.

Neumark-Sztainer, D., Sherwood, N., Coller, T., & Hannan, P. J. (2000). Promoting media literacy and advocacy skills: A community-based intervention to enhance body acceptance and prevent unhealthy weight control behaviors among pre-adolescent girls. *Journal of the American Dietetic Association, 100,* 1466–1473.

Nichter, M., Vuckovic, N., & Parker, S. (1999). The Looking Good, Feeling Good program: A multiethnic intervention for healthy body image, nutrition, and physical activity. In N. Piran, M. P. Levine, & C. Steiner-Adair (Eds.), *Preventing eating disorders: A handbook of interventions and special challenges* (pp. 175–193). Philadelphia: Brunner/Mazel.

O'Dea, J., & Abraham, S. (2000). Improving the body image, eating attitudes and behaviors of young and behaviors of young male and female adolescents: A new educational approach which focuses on self esteem. *International Journal of Eating Disorders, 28,* 43–57.

O'Dea, J., & Maloney, D. (2000). Preventing eating and body image problems in children and adolescents using the health promoting schools framework. *Journal of School Health, 70,* 18–21.

Peirce, K. (1990). A feminist theoretical perspective on the socialization of teenage girls through Seventeen magazine. *Sex Roles, 23,* 491–500.

Pipher, M. (1994). *Reviving Ophelia: Saving the selves of adolescent girls.* New York: Ballatine Books.

Piran, N. (1996). The reduction of preoccupation with body weight and shape in schools: A feminist approach. *Eating Disorders: The Journal of Treatment & Prevention, 4,* 323–330.

Piran, N. (1999). Eating disorders: A trial of prevention in a high risk school setting. *Journal of Primary Prevention, 20,* 75–90.

Piran, N., Levine, M. P., Irving, L., & EDAP (2000, May). GO GIRLS™! Preventing negative body image through media literacy. Paper/workshop presented at the Summit 2000 (Children, Youth, and the Media Beyond the Millennium) conference, Toronto.

Piran, N., Levine, M. P. & Steiner-Adair, C. (Eds.). (1999). *Preventing eating disorders: A handbook of interventions and special challenges.* Philadelphia: Brunner/Mazel.

Porter, J., Morrell, T., & Moriarty, D. (1986). Primary prevention of anorexia nervosa: Evaluation of a pilot project for early and pre-adolescents. *The Canadian Association for Health, Physical Education, and Recreation Journal, 52*, 21–26.

Richman, R. D. (1993). *Primary prevention of eating disorders: A pilot program.* Unpublished master's thesis, Simon Fraser University, British Columbia, Canada.

Richman, R. D. (1997). *Preventing eating disorders; promoting healthy attitudes and behaviors: A school-based program.* Unpublished doctoral dissertation, Simon Fraser University, British Columbia, Canada.

Robinson, T., Killen, J., Litt, R., Hammer, L., Wilson, D., Hayden, K., Hayward, C., & Taylor, C. B. (1996). Ethnicity and body dissatisfaction: Are Hispanic and Asian girls at increased risk? *Journal of Adolescent Health, 19*, 384–393.

Santonastaso, P., Zanetti, T., Ferrara, S., Olivetto, M. C., Magnavita, N., & Favaro, A. (1999). A preventive intervention program in adolescent schoolgirls: A longitudinal study. *Psychotherapy and Psychosomatics, 68*, 46–50.

Shisslak, C. M., Crago, M., & Estes, L. (1995). The spectrum of eating disturbances. *International Journal of Eating Disorders, 18*, 209–219.

Shisslak, C. M., Crago, M., Estes, L., & Gray, N. (1996). Content and method of developmentally appropriate prevention programs. In L. Smolak, M. P. Levine, & R. Striegel-Moore (Eds.), *The developmental psychopathology of eating disorders: Implications for research, prevention, and treatment* (pp. 341–363). Mahwah, NJ: Erlbaum.

Shisslak, C., Crago, M., Renger, R., & Clark-Wagner, A. (1998). Self-esteem and the prevention of eating disorders. *Eating Disorders: The Journal of Treatment & Prevention, 6*, 105–117.

Smolak, L. (1999). Elementary school curricula for the primary prevention of eating problems. In N. Piran, M. P. Levine, & C. Steiner-Adair (Eds.), *Preventing eating disorders: A handbook of interventions and special challenges* (pp. 85–104). Philadelphia: Brunner/Mazel.

Smolak, L., & Levine, M. P. (1994). Toward an empirical basis for primary prevention of eating problems with elementary school children. *Eating Disorders: The Journal of Treatment & Prevention, 2*, 293–307.

Smolak L., & Levine, M. P. (1996). Adolescent transitions and the development of eating problems. In L. Smolak, M. P. Levine, & R. Striegel-Moore (Eds.), *The developmental psychopathology of eating disorders: Implications for research, prevention, and treatment* (pp. 207–233). Mahwah, NJ: Erlbaum.

Smolak, L., & Levine, M. P. (in press). A two-year follow-up of a primary prevention program for negative body image and unhealthy weight regulation: *Eating Disorders: The Journal of Treatment & Prevention.*

Smolak, L., Levine, M. P., & Schermer, F. (1998a). A controlled evaluation of an elementary school primary prevention program for eating problems. *Journal of Psychosomatic Research, 44*, 339–353.

Smolak, L., Levine, M. P., & Schermer, F. (1998b). Lessons from lessons: An evaluation of an elementary school prevention program. In W. Vandereycken

& G. Noordenbos (Eds.), *The prevention of eating disorders* (pp. 137–172). London: Athlone.

Smolak, L., & Murnen, S. (2001). Gender and eating problems. In R. Striegel-Moore & L. Smolak (Eds.), *Eating disorders: Innovative directions for research and practice* (pp. 91–110). Washington, DC: American Psychological Association.

Smolak, L., & Striegel-Moore, R. (2001). Challenging the myth of the golden girl: Ethnicity and eating disorders. In R. Striegel-Moore & L. Smolak (Eds.), *Eating disorders: Innovative directions for research and practice* (pp. 111–132). Washington, DC: American Psychological Association.

Steiner-Adair, C., & Vorenberg, A. P. (1999). Resisting weightism: Media literacy for elementary school children. In N. Piran, M. P. Levine, & C. Steiner-Adair (Eds.), *Preventing eating disorders: A handbook of interventions and special challenges* (pp. 105–121). Philadelphia: Brunner/Mazel.

Stewart, A. (1998). Experience with a school-based eating disorders prevention programme. In W. Vandereycken & G. Noordenbos (Eds.), *The prevention of eating disorders* (pp. 99–136). London: Athlone.

Stewart, D. A., Carter, J. C., Drinkwater, J., Hainsworth, J., & Fairburn, C. G. (in press). Modification of eating attitudes and behaviour in adolescent girls: A controlled study. *International Journal of Eating Disorders*.

Stice, E. (1994). Review of the evidence for a sociocultural model of bulimia nervosa and an exploration of the mechanisms of action. *Clinical Psychology Review, 14*, 633–661.

Stice, E., Mazotti, L., Weibel, D., & Agras, W. S. (2000). Dissonance prevention program decreases thin-ideal internalization, body dissatisfaction, dieting, negative affect, and bulimic symptoms: A preliminary experiment. *International Journal of Eating Disorders, 27*, 206–217.

Striegel-Moore, R., & Smolak, L. (1996). The role of race in the development of eating disorders. In L. Smolak, M. P. Levine, & R. Striegel-Moore (Eds.), *The developmental psychopathology of eating disorders: Implications for research, prevention, and treatment* (pp. 259–284). Mahwah, NJ: Erlbaum.

Thoman, E. (1998, June). *What's it all about? A crash course in core principles and key concepts* [of media education]. Workshop presented at the National Media Education Conference ("A Paradigm for Public Health"), Colorado Springs, CO.

Thompson, J. K., Heinberg, L. J., Altabe, M., & Tantleff-Dunn, S. (1999). *Exacting beauty: Theory, assessment, and treatment of body image disturbance*. Washington, DC: American Psychological Association.

Toledo, T., & Neumark-Sztainer, D. (1999). Weighting for you! Training for high school faculty and staff in the prevention and detection of weight-related disorders among adolescents. *Journal of Nutrition Education, 31*, 283A.

Vandereycken, W., & Noordenbos, G. (Eds.) (1998). *Prevention of eating disorders*. London: Athlone.

Winzelberg, A. J., Taylor, C. B., Sharpe, T., Eldredge, K. L., Dev, P., & Constantinou, P. S. (1998). Evaluation of a computer-mediated eating disorder intervention program. *International Journal of Eating Disorders, 24*, 339–349.

11

OBESITY PREVENTION FOR CHILDREN AND ADOLESCENTS

THOMAS N. ROBINSON AND JOEL D. KILLEN

There are compelling reasons for attacking childhood and adolescent obesity with population-based prevention efforts. First, obesity has become one of the most important public health problems in the United States and around the world (World Health Organization, 1998). In the past two decades, the United States has experienced dramatic increases in obesity among both children and adults. In the recent Third National Health and Nutrition Examination Survey (NHANES III, 1988–1994) from 12% to 35% of American children and adolescents were found to be obese, depending on the reference data used, and more than half of American adults were found to be overweight (Centers for Disease Control and Prevention, 1997; Troiano & Flegal, 1998). Second, in the traditional medical treatment model, it is necessary to identify a high-risk group to target with treatment. In the case of childhood obesity, it is difficult to identify a true high-risk group. Although being overweight represents an immediate health risk to some children and adolescents and confers a substantial increased relative risk for adult obesity, known factors are unable to discriminate, with reasonable sensitivity and specificity, which children will go on to develop obesity-related clinical complications, persistent obesity, or adult-onset obesity (Robinson, 1993). Third, although some intensive childhood obesity treat-

This work was supported in part by grants from the National Heart, Lung, and Blood Institute (RO1 HL54102), the National Cancer Institute (RO1 CA68082), and the American Heart Association, California Affiliate.

We are indebted to many collaborators, past and present, whose influences are evident in this chapter. In particular, Helena C. Kraemer, PhD; C. Barr Taylor, MD; David G. Altman, PhD; and Ellen Feighery, RN, MS; and the research staff who have made our work possible, K. Farish Haydel; Ann Varady, MS; Sally McCarthy; Sarah Erickson, PhD; Cindy Zedeck, MA; Christina Russell; Kathy Valenzuela; Mireya Samaniego; Connie Watanabe, MS; Elsy Ochoa-Martelli; W. Elizabeth Shepard, MD; Dina Borzekowski, EdD; Donna Matheson, PhD; Andrea Romero, PhD; Michael Kubalik; Imelda Gonzalez; Bernadette Whitman; Marta Wilde, MA; and Elizabeth Klein.

ment programs have demonstrated long-term success in up to a third of research participants (Epstein, Valoski, Wing, & McCurley, 1994), most available treatments have produced disappointing long-term results, including some significant adverse effects (Epstein, Myers, Raynor, & Saelens, 1998; Haddock, Shadish, Klesges, & Stein, 1994), and we are unable to accurately identify those individuals most likely to benefit from treatment (Robinson, 1993). Adult treatment results have generally been even more disappointing (National Institutes of Health Technology Assessment Conference Panel, 1993). These observations suggest that a population-based approach emphasizing both primary and secondary prevention may hold the greatest promise for resolving the long-term problem of obesity among children and adolescents.

THE CURRENT STATUS OF OBESITY PREVENTION

Past attempts to prevent obesity in children and adolescents have produced only modest results. Traditional health education approaches have been relatively unsuccessful in producing any significant changes in adiposity or obesity-related behaviors, and short-term effects consistently decay over time. This was clearly illustrated in a recent review of school-based prevention studies targeting risk factors for cardiovascular disease, including obesity (Resnicow & Robinson, 1997). It included all published, controlled studies dating back to 1980 that assessed at least one physiologic risk factor, including blood lipids, blood pressure, body fatness, or cardiorespiratory fitness—a total of 12 U.S. studies and 7 international studies, including 3 studies that intervened exclusively in physical education or school food service. For each outcome, the percentage of positive results was calculated across all studies combined. There were statistically significant positive results in 80% of the smoking outcomes reported; 65% of attitudes, beliefs, or knowledge outcomes reported; 36% of physical fitness outcomes; 34% of dietary intake outcomes; 31% of blood lipids outcomes; 30% of physical activity outcomes; and 18% of blood pressure outcomes reported. Adiposity outcomes were at the bottom of the list. Significant reductions in adiposity were achieved in only 16% of the body fatness measures reported from these studies (Resnicow & Robinson, 1997).

School Curriculum Interventions

A number of school curriculum programs have attempted to influence children's and adolescents' diet and activity patterns, and ultimately prevent obesity (Jackson, Proulx, & Pelican, 1991; Resnicow, 1993; Resnicow & Robinson, 1997). Although most have been successful in increasing knowledge or improving attitudes about healthful behaviors, and many have been successful in changing health behaviors, they have generally not been successful in reducing adiposity (Resnicow, 1993; Resnicow & Robinson, 1997). One exception to this is our own study of a multiple risk factor intervention for adolescents. This study involved all 10th graders in four high schools (N = 1447) from two ethnically diverse school districts (Killen & Robinson, 1989; Killen et al., 1988). Within each district, one school was assigned at random to receive a 20-session cardiovascular disease risk reduction intervention and one school served as a control. The educational methods were derived from the conceptual perspectives provided by social cognitive theory (Bandura, 1986) and social inoculation theory (McGuire, 1964). The sessions were divided among five program modules: physical activity, nutrition, cigarette smoking, stress, and personal problem solving. At a two-month follow-up, compared to controls, the treatment group demonstrated large significant gains in knowledge, adoption of regular aerobic exercise, cessation of experimental smoking, and increased heart-healthy snack consumption. Significant beneficial treatment effects were also observed for resting heart rate, body mass index, triceps skinfold thickness, and subscapular skinfold thickness (Killen et al., 1988).

Physical Education (PE) Interventions

U.S. children get 20 to 40% of their total physical activity at school, and many children are active only during PE classes (Simons-Morton et al., 1990). However, PE classes may average as few as 10 minutes of moderate to vigorous activity per week (DeMarco & Sidney, 1989; Simons-Morton, Taylor, Snider, & Huant, 1993). Interventions targeting PE have been somewhat effective at improving physical activity and fitness levels (McKenzie et al., 1996; Sallis et al., 1997; Simons-Morton, Parcel, Baranowski, Forthofer, & O'Hara, 1991), though without producing changes in adiposity (Resnicow & Robinson, 1997). One exception was a study in Adelaide, Australia, in which fifth graders who received an intensive, 1.25 hour, daily endurance fitness program had significant decreases in skinfold thicknesses and improvements in endurance, compared to controls (T. Dwyer, Coonan, Leitch, Hetzel, & Baghurst, 1983). Unfortunately, political, financial, and educational priorities have limited the opportunities to provide sufficient physical activity during PE classes in many schools.

School Food Service Interventions

School lunches are estimated to provide one fourth to one third of total school day calories for participating children. Changes in school food service can passively influence children's consumption of fat while at school

(J. Dwyer et al., 1996; Ellison, Capper, Goldberg, Witschi, & Stare, 1989; Osganian et al., 1996; Whitaker, Wright, Finch, & Psaty, 1993). However, to date, school food service interventions have not had effects on adiposity.

Parent and Family Interventions

Parents are influential in the development of children's health-related behaviors (Perry, Luepker, Murray, & Hearn, 1989). However, research on parent and family interventions has been hindered by the difficulty of getting parents to participate. Interventions targeting families have generally produced modest short-term effects on dietary behaviors but not on anthropometric measures (Hearn et al., 1992; Luepker et al., 1996; Nader et al., 1983; Perry, Crockett, & Pirie, 1987; Perry et al., 1989; Stolley & Fitzgibbon, 1997; Vega et al., 1988).

Multiple-Component Interventions

The National Heart, Lung, and Blood Institute (NHLBI) Child and Adolescent Trial for Cardiovascular Health (CATCH) represents the state-of-the-art multiple component intervention for improving diet and increasing physical activity in children (Luepker et al., 1996; Resnicow, Robinson, & Frank, 1996). The CATCH intervention included school curricula, school food service, physical education and, in half of the intervention schools, family-based components. However, despite producing significant modifications in school lunches, reductions in fat intake, increased activity during PE classes and increased total daily vigorous activity, these changes resulted in no significant decreases in BMI or triceps or subscapular skinfold thicknesses (Luepker et al., 1996; Webber et al., 1996). However, CATCH did not specifically target obesity prevention as an objective (its primary objective was to decrease total cholesterol) and did not specifically address secondary prevention.

THE STANFORD OBESITY PREVENTION FOR PRE-ADOLESCENTS (OPPrA) TRIAL

The Stanford OPPrA trial was funded by the National Heart, Lung, and Blood Institute to test an integrated, sustained, multiple-component intervention emphasizing both primary and secondary prevention of obesity, in an ethnically and socioeconomically diverse sample of children. The OPPrA intervention model includes concurrent activities on three "fronts": the school, the home, and high-risk children. In addition, the intervention is being delivered over a three-year period, as children progress from the third grade through the fifth grade. The school component includes (a) a classroom curriculum, (b) a physical education intervention, and (c) a school lunch intervention. The home component includes newsletters for parents and videotapes delivered to each household. Finally, children identified as "high risk," based on their own obesity and their parent's obesity, are eligible to participate with a parent in an intensive, treatment-oriented intervention. As a result of the past experience described earlier, we believe this model represents the current state-of-the-art for population-based obesity prevention programs for children.

TARGETING PREADOLESCENTS

An intervention targeting preadolescents has the greatest potential to limit the tracking of obesity from childhood and adolescence into adulthood. There is evidence that early adolescence is an important period for the development of obesity (Dietz, 1994). Puberty is one of only a few periods during childhood and adolescence normally associated with fat cell hyperplasia (Knittle, Timmers, Ginsberg-Fellner, Brown, & Katz, 1979). These physiologic changes may explain the jump in tracking of overweight from childhood to adulthood that occurs around puberty. For example, in the Fels longitudinal cohort the risk of obesity at age 35 for children with BMIs above the 95th percentile increased from 20 to 30% at 6 years of age to 40 to 80% after 10 years of age (Guo, Roche, Chumlea, Gardner, & Siervogel, 1994), and in a recent retrospective cohort study, 55% of obese 6 to 9 year olds became obese young adults compared to 75% of obese 10 to 14 year olds (Whitaker, Wright, Pepe, Seidel, & Dietz, 1997). Other studies have demonstrated similar patterns (Braddon, Rodgers, Wadsworth, & Davies, 1986; Clarke & Lauer, 1993). After this initial jump, risks tend to mostly flatten out between the ages of about 12 to 18 years.

An intervention targeting preadolescents may produce exaggerated effects on preventing the excess morbidity and mortality associated with central obesity in adults. Obesity acquired during the preadolescent period may also be associated with increased risks of future morbidity and mortality. In a 33- to 40-year follow-up of 9- to 13-year-old White boys from Hagerstown, Maryland (Abraham, Collins, & Nordsieck, 1971), those with the highest preadolescent weights had the greatest mean levels of adult fasting blood sugar and blood pressures, and adult prevalences of diabetes, coronary heart disease, renal disease, and peripheral vascular disease. In a 55-year follow-up study of another sample, both morbidity and mortality were increased in males and females who were overweight during adolescence, compared to their lean classmates (Must, Jacques, Dallal, Bajema, & Dietz, 1992). This excess morbidity and mortality may result from a change in the pattern of fat distribution occurring with puberty. Starting in late childhood and continuing through adolescence, males demonstrate a redistribution of body fat away from the extremities and to the trunk. The same process may occur at a slower pace in adolescent females (Mueller, 1982).

An intervention targeting preadolescents, emphasizing healthful methods of weight control, may be effective at preventing the adoption of unhealthful weight control behaviors and attitudes, and psychosocial morbidities associated with obesity in adolescents. The onset of obesity during early adolescence may also be associated with increased psychosocial morbidity. Our own longitudinal studies of body dissatisfaction, weight concerns, and eating disorders among adolescent girls suggest that puberty may play an important role in the development of disordered eating behaviors (Killen et al., 1992). In addition, attitudes and behaviors related to dieting and thinness often start in childhood (Robinson, Chang, Haydel, & Killen, in press). Obesity prevention programs for preadolescents may help to preempt this potentially vulnerable period. By instilling healthful attitudes, behaviors, and social and environmental influences during the preadolescent period we intend to prevent the complications associated with onset or acceleration of obesity during puberty.

In addition, an intervention targeting preadolescents has several practical and theoretical advantages for influencing school and family environments: (a) preadolescents are more likely to be in school—as adolescents progress into junior high school and high school, absence and drop-out rates increase, particularly for minority adolescents, among whom obesity prevalence rates are greater than in the overall population; (b) diet and activity patterns of preadolescents are still heavily influenced by their parents—in general, the number of meals consumed outside of the home and the amount of unsupervised discretionary time increases through the adolescent years; (c) parents of elementary and middle school students are more likely to participate in school activities than parents of older students; and (d) elementary school students are more likely to eat school lunches than older students (Olsen, 1984).

SOCIAL COGNITIVE THEORY: THE CONCEPTUAL MODEL FOR THE INTERVENTION

The design of integrating multiple interventions and targeting both primary and secondary prevention, is not simply motivated by a desire to throw everything possible at a difficult problem. The intervention model is an attempt to most faithfully apply principles of social cognitive theory. Bandura's social cognitive model specifies three domains to consider in the design of behavior change and prevention interventions (Bandura, 1986). In social cognitive theory, behavior develops, is altered and maintained through the interplay of personal, behavioral, and environmental factors. With respect to the focus on obesity prevention, *personal factors* include children's, parents', teachers', and food service workers' own value systems, which determine the nature of the incentives that sustain behavior, expectations derived from observation and experience about the consequences of different behaviors (outcome expectancies), and expectations about personal abilities to perform behaviors that will secure desired outcomes (efficacy expectancies). *Behavioral factors* include the skills available in the behavioral repertoire of the child, parent, teacher, or food service worker, and the degree of competence attained in using these skills. *Environmental factors* include peers, family members, teachers, supervisors, and media representations who model various attitudes and behaviors regarding diet, physical activity, television viewing, parenting behaviors, food preparation, and so forth, and are in a position, through their own actions, judgments, or social positions, to influence the development of the participant's value systems and standards of conduct regarding those attitudes and behaviors. Environmental factors also include environmental or structural influences such as fat content in school lunches or safe playgrounds.

DEVELOPING THE INTERVENTION

Social cognitive theory is particularly helpful in planning interventions. The social cognitive model suggests four processes are important in learning and adopting new behaviors: attention, retention, production, and motivation (Bandura, 1986). We have organized our intervention development around these four processes, whose operationalizations guide the macro and micro development and implementation of all components of the overall program. *Attention* regulates exploration and perception and is highly influenced by factors such as salience, conspicuousness, functional value, affective valence, and attractiveness (e.g., the use of color, graphics, and interactivity in instruction, emphasis on meaningful short-term consequences of behaviors instead of future health outcomes, use of the video medium for parent intervention, incentives specified prior to learning activities). *Retention*, or memory, is influenced by the processes of symbolic coding, organization of information, cognitive or imagined rehearsal, and enactive rehearsal (e.g., linking explicit instruction with visual demonstration, allowing observers to infer messages from simulations). *Production* is the conversion of conceptual representations into actions, and is influenced by immediate intrinsic and extrinsic feedback (e.g., role playing with feedback highlighting successes while correcting deficiencies, menu planning and meal preparation in the classroom or intensive intervention group). Production is the process most closely linked to efficacy expectancies. *Motivation* is most directly linked to outcome expectancies and is strongly influenced by external, vicarious, and internal incentives (e.g., peer, parent, or teacher approval or disapproval, material rewards, observation of modeled behavior linked to desirable outcomes, control over events, and perceived choice).

Therefore, at each stage in the construction of our interventions we are careful to ask (a) whether the stimulus material and methods are appropriate to engage and direct the attention of our target audience; (b) whether the form of the intervention (i.e., language and skill demands, information level) is a match for the cognitive and behavioral skill attainments of our target audience; (c) whether sufficient performance (cognitive and behavioral) opportunities are provided; and (d) whether the incentives are relevant and attractive to our target audience and thus more likely to serve as prompts for action. To be sure that we are satisfactorily addressing these questions it is necessary, at each stage of intervention construction, to submit the program materials for formative evaluation–testing. This consists of focus groups with small numbers of same-aged children, parents, teachers and food service workers to obtain information about the factors that are most likely to influence attention, retention, production, and motivation. For example, for students this would include food and activity preferences, the perceived positive and negative consequences of developing and maintaining healthful physical activity and dietary regimens, perceived parental influences on behavior, relevant incentives for behavior and general interests and concerns. For teachers this includes brainstorming regarding program content and problem-solving regarding resources and logistics critical to implementation. Previous experience persuades us that the information obtained via focus groups is often critical to developing salient and successful interventions.

Focus group results help drive content specification and materials design. Initial intervention design and development is aided by continuous and extensive formative testing with additional groups of the intended target audiences. For example, we use paid teacher consultants to review and critique lesson plans, manuals, workbooks, and teacher training protocols. This process leads to multiple revisions before final production of intervention materials and protocols. This is then followed by training for implementation (e.g., intensive intervention group leader training, physical education and classroom teacher training, food service worker training) and actual implementation and booster training.

THE CLASSROOM INTERVENTION

The classroom curriculum is intended to help students (a) learn about the short- and long-term consequences of healthful and unhealthful diet and activity behaviors; (b) develop positive attitudes about healthful diet and activity behaviors; (c) develop preferences for healthful foods; (d) develop the skills necessary to adopt and maintain healthful diet and activity behaviors; (e) develop skills to influence their family, peer, and school environments; (f) develop skills to resist unhealthful environmental influences; and (g) develop high levels of perceived self-efficacy for performing the skills learned. The classroom curriculum consists of 16 or 17 30- to-50-minute class sessions each, in the third, fourth, and fifth grades, delivered throughout the entire school years. Regular classroom teachers lead these sessions following a detailed teacher's manual, with the assistance of a teaching assistant. A single teaching assistant is assigned to each school to help prepare materials and implement classroom lessons. This approach was based on earlier research and extensive formative work in methods to improve curriculum adoption, implementation fidelity, and maintenance.

In the third grade the curriculum focuses on increasing fruit and vegetable intake. Although data are lacking on the efficacy of increasing fruit and vegetable intake for obesity prevention, it is widely believed that increasing children's high fiber, fruit, and vegetable consumption will displace higher calorie, high-fat foods in the diet. In addition, a five-a-day fruit and vegetable message was judged, through formative research, to be appropriate for this age group. Children this age have difficulty assessing serving sizes, but if serving sizes are ignored they can more easily count their intakes of fruits and vegetables, allowing self-monitoring, goal setting, feedback, and rewards for behavior changes. In the fourth grade the curriculum focuses on reducing television, videotape, and video game use, based on our own pilot studies described later in the chapter. In the fifth grade the curriculum focuses on reducing dietary fat intake. Even by the fifth grade, however, children participating in our formative research were unable to grasp the more abstract goal of reducing fat intake. Therefore, it was important to translate fat intake into understandable, specific, countable behaviors. This was achieved by defining types of foods to target: substituting fat free milk for higher fat milks; substituting fruits and vegetables for heavily processed and packaged snack foods; and finding alternatives to fast food. In addition, to build perceived incentive value, desirable foods were classified as "green foods" by being both good for health and also good for the environment.

An emphasis on personal goal setting and problem solving is woven through all three years of the classroom curriculum. Although focusing on individual changes, these elements are usually performed as a whole classroom activity. Class participation in goal setting and problem solving is desirable because the process is often enhanced through group participation, as students learn from the experiences of their peers, as well as the teacher. These activities are designed to facilitate the transition from knowledge and attitude change to behavior change, and emphasize self-evaluation, identifying behavior change areas, developing action plans, identifying barriers to change, and overcoming barriers to change (Killen et al., 1989).

THE PHYSICAL EDUCATION INTERVENTION

The physical education intervention is intended to (a) increase moderate and vigorous physical activities during the school day; (b) increase enjoyable experiences with moderate and vigorous physical activities; (c) help students develop a variety of skills associated with moderate and vigorous physical activities, enhancing performance mastery and self-efficacy; and (d) increase light, moderate, and vigorous activity outside of the school day. The physical education intervention was adapted from the state-of-the-art CATCH PE (from the NHLBI) and SPARK PE (from San Diego State University) programs. Because neither of these interventions has previously produced reductions in adiposity (Luepker et al., 1996; Sallis et al., 1997; Webber et al., 1996), though a more intensive aerobic training intervention has (T. Dwyer et al., 1983), it was our goal to modify these programs to increase the level of activity that would result. However, the main principles and methods of CATCH PE and SPARK PE are maintained. The major focus is to encourage maximum student participation during class time. This is primarily achieved by increasing available equipment, so all children can participate in activities simultaneously, and improving the class management methods of teachers to minimize the amount of time any individual student is not moving. Lessons are delivered two days per week in the experimental group, which is the standard PE for all elementary schools in the participating school district. In the fifth grade, students are also given pedometers to monitor their movement both during PE and throughout the rest of their day. Pedometer totals are recorded to help children monitor their progress toward individual and combined class goals.

THE SCHOOL LUNCH INTERVENTION

Previous school lunch interventions have altered the content of the meals prepared and served at school (J. Dwyer et al., 1996; Ellison et al., 1989; Osganian et al., 1996; Whitaker et al., 1993). However, many schools, including the schools participating in this trial, now use vendor-prepared meals that are delivered to schools prepackaged. As a result, the feasibility of altering school lunch content is limited in this setting. In addition, passive change of school meal content alters only a small minority of meals eaten, without enhancing skills for more healthful eating outside of school. As a result, the school lunch intervention was designed to help students learn to make lower fat lunch choices via point-of-choice education and physical changes, in addition to attempts to enhance taste preferences for fruits and vegetables. This includes posters and aprons promoting fruit and vegetable intake, weekly taste tests of fruits and vegetables to encourage children to try novel tastes in a supportive and encouraging social environment, moving fruits and vegetables to the front of the food line so children will leave less room on their plates for higher fat, higher calorie foods, and, coordinated with the fifth grade classroom curriculum, switching the school milk supply to fat free white and chocolate milk.

THE PARENT INTERVENTION

The parent intervention is intended to (a) teach parents basic parenting skills (e.g., monitoring their child's behavior, negotiating, using contingencies, setting explicit limits and explicit consequences for violating those limits, and using praise); (b) help parents provide a healthful, low-fat diet for their family; (c) help parents promote the development of healthful food preferences in their child; (d) help parents reduce sedentary activity, particularly television viewing, by their children; and (e) help parents build regular moderate to vigorous physical activity into their children's and family's routine. This is attempted with weekly newsletters that are linked to the classroom curriculum and an instructional videotape.

In a recent review of parent intervention research, Perry et al. concluded that (a) children are able to influence the attitudes and behaviors of their parents, (b) poor parent participation rates are a substantial barrier to implementing parent and/or family-based interventions, and (c) parents prefer interventions that can be completed at home and that involve their children (Perry et al., 1987). Our experience has been consistent with these conclusions; most families are unlikely to accept face-to-face interventions, given their inherent intrusiveness. Correspondence interventions and videotapes for parents provide a self-help instructional format and enable families to receive training in private, under less threatening conditions.

Our formative research with parents suggests that video, as compared to other approaches such as workbook-based educational interventions, is more likely to get attention and be used in the home. For the Stanford OPPrA trial, a 12-minute parent videotape, "What's to Eat?" has been produced in both English and Spanish. Through a series of vignettes with accompanying testimonials, "What's to Eat?" encourages parents to adopt three primary strategies to help their children develop healthful eating habits: (a) fill your kitchen with fruits and vegetables that are easy for your kids to eat, and keep junk food out of your house; (b) eat the foods you want your children to eat (modeling); and (c) do not use food as a reward, particularly do not use sweets to bribe your child to eat more healthy foods like vegetables. These strategies were identified from research on the development of food preferences in children, as described later, in addition to extensive formative research with families of third-, fourth-, and fifth-grade students (see also chapter 1, this volume).

THE INTENSIVE INTERVENTION FOR HIGH-RISK CHILDREN AND THEIR FAMILIES

The growing prevalence of obesity among children compels prevention researchers to consider interventions for both primary and secondary prevention. As a result, a recent NHLBI Strategy Development Workshop for Public Education on Weight and Obesity recommended combing high-risk targeting with population-based primary prevention (NHLBI, 1994). The feasibility of school-based treatment programs has been demonstrated by previous studies of self-selected participants who achieved modest short-term improvements in obesity (Epstein et al., 1998). After formative research, we decided that the intervention for high-risk students should be scheduled outside of the regular school day, to avoid possible stigmatization. However, we have found that, over time, the participating children do not tend to hide their participation from their classmates.

In the Stanford OPPrA trial, high risk is defined as those students whose body mass index (BMI) exceeds the 85th percentile for age and gender and those with a BMI greater than 75th percentile plus at least one obese parent. These children and their families are eligible to enroll in a voluntary, family-based, group behavioral treatment program that is conducted at one of the school sites. New groups are started in the fall and winter of the fourth and fifth grades. The treatment program is a less intensive adaptation of Epstein's Traffic Light Diet program (Epstein, 1996; Epstein et al., 1998), and is the same treatment used in the clinic-based Stanford Pediatric Weight Control Program (Robinson, 1999a), which has been successful at producing significant decreases in overweight. The core of the program involves 14 weekly sessions followed by weekly maintenance sessions that last for up to 18 months. At least one parent must agree to attend all sessions with his or her child. Children and parents meet separately and together at each session.

INNOVATIVE APPROACHES FOR OBESITY PREVENTION

In addition to more traditional approaches for altering diet and physical activity behaviors, we have identified several innovative intervention approaches that we believe hold promise for improving the effects of obesity prevention programs for children. These include interventions to alter food preferences; interventions to reduce television, videotape, and video game use; and the use of advocacy experiences to increase motivation and rehearsal opportunities.

Altering Food Preferences

Despite available research on the determinants of food preferences in children, we are aware of no previous prevention trials that have specifically attempted to apply this approach. There are some data associating obesity with increased preferences for high-fat foods (Drewnowski, Brunzell, Sande, Iverius, & Greenwood, 1985), though causality has not been demonstrated. In addition, children with at least one overweight parent have been shown to consume greater percentages of calories from fat (Eck, Klesges, Hanson, & Slawson, 1992). However, food preferences tend to be malleable, and several factors have been identified that are of theoretical value for designing interventions. Factors found to have the greatest influence on young children's food preferences are (a) repeated exposure–ingestion; (b) postingestive satiety—most clearly demonstrated with the energy density of foods consumed over consecutive meals; and (c) the social context of food consumption—preferences increase for foods presented in positive social contexts, as rewards, or with adult attention, whereas preferences decrease when rewards are made contingent on food consumption (Birch & Fisher, 1998). There is also evidence that parent monitoring and modification of food choices, both actual and threatened, can affect the foods selected by children (Klesges, Stein, Eck, Isbell, & Klesges, 1991). As described earlier, we have attempted to translate these laboratory findings into practical intervention strategies. In particular, these findings help to shape content for the parent newsletters and the parent videotape, and they are the basis for the taste tests offered in the schools.

Television Viewing

Children spend a substantial part of their lives in front of the television set. Recent national data indicate that children watch an average of more than 24 hours of television per week (written communication, Nielsen Media Research, 1997). Extrapolation of age-specific viewing data reveals that between the ages of 2 and 17 years, the average U.S. child spends more than three years of his or her waking life watching television (Robinson, 1998). In addition, American children spend an average of more than seven hours per week watching videotapes and more than five hours per week playing video games (Annenberg Public Policy Center, 1997). Three possible mechanisms have been suggested to link television viewing and obesity (Robinson, 1998): First, reduced energy expenditure by displacing physical activity; second, increased energy intake from eating while viewing or as a result of food advertising; third, the suggestion that watching television decreases resting metabolic rate.

Epidemiological studies examining the association between television viewing and childhood obesity have found relatively weak and variable associations (Robinson, 1998). To overcome the limitations of these epidemiological studies, we performed an experimental pilot study to examine the effects of reducing television, videotape, and video game use on body composition, diet, and physical activity. Initial formative research tested multiple intervention approaches and demonstrated the feasibility of reducing children's television viewing through self-help behavioral methods. These findings led to a classroom-based curriculum that was tested in a controlled trial involving third and fourth graders in two matched elementary schools. Over the course of the school year, children in the intervention school reduced their television, videotape, and video game use by about one fourth to one third, compared to controls. These changes were accompanied by statistically significant and clinically significant relative decreases in BMI, triceps skinfold thickness, waist circumference, and waist-to-hip ratio, compared to controls. There were also significant decreases in eating while watching television and a trend toward reduced high-fat food intake. There were no accompanying changes in physical activity or physical fitness (Robinson, 1999b). These results strongly demonstrate the feasibility of decreasing weight gain by reducing television viewing, and the curriculum was adapted for use in the OPPrA trial during the fourth grade.

Health Advocacy

Colleagues at the Stanford Center for Research in Disease Prevention have demonstrated that involving youth in antitobacco advocacy activities may be particularly effective in reducing youth smoking (Altman, Foster, Rasenick-Douss, & Tye, 1989). In addition, classroom learning effects are likely to be greater where most students have bonded with the school (Hawkins, Lishner, & Catalano, 1985) and peer group support exists for the goals of prevention programs (Cauce & Srebnik, 1989). The Stanford OPPrA intervention includes advocacy activities, organized from the classroom and included in the parent intervention, specifically designed to promote environmental changes, and increasing both internal and social pressures to adopt and maintain healthful behaviors. Examples of advocacy activities include the focus on environmentally friendly foods during the fifth grade and fourth graders' efforts to persuade other students to reduce television viewing.

CULTURAL APPROPRIATENESS

Prevention interventions need to become more culturally appropriate by taking into consideration ethnic group differences in social, psychological, environmental, and cultural aspects of health (Landrine & Klonoff, 1992; Marin, 1993). This has particular relevance for obesity prevention interventions, as Latino boys and girls and African American girls represent the groups at highest risk (Troiano & Flegal, 1998; Winkleby, Robinson, & Sundquist, 1999), and there are known cultural differences that may affect intervention design and implementation. For example, body weight and weight loss tend to be less important among African American women and girls, the ideal or desired body weight–shape is heavier, and overweight African American girls are less dissatisfied with their weight than girls of other ethnicities (Centers for Disease Control, 1991). To adequately incorporate the complexity of culture into health interventions, it is important to address both changes in surface structure (culturally matched models, music, language) and deep structure (values, social and historical influences; Resnicow, Baranowski, Ahluwalia, & Braithwaite, 1999). Surface structure can be addressed through culturally matched intervention providers, intervention content chosen by the participants, intervention materials that are in appropriate languages, and so forth. However, to appropriately address deep structure, Marin suggested that cultural values, norms, attitudes, and expectancies be assessed and then integrated into the goals and strategies of the intervention (Marin, 1993). When working with African Americans, for example, it may be important to take into account the collectivistic nature of the culture, importance of family, present orientation, importance of religiosity, sense of historical racism and prejudice, and use of social support as a coping mechanism (Gaines et al., 1997; Harrison, Wilson, Pine, Chan, & Buriel, 1990; Resnicow, Braithwaite, & Kuo, 1997). To adequately address cultural appropriateness, formative research needs to be performed on the subjective culture of the group as related to obesity, physical activity, and diet. The results of the formative research should guide intervention strategies to focus on relevant issues for the participants.

STRATEGIES TO PROMOTE PROGRAM IMPLEMENTATION

Failure to plan for effective implementation is often the major reason new programs fail (Parcel, Perry, & Taylor, 1990). Program adoption, whether by school administrators or teachers, does not guarantee implementation. Likewise, teachers' initial attempts at implementation will not necessarily result in continued use of the program. Thus it is critical that developers of obesity-prevention programs pay close attention to issues of implementation and maintenance if long-term effects on students are to be achieved (Basch, Eveland, & Portnoy, 1986).

Educational research has shown that a combination of organizational and individual (i.e., teacher) variables predict implementation of innovative programs. Organizational factors that are positively correlated with implementation include strong teacher morale, a high degree of teacher involvement in decision making, active support for the innovation from school principals, general support from district superintendents, and a good fit between the innovation and local needs (Anderson et al., 1987; Berman & Pauly, 1975; Gold et al., 1991). Principals, in particular, appear to be "gatekeepers" of new curricula; their attitudes and behaviors have been shown to significantly facilitate or inhibit implementation (Fullan & Pomfret, 1977; Huberman & Miles, 1984).

At the program provider level, adoption and implementation of innovative programs are related to attributes of the innovation as well as cognitive, social, and psychological attributes of the providers themselves. Classroom teachers are most likely to implement educational innovations that are well specified and require the same teaching strategies they normally use. Other teacher variables mediating program implementation include the teacher's enthusiasm, preparedness, comfort with and acceptance of the program, and confidence in their ability to implement the program effectively (Levenson-Gingiss & Hamilton, 1989). Recent studies of smoking prevention program facilitators, who are not regular classroom teachers, have shown that program integrity is positively associated with an enthusiastic, confident, and nonauthoritarian teaching style (Sobol et al., 1989) and characteristics such as being outgoing, adventurous, and organized (Young et al., 1990).

In the Stanford OPPrA trial incentive systems are built into all levels of program implementation. The current political and social environment is abundant with criticism of the public education system. As a result, demands are being made for districts, schools, and teachers to improve the quality of curricula and teaching methods, provide innovative curricula sensitive to the needs of students, and demonstrate results. In addition, budget cuts threaten the jobs of administrators and teachers. Our program provides district and school administrators and classroom and physical education teachers with a direct response to these political demands, with a university–public schools partnership to implement an innovative curriculum and improve teaching methods. In addition, the setting of a research partnership demonstrates interest in "results" and commitment to objective evaluations.

We have also identified specific incentives to be emphasized for teachers (e.g., perception of high value to the district, use of innovative teaching methods and technology, responsiveness to teacher feedback, feedback to teachers regarding program effects on students). In addition, the performance of participant teachers may be enhanced by the opportunity to develop "joint ownership" of the curriculum. To achieve this, we meet with all teachers in the early stages of the project, and all teachers are invited to be paid consultants on curriculum development. As the project progresses, we continue to give teachers and administrators frequent opportunities to ask questions and make suggestions regarding logistics.

Teacher Training and Support

We expect that some teachers will be hostile to, or suspicious of, curriculum innovation, particularly when the subject matter and teaching methods are unfamiliar. Therefore, it is not surprising that teacher training is considered critical to effective program implementation (Fullan & Pomfret, 1977; Huberman, Miles, Taylor, & Goldberg, 1983). Teacher training interventions are designed to equip teachers with the knowledge, skills, and resource support necessary to conduct a new program so that all program components are included and so that there is fidelity to the content of the program (Parcel et al., 1990). It has been shown that for curriculum innovations in general, and school health innovations in particular, providing preimplementation training increases the likelihood that teachers will implement the curriculum fully and with integrity (Anderson et al., 1987; Berman & McLaughlin, 1976; Connell, Turner, & Mason, 1985; Flay et al., 1987; Fullan & Pomfret, 1977). From a cognitive social learning perspective (Bandura, 1986), an effective training program would provide teachers with mastery experiences to boost perceived efficacy for implementing a curriculum with success. Mastery experiences would also be expected to have a positive impact on other variables important to program implementation, such as teacher enthusiasm and perceived preparedness to deliver the curriculum.

In our school-based trials, participating classroom teachers are paid consultants in the development of curriculum materials and implementation plans for the classroom intervention. We have found this to be valuable for improving the quality of a curriculum. In addition, it has proven beneficial for engaging the commitment and enthusiasm of the consultant teachers as well as their teaching colleagues. Then each year before the intended start date of the intervention, we deliver copies of the curriculum materials to all participating teachers and provide a half-day paid training workshop emphasizing the teaching–classroom management skills used in the curriculum. This reduces anxiety about delivering a "new" curriculum and helps teachers to prepare. Our experience suggests teachers are enthusiastic to have the opportunity to brush up on teaching skills, and we believe this enhances their morale and subsequent enthusiasm for implementing the curriculum. After the intervention begins, we adopt the "customer support" or "resource support" model often used by computer software distributors. Providing resource and technical support may increase the likelihood that programs will be implemented with completeness and integrity (Parcel et al., 1990).

EVALUATION ISSUES FOR OBESITY PREVENTION PROGRAMS

The efficacy of the Stanford OPPrA intervention is being evaluated in a cohort of approximately 1000 third graders in 13 ethnically and socioeconomically diverse elementary schools. As noted earlier, the intervention runs from the fall of the third grade to the spring of the fifth grade. Six schools were randomly assigned to receive the comprehensive obesity prevention intervention, and the remaining seven schools were assigned to receive an attention–placebo smoking and alcohol use prevention intervention. Assessments of children's height, weight, triceps skinfold thickness, waist and hip circumferences, food preferences, activity preferences, cardio–respiratory fitness, and self-reported diet, activity, and sedentary behaviors occur every six months, and six-months following the end of the intervention (in the sixth grade). Parent telephone interviews are performed at baseline and at the end of the fifth grade. An assessment of effects on parents and school personnel (administrators, teachers, food service) will also be completed. However, the crucial question is whether the overall intervention has an impact on student obesity and obesity-related behaviors. The primary objective of the intervention is to significantly reduce the prevalence of obesity, compared to controls, at the end of the three-year intervention. This design is typical of many school-based prevention programs. However, it brings up a number of important evaluation issues that deserve discussion.

CHOOSING AN APPROPRIATE CONTROL CONDITION

In all of our school-based prevention trials we include an attention–placebo control condition. We feel this is important for several reasons. First, we know there is communication among teachers from schools in the same district. Use of an untreated control condition might produce either resentful demoralization or even compensatory rivalry among teachers in schools assigned to no treatment (Campbell & Stanley, 1963; Cook & Campbell, 1979). We need to control for these plausible rival hypotheses not only for the integrity of the proposed trial but also to remain sensitive to the political realities of working in school districts. This may be most important when working in ethnic minority communities. In times past, the rights of ethnic minorities have been trampled on and ignored in the pursuit of questionable scientific objectives. As a result, many minority groups, and many people in general, have come to view the scientific enterprise with suspicion. Failure to consider and attend to the negative attitudes toward science that exist will seriously jeopardize the ability of any investigators to successfully evaluate their intervention. The attention–placebo control intervention is also necessary to control for potential effects associated with the use of innovative teaching methods. Because of this, we provide a control intervention that parallels the treatment intervention in materials, methods of instruction, teacher consulting, and teacher training and support. It is also important that the control intervention is perceived as being as desirable as the treatment intervention. Therefore, school personnel participate in identifying the specific goals of the control intervention. In addition to methodological benefits, this design also allows for the conduct of two controlled trials in which each intervention is the control for the other.

CHOOSING AN APPROPRIATE PRIMARY OUTCOME MEASURE

On the bases of accessibility, reliability, measurement validity, and clinical validity, the BMI is preferable to other available indirect measures of body fatness in common use in children and adolescents (Dietz & Robinson, 1998; Kraemer, Berkowitz, & Hammer, 1990). Therefore, we recommend the use of BMI (also referred to as the Quetelet Index, and defined as the weight in kilograms divided by the square of the height in meters) as the primary outcome measure for obesity-prevention trials. Unlike laboratory measures, BMI is obtained noninvasively and is therefore more accessible. Measures of height and weight are more reliably obtained than skinfold thicknesses (Marks, Habicht, & Mueller, 1989; USDHEW, 1974), and BMI demonstrates high measurement validity, correlating well with estimates of percentage body fat from densitometry (Himes & Bouchard, 1989), total body water (Dietz, Bandini, Schoeller, & Gortmaker, 1988), dual energy x-ray absorptiometry (Daniels, Khoury, & Morrison, 1997; Pietrobelli et al., 1998), and skinfold thicknesses (Killeen, Vanderburg, & Harlan, 1978) among children and adolescents of both sexes and multiple races. Most important, BMI has demonstrated clinical validity in its associations with blood pressure and hypertension (J. Dwyer et al., 1998; T. Dwyer & Blizzard, 1996; Lauer, Clarke, & Witt, 1989), adverse lipoprotein profiles (J. Dwyer et al., 1998; T. Dwyer & Blizzard, 1996), Type 2 diabetes (Pinhas-Hamiel et al., 1996), and early atherosclerotic lesions (McGill et al., 1995) among children and adolescents. In addition, BMI tracks more strongly from childhood to adulthood than skinfold thicknesses in both boys and girls (Clarke & Lauer, 1993; Rolland-Cachera, Bellisle, & Sempe, 1989), and adolescent BMI has been associated with future morbidity and mortality (Must et al., 1992).

ASSESSING EFFECTS OF THE INTERVENTION ON THE PRIMARY OUTCOME

The medical model tends to define outcomes dichotomously (i.e., disease or no disease, obese or not obese). Though it may seem appealing to choose a single cut-off definition of obesity (e.g., the 85th percentile of BMI), evaluation of program effects using a dichotomous outcome ignores the potential effects of the intervention on research participants at other points along the continuous distribution—it sacrifices the sensitivity of measurement necessary to recognize individual differences in response, both within and between groups, introduces misclassification errors as a result of the limited precision of both the measurements and the reference data used to define cut-offs, and sacrifices statistical power in establishing statistical significance (Cohen, 1983). Use of a threshold definition limits the test of the intervention to only the small number of participants hovering near the cut-off level who have a greater opportunity to jump from one side to the other. In addition, a cut-off definition has limited clinical validity because it assumes that children above the cut-off are at clearly greater risk than those below the cut-off (Kraemer et al., 1990; Power, Lake, & Cole, 1997; Robinson, 1993), which is not the case. BMI and other measures of body fatness are associated with clinically important outcomes, morbidity, and mortality in a continuous curvilinear manner, with no apparent threshold (Bray, 1985; T. Dwyer & Blizzard, 1996). Thus for purposes of establishing the efficacy of an obesity prevention program it is most appropriate to compare the full distributions of BMI between treatment and control groups. This is illustrated in Figure 11-1 displaying a hypothetical outcome distribution of BMI in treatment and control groups. In a prevention program, intervention effects may occur, and are intended to occur, throughout the distribution of BMI in the sample, not just around a standard (and necessarily arbitrary) threshold.

However, reductions in BMI among the leanest children may not be desirable. As illustrated in Figure 11-1, greater relative reductions in BMI are expected at higher levels of the BMI distribution. Therefore, it is informative to perform additional descriptive analyses to better characterize the clinical significance of the results. For descriptive analyses, effects are characterized not by statistical significance but by judgments of clinical significance. In this analysis one examines treatment effects based on thresholds of BMI. Figure 11-2 illustrates the desired hypothetical result of the intervention. It plots the risk ratios (vertical axis) associated with having a BMI greater than the specified threshold (horizontal axis) at the study endpoint (i.e., comparing prevalences of overweight as defined by various thresholds). The hypothetical figure shows minimal treatment effects on the proportion of

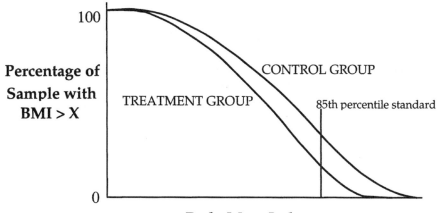

Figure 11-1. Hypothetical Outcome Distributions of BMI in the Treatment and Control Groups

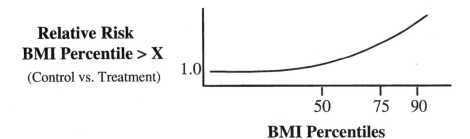

Figure 11-2. Hypothetical Descriptive Analysis of Treatment Effects Based on Thresholds of BMI

children with low and normal levels for BMI with increasing effects on the prevalence of high BMI.

ADDITIONAL MEASURES OF BODY COMPOSITION

Multiple skinfold thicknesses are often added as a more direct measure of subcutaneous fat or as an indirect assessment of body fat distribution. However, because of the difficulties in producing highly reliable skinfold measurements, introducing substantial measurement error, their added bene-fits are often unjustified outside of a controlled research setting. There has also been interest in including measures of abdominal adiposity, or visceral fat. Abdominal adiposity is related to metabolic risk factors in children

(Freedman et al., 1987; Freedman, Srinivasan, Harsha, Webber, & Berenson, 1989). Waist and hip circumferences can be measured reliably in field settings (Lohman, Roche, & Martorell, 1988), though evidence to date suggests that anthropometric measures tend to only moderately predict visceral fat compared to the gold standards of quantitative computed tomography and magnetic resonance (Goran, 1998). Finally, dual-energy x-ray absorptiometry (DXA) is commonly used in research settings to assess bone mass, fat mass, and lean body mass. However, normal growth in children introduces considerable error in DXA estimates of body composition, making DXA inappropriate for longitudinal studies (Gilsanz, 1998).

MEASURES OF DIET AND ACTIVITY

It is not uncommon to hear investigators speculate that choosing BMI as a primary outcome measure is, in effect, setting the bar too high—as an explanation for the limited past success of obesity prevention programs. They often suggest, instead, more "proximal" measures of behavior such as diet and activity levels. However, we believe that this argument is misinformed. First, it is important to acknowledge the potential for reporting bias in individuals who, by the nature of the intervention, are not blinded to the "right" answers. Perhaps even more important is the measurement error associated with self-reports of behavior. As noted previously, height and weight, the components of BMI, are reliably and validly measured in field settings. The reliability and validity of measures is particularly important in assessing the effects of population-based behavioral prevention programs because the resultant effect sizes may be relatively small, in comparison, for example, to many pharmacologic treatments. In contrast, interview and self-report measures of physical activity and dietary intake are notoriously prone to measurement error. Existing measures of physical activity and dietary intake all lack the requisite accuracy to distinguish the subtle changes in energy balance that may lead to changes in adiposity. In fact, it has been suggested that even the most accurate laboratory measurements of energy intake and expenditure are not sensitive enough to detect differences responsible for weight gain and loss over time in free-living samples (Liebel, 1995). As a result, choosing activity and diet measures as primary outcomes may really be setting the bar *even higher* than using BMI, because the added measurement error will demand even greater effect sizes to achieve statistical significance.

We recommend that measures of physical activity and dietary intake be included as secondary outcome variables, to attempt to describe more proximal effects of the intervention and mechanisms of change. Therefore, the choice of specific measures will depend on the specific goals of the intervention. For example, a program intended to promote substitution of fruits and vegetables for high-fat foods may be assessed best by a food frequency questionnaire containing the specific foods that are targeted in the intervention. The additional calorie, fat, fiber, vitamin, and mineral estimates that would come from much more expensive and time-consuming multiple 24-hour recalls would not match the intervention, and therefore may even be less sensitive to change. Similarly, if a physical activity intervention is targeting lifestyle activities, then activity monitoring is likely to be a better measure than an endurance running test, which would be better for assessing the effects of an endurance training intervention including a lot of running. In addition, as suggested previously, measures should be chosen that will provide the greatest reliability, accuracy, and sensitivity to change in the intended sample. In many cases, this is best served by extensive formative evaluation and pilot testing before the evaluation.

IMPLEMENTATION ASSESSMENTS

Because implementation is crucial to program success, implementation assessment is necessary to know whether the effects (or lack of effects) of an intervention can be attributed to the intervention itself or to some other factor (such as poor implementation). Therefore, implementation assessments should generally include measures of implementation fidelity as well as surveillance for potential outside influences. In our school-based prevention programs these consist of (a) direct, systematic classroom, PE, and school lunch observations to assess whether teachers facilitate delivery of program lessons, how completely lessons are delivered, and the quality–integrity of delivery (Tortu & Botvin, 1989); (b) assessments of teacher and organizational variables (e.g., sociodemographic variables, self-reported health behaviors and attitudes, teacher morale, compatibility of teaching methods, enthusiasm for the program, perceived preparedness, etc.), which may help us understand any observed variation in implementation; and (c) active surveillance of schools for events, new programs, or curricula that may pose threats to internal validity (e.g., serious illnesses or death among students or staff, other health-oriented curricula, physical education programs or sports programs at the participating schools).

CONCLUSION

Obesity prevention represents a challenging, and largely new, direction for applied psychological research. We believe that success in establishing effective obesity prevention programs will be achieved to the degree that investigators pay more than lip service to the importance of carefully translating behavior change theory into innovative practice. We have discussed some promising approaches: altering food preferences; reducing television, videotape, and video game use; and involving children as health advocates. Instead of directly targeting broad diet and activity changes, these approaches target specific behavior changes that will, in turn, indirectly influence dietary intake and activity levels. Our study of reducing television viewing is one of the first successful examples of this approach. By identifying a potential mediating behavior that is susceptible to change with a behavioral intervention, we were able to influence body composition without addressing diet or physical activity directly. Similarly, we are conducting an intervention using young adult African American female role models to lead traditional African dance classes and popular hip-hop dance classes for African American preadolescent girls, thereby avoiding the usual emphasis on weight control, diet, and exercise that has been mostly unsuccessful in the past. However, these same principles can be applied more directly to diet and activity behaviors as well, if they are sufficiently defined and subject to monitoring. In the Stanford OPPrA trial we chose fruit and vegetable intake, switching to low-fat milk, reducing fast food meals, and reducing heavily processed and packaged snack foods as discrete behavioral targets, for example, in contrast to trying to promote overall lower fat intake. In the PE intervention, instead of trying to persuade children to exercise more, we are making physical activity more enjoyable, and challenging them to increase their daily steps with pedometers. Our belief, increasingly supported by our results, is that greater attention to principles of behavior change will result in more innovative, effective, and generalizable approaches to prevent obesity.

REFERENCES

Abraham, S., Collins, G., & Nordsieck, M. (1971). Relationship of childhood weight status to morbidity in adults. *HSMHA Health Reports, 86,* 273–284.

Altman, D. G., Foster, V., Rasenick-Douss, L., & Tye, J. B. (1989). Reducing the illegal sales of cigarettes to minors. *Journal of the American Medical Association, 261,* 80–83.

Anderson, B., Odden, A., Farrar, E., Fuhrman, S., Davis, A., Huddle, E., Armstrong, J., & Flakus-Mosqueda, P. (1987). State strategies to support local school improvement. *Knowledge: Creation, Diffusion, Utilization, 9,* 42–86.

Annenberg Public Policy Center. (1997). *Television in the home: The 1997 survey of parents and children.* Philadelphia: University of Pennsylvania.

Bandura, A. (1986). *Social foundations of thought and action.* Englewood Cliffs, NJ: Prentice-Hall.

Basch, C. E., Eveland, J. D., & Portnoy, B. (1986). Diffusion systems for education and learning about health. *Family and Community Health, 9,* 1--6.

Berman, P., & McLaughlin, M. W. (1976). Implementation of educational innovation. *Education Forum, 40,* 347–370.

Berman, P., & Pauly, E. W. (1975). *Federal Programs Supporting Educational Change, Vol II: Factors affecting change agent projects.* Santa Monica, CA: RAND.

Birch, L. L., & Fisher, J. O. (1998). Development of eating behaviors among children and adolescents. *Pediatrics, 101,* 539–549.

Braddon, F. E. M., Rodgers, B., Wadsworth, M. E. J., & Davies, J. M. (1986). Onset of obesity in a 36-year birth cohort study. *British Medical Journal, 293,* 299–303.

Bray, G. A. (1985). Complications of obesity. *Annals of Internal Medicine, 103,* 1052–1062.

Campbell, D. T., & Stanley, J. C. (1963). *Experimental and Quasi-Experimental Designs for Research.* Boston: Houghton Mifflin.

Cauce, A. M., & Srebnik, D. S. (1989). Peer networks and social support: a focus for preventive efforts with youths. In L. A. Bond & B. E. Compas (Eds.), *Primary prevention and health promotion in the schools* (pp. 235–254). Newbury Park, CA: Sage.

Centers for Disease Control. (1991). Body weight perceptions and selected weight management goals and practices of high school students—United States, 1990. *Morbidity and Mortality Weekly Report, 40,* 741–750.

Centers for Disease Control and Prevention. (1997). Update: Prevalence of overweight among children, adolescents, and adults—United States, 1988–1994. *Morbidity and Mortality Weekly Report,46,* 199–202.

Clarke, W. R., & Lauer, R. M. (1993). Does childhood obesity track to adulthood? *Critical Reviews in Food Science and Nutrition, 33,* 423–430.

Cohen, J. (1983). The cost of dichotomization. *Applied Psychological Measurement, 7,* 249–253.

Connell, D. B., Turner, R. R., & Mason, E. F. (1985). Summary of findings of the school health education evaluation: health promotion effectiveness, implementation, and costs. *Journal of School Health, 55,* 316–321.

Cook, T. D., & Campbell, D. T. (1979). *Quasi-experimentation. Design & analysis issues for field settings.* Boston: Houghton Mifflin.

Daniels, S. R., Khoury, P. R., & Morrison, J. A. (1997). The utility of body mass index as a measure of body fatness in children and adolescents: Differences by race and gender. *Pediatrics, 99,* 804–807.

DeMarco, T., & Sidney, K. (1989). Enhancing children's participation in physical activity. *Journal of School Health, 59,* 337–340.

Dietz, W. H. (1994). Critical periods in childhood for the development of obesity. *American Journal of Clinical Nutrition, 59,* 995–999.

Dietz, W. H., Bandini, L., Schoeller, D. A., & Gortmaker, S. L. (1988). Diagnosis of obesity in adolescents and young adults. In E. M. Berry, S. H. Blondheim,

H. E. Eliahou, & E. Shafrir (Eds.), *Recent Advances in Obesity Research: V: Proceedings of the 5th International Congress on Obesity, Jerusalem, Israel, 1986* (pp. 9–15). London: John Libbey.

Dietz, W. H., & Robinson, T. N. (1998). Use of the body mass index (BMI) as a measure of overweight in children and adolescents. *Journal of Pediatrics, 132*, 191–193.

Drewnowski, A., Brunzell, J. D., Sande, K., Iverius, P. H., & Greenwood, M. R. C. (1985). Sweet tooth reconsidered: Taste responsiveness in human obesity. *Physiology and Behavior, 35*, 617–622.

Dwyer, J. T., Hewew, L. V., Mitchell, P. D., Nicklas, T. A., Montgomery, D. H., Lytle, L. A., Snyder, M. P., Zive, M. M., Bachman, K. J., Rice, R., & Parcel, G. S. (1996). Improving school breakfasts: Effects of the CATCH Eat Smart program on the nutrient content of school breakfasts. *Preventive Medicine, 25*, 413–422.

Dwyer, J. T., Stone, E. J., Yang, M., Feldman, H., Webber, L. S., Must, A., Perry, C. L., Nader, P. R., & Parcel, G. S. (1998). Predictors of overweight and overfatness in a multiethnic pediatric population. *American Journal of Clinical Nutrition, 67*, 602–610.

Dwyer, T., & Blizzard, C. L. (1996). Defining obesity in children by biological endpoint rather than population distribution. *International Journal of Obesity, 20*, 472–480.

Dwyer, T., Coonan, W. E., Leitch, D. R., Hetzel, B. S., & Baghurst, R. A. (1983). An investigation of the effects of daily physical activity on the health of primary school students in South Australia. *International Journal of Epidemiology, 12*, 308–313.

Eck, L. H., Klesges, R. C., Hanson, C. L., & Slawson, D. (1992). Children at familial risk for obesity: An examination of dietary intake, physical activity and weight status. *International Journal of Obesity, 16*, 71–78.

Ellison, R. C., Capper, A. L., Goldberg, R. J., Witschi, J. C., & Stare, F. J. (1989). The environmental component: changing school food service to promote cardiovascular health. *Health Education Quarterly, 16*, 285–297.

Epstein, L. H. (1996). Family-based behavioral intervention for obese children. *International Journal of Obesity, 20*(Suppl. 1), S14–S21.

Epstein, L. H., Myers, M. D., Raynor, H. A., & Saelens, B. E. (1998). Treatment of pediatric obesity. *Pediatrics, 101*, 554–570.

Epstein, L. H., Valoski, A., Wing, R. R., & McCurley, J. (1994). Ten-year outcomes of behavioral family-based treatment for childhood obesity. *Health Psychology, 13*, 373–383.

Flay, B. R., Hansen, W. B., Johnson, C. A., Collins, L. M., Dent, C. W., Dwyer, K. M., Grossman, L., Hockstein, G., Rauch, J., Sobel, J., Sobol, D. F., Sussman, S., & Ulene, A. (1987). Implementation effectiveness trial of a social influences smoking prevention program using schools and television. *Health Education Research, 2*, 385–400.

Freedman, D. S., Srinivasan, S. R., Burke, G. L., Shear, C. L., Smoak, C. G., Harsha, D. W., Webber, L. S., & Berenson, G. S. (1987). Relation of body fat distribution to hyperinsulinemia in children and adolescents: the Bogalusa Heart Study. *American Journal of Clinical Nutrition, 46,* 403–410.

Freedman, D. S., Srinivasan, S. R., Harsha, D. W., Webber, L. S., & Berenson, G. S. (1989). Relation of body fat patterning to lipid and lipoprotein concentrations in children and adolescents: the Bogalusa Heart Study. *American Journal of Clinical Nutrition, 50,* 930–939.

Fullan, M., & Pomfret, A. (1977). Research on curriculum and instruction implementation. *Reviews of Educational Research, 47,* 335–397.

Gaines, S. O., Marelich, W. D., Bledsoe, K. L., Steers, W. N., Henderson, M. C., Granrose, C. S., & Barajas, L. (1997). Links between race/ethnicity and cultural values as mediated by race/ethnicity identity and moderated by gender. *Journal of Personality and Social Psychology, 72,* 1460–1476.

Gilsanz, V. (1998). Bone density in children: a review of the available techniques and indications. *European Journal of Radiology, 26,* 177–182.

Gold, R. S., Parcel, G. S., Walberg, H. J., Luepker, R. V., Pornoy, B., & Stone, E. J. (1991). Summary and conclusions of the THTM evaluation: The expert work group perspective. *Journal of School Health, 61,* 39–42.

Goran, M. I. (1998). Measurement issues related to studies of childhood obesity: Assessment of body composition, body fat distribution, physical activity, and food intake. *Pediatrics, 101,* 505–518.

Guo, S. S., Roche, A. F., Chumlea, W. C., Gardner, J. D., & Siervogel, R. M. (1994). The predictive value of childhood body mass index values for overweight at age 35y. *American Journal of Clinical Nutrition, 59,* 810–819.

Haddock, C. K., Shadish, W. R., Klesges, R. C., & Stein, R. (1994). Treatments for childhood and adolescent obesity. *Annals of Behavioral Medicine, 16,* 235–244.

Harrison, A. O., Wilson, M. N., Pine, C. J., Chan, S. Q., & Buriel, R. (1990). Family ecologies of ethnic minority children. *Child Development, 61,* 347–362.

Hawkins, J. D., Lishner, D., & Catalano, R. F. (1985). Childhood predictors and the prevention of adolescent substance use. In D. L. Jones & R. J. Battjes (Eds.), *Etiology of drug use: Implications for prevention (NIDA Research Monograph 56)* (pp. 75–126). Washington, DC: U.S. Government Printing Office. (DHHS Pub. No. (ADM)85-1335)

Hearn, M. D., Bigelow, C., Nader, P. R., Stone, E., Johnson, C., Parcel, G., Perry, C. L., & Luepker, R. V. (1992). Involving families in cardiovascular health promotion: the CATCH feasibility study. *Journal of Health Education, 23*(1), 22–31.

Himes, J. H., & Bouchard, C. (1989). Validity of anthropometry in classifying youths as obese. *International Journal of Obesity, 13,* 183–193.

Huberman, A. M., & Miles, M. B. (1984). *Innovations up close.* New York: Plenum Press.

Huberman, A. M., Miles, M. B., Taylor, B. L., & Goldberg, J. A. (1983). Innovation up close: a field study in 12 school settings. In D. P. Crandall (Ed.), *People, Policies and Practices: Examining the chain of school improvement* . Andover, MA: The Network.

Jackson, M. Y., Proulx, J. M., & Pelican, S. (1991). Obesity prevention. *American Journal of Clinical Nutrition, 53*, 1625S–1630S.

Killeen, J., Vanderburg, D., & Harlan, W. R. (1978). Application of weight-height ratios and body indices to juvenile populations—The National Health Examination Survey data. *Journal of Chronic Disease, 31*, 529–537.

Killen, J. D., Hayward, C., Litt, I., Hammer, L. D., Wilson, D. M., Miner, B., Taylor, C. B., Varady, A., & Shisslak, C. (1992). Is puberty a risk factor for eating disorders? *American Journal of Diseases of Children, 146*, 323–325.

Killen, J. D., & Robinson, T. N. (1989). School-based research on health behavior change: the Stanford adolescent heart health program as a model for cardiovascular disease risk reduction. In E. Rothkopf (Ed.), *Review of research in education* (Vol. 15, pp. 171–200). Washington, DC: American Educational Research Association.

Killen, J. D., Robinson, T. N., Telch, M., Saylor, K. E., Maron, D. J., Rich, T., & Bryson, S. (1989). The Stanford Adolescent Heart Health Program. *Health Education Quarterly, 16*(2), 265–283.

Killen, J. D., Telch, M. J., Robinson, T. N., Maccoby, N., Taylor, C. B., & Farquhar, J. W. (1988). Cardiovascular disease risk reduction for tenth graders. *Journal of the American Medical Association, 260*(12), 1728–1733.

Klesges, R. C., Stein, R. J., Eck, L. H., Isbell, T. R., & Klesges, L. M. (1991). Parental influence on food selection in young children and its relationships to childhood obesity. *American Journal of Clinical Nutrition, 53*, 859–864.

Knittle, J. L., Timmers, K., Ginsberg-Fellner, F., Brown, R. E., & Katz, D. P. (1979). The Growth of Adipose Tissue in Children and Adolescents: Cross-sectional and Longitudinal Studies of Adipose Cell Number and Size. *Journal of Clinical Investigation, 63*, 239–246.

Kraemer, H. C., Berkowitz, R. I., & Hammer, L. D. (1990). Methodological difficulties in studies of obesity. I. measurement issues. *Annals of Behavioral Medicine, 12*, 112–118.

Landrine, H., & Klonoff, E. A. (1992). Culture and health-related schemas: a review and proposal for interdisciplinary integration. *Health Psychology, 11*, 267–276.

Lauer, R. M., Clarke, W. R., & Witt, J. (1989). Childhood risk factors for high adult blood pressure: the Muscatine study. *Pediatrics, 84*, 633–641.

Levenson-Gingiss, P., & Hamilton, R. (1989). Determinants of teachers' plans to continue teaching a sexuality education course. *Family and Community Health, 12*, 40–53.

Liebel, R. L. (1995). Obesity: a game of inches. *Pediatrics, 95*, 131–132.

Lohman, T. G., Roche, A. F., & Martorell, R. (1988). *Anthropometric Standardization Reference Manual*. Champaign, IL: Human Kinetics.

Luepker, R. V., Perry, C. L., McKinlay, S. M., Nader, P. R., Parcel, G. S., Stone, E. J., Webber, L. S., Elder, J. P., Feldman, H. A., Johnson, C. C., Kelder, S. H., & Wu, M. (1996). Outcomes of a field trial to improve children's dietary patterns and physical activity. The Child and Adolescent Trial for Cardiovascular Health (CATCH). *Journal of the American Medical Association, 275,* 768–776.

Marin, G. (1993). Defining culturally appropriate community interventions: Hispanics as a case study. *Journal of Community Psychology, 21,* 149–161.

Marks, G. C., Habicht, J.-P., & Mueller, W. H. (1989). Reliability, dependability, and precision of anthropometric measurements. *American Journal of Epidemiology, 130*(3), 578–587.

McGill, H. C. J., McMahan, C. A., Malcom, G. T., Oalmann, M. C., Strong, J. P., & and the Pathobiological Determinants of Atherosclerosis in Youth (PDAY) Research Group. (1995). Relation of glycohemoglobin and adiposity to atherosclerosis in youth. *Arteriosclerosis, Thrombosis, and Vascular Biology, 15,* 431–440.

McGuire, W. (1964). Inducing resistance to persuasion. In L. Berkowitz (Ed.), *Advances in Experimental Social Psychology* (pp. 191–229). New York: Academic Press.

McKenzie, T. L., Nader, P. R., Strikmiller, P. K., Yang, M., Stone, E. J., Perry, C. L., Taylor, W. C., Epping, J. N., Feldman, H. A., Luepker, R. V., & Kelder, S. H. (1996). School physical education: Effect of the Child and Adolescent Trial for Cardiovascular Health. *Preventive Medicine, 25,* 423–431.

Mueller, W. H. (1982). The changes with age of the anatomical distribution of fat. *Social Science and Medicine, 16,* 191–196.

Must, A., Jacques, P. F., Dallal, G. E., Bajema, C. J., & Dietz, W. H. (1992). Long-term morbidity and mortality of overweight adolescents: A follow-up of the Harvard Growth Study of 1922 to 1935. *New England Journal of Medicine, 327,* 1350–1355.

Nader, P. R., Baranowski, T., Vanderpool, N. A., & Dunn, K., Dworkin, R., & Ray, L. (1983). The family health project: cardiovascular risk reduction education for children and parents. *Journal of Developmental and Behavioral Pediatrics, 4,* 3–10.

National Institutes of Health Technology Assessment Conference Panel. (1993). Methods for voluntary weight loss and control. *Annals of Internal Medicine, 119,* 764–770.

NHLBI. (1994). *Strategy Development Workshop for Public Education on Weight and Obesity: Summary Report.* Bethesda, MD: U.S. Department of Health and Human Services, PHS, National Institutes of Health, National Heart, Lung and Blood Institute. (NIH Publication No. 94-3314)

Olsen, L. (1984). *Food Fight: A report on teenagers' eating habits and nutritional status:* Oakland, CA: Citizen's Policy Center.

Osganian, S. K., Ebzery, M. K., Montgomery, D. H., Nicklas, T. A., Evans, M. A., Mitchell, P. D., Lytle, L. A., Snyder, M. P., Stone, E. J., Zive, M. M., Bachman,

K. J., Rice, R., & Parcel, G. S. (1996). Changes in nutrient content of school lunches: results from the CATCH Eat Smart foods service intervention. *Preventive Medicine, 25*, 400–412.

Parcel, G. S., Perry, C. L., & Taylor, W. C. (1990). Beyond demonstration: diffusion of health promotion innovations. In N. Bracht (Ed.), *Health Promotion at the Community Level* . Newbury Park, CA: Sage.

Perry, C. L., Crockett, S. J., & Pirie, P. (1987, October/November). Influencing parental health behavior: implications of community assessments. *Health Education* 68–77.

Perry, C. L., Luepker, R. V., Murray, D. M., & Hearn, M. D. (1989). Parent involvement with children's health promotion: a one-year follow-up of the Minnesota Home Team. *Health Education Quarterly, 16*, 1156–1160.

Pietrobelli, A., Faith, M. S., Allison, D. B., Gallagher, D., Chiumello, G., & Heymsfield, S. B. (1998). Body mass index as a measure of adiposity among children and adolescents: a validation study. *Journal of Pediatrics, 132*, 204–210.

Pinhas-Hamiel, O., Dolan, L. M., Daniels, S. R., Standiford, D., Khoury, P. R., & Zeitler, P. (1996). Increased incidence of non-insulin dependent diabetes mellitus among adolescents. *Journal of Pediatrics, 128*, 608–615.

Power, C., Lake, J. K., & Cole, T. J. (1997). Measurement and long-term health risks of childhood and adolescent fatness. *International Journal of Obesity, 21*, 507–526.

Resnicow, K. (1993). School-based obesity prevention. Population versus high-risk interventions. *Annals of the New York Academy of Sciences, 699*, 154–166.

Resnicow, K., Baranowski, T., Ahluwalia, J. S., & Braithwaite, R. L. (1999). Cultural sensitivity in public health: Defined and demystified. *Ethnicity and Disease, 9*, 10–21.

Resnicow, K., Braithwaite, R. L., & Kuo, J. (1997). Interpersonal interventions for minority adolescents. In D. K. Wilson, J. R. Rodrigue, & W. C. Taylor (Eds.), *Health Promoting and Health Compromising Behaviors Among Minority Adolescents*. Washington, DC: American Psychological Association.

Resnicow, K., & Robinson, T. N. (1997). School-based cardiovascular disease prevention studies: review and synthesis. *Annals of Epidemiology, S7*, S14–S31.

Resnicow, K., Robinson, T. N., & Frank, E. (1996). Advances and future directions for school-based health promotion research: commentary on the CATCH intervention trial. *Preventive Medicine, 25*, 378–383.

Robinson, T. N. (1993). Defining obesity in children and adolescents: clinical approaches. *Critical Reviews in Food Science and Nutrition, 33*, 313–320.

Robinson, T. N. (1998). Does television cause childhood obesity? *Journal of the American Medical Association, 279*, 959–960.

Robinson, T. N. (1999a). Behavioural treatment of childhood and adolescent obesity. *International Journal of Obesity, 23*(Suppl. 2), S52–S57.

Robinson, T. N. (1999b). Reducing children's television to prevent obesity: a randomized controlled trial. *Journal of the American Medical Association, 282,* 1561–1567.

Robinson, T. N., Chang, J. Y., Haydel, K. F., & Killen, J. D. (in press). Overweight concerns, body dissatisfaction, and desired body shape among 3rd grade children: The impacts of ethnicity and socioeconomic status. *Journal of Pediatrics.*

Rolland-Cachera, M. F., Bellisle, F., & Sempe, M. (1989). The prediction in boys and girls of the weight/height^2 index and various skinfold measurements in adults: A two-decade follow-up study. *International Journal of Obesity, 13,* 305–311.

Sallis, J. F., McKenzie, T. L., Alcaraz, J. E., Kolody, B., Faucette, N., & Hovell, M. F. (1997). The effects of a 2-year physical education program (SPARK) on physical activity and fitness in elementary school students. *American Journal of Public Health, 87,* 1328–1334.

Simons-Morton, B. G., O'Hara, N. M., Parcel, G. S., Huang, I. W., Baranowski, T., & Wilson, B. (1990). Children's frequency of participation in moderate to vigorous physical activities. *Research Quarterly for Exercise and Sport, 61,* 307–314.

Simons-Morton, B. G., Parcel, G. S., Baranowski, T., Forthofer, R., & O'Hara, N. M. (1991). Promoting physical activity and a healthful diet among children: results of a school-based intervention study. *American Journal of Public Health, 81,* 986–991.

Simons-Morton, B. G., Taylor, W. C., Snider, S. A., & Huant, I. W. (1993). The physical activity of fifth-grade students during physical education classes. *American Journal of Public Health, 83,* 262–264.

Sobol, D. F., Rohrbach, L. A., Dent, C. W., Gleason, L., Brannon, B. R., Johnson, C. A., & Flay, B. R. (1989). The integrity of smoking prevention curriculum delivery. *Health Education Research, 4,* 59–67.

Stolley, M. R., & Fitzgibbon, M. L. (1997). Effects of an obesity prevention program on the eating behavior of African American mothers and daughters. *Health Education and Behavior, 24,* 152–164.

Tortu, S., & Botvin, G. J. (1989). School-based smoking prevention: The teacher training process. *Preventive Medicine, 18,* 280–289.

Troiano, R. P., & Flegal, K. M. (1998). Overweight children and adolescents: description, epidemiology, and demographics. *Pediatrics, 101,* 497–504.

USDHEW. (1974). *Skinfold Thickness of Youths 12–17 Years, United States: Vital and Health Statistics.* Washington, DC: National Center for Health Statistics. (Series 11, Number 132, DHEW Publication Number (HRA) 74-1614)

Vega, W. A., Sallis, J. F., Patterson, T. L., Rupp, J. W., Morris, J. A., & Nader, P. R. (1988). Predictors of dietary change in Mexican-American families participating in a health behavior change program. *American Journal of Preventive Medicine, 4,* 194–199.

Webber, L. S., Osganian, S. K., Feldman, H. A., Wu, M., McKenzie, T. L., Nichaman, M., Lytle, L. A., Edmundson, E., Cutler, J., Nader, P. R., & Luepker,

R. V. (1996). Cardiovascular risk factors among children after a 2 1/2-year intervention—The CATCH study. *Preventive Medicine, 25*, 432–441.

Whitaker, R. C., Wright, J. A., Finch, A. J., & Psaty, B. M. (1993). An environmental intervention to reduce dietary fat in school lunches. *Pediatrics, 91*, 1107–1111.

Whitaker, R. C., Wright, J. A., Pepe, M. S., Seidel, K. D., & Dietz, W. H. (1997). Predicting obesity in young adulthood from childhood and parental obesity. *New England Journal of Medicine, 337*, 869–873.

Winkleby, M. A., Robinson, T. N., & Sundquist, J. (1999). Ethnic variation in cardiovascular disease risk factors among children and young adults: Findings from the Third National Health and Nutrition Examination Survey, 1988–1994. *Journal of the American Medical Association, 281*, 1006–1013.

World Health Organization. (1998). *Obesity. Preventing and Managing the Global Epidemic. Report of a WHO Consultation on Obesity.* Geneva: World Health Organization.

Young, R. L., deMoor, C., Wildey, M. B., Gully, S., Hovell, M. F., & Elder, J. P. (1990). Correlates of health facilitator performance in a tobacco use prevention program: implications for recruitment. *Journal of School Health, 60*, 463–467.

12

TREATMENT OF EATING DISORDERS IN CHILDREN AND ADOLESCENTS

STACY A. GORE, JILLON S. VANDER WAL, AND MARK H. THELEN

Few controlled studies of treatment of children and adolescents with eating disorders have been conducted. Nonetheless, this population continues to present for treatment, and effective methods of treatment are needed. Given the sparse nature of the literature, a review of adult research can help identify potential interventions for children and bring to light common methodological problems in this type of research, regardless of the age of the participants. The adult literature contains three major treatment modalities that have shown the most promise and are applicable to children. These modalities are behavioral therapy (BT), cognitive–behavioral therapy (CBT), and interpersonal therapy (IPT). First, outcome studies of these treatments with adult participants will be briefly reviewed. Second, studies more closely related to children that focus on family therapy and treatment of body image disturbance will be explored. Third, studies addressing the use of hospitalization and medication in treatment will be reviewed. In each of these areas, suggestions will be made regarding possible applications to children.

BEHAVIORAL THERAPY

Behavioral therapy for bulimia nervosa typically involves exposure and response prevention, during which clients eat feared foods in the presence of the therapist while purging is prevented. The outcome studies of BT for bulimia nervosa among adult participants have shown mixed results. BT has been found to result in decreased vomiting and to favorably change obsessive thoughts, interpersonal sensitivity, depression, and binge eating (Cooper, Cooper, & Hill, 1989; Johnson, Sclundt, & Jarrell, 1986). The urge to binge, as well as feelings of guilt, tension, and lack of control decreased after every session according to Kennedy, Katz, Neitzert, Ralevski, and Mendlowitz (1985). However, depression, feelings of being fat, urge to exercise, and food intake have not been found to change following a course of BT (Johnson et al., 1986; Kennedy et al., 1985). Given that BT does not target these characteristics, it is not surprising that BT does not appear to affect many of the major beliefs and emotions that are thought to underlie bulimia nervosa. BT for anorexia nervosa often takes the form of granting privileges for weight gain. Channon, de Silva, Hemsley, and Perkins (1989) compared BT to CBT and a control treatment in an outpatient setting. Participants in the control group received an eclectic treatment. No differences were found between CBT, BT, or control treatments on measures of eating disorder symptomatology. Although improvements occurred in weight, nutritional functioning, menstrual functioning, psychosexual functioning, preferred weight, drive for thinness, and depressed mood regardless of group membership, the majority of participants could not be considered recovered. Hence BT may not be effective as the sole treatment for anorexia nervosa.

Given the frequent use of behavioral techniques in treating various childhood disorders, it is likely that these techniques could be effective when incorporated in the treatment of eating disorders. For example, behavioral techniques such as exposure, relaxation, modeling, visualization, and role playing have been used to treat simple phobia and other anxiety disorders in childhood (e.g., Silverman & Nelles, 1990; Thyer, 1991). Children with eating disorders may benefit from gradual exposure to feared foods coupled with relaxation training. Moreover, they could learn to address social and familial problems via role-playing. Celebrities who promote a strong and healthy body image may be used as role models. Finally, reinforcements can be used to promote positive behavioral change or weight gain.

COGNITIVE–BEHAVIORAL TREATMENT

Cognitive–behavioral treatment is a problem-focused therapy based on the premise that treatment should modify extreme attitudes about eating and the body (Wilson & Pike, 1993). The therapy typically combines behavioral techniques, such as self-monitoring of food intake, avoidance of high-risk situations, and stimulus control, with cognitive strategies to combat dysfunctional thoughts related to food and weight. In addition, coping skills training and relapse prevention techniques are typically included. Behavioral techniques are often used in the beginning of treatment, whereas cognitive interventions dominate in the middle and late stages. CBT has been found to decrease bulimic symptomatology (Fairburn, Kirk, O'Connor, & Cooper,

1986; Garner et al., 1983; Ordman & Kirschenbaum, 1985), increase overall adjustment, decrease depressive symptomatology, and improve body image (Fairburn et al., 1986; Garner et al., 1983; Ordman & Kirschenbaum, 1985). Further, these improvements have been found to be maintained one year after treatment (Fairburn et al., 1986; Garner et al., 1983). CBT has also been shown to be superior to educational approaches, brief psychoanalysis, and supportive psychotherapy (Garner et al., 1983; Ordman & Kirschenbaum, 1985). Although the mechanism by which CBT achieves its effect is unclear, explanatory theories tend to emphasize the importance of changing beliefs and behaviors. For example, one theory suggests that changing beliefs about the body leads to changes in eating, whereas another suggests that changes in eating and purging behavior are themselves the important component through exposure or increased self-efficacy (Wilson & Fairburn, 1993).

There are significantly fewer studies of CBT for anorexia nervosa. As discussed earlier, Channon et al. (1989) found that CBT was no more effective than BT and eclectic therapy. However, in a preliminary application of an effective treatment regime for bulimia nervosa, Cooper and Fairburn (1984) suggested that CBT may be effective in treating anorexia nervosa, especially in women who also suffer from bulimic episodes.

Although the outcome studies reviewed included adults, there are applications for children and adolescents. It should be noted that many of the studies included women who were 17 or 18 years old. Because of adolescents' difficulty with metacognition, some cognitive components may not be applicable (Schrodt, 1992; Wilkes & Rush, 1988). However, using modified CBT, it is likely that adolescents could be treated as effectively as adults. For example, adolescents would be able to develop alternative ways of thinking about a situation and participate in problem solving exercises (Schrodt, 1992; Wilkes & Rush, 1988). Robin, Gilroy, and Dennis (1998) give two guidelines for determining if CBT is an appropriate treatment of choice. First, one must have the ability to think abstractly. Second, one must be able to develop and test alternative hypotheses. Typically, these skills are developed by the age of 14 or 15. Hence it is likely that older adolescents may be treated as effectively as adults with CBT. However, CBT must be modified to meet the developmental level of young adolescents and children. Techniques such as identifying and correcting cognitions and developing cognitive coping strategies have been used in the treatment of children with anxiety disorders and could improve the efficacy of the behavioral techniques discussed earlier (Silverman & Nelles, 1990). In addition, behavioral experimentation could be used to disconfirm distortions. Other cognitive techniques could be taught using games or fables (Robin et al., 1998).

INTERPERSONAL THERAPY

Unlike the treatment modalities just reviewed, IPT does not directly address eating attitudes and behaviors. Instead, the symptoms are placed in a larger interpersonal context. Thus the focus of treatment is on interpersonal events that seem to trigger problematic behaviors. These events fall into four categories: grief, interpersonal role disputes, role transitions, and interpersonal deficits. Treatment involves exploring individual events, defining the client's expectations, developing alternative ways of handling the problems, and practicing new behaviors. The therapist reinforces attempts to change without making specific recommendations (Fairburn, 1985). IPT has shown promise in treating bulimia nervosa in adults, although Fairburn (1993) stated that interpersonal role disputes and role transitions are most often the focus in therapy with clients suffering from bulimia nervosa. In an initial study, Fairburn et al. (1991) found that IPT was comparable with BT at reducing dietary restraint, although it was inferior to CBT. IPT was less effective than CBT and BT at decreasing vomiting frequency. IPT also was less effective than CBT in changing concerns about weight and decreasing scores on a global measure of disturbed eating habits and attitudes. However, IPT was as effective as CBT and more effective than BT in decreasing participants' concerns about their body shape. Although this study seems to demonstrate the superiority of CBT, results obtained on follow-up tell a different story (Fairburn, Jones, Peveler, Hope, & O'Connor, 1993). At the 12-month follow-up, IPT and CBT groups showed a significant and comparable reduction in dietary restraint and shape and weight concerns compared to pretreatment assessments. The trend for IPT clients to improve over the follow-up period and have similar results to CBT clients was replicated by Fairburn et al. (1995).

The potential of IPT as a treatment of adolescents suffering from bulimia nervosa looks promising. An IPT treatment for adolescents suffering from depression has been developed using the same concepts used in treating adults (Mufson, Woreau, Weissman, & Klerman, 1993). This treatment involves a focus on present and future role disputes and life choices. Treatment is similar to that used with adults, with the primary difference involving a focus on developmental changes experienced in adolescence. This advancement suggests that the same could be done for treating adolescents suffering from an eating disorder. The applicability of IPT to children is less certain, because IPT has not been modified to treat children. Further, two (role disputes and role transitions) of the four focus areas of IPT do not appear to be relevant for children. However, interpersonal deficits and grief could be appropriate topics for treatment.

FAMILY THERAPY

Unlike the other treatment modalities, family therapy research has included children and adolescents. The treatment was originally developed for anorexia nervosa but has been applied to bulimia nervosa. However, little controlled outcome research on the treatment of bulimia nervosa has been conducted.

Shugar and Kruegar (1995) focused on specific types of family communication, specifically confrontation, hostility, and aggressiveness, as a means of assessing the outcome of systemic therapy in the treatment of anorexia nervosa for 13- to 16-year-old adolescents. At the end of treatment, all participants had gained some weight. Those adolescents who had the most weight gain and significant improvements in eating attitudes had families who exhibited the least amount of indirect aggression in any phase of therapy. There was a significant change in all components of aggression in each phase of treatment as overt aggression increased and indirect aggression decreased. The results of this study seem to indicate that family interactions could be an indicator of improvement in therapy.

To determine the most effective aspects of family therapy, le Grange, Eisler, Dare, and Russell (1992) compared one condition, in which the whole family was seen together (conjoint family therapy), with a condition in which the parents and patients are seen separately (family counseling). Participants included 18 anorexic adolescents ranging in age from 12 to 17. The conjoint therapy required that the family attend all sessions; therefore, the therapist was able to observe interactions directly. In addition, the treatment used the family meal as an important focus of therapy. In family counseling the therapist was unable to directly observe family interactions. Results indicate that improvements occurred in reported eating disorder symptomatology, self-esteem, and overall psychological adjustment in both conditions, and adolescents in both conditions achieved an equal amount of weight gain. In the conjoint therapy, critical comments from fathers and mothers increased. These comments in the family counseling condition decreased. There was no change in ratings of dissatisfaction with family cohesion and adaptability in either group. At the very least, the study demonstrates the usefulness of including parents in treatment. What is not so clear is whether or not the whole family must be seen together.

Hall (1987) evaluated family therapy research and found that when comparing adolescents of different ages involved in family therapy, those younger than 18 had better outcomes with regard to decreases in symptomatology. Given this finding and the tendency of family therapy research to include a disproportionate number of families with younger daughters, a study was designed to compare families whose anorexic daughters were 18 years old or younger with those whose daughters were older than 18. The results indicate that few families actually participated, and those families that did participate were two-parent families with younger children. Thus many studies of family therapy may not include a representative sample but rather a group that is most likely to benefit from family therapy.

The greater effectiveness of family therapy with younger clients was also demonstrated in a long-term study of 80 adolescents suffering from anorexia nervosa or bulimia nervosa (Russell, Szmukler, Dare, & Eisler, 1987). Clients were randomly assigned to either the family therapy or individual therapy group. After one year, the majority of participants were classified as having a poor outcome. When comparing the treatments, younger, early onset participants in the family therapy condition showed a better outcome and gained more weight. There was no significant difference in outcome among the older anorexic participants or bulimic participants. At the five-year follow-up, the difference between the two treatment conditions among younger participants was not significant.

Family therapy appears to be especially suited for treatment of families of anorexic women who are 18 years old or younger and who have had symptoms for a relatively short amount of time. This finding, along with the fact that the majority of family therapy research includes children and adolescents, suggests that family therapy is appropriate and can be effective when included in the treatment of children and adolescents with bulimia nervosa. Specifically, therapy that addresses family conflict, criticism, and cohesion could be beneficial. However, the literature on the treatment of bulimia nervosa is sparse and the appropriateness of family therapy as the sole treatment for bulimia nervosa is still unclear.

TREATMENT OF BODY IMAGE DISSATISFACTION

Many children are dissatisfied with their weight, desire a thinner physique, use various weight control measures, and endorse symptoms of disordered eating (Collins, 1991; Davies & Furnham, 1986; Flannery-Schroeder & Chrisler, 1996; Hill & Bhatti, 1995; Hill, Draper, & Stack, 1994; Koff & Rierdan, 1991; Maloney, McGuire, Daniels, & Specker, 1989; Mellin, Irwin, & Scully, 1992; Thelen, Powell, Lawrence, & Kuhnert, 1992; Tiggemann & Pennington, 1990; Vander Wal & Thelen, 2001; Wardle & Marsland, 1990). As discussed in earlier chapters, a relationship has been found between body image dissatisfaction of childhood and the development of eating disorders (Flannery-Schroeder & Chrisler, 1996; Lawrence & Thelen, 1995). Longitudinal research supports the role of body image dissatisfaction as an important predictor of eating disorder development (e.g. Attie & Brooks-Gunn, 1989; Cattarin & Thompson, 1994). Indeed, body image dissatisfaction is thought to be one of the most relevant and immediate causes of eating disorders (Leon, Fulkerson, Perry, & Cudeck, 1993; Rosen, 1997). Therefore, the amelioration of body image concerns has tremendous potential for the prevention of eating disorders and related concerns. To date, however, no studies have addressed the treatment of body image dissatisfaction in children. Further, the treatment of body image dissatisfaction in adults is a relatively new area of research and intervention. As in previous sections, studies reviewing the treatment efficacy of various interventions for body image dissatisfaction in adults are reviewed and applications are made to child treatment approaches. The majority of available interventions involve some form of CBT.

CBT has been found to be superior to a wait list control condition (WLC) in improving overall body image, body image affect, and body image cognitions (Butters & Cash, 1987; Dworkin & Kerr, 1987). However, when comparing CBT, WLC, cognitive therapy (CT), and reflective therapy (RT), Dworkin and Kerr (1987) found CT to be superior to RT and CBT for improving body image and all were better than WLC. There were no significant differences between RT and CBT. Further, Rosen, Salzberg, and Srebnik (1989) compared the efficacy of CBT to a minimum treatment condition (MTC) that was similar to the RT used by Dworkin and Kerr (1987). Unlike Dworkin and Kerr (1987), Rosen et al. (1989) found a significant improvement in body image satisfaction in the CBT group compared to the MTC group (akin to reflective therapy), whereas Dworkin and Kerr (1987) did not find a difference. The failure of the minimum treatment group to respond in Rosen et al.'s (1989) study suggests that education and support alone are likely insufficient to effect significant change.

An examination of different variations of CBT indicates that exercises that facilitate realistic appraisal of body weight and shape may not be necessary to bring about positive change in body image, psychological adjustment, and dysfunctional eating patterns (Rosen, Cado, Silberg, Srebnik, & Wendt, 1990). Treatments that did and did not include these exercises resulted in improvements in all areas. Further, these improvements were maintained at three-month follow-up. In addition, Grant and Cash (1995) found that 65% of participants who participated in CBT with limited therapist contact were functionally recovered as defined by a "recovery" index (signifying a shift toward the mean of a "normally" functioning population).

As opposed to treatments that focus on the appraisal of body weight, Stice, Mazotti, Weibel, and Agras (2000) examined a prevention program that targeted the internalization of the thin ideal. The study used a dissonance-based approach by asking participants to help develop a program that combated the thin ideal in high school girls. Participants were 30 undergraduate women who were assigned to an intervention or delayed intervention condition. Results indicated that thin-ideal internalization, dieting behaviors, body image dissatisfaction and bulimic symptomatology decreased during the three-session intervention period, and that this decrease was maintained at the one-month follow-up. Although negative affect also decreased, this improvement was not maintained at follow-up. When compared to the control group, the intervention group reported significantly fewer bulimic symptoms. Stice et al. (2000) suggested that this finding could indicate the intervention's ability to prevent the normal progression of bulimia. Although this specific intervention may not be directly applicable to children, it seems feasible that focused and developmentally appropriate dissonance-based programs could be developed.

Training in physical fitness as an intervention strategy for body image dissatisfaction has received little attention (Thompson, 1990). However, Fisher and Thompson (1994) compared the efficacy of physical training in the treatment of body image dissatisfaction with CBT. Members of the CBT and exercise therapy (ET) groups, but not the WLC group, showed decreased trait and state body image anxiety and dissatisfaction. All groups showed a decrease in behavioral avoidance, but there were no between-group differences. All groups showed increases in perceptual accuracy, but the exercise group overestimated their size to a greater extent than the CBT or WLC groups. There is concern that some clients may interpret the assignment of an exercise program as validation of their appearance concerns (Fisher & Thompson, 1994). Also, some research suggests that exercise may contribute to the development of eating disorders (Davis, Fox, Cowles, Hastings, & Schwass, 1990). Perhaps some types of physical activity decrease body image dissatisfaction, whereas other types heighten body image anxiety. Also, the fit between one's body build and the body build required by the sport is an important consideration.

Because there are no controlled studies of interventions for body image dissatisfaction among children, clinicians must rely on case reports, uncontrolled trials, and extrapolations drawn from treatment with adults (Robin et al., 1998). Although cognitive–behavioral treatments have been shown to reduce body image dissatisfaction in adult women, research is needed to test these interventions with younger populations and to determine whether these techniques would constitute an effective prevention program (Freedman, 1990).

Treatment of child body image dissatisfaction may be conducted individually with the child, in conjunction with a class, or in small groups. Whichever treatment course is used, parental involvement is necessary for treatment success, because the efficacy of treatment is weakened without parental support (Lask & Bryant-Waugh, 1997; Robin et al., 1998). After introducing the child to treatment and administering a thorough body image assessment, the child should be provided with information on body image. One should then investigate reasons that make children feel both satisfied and dissatisfied with their bodies. Information may be sought from children, parents, or teachers. Next, children can be desensitized to body parts and to situational events that elicit body image dysphoria. Even young children may be taught relaxation programs that include simple guided imagery, progressive muscle relaxation, and deep breathing. If the child is older, such as a fifth or sixth grader, she may be able to engage in a desensitization protocol described by Cash and Grant (1996). Kearney-Cooke and Striegel-Moore (1997) suggested developing an alternative cognitive schema by envisioning one's self handling a difficult situation in a competent manner. This principle could be applied to children who could be instructed to envision themselves as brave and strong with skills for handling the situation. The child's assumptions about appearance could then be addressed. Next, it is helpful to incorporate pleasurable body-related activities. Suitable activities for children may include bike riding, roller skating, swimming, wearing favorite clothing, getting a new haircut, experimenting with hand lotions, or engaging in various physical activities. Children may be able to generate possible solutions to difficult situations through a problem-solving approach or may be able to practice their solutions to difficult situations through role playing.

In summary, it appears that the treatment of body image dissatisfaction is an important area of intervention that has only recently received attention. It is apparent that cognitive behavioral programs have proven successful for producing statistically and clinically significant improvements on various aspects of body image dissatisfaction among adults. Treatment protocols for the cognitive–behavioral treatment of body image dissatisfaction in adults have been outlined in various locations and are easily accessible (Cash, 1991; Cash & Grant, 1996; Rosen, 1997). The challenge before us is to develop prevention and intervention programs for children by adapting effective procedures with adults.

HOSPITALIZATION

Hospitalization is sometimes necessary, especially in the case of anorexia nervosa. Fairburn and Cooper (1989) outlined some factors that indicate when hospitalization is needed. These factors include severe or rapid weight loss, life-threatening physical complications, and suicide risk. In addition, hospitalization may be necessary if the client's social situation significantly interferes with outpatient treatment or when outpatient treatment has been unsuccessful. Treatment in inpatient facilities typically involves a behavioral component where weight gain leads to an increase in privileges. The actual privileges used and the amount of weight gain expected varies.

Inpatient treatment often includes family therapy. The family may participate in the refeeding process as a way of gradually transferring this responsibility from the hospital staff to the client. In addition, treatment often involves some form of individual therapy. Several studies examined the effectiveness of specific aspects of hospitalization. All of the studies include only anorexic participants, probably because they are most likely to be hospitalized.

Seltzer (1984) examined the effectiveness of parental participation in the refeeding process in five clients ranging in age from 9 to 15. The program used a family systems approach coupled with a behavioral component in which weight increases were a requirement for hospital privileges. The families lived in the hospital for the first one to two weeks of treatment. During hospitalization, the responsibility for feeding moved from the medical team to the parents. In addition, the whole family took part in therapy sessions. At the end of treatment, four out of five of the clients were in symptom remission.

Although Seltzer (1984) included refeeding and therapy in the treatment process, others examined whether or not psychotherapy is even necessary when clients are hospitalized for refeeding (Danziger, Carel, Tyano, & Mimouni, 1989). Participants ranged in age from 10 to 17. Like typical inpatient treatments, weight increases led to privileges. Participants were divided into two groups: a family therapy group and a group that received no therapy until two months after refeeding. Results indicated that the refeeding group had higher weight gain initially. However, at six-month and one-year follow-ups, weight gain was similar between the groups. Although the long-term outcome was similar, given the dangerousness of low weight, choosing a course of therapy that leads to weight gain in the faster manner seems prudent. Thus the results suggest that family therapy should be delayed until refeeding has been completed. The authors hypothesize that family therapy may be too stressful early in treatment and better tolerated after the client has gained weight.

In a study that targeted refeeding, Kreipe and Kidder (1986) compared two different inpatient treatment programs for weight gain in adolescents. In one program, the focus was on metabolic balance and clients had to eat a certain amount of food per day to earn privileges. The second focused on weight gain. Both groups received psychotherapy. When comparing the groups, the weight gain was similar, although there was less variability for the metabolic group. In addition, weight gain was less sporadic and more predictable in the metabolic group, suggesting that this method of weight gain may be more desirable than the traditional weight gain method.

Powers and Powers (1984) compared the effectiveness of inpatient and outpatient treatments for anorexia nervosa. Inpatient treatment consisted of behavior management, psychotherapy, and family therapy. Outpatient treatment involved individual insight-oriented therapy and family systems therapy. Participants ranged in age from 11 to 25. At the end of treatment, the hospitalization group had more participants who were below their ideal body weight than the outpatient group, although most clients gained some weight. In addition, clients in the outpatient group gained more weight than the inpatient group during the course of therapy.

In summary, although hospitalization appears to help clients return to more healthy weights, these studies suggest that alternative management techniques could be helpful. It is possible that including parents in treatment, delaying therapy until discharge, and focusing on food consumed rather than actual weight gain may result in more predictable weight gain.

USE OF MEDICATIONS

There are no outcome studies on the use of pharmacotherapy for the treatment of eating disorders in adolescents and children. However, as in the case of therapy, a brief examination of the adult literature could offer guidelines that are applicable to adolescents and children. The majority of studies to date have focused on bulimia nervosa. Typically, antidepressants are used, but studies have shown mixed results for both anorexia nervosa and bulimia nervosa. For example, medications have been shown to be effective at decreasing bulimic symptoms, but clients often relapse after the medication is terminated (Agras, 1997). However, the length of treatment has been found to affect results (Agras et al., 1992, 1994). Although clients taking a 16-week course of medication were likely to experience a relapse of bulimic symptoms, participants who had a 24-week course were less likely to relapse after a one-year follow-up. On the other hand, studies have shown that even if clients are kept on medication, one third relapse (Pyle et al., 1990; Walsh, Hadigan, Devlin, Gladis, & Roose, 1991). For anorexia nervosa, neither the addition of medication to the treatment regimen nor the use of medication to bring about weight gain have augmented treatment gains (Strober, Freeman, DeAntonio, Lampert, & Diamond, 1997).

As stated earlier, no research has exclusively targeted children and adolescents, although they have been included in some samples. There is no reason to think that the outcome would not be similar for adolescents. Antidepressants have been recommended for use in children, and McDaniel (1986) reported that antidepressants with less anticholinergic action are tolerated best. The use of medication may be considered a last resort when the client has not responded to psychological treatments in the past or if there is also severe depression (Robin et al., 1998).

METHODOLOGICAL PROBLEMS

Treatment outcome studies involve certain methodological issues that can affect the outcome and interpretations drawn from the results of studies such as those reviewed in this chapter. Such issues include sample size, the method of measuring outcome, and use of a control group.

Most likely because of the expense of treatment outcome studies, many of the studies reviewed had small sample sizes. When participants are randomly assigned to treatment groups, the number of participants in each group may be quite small, resulting in insufficient power to detect group differences. In addition, small samples my not represent the eating disordered population. Because anorexia nervosa and bulimia nervosa are heterogeneous disorders, the full range of symptom profiles may not be represented in small samples.

Another problem is several treatment studies lack a comparison group. Some of the studies only included a group of women who were engaged in treatment and did not include a wait-list control group or another treatment condition. Therefore, for these studies one cannot determine if the improvements seen in the participants were a result of the treatment, nonspecific treatment effects, or to a placebo effect. Because of the dangers caused by eating disordered behaviors, wait-list control groups may not be considered ethical. However, several other studies reviewed included more than one treatment condition. Although this method does not rule out the possibility of a placebo effect, it does allow for between-group comparisons. Therefore, differences seen between the groups demonstrate the effectiveness of one treatment over another. Inasmuch as the treatments are different, one can conclude that group differences are a result of the specific interventions of the treatment as opposed to a placebo effect. In addition, comparing different treatments may shed light on the effectiveness or ineffectiveness of specific treatment techniques. This concept was demonstrated by studies performed by Fairburn and colleagues (Fairburn et al., 1991; Fairburn et al., 1993; Fairburn, 1995) that compared BT and CBT. Because the only differences in the two conditions were the presence or absence of cognitive techniques, the authors could draw conclusions concerning whether behavioral techniques were sufficient to create desired effects or whether cognitive techniques were necessary.

An additional methodological area that should be discussed is the way in which outcome is measured. One issue involves the factors that are considered indicators of outcome. Often, treatment outcome is confined to eating disorder symptomatology or behaviors. Although these factors would obviously be an appropriate indicator of treatment success or failure, there are other areas of functioning that could serve as indexes of outcome. Because it appears that body image dissatisfaction may constitute an important determinant of treatment outcome, it is prudent to include both pre- and posttreatment assessments of this construct. Other relevant features such as social functioning, self-esteem, and levels of depression and general psychopathology have been used as measures of outcome. These and other features are often related to bulimia nervosa and anorexia nervosa. In addition, because of the possibility that there are comorbid diagnoses, it is important to know if treatments are addressing these other symptoms. Treatment may not be effective if the comorbid diagnosis is not first addressed. The current emphasis on short-term, problem-focused psychotherapy may not give sufficient attention to issues of comorbidity. It is important to consider these other areas of functioning when performing studies of treatment effectiveness, especially when comparing different treatment modalities. As has been demonstrated, treatments that do focus on bulimia nervosa can also lead to improvements in other areas (e.g. Fairburn et al., 1986; Ordman & Kirschenbaum, 1985).

Another issue involving outcome is the appropriateness of the outcome measures chosen. Often, the outcome measures used do not represent the focus of all therapies included in the study. This problem could adversely affect conclusions drawn in studies including IPT, because this treatment modality often does not focus directly on bulimic symptoms. Although the treatment should result in decreased bulimic symptomatology, it may also affect other important areas, including social functioning. In addition, it is possible that certain changes, such as improved interpersonal functioning, lead to changes in bulimic symptomatology. This might mean that changes in interpersonal functioning are a marker for treatment success and predict future reductions in bulimic symptomatology. Fairburn et al. (1995) suggested this hypothesis in reference to the long-term improvements in participants who received IPT. Finally, attention should be given to the issue of clinical versus statistical significance as was done by Grant and Cash (1995).

Long-term improvement is not measured in many of the studies and represents another area of concern. Conclusions that treatment resulted in permanent changes in eating disorder symptomatology cannot be made without long-term outcome results. In addition, because it is possible that different treatment modalities result in different rates of change, longer term outcomes are needed to track these differences. As discussed earlier, this possibility was made especially clear in the results of Fairburn et al. (1995), who found that the group that received IPT did not improve as much as the CBT group immediately after treatment, but after time improvements in the two groups were quite similar. If there had been no long-term follow-up, the authors would have concluded that CBT was the most effective treatment, overlooking the efficacy of IPT. Long-term follow-up would also be beneficial for evaluating inpatient treatment. Further, long-term follow-up is especially important for evaluation of pharmacotherapy, given the higher risk of relapse after medication has been discontinued.

A problem that seems to occur with family therapy and BT research is the blending of techniques from various modalities. For example, many inpatient programs use behavioral and family therapy techniques to promote weight gain. Therefore it is not always clear how much of the progress of therapy is a result of which techniques. Further, more studies like that of le Grange et al. (1992) should be developed to investigate which components of therapy programs promote change.

CONCLUSION

Overall, the literature on the treatment of children and adolescents is quite limited, with few well-controlled outcome studies. There are many opportunities for research in the area of treating children and adolescents suffering from eating disorders. Future research should include several components that may add to the current state of the literature. These components include long-term follow-up and multiple treatment groups. Research that includes and compares participants of various ages would be invaluable in identifying those techniques that are most effective at various stages of the life span. In addition, if children, like adults, are found to have high rates of comorbid diagnoses, examining the influences of comorbid diagnoses on treatment outcome would also be helpful.

In terms of the type of treatment included in future studies, it seems that research on BT alone as a treatment or as a method for weight gain is not crucial. BT has been shown to be less effective than other treatments in bringing about long-term changes. Research should focus on treatments that show more promise, such as CBT, IPT, or family therapy. In addition, it is unclear what aspects of treatment are most vital for change; hence research that compares the effectiveness of the different components of treatment is needed. Finally, additional research is needed that compares family therapy for women suffering from anorexia nervosa or bulimia nervosa to other treatment modalities. Future research should also test family therapy in isolation to determine if it can be effective without the inclusion of CBT and BT techniques.

In the area of body image dissatisfaction, future research should be directed toward identifying possible causal influences, the generation of reliable and valid assessment inventories, the development of treatment protocols, and the evaluation of treatment efficacy. Perhaps additional research and clinical observations will enable the development of effective prevention programs that will decrease the incidence of body image dissatisfaction and related concerns.

Despite the gaps in the literature, research on adults with eating disorders and children suffering from other disorders offers clues to possible intervention strategies. Clearly, the current treatment of choice is CBT. However, given developmental considerations such as level of cognitive ability required, adjustments must be made for younger children. Techniques such as cognitive coping, modeling, problem solving, and skills training may be effective with adolescents and children, whereas tasks that require metacognition may be less applicable. The research also suggests that including the family in treatment is a promising option. Further, IPT may be indicated for difficult to engage adolescents because of its focus on peer relationships that are so important to teenagers. Regardless of the techniques used, treatment of children and adolescents should include a unique component: education of parents and other adults involved in the client's life. This education can be valuable because adults can, at the very least, help reinforce and prompt adaptive behaviors and cognitions (Robin et al., 1998).

REFERENCES

Agras, W. S. (1997). Pharmacotherapy of bulimia nervosa and binge eating disorder: Longer-term outcomes. *Psychopharmocology Bulletin, 33*(3), 433–436.

Agras, W. S., Rossiter, E. M., Arnow, B., Schneider, J. A., Telch, C. F., Raeburn, S. D., Bruce, B., Perl, M., & Koran, L. M. (1992). Pharmacologic and cognitive-behavioral treatment for bulimia nervosa: A controlled comparison. *American Journal of Psychiatry, 149,* 82–87.

Agras, W. S., Rossiter, E. M., Arnow, B., Telch, C. F., Raeburn, S. D., Bruce, B., & Koran, L. M. (1994). One-year follow-up of psychosocial and pharmacologic treatment for bulimia nervosa. *Journal of Clinical Psychiatry, 55,* 179–183.

Attie, I., & Brooks-Gunn, J. (1989). Development of eating problems in adolescent girls: A longitudinal study. *Developmental Psychology, 25*(1), 70–79.

Butters, J. W., & Cash, T. F. (1987). Cognitive-behavioral treatment of women's body-image dissatisfaction. *Journal of Consulting and Clinical Psychology, 55,* 889–897.

Cash, T. F. (1991). *Body-image therapy: A program for self-directed change.* New York: Guilford Press.

Cash, T. F., & Grant, J. R. (1996). Cognitive-behavioral treatment of body-image disturbances. In V. B. Van Hasselt & M. Hersen (Eds.), *Sourcebook of psychological treatment manuals for adult disorders* (pp. 567–614). New York: Plenum Press.

Cattarin, J. A., & Thompson, J. K. (1994). A three-year longitudinal study of body image, eating disturbance, and general psychological functioning in adolescent females. *Eating Disorders: The Journal of Treatment and Prevention, 2*(2), 114–125.

Channon, S., de Silva, P., Hemsley, D., & Perkins, R. (1989). A controlled trial of cognitive behavioral and behavioral treatment of anorexia nervosa. *Behavior Research and Therapy, 27,* 529–535.

Collins, M. E. (1991). Body figure perceptions and preferences among preadolescent children. *International Journal of Eating Disorders, 10*(2), 199–208.

Cooper, P. J., Cooper, Z., & Hill, C. (1989). Behavioral treatment of bulimia nervosa. *International Journal of Eating Disorders, 8*(1), 87–92.

Cooper, P. J., & Fairburn, C. G. (1984). Cognitive behaviour therapy for anorexia nervosa: Some preliminary findings. *Journal of Psychosomatic Research, 28,* 493–499.

Danziger, Y., Carel, C. A., Tyano, S., & Mimouni, M. (1989). Is psychotherapy mandatory during the acute refeeding period in the treatment of anorexia nervosa? *Journal of Adolescent Health Care, 10,* 328–331.

Davies, E., & Furnham, A. (1986). The dieting and body shape concerns of adolescent females. *Journal of Child Psychology and Psychiatry, 27*(3), 417–428.

Davis, C., Fox, J., Cowles, M., Hastings, P., & Schwass, K. (1990). The functional role of exercise in the development of weight and diet concerns in women. *Journal of Psychosomatic Research, 34,* 563–574.

Dworkin, S. H., & Kerr, B. A. (1987). Comparison of interventions for women experiencing body image problems. *Journal of Counseling Psychology, 34*(2), 136–140.

Fairburn, C. G. (1985). Interpersonal psychotherapy for bulimia nervosa. In D. M. Garner & P. E. Garfinkel (Eds.), *Handbook of Treatment for Eating Disorders* (2nd ed., pp. 278–294). New York: Guilford Press.

Fairburn, C. G. (1993). Interpersonal psychotherapy for bulimia nervosa. In G. L. Klerman & M. M. Weissman (Eds.), *New applications of interpersonal psychotherapy* (pp. 353–378). Washington, DC: American Psychiatric Press.

Fairburn, C. G., & Cooper, P. J. (1989). Eating disorders. In K. Hawton & P. M. Salkovskis (Eds.), *Cognitive behaviour therapy for psychiatric problems: A practical guide* (pp. 277–314). Oxford: Oxford Medical.

Fairburn, C. G., Jones, R., Peveler, R. C., Carr, S. J., Solomon, R. A., O'Connor, M., & Hope, R. A (1991). Three psychological treatments for bulimia nervosa. *Achieves of General Psychiatry, 48,* 463–469.

Fairburn, C. G., Jones, R., Peveler, R. C., Hope, R. A., & O'Connor, M. (1993). Psychotherapy and bulimia nervosa: Longer-term effects of interpersonal psychotherapy, behavior therapy, and cognitive behavior therapy. *Achieves of General Psychiatry, 50,* 419–428.

Fairburn, C. G., Kirk, J., O'Connor, M., & Cooper, P. J. (1986). A comparison of two psychological treatments for bulimia nervosa. *Behavior Research and Therapy, 24*(6), 629–643.

Fairburn, C. G., Norman, P. A., Welsh, S. L., O'Connor, M. E., Doll, H. A., & Peveler, R. C. (1995). A prospective study of outcome in bulimia nervosa and the long-term effects of three psychological treatments. *Archives of General Psychiatry, 52,* 304–312.

Fisher, E., & Thompson, J. K. (1994). A comparative evaluation of cognitive-behavioral therapy (CBT) vs. exercise therapy (ET) for the treatment of body image disturbance: Preliminary findings. *Behavior Modification, 18*(2), 171–185.

Flannery-Schroeder, E. C., & Chrisler, J. C. (1996). Body esteem, eating attitudes, and gender-role orientation in three age groups of children. *Current Psychology: Developmental, Learning, Personality, Social, 15*(3), 235–248.

Freedman, R. (1990). Cognitive-behavioral perspectives on body-image change. In T. F. Cash & T. Pruzinsky (Eds.), *Body images: Development, deviance, and change* (pp. 272–295). New York: Guilford Press.

Garner, D. M., Rockert, W., Davis, R., Garner, M. V., Olmsted, M. P., & Eagle, M. (1983) Comparison of cognitive-behavioral and supportive-expressive therapy for bulimia nervosa. *American Journal of Psychiatry, 150*(1), 37–46.

Grant, J. R., & Cash, T. F. (1995). Cognitive-behavioral body image therapy: Comparative efficacy of group and modest-contrast treatments. Special Series: Body dissatisfaction, binge eating, and dieting as interlocking issues in eating disorders research. *Behavior Therapy, 26*(1), 69–84.

Hall, A. (1987). The place of family therapy in the treatment of anorexia nervosa. *Australian and New Zealand Journal of Psychiatry, 21,* 568–574.

Hill, A. J., & Bhatti R. (1995). Body shape perception and dieting in preadolescent British Asian girls: Links with eating disorders. *International Journal of Eating Disorders, 17*(2), 175–183.

Hill, A. J., Draper, E., & Stack, J. (1994). A weight on children's minds: Body shape dissatisfaction at 9 years old. *International Journal of Obesity and Related Metabolic Disorders, 18*(6), 383–389.

Johnson, W. G., Sclundt, D. G., & Jarrell, M. P. (1986). Exposure with response prevention, training in energy balance, and problem solving therapy for bulimia nervosa. *International Journal of Eating Disorders, 5*(1), 35–45.

Kearney-Cooke, A., & Striegel-Moore, R. (1997). The etiology and treatment of body image disturbance. In D. M. Garner & P. E. Garfinkel (Eds.), *Handbook of treatment for eating disorders* (2nd ed., pp. 295–306). New York: Guilford Press.

Kennedy, S. H., Katz, R., Neitzert, C. S., Ralevski, E., & Mendlowitz, S. (1985). Exposure with response prevention treatment of anorexia nervosa-bulimic subtype and bulimia nervosa. *Behavior Research and Therapy, 33*(6), 685–689.

Koff, E., & Rierdan, J. (1991). Perceptions of weight and attitudes toward eating in early adolescent girls. *Journal of Adolescent Health, 12,* 307–312.

Kreipe, R. E., & Kidder, F. (1986). Comparison of two hospital treatment programs for anorexia nervosa. *International Journal of Eating Disorders, 5,* 649–657.

Lask, B., & Bryant-Waugh, R. (1997). Prepubertal eating disorders. In D. M. Garner & P. E. Garfinkel (Eds.), *Handbook of treatment for eating disorders* (2nd ed., pp. 476–483). New York: Guilford Press.

Lawrence, C. M., & Thelen, M. H. (1995). Body image, dieting, and self-concept. Their relation in African-American and Caucasian children. *Journal of Clinical Child Psychology, 24*(1), 41–48.

le Grange, D., Eisler, I., Dare, C., & Russell, G. F. M. (1992). Evaluation of Family Treatments in Adolescent Anorexia Nervosa: A Pilot Study. *International Journal of Eating Disorders, 12*(4), 347–357.

Leon, G. R., Fulkerson, J. A., Perry, C. L., & Cudeck, R. (1993). Personality and behavioral vulnerabilities associated with risk status for eating disorders in adolescent girls. *Journal of Abnormal Psychology, 102*(3), 438–444.

Maloney, M. J., McGuire, J., Daniels, S. R., & Specker, B. (1989). Dieting behavior and eating attitudes in children. *Pediatrics, 84*(3), 482–487.

McDaniel, K. D. (1986). Pharmacologic treatment of psychiatric and neurodevelopmental disorders in children and adolescents. *Pharmacologic Treatment, 25*, 198–204.

Mellin, L. M., Irwin, C. E., & Scully, S. (1992). Prevalence of disordered eating in girls: A survey of middle-class children. *Journal of the American Dietetic Association, 92*, 851–853.

Mufson, L. H., Woreau, D., Weissman, M. M., & Klerman, G. L. (1993). Interpersonal Psychotherapy for Adolescent Depression. In G. L. Klerman & M.M Weissman (Eds.), *New applications of interpersonal psychotherapy* (pp. 129–166). Washington, DC: American Psychiatric Press.

Ordman, A. M., & Kirschenbaum, D. S. (1985). Cognitive-behavioral therapy for bulimia: An initial outcome study. *Journal of Consulting and Clinical Psychology, 33*(3), 305–313.

Powers, P. S., & Powers, H. P. (1984). Inpatient treatment of anorexia nervosa. . *Psychosomatics, 25*, 512–527.

Pyle, R. L., Mitchell, J. E., Eckert, E. D., Hatsukami, D., Pomeroy, C., & Zimmerman, R. (1990). Maintenance treatment and 6 month outcome for bulimic patients who respond to initial treatment. *American Journal of Psychiatry, 147*, 871–875.

Robin, A. L., Gilroy, M., & Dennis, A. B. (1998). Treatment of eating disorders in children and adolescents. *Clinical Psychology Review, 18*(4), 421–446.

Rosen, J. C. (1997). Cognitive-behavioral body image therapy. In D. M. Garner & P. E. Garfinkel (Eds.), *Handbook of treatment for eating disorders* (2nd ed., pp. 188–201). New York: Guilford Press.

Rosen, J. C., Cado, S., Silberg, N. T., Srebnik, D., & Wendt, S. (1990). Cognitive behavior therapy with and without size perception training for women with body image disturbance. *Behavior Therapy, 21*, 481–498.

Rosen, J. C., Salzberg, E., & Srebnik, D. (1989). Cognitive behavior therapy for negative body image. *Behavior Therapy, 20*, 393–404.

Russell, G. F. M., Szmukler, G. I., Dare, C., & Eisler, I. (1987). An evaluation of family therapy in anorexia nervosa and bulimia nervosa. *Archives of General Psychiatry, 44*, 1047–1056.

Seltzer, W. J. (1984). Treating anorexia nervosa in the somatic hospital: A multisystemic approach. *Family Systems Medicine, 2,* 195–207.

Schrodt (1992). Cognitive therapy of depression. In M. Shafii & S. L. Shafii (Eds.), *Clinical guide to depression in children and adolescents* (pp. 197–218). Washington, DC: American Psychiatric Press.

Shugar, G., & Kruegar, S. (1995). Aggressive family communication, weight gain, and improved eating attitudes during systemic family therapy for anorexia nervosa. *International Journal of Eating Disorders, 17,* 23–31.

Silverman, W. K., & Nelles, W. B. (1990). Simple Phobia in Childhood. In M. Hersen & C. B. Last (Eds.), Handbook of childhood and adult psychopathology (pp. 183–193). New York. Pergamon Press.

Stice, E., Mazotti, L., Weibel, D., & Agras, W. S. (2000). Dissonance prevention program decreases thin-ideal internalization, body dissatisfaction, dieting, negative affect, and bulimic symptoms: A preliminary experiment. *International Journal of Eating Disorders, 27,* 206–217.

Strober, M., Freeman, R., DeAntonio, M., Lampert, C., & Diamond, J. (1997). Does adjunctive fluoxetine influence the post-hospital course for restrictor-type anorexia nervosa: A 24 month prospective longitudinal follow-up and comparison with historical controls. *Psychopharmacology Bulletin, 33,* 425–431.

Thelen, M. H., Powell, A. L., Lawrence, C., & Kuhnert, M. E. (1992). Eating and body image concern among children. *Journal of Clinical Psychology, 21*(1), 41–46.

Thompson, J. K. (1990). *Body image disturbance: Assessment and treatment.* New York: Pergamon Press.

Thyer, B. A. (1991). Diagnosis and treatment of child adolescent anxiety disorders. *Behavior Modification, 15,* 310–325.

Tiggemann, M., & Pennington, B. (1990). The development of gender differences in body-size dissatisfaction. Special section: Women and psychology. *Australian Psychologist, 25*(3), 306–313.

Vander Wal, J. S., & Thelen, M. H. (2001). Eating and body image concerns among obese and non-obese children. *Eating Behaviors, 1,* 1–18.

Walsh, B. T., Hadigan, C. M., Devlin, M. J., Gladis, M., & Roose, S. P. (1991). Long-term outcome of antidepressant treatment for bulimia nervosa. *American Journal of Psychiatry, 148,* 1206–1212.

Wardle, J., & Marsland, L. (1990). Adolescent concerns about weight and eating; A social-developmental perspective. *Journal of Psychosomatic Research, 34*(4), 377–391.

Wilkes, T. C., & Rush, A. J. (1988). Adaptations of cognitive therapy for depression in adolescents. *Journal of the American Academy of Child and Adolescent Psychiatry, 27,* 381–386.

Wilson, G. T., & Fairburn, C. G. (1993). *Journal of Consulting and Clinical Psychology, 61,* 261–269.

Wilson, G. T., & Pike, K. M. (1993). Eating disorders. In D. H. Barlow (Ed.), *Clinical handbook of psychological disorders*(2nd ed., pp. 278–317). New York: Guilford Press.

13

BEHAVIORAL TREATMENT OF CHILDHOOD AND ADOLESCENT OBESITY: CURRENT STATUS, CHALLENGES, AND FUTURE DIRECTIONS

MYLES S. FAITH, BRIAN E. SAELENS, DENISE E. WILFLEY,
AND DAVID B. ALLISON

Addressing the problems of childhood obesity has become a major focus of attention for practitioners and public health officials in recent years and will remain so well into the twenty-first century. There are several reasons for this: . The first concerns the increasing prevalence of childhood obesity in recent decades (Troiano & Flegal, 1998). A second reason concerns the health complications associated with childhood obesity (Faith, Pietrobelli, Allison, & Heymsfield, 1997; Freedman, Dietz, Srinivasan, & Berenson, 1999), including elevated blood pressure, hyperinsulinemia and glucose intolerance, respiratory abnormalities, poor body image, and increased adulthood mortality in females. Third, as this chapter will illustrate, many questions concerning treatment efficacy, maintenance, and mechanisms remain unanswered (Epstein, Myers, Raynor, & Saelens, 1998).

This chapter addresses current approaches to the behavioral treatment of childhood and adolescent obesity. It begins with a discussion of the children who may be the most appropriate candidates for treatment, followed by an overview of the effectiveness of current behavioral interventions for childhood obesity. Data on core treatment components are then presented along with practical clinical recommendations. Following this, potential barriers to behavioral intervention are outlined. Finally, directions for future research are discussed. Given the limited data on surgical and pharmacological

This chapter was supported in part by grants 1K08 MH01530, R29MH51384, 1R03DK51931, R29DK47256, R01DK51716, P30DK26687, R01HD36904, and a NAASO Young Investigators Grant. The authors would like to thank Richanne Sniezek for her assistance with the table and manuscript preparation.

interventions in children (Epstein et al., 1998), we restrict our discussion to nonpharmacological, primarily behavioral and "lifestyle," interventions. *Lifestyle intervention* broadly refers to a range of behavioral changes that are compatible with everyday living and daily activities and, therefore, are sustained over longer time periods. Examples include decisions to use stairs rather than escalators, to take short walks after dinner rather than watch television, and to replace high-fat snack foods with fruits and vegetables at home. Moreover, lifestyle interventions integrate physical activity into situations wherever there is a choice between being active versus sedentary. When driving to a mall, for example, one can park the car close to the entrance or further away so that some walking becomes necessary. Lifestyle interventions promote choices that favor physical activity over inactivity.

DETERMINING WHICH CHILDREN SHOULD RECEIVE TREATMENT

For determining whether a given child is a reasonable candidate for treatment, available guidelines come from a recent expert panel consensus report (Barlow & Dietz, 1998). Figures 13-1 and 13-2 present a subset of these guidelines.

Borrowing from a previous model (Himes & Dietz, 1994), the consensus report recommends a two-stage screening process (see Figure 13-1). The initial screen focuses on the child or adolescent's body mass index (BMI: kg/m^2), with an in-depth medical assessment recommended for any child whose BMI exceeds the 95th percentile (age- and sex-specific), as per the First National Health and Nutrition Examination Survey (Must, Dallal, & Dietz, 1991). For any child whose BMI falls between the 85th and 94th percentiles (so-called at-risk for overweight), a second-level screen determines if an in-depth medical assessment is warranted. This second-level screen examines the following five domains:

- Family history of cardiovascular disease, parental hypercholesterolemia, or unknown family history (see American Academy of Pediatrics, 1992), or family history of diabetes mellitus or parental obesity;
- High blood pressure (see Second Task Force on Blood Pressure Control in Children, 1987);
- Elevated total cholesterol—in other words, 5.2 mmol/L or 200 mg/dL (see National Cholesterol Education Program, 1991);
- A large recent increase in BMI (e.g., an annual increase of 3 to 4 BMI units); and
- Child–adolescent concerns about weight or display of any emotional or psychological manifestations possibly related to overweight or perceptions of overweight.

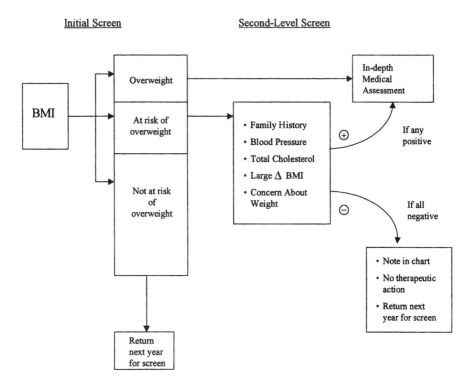

Figure 13-1. Proposed Two-Stage Screen for Determination of Childhood and Adolescent Obesity Treatment
From Barlow and Dietz (1998). Used with permission of the authors.

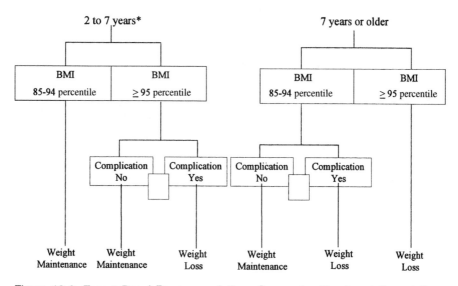

Figure 13-2. Expert Panel Recommendations Concerning Treatment Prescriptions for Childhood and Adolescent Obesity
From Barlow and Dietz (1998). Used with permission of the authors.

"At-risk" children who show *any* of these characteristics would be recommended for further medical assessment.

Information from this two-stage screen and, if conducted, the in-depth medical examination, would guide treatment prescriptions. As Figure 13-2 illustrates, treatment prescriptions are broadly broken down into guidelines for children who are 2 to 7 years old versus children who are 7 years and older, with clinical recommendations for weight maintenance versus weight loss depending on the BMI percentile and the presence of medical complications (see Dietz, 1983).

Several other indexes are also available to track the growth and development of children that provide referents for childhood overweight and obesity. For example, the National Center for Health Statistics published revised growth charts for individuals 2 to 20 years old (see the Website at www.cdc.gov/nchs/about/major/nhanes/growthcharts/charts.htm). Originally developed in 1977, these charts have been used widely by pediatricians and other health professionals to gauge the developmental trajectory of individual children. In the most current release (2000), growth charts pertaining to the 5th, 10th, 25th, 50th, 75th, 85th, 90th, and 95th percentiles are presented for various growth parameters: weight-for-age, length-for-age, stature-for-age, weight-for-stature, head circumference-for-age, and BMI-for-age. This last category, BMI-for-age, is most pertinent for the classification of overweight and obesity. Figure 13-3 presents BMI-for-age percentile growth charts for boys, and Figure 13-4 presents BMI-for-age percentile growth charts for girls.

Finally, the first set of international guidelines for defining overweight and obesity in children and adolescents were recently published (Cole, Bellizzi, Flegal, & Dietz, 2000). Using data from Brazil, Great Britain, Hong Kong, Netherlands, Singapore, and the United States, growth curves were constructed for each age group to identify those BMI scores that would "project" to a BMI of 25 (i.e., overweight) or 30 (i.e., obese) at 18 years of age. Thus they provide BMI cutoffs for overweight and obesity from age 2 to 18 by half years for males and females. Table 13-1 illustrates several gender-specific cut-offs for defining overweight and obesity in children and adolescents. Alternatively, one could use the aforementioned BMI cutoffs that were developed by Must et al. (1991) on a nationally representative U.S. sample (also see Barlow & Dietz, 1998). At the present, the practical implications of using one set of criteria versus the other may be negligible.

CDC Growth Charts: United States

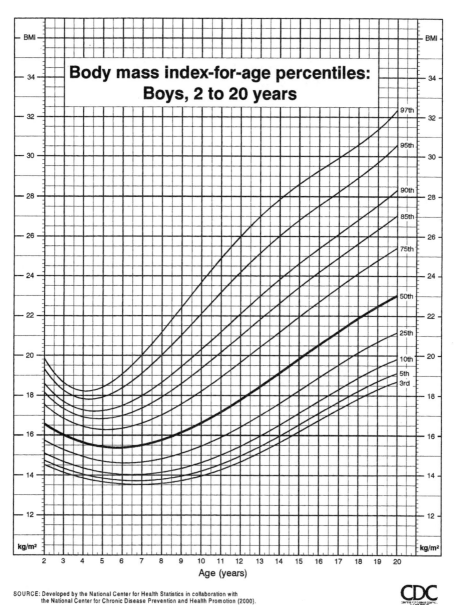

Body mass index-for-age percentiles:
Boys, 2 to 20 years

SOURCE: Developed by the National Center for Health Statistics in collaboration with
the National Center for Chronic Disease Prevention and Health Promotion (2000).

CDC

Figure 13-3. BMI-for-Age Growth Charts for 2- to 20-Year-Old Males
From National Center for Health Statistics.

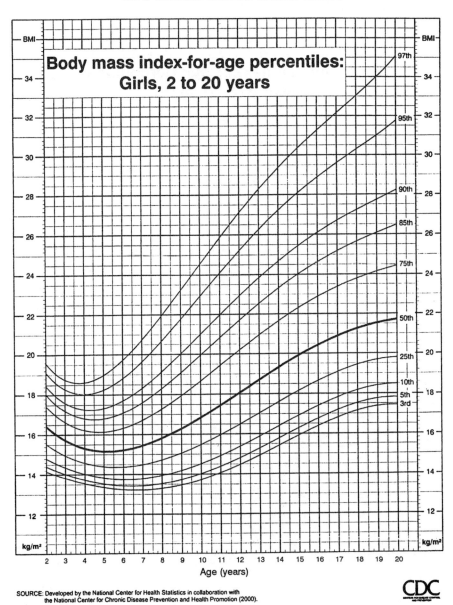

Figure 13-4. BMI-for-Age Growth Charts for 2- to 20-Year-Old Females From National Center for Health Statistics.

TABLE 13-1
International BMI Cutoffs for Defining Overweight and Obesity
in Children and Adolescents

Age	Males		Females	
	Overweight	Obesity	Overweight	Obesity
5	17.4	19.3	17.1	19.2
6	17.6	19.8	17.3	19.7
7	17.9	20.6	17.8	20.5
8	18.4	21.6	18.3	21.6
9	19.1	22.8	19.1	22.8
10	19.8	24.0	19.9	24.1
11	20.6	25.1	20.7	25.4
12	21.2	26.0	21.7	26.7
13	21.9	26.8	22.6	27.8

From: Cole et al. (2000). With permission from the British Medical Journal Publishing Group.

THE EFFICACY OF BEHAVIORAL TREATMENT
FOR CHILDHOOD OBESITY

Compared to medical, educational, and school-based treatments, family-based behavioral treatment programs have been the most studied intervention for childhood obesity, and have reliably produced the best short- and long-term treatment effects on weight (Jelalian & Saelens, 1999). Moreover, treatment of childhood obesity is associated with significant health benefits, including decreases in systolic and diastolic blood pressure, better physical fitness, and improved lipid profiles. Table 13-2 summarizes changes in common health outcomes from studies reported in three recent reviews (Epstein et al., 1998; Haddock, Shadish, Klesges, & Stein, 1994; Jelalian & Saelens, 1999).

The most effective behavioral weight control programs show promising results even at 10-year follow-up for overweight children, but not for their overweight parents even though parents often have initial success (Epstein, Valoski, Kalarchian, & McCurley, 1995). Several reasons have been posited for the superior outcomes obtained with children compared with adults (Epstein, Valoski, Kalarchian et al., 1995; Wilson, 1994). First, children may require less self-motivation than adults to maintain behavior change because the primary agent of change is external (typically the parent). Second, children may have less ingrained and therefore more malleable dietary and physical activity habits than adults. Children are generally more physically active than adults (U.S. Department of

TABLE 13-2

Common Physical Health Outcomes Investigated Among Nonpharmacological Interventions for Childhood and Adolescent Obesity

Blood Pressure	Physical Fitness[a]	Body Fat Mass[b]	Cholesterol (CHOL), Triglycerides (TRI), and Lipoproteins (LDL, HDL)	Insulin and Fasting Glucose
Coates, Jeffery, et al. (1982) (+) Brownell et al. (1983) (+) Rocchini et al. (1987) —Tx groups (+) —No-tx (0) Rocchini et al. (1988) —Tx (+) —No-tx (0) Becque et al. (1988) —Exercise plus diet (++) —Diet only, No-tx. (0) —No-tx (0) Marshall Hoerr et al. (1988) (+) Figueroa-Colon et al. (1993) (+) Hoffman et al. (1995) (+)	Blomquist et al. (1965) —Exercise (+)* —No-tx (+)* Epstein et al. (1982) —Lifestyle exercise (+) —Programmed exercise (0) Archibald et al. (1983) (0) Epstein et al. (1985) —Diet plus exercise (+) —Diet only (0) Epstein, Wing, et al. (1985) —Lifestyle exercise (0) —Programmed exercise (+) —Calisthenics (0) Sasaki et al. (1987) (+) Rocchini et al. (1987) —Exercise plus diet (+) —Diet only, No-tx (0) Rocchini et al. (1988) —Exercise plus diet (+) —Diet only, No-tx. (0) Becque et al. (1988) (0)	Blomquist et al. (1965) —Exercise (+), Control (0) Archibald et al. (1983) (+)* Brown et al. (1983) (−)* Senediak & Spence (1985) —Tx groups (+), Non-specific control (0) Rocchini et al. (1987) (+) Sasaki et al. (1987) (+) Stallings et al. (1988) (+) Becque et al. (1988) (0) Marshall Hoerr et al. (1988) (+) Hills & Parker (1988) (+) Katch et al. (1988) —Exercise & diet (+), diet alone (+), No-tx (0) Pena et al. (1989) —Exercise (+), No exercise (0)	Coates, Killen, et al. (1982) —CHOL (0), LDL (0), HDL (0) Coates, Jeffery, et al. (1982) —CHOL (+), LDL (+), HDL (0) Sasaki et al. (1987) —HDL (+), CHOL (0), TRI (+, girls only) Becque et al. (1988) —CHOL (0), TRI (0) —HDL Epstein et al. (1989) —Exercise plus diet (+) —Diet only (0), No-tx (0) Epstein et al. (1989) —CHOL, HDL, TRI —Tx, (+), No-tx (0) Zwiauer et al. (1989) —CHOL, TRI, LDL (+) —HDL (−), HDL_2 (0) Endo et al. (1992) —CHOL, TRI (+) —HDL (0) Figueroa-Colon et al. (1993) —CHOL (+), TRI (0)	*Insulin* Rocchini et al. (1987) (++) —Diet only (+) —No-tx. (0) Knip et al. (1993) —occurrence of hyperinsulinemia (+) —plasma insulin (0) Hoffman et al. (1995) —Insulin sensitivity (+) Gutin et al. (1996) (0) *Fasting glucose* Rocchini et al. (1987) (0) Hoffman et al. (1995) (0) Gutin et al. (1996) —Exercise training (0) —Lifestyle education (+)

Marshall Hoerr et al. (1988)
—Tx group (+)
—No tx (0)

Katch et al. (1988)
—Exercise plus diet (+)
—Diet only, No-tx (0)

Epstein et al. (1989)
—Tx group (+)
—No-tx (0)

Emes et al. (1990) (0)

Flodmark et al. (1993)
—Family Tx. (+)
—Dietary & pediatrician counseling (0)

Epstein et al. (1995) (+)

Gutin et al. (1996)
—Exercise training (+)
—Lifestyle education (0)

Amador et al. (1990)
—Higher (0) or lower (+) caloric restriction

Emes et al. (1990) (+)

Endo et al. (1992) (+)*

Flodmark et al. (1993)
—Family Tx (+), Diet & physician counseling (0)

Figueroa-Colon et al. (1993)
—PSMF (+), Hypocaloric diet (0)

Suskind et al. (1993) (+)

Israel et al. (1994) (+)

Hoffman et al. (1995) (0)

Gutin et al. (1996)
—Exercise (+), Lifestyle education (0)

Wabitsch et al. (1996) (+)

Johnson et al. (1997)
—Target diet & exercise (+), Info only (0)

Fanari et al. (1993)
—CHOL (+), TRI (0)

Suskind et al. (1993)
—CHOL, LDL, TRI (+)
—HDL (0)

Knip et al. (1993)
—HDL (+), TRI (0), LDL (0) HDL/CHOL ratio (0)

Hoffman et al. (1995)
—CHOL (+), TRI (0)

Gutin et al. (1996)
—TRI, CHOL/HDL ratio (+)

Johnson et al. (1997)
—CHOL
—Target diet & exercise (+)
—Info only (0)

[a]Various methods were used to assess children's physical fitness, with the most common method being submaximal ergometer fitness testing.
[b]Body fat was typically estimated via single- or multiple-site skinfold measures. Results reflect those obtained at post-treatment or at the most distal follow-up reported in the cited article.

Note. (+) positive change in outcome (e.g., increase in fitness, decrease in body fat); (++) significant improvement above and beyond any other treatment group also demonstrating improvement; (−) negative change in outcome; (0) no significant change in outcome; * significance testing not reported. Group differences in outcome measures are noted when presented; group differences are not given for studies that did not have multiple treatment groups, did not find group differences for a given outcome, or did not statistically examine group differences on a given outcome. Additional information can be retrieved from the original articles. These primary articles were selected from three review articles (Epstein et al., 1998; Haddock et al., 1994; Jelalian & Saelens, 1999).

Health and Human Services, 1996), and this may be beneficial for their long-term weight maintenance. Finally, children often have the benefit of incurring percentage overweight changes while maintaining their weight as a result of increases in height.

Although behavioral treatments show promising efficacy on average for overweight children, substantial work is needed to reduce the considerable relapse that occurs for some treated children (Epstein et al., 1998). Three indexes are useful in evaluating outcome: (a) change in average percentage overweight (with 20% change considered the standard for a large effect; Epstein, Valoski, Kalarchian, et al., 1995), as this measure accounts for changes in expected weight as a result of developmental increases in height (Epstein, Valoski, Wing, & McCurley, 1990); (b) the proportion of children maintaining large changes in percentage overweight (Epstein, Valoski, Kalarchian, et al., 1995); and (c) long-term follow-up of at least one year or longer, as many obesity treatment programs are able to delay relapse for approximately six months (Wilson, 1994). Recent reviews of the pediatric obesity treatment literature (Epstein et al., 1998; Haddock et al., 1994; Jelalian & Saelens, 1999) identified 14 published studies that evaluated changes in percentage overweight for at least one year and included some follow-up evaluation. Of these, three studies reported poor maintenance (i.e., research participants maintained less than a 10% decrease in percentage overweight), eight studies reported moderate maintenance (i.e., participants maintained a 10% to 20% decrease in percentage overweight), and only three studies reported good maintenance (i.e., participants maintained a 20% or greater decrease in percentage overweight). Among those achieving good maintenance, one treatment study by Brownell, Kelman, and Stunkard (1983) achieved an average of 20.5% change in percentage overweight in the most effective treatment group for the 12 of 14 adolescents who were still available for follow-up. Whereas another study (Epstein, Wing, Koeske, & Valoski, 1985) reported an average 20% decrease in children's percentage overweight that was even maintained at 10-year follow-up (Epstein, Wisniewski, & Wing, 1994). Of note, the most effective interventions tended to have parental involvement incorporated into the treatment program (although some had separate parental participation; e.g., Brownell et al., 1983), whereas interventions with the lowest relative long-term success generally either did not include a specific parental component or placed more responsibility for behavior change directly on the child. Nonetheless, despite this variability in treatment response, long-term outcomes for behavioral weight control treatment for children are particularly encouraging relative to the poor long-term outcomes obtained by adult weight-control programs (Jeffery et al., 2000).

EFFICACY AND PRACTICAL RECOMMENDATIONS
FOR KEY TREATMENT COMPONENTS

Behavioral interventions often target changes in both diet and physical activity to foster weight loss. The independent contribution of these components remains unclear because of the many permutations of the presence and absence of these components within more comprehensive treatment programs, evaluated across various follow-up periods.

The most robust and longest term outcomes exist for interventions targeting changes in both eating and physical activity (Epstein et al., 1990; Epstein et al., 1994). Indeed, dietary and activity change may work synergistically (Epstein & Goldfield, 1999) to maximize weight loss. In addition, results from Epstein, Valoski, Vara, et al. (1995) suggest that reductions in sedentary behavior may disrupt the potent connection between engaging in sedentary activity (e.g., television watching) and higher caloric consumption.

Diet Modification

Obese children consume more calories than their nonobese counterparts. For this reason, reducing energy intake is fundamental to weight loss. In this section we summarize the empirical research on dieting modifications for childhood obesity and offer some practical clinical suggestions.

Review of Empirical Literature

Research suggests that dietary modification is a powerful and necessary component for child weight loss. There are short- (Epstein, Wing, Penner, & Kress, 1985; Rocchini et al., 1988) and long-term decreases in adiposity (Epstein at al., 1994) for treatments focusing solely on dietary modification. Short-term effects for interventions lacking a dietary component are mixed (Blomquist, Borjeson, Larsson, Persson, & Sterky, 1965; Epstein, Vara, et al., 1982), but there is no evidence to date of long-term efficacy for the outcome of percentage overweight among treatments lacking a dietary component.

Nutrition education–instruction alone as a dietary component of treatment appears inadequate for overweight children to incur weight loss. Behavior modification strategies, such as behavioral contracting, stimulus control, or a specific dietary plan are required to help children lose weight (Coates et al., 1982; Epstein, Wing, Steranchak, Dickson, & Michelson, 1980; Johnson et al., 1997). Many different dietary components have been attempted, including moderate caloric restriction, protein-sparing modified fast (PSMF), and very low calorie diets. Aside from differences in prescribed caloric restriction (e.g., Amador, Ramos, Morono, & Hermelo, 1990), few studies have evaluated different nutrition plans or tested particular aspects of the overall dietary component while keeping constant other treatment components (Epstein et al, 1998). In their meta-analysis, Haddock and colleagues (1994) found little evidence that any particular aspect of dietary intervention is maximally effective for inducing child weight loss. Controlled trials are needed as long-term outcomes remain unknown for some dietary modification plans (e.g., Brown, Klish, Hollander, Campbell, & Forbes, 1983).

Practical Treatment Recommendations

Increasing children's awareness of eating habits through self-monitoring, with parental help, is a recommended first step for dietary change. By moderate caloric restriction and reductions in fat intake, children can meet their nutritional needs through increasing the nutrient density of foods eaten, shift toward negative energy balance, and gradually substitute for unhealthy food choices. A healthful target range for moderate caloric reduction can be selected based on children's initial weight, some expected underreporting of caloric intake (Bandini, Vu, Must, Cyr, Goldberg, & Dietz, 1999), and gradual weight loss (Barlow & Dietz, 1998). Many programs targeting preadolescents up to 100% overweight have used Epstein's Traffic Light or Stoplight diet approach (Epstein & Squires, 1988), which used the Food Guide Pyramid as a basis to maintain dietary reference intakes and provides a readily understandable food categorization system.

Expert consensus suggests that a lifestyle approach to changing overweight children's eating habits has the potential to gradually decrease overall caloric intake, to minimize the risk of youths' failing to meet recommended nutrient intake, and to maximize the likelihood of long-term weight control (Barlow & Dietz, 1998). This may be especially true for children who are mildly to moderately obese. More restrictive approaches, such as PSMF and very low calorie diets, have been less frequently investigated. Those studies conducted suggest similar long-term outcomes to those induced by moderate caloric restrictive diets among moderately overweight adolescents (Figueroa-Colon, von Almen, Franklin, Schuftan, & Suskind, 1993). These more restrictive dietary plans have been recommended in combination with careful physician monitoring for severely obese adolescents or less overweight adolescents with major health complications secondary to obesity (Stallings, Archibald, Pencharz, Harrison, & Bell, 1988).

Physical Activity

Aside from diet modification, increased activity is the other hallmark component of behavior therapy for childhood obesity. In this section we summarize research on physical activity prescribed as treatment and offer some practical clinical suggestions.

Review of Empirical Literature

Physical activity appears essential to maintaining weight loss among adults (National Institutes of Health, 1998), but the long-term impact of physical activity in the treatment of childhood obesity is less clear (Kohl & Hobbs, 1998). The most successful pediatric obesity programs have included a physical activity component (e.g., Epstein, Wing, et al. 1985; Epstein, Valoski, Wing, & McCurley, 1994), but physical activity components have not always augmented the effects of dietary modification (Epstein et al., 1984; Hills & Parker, 1988; Rocchini, Katch, Schork, & Kelch, 1987). There appear to be consistent short-term effects of physical activity interventions on both children's weight status as well as cardiorespiratory fitness (e.g., Epstein, Valoski, Vara et al., 1995) and other cardiovascular health benefits (Rocchini et al., 1988; Sasaki, Shindo, Tanaka, Ando, & Arakawa, 1987). However, more research is needed to clarify the long-term effects on overweight children's weight status after receiving physical activity modification alone and to determine physical activity programs that maximize outcomes (Epstein & Goldfield, 1999).

Programmed exercise programs that stress planned aerobic bouts of physical activity seem to contribute to children's weight loss more significantly than lower energy expenditure calisthenics programs (Epstein, Wing, Koeske, et al., 1985; Epstein et al., 1994). Epstein and colleagues (Epstein et al., 1982; Epstein, Wing, Koeske, et al., 1985; Epstein et al., 1994) report some success with lifestyle physical activity interventions, but few other studies have explored such approaches. Lifestyle interventions work to integrate more physical activity into daily activities, such as climbing stairs instead of taking the elevator. Recent research suggests that targeting reductions in sedentary activity (e.g., positively reinforcing decreases in television watching time), an innovative strategy for increasing physical activity (Epstein, Saelens, & Giancola O'Brien, 1995), can produce weight loss (Epstein, Valoski, Vara, et al., 1995; Epstein, Paluch, Gordy, & Dorn, 2000). There seems to be a reliable, albeit moderate, association between the sedentary activity of television watching and adiposity among children (Andersen, Crespo, Bartlett, Cheskin, & Pratt, 1998). Based on these data, we tested a home-based exercise device designed to increase physical activity while decreasing children's television viewing. This device consists of a cycle ergometer electronically connected to a television, thus rendering television viewing fully contingent on pedaling. When placed in the homes of obese children, their physical activity increased and television viewing decreased (Faith et al., in press).

Practical Treatment Recommendations

Current American College of Sports Medicine and Center for Disease Control recommendations for children's physical activity are similar to those of adults (see U.S. Department of Health and Human Services, 1996). Specifically, children 2 years of age and older are encouraged to engage in moderate- to vigorous-intensity physical activity for at least ½ hour on most days. However, this recommendation is for the goal of long-term health promotion, and no specific physical activity guidelines exist for adults', adolescents', or children's weight loss. In fact, others have recommended higher levels of physical activity for youth and the inclusion of physical activity focusing on maintaining or increasing strength as well as cardiorespiratory fitness, particularly among adolescents (Pate, Trost, & Williams, 1998). It is reasonable to assume that most overweight children's level of physical activity is initially inadequate for weight loss and that approaches to increase duration, frequency, and ultimately intensity of physical activity are warranted.

As with dietary modification, self-monitoring of children's physical activity is a reasonable initial step in modifying their physical activity. In addition, helping children become more cognizant of their sedentary behavior may provide them the opportunity to consider changes in physical activity patterns. In our experience, effective strategies include identifying physical activities that can be done by the family (e.g., family hikes, bicycle rides), increasing cues for and providing access to physical activity (e.g., bringing child to the park instead of the video arcade), parental modeling of habitual physical activity, and initiating lifestyle and moderate physical activity (e.g., walking) before moving into more vigorous physical activity (e.g., running, swimming laps). Parents can be instrumental in providing opportunities, safe environments, and support for their children's physical activity, particularly when physical activity is perceived as a family health priority.

Parent Participation

Children attempting to lose weight must depend on their parents at least to some extent. This section reviews data on the extent to which parental involvement in treatment enhances children's weight loss and summarizes some practical clinical suggestions for parents.

Review of Empirical Literature

Parental participation in childhood and adolescent weight loss programs has received considerable attention. Some treatments have targeted parents exclusively (Golan, Weizman, Apter, & Fainarn, 1998), the child or adolescent exclusively (e.g., Brownell et al., 1983; Kirschenbaum, Harris,

& Tomarken, 1984), the parent and the child or adolescent seen primarily together (e.g., Wadden et al., 1990), or most commonly the parent and child or adolescent participating separately for at least part of the treatment session (e.g., Epstein, Valoski, Vara, et al., 1995). Some studies found that parent participation did not improve effects found for treating children alone, although other data suggest that treating parents alone may be more effective for inducing child weight loss (Golan et al., 1998). However, the most robust weight control programs for prepubertal children have included at least some separate, concurrent participation by parents (Epstein et al., 1990). Among obese adolescents, there is some evidence that parents' separate concurrent participation is valuable (Brownell et al., 1983), but not all studies support this conclusion (Coates et al., 1982; Wadden et al., 1990).

Clinical experience also suggests that active parent participation is an important component of children's long-term weight control. Parenting skills training is a common component of treatment (e.g., Barlow & Dietz, 1998; Epstein, Wing, Koeske, et al., 1985; Israel, Stolmaker, & Andrian, 1985), particularly focusing on increasing praise for children's healthful eating and activity choices, better control of the familial eating and physical activity environment, and parental modeling. Others highlight additional parenting skills frequently taught in child and adolescent weight control programs (Barlow & Dietz, 1998). Parental participation is likely especially necessary for young children to be successful at weight control. Some research suggests at least short-term weight control and other health benefits for parents and overweight siblings of children targeted for weight loss (see Table 13-3).

Practical Treatment Recommendations

Practical recommendations for parental feeding practices are provided by Barlow and Dietz (1998). Among other practices, they recommend the following: Never use food as a reward; establish daily family meal and snack times; offer only healthy food options; be a role model for children; parents or caregivers should determine what food is offered and when, and the child should decide whether to eat.

CHALLENGES TO BEHAVIORAL INTERVENTION WITH OBESE CHILDREN AND ADOLESCENTS

Elsewhere we have conceptualized four potential barriers to treating obese children and adolescents (Faith & Allison, 1997): macro-level environmental barriers, family-specific barriers, peer-specific barriers, and child-specific barriers. With regard to macro-level environmental barriers, the current environment is arguably conducive to weight regain. The increasing

TABLE 13-3
Weight Outcomes for Parents of and Nontargeted Siblings of Children Receiving Obesity Treatment

Parent or Other Family Member Change in Percentage Overweight (% OV)

Kingsley & Shapiro (1977)
• Mothers in all tx. groups (+)*

Brownell, Kelman, Stunkard (1983)*
• Mother % OV (+)*

Kirschenbaum, Harris, & Tomarken (1984)
• Parent % OV
  • Child participates only (0)
  • Parent & child participate (+)

Israel et al. (1985)
• Participating parent % OV
  • Parent training plus weight loss (+)
  • Weight loss tx. only (+)
  • Wait-list control (0)

Epstein, Nudelman, & Wing (1987)
• Obese non-participating sibling % OV
  • Parent plus child targeted for weight loss (+)
  • Child alone targeted for weight loss (0)
  • Non-specific target for weight loss (0)

Nuutinen & Knip (1992)
• Maternal BMI (0)

Epstein, Valoski, Kalarchian, & McCurley (1995)**
• Various Tx. groups
  • post-tx. parent % OV (+)
  • 5 year follow-up parent % OV (0)
  • 10-year follow-up parent; % OV (–)

Golan et al. (1998)
• Parent only Tx.
  • father % OV (+)
  • mother % OV (0)

Note. (+) positive change in outcome (e.g., increase in fitness, decrease in body fat; (–) negative change in outcome; (0) no significant change in outcome; * significance testing not reported; ** Epstein and colleagues review their numerous findings regarding parent weight, with short-term results available in many of the original outcome reports.

Group differences in outcome measures are noted when presented; group differences are not given for studies that did not have multiple treatment groups, did not find group differences for a given outcome, or did not statistically examine group differences on a given outcome. Additional information can be retrieved from the original articles.

availability of energy-dense food and provisions for inactivity pose widespread challenges for those attempting weight control (Hill & Peters, 1998). These factors may be especially pertinent for families living in lower socioeconomic environments, in which limited financial constraints may favor purchasing less expensive yet more fattening foods. On a related level, the safety of the broader physical environment can encourage or discourage a child from being physically active (Sallis, 1995).

With regard to family-specific barriers, a number of potential variables are suggested from the literature. These factors include but may not be limited to a chaotic family home environment (Banis et al., 1988), parental neglect (Lissau & Sørensen, 1994), parental psychopathology and neuroticism (Epstein et al., 1994),and a controlling style of child feeding (Johnson & Birch, 1994). The strength of evidence concerning these variables is currently modest. Nonetheless, clinicians working with individual families may wish to assess their presence and potential impact on intervention.

Peer-specific barriers refer to the ways in which friends and acquaintances can impede weight loss efforts. The impact of such variables has not been formally assessed in controlled weight loss trials among children, however some data suggest that children are more likely to engage in exercise if they receive social support from peers to do so (Sallis, Prochaska, Taylor, Hill, & Geraci, 1999). Weight teasing may be one concrete example of a peer-specific barrier to exercise and hence weight control. One correlational study has shown that children who were teased about their body weight held more negative attitudes toward physical activity and reported less participation in physical activity compared to those who were teased less often (Pietrobelli, Leone, Heymsfield, & Faith, 1998). These associations were less pronounced among children who were better able to cope with weight teasing from peers. In a separate study, obese children attending a camp reported reluctance to expose their bodies or demonstrate their abilities in physical activity situations (Wilfley et al., 1998). Finally, increases in adiposity are prospectively associated with lower body image satisfaction and poor athletic competence (Kolody & Sallis, 1995), which may discourage participation in vigorous physical activity (Wilfley et al., 1998).

Child-specific barriers refer to those factors internal to the child that operate to hinder initial weight loss and maintenance. Perhaps the most powerful of such barriers is a genetic predisposition to obesity (Comuzzie & Allison, 1998; Faith et al., 1999; Rosenbaum & Leibel, 1998). Current molecular research is moving beyond broad heritability estimates of body weight and is focusing on specific genes that are suspected to influence obesity (Comuzzie & Allison, 1998). As discussed next, advances on this front may have implications for behavioral interventions with children.

FUTURE DIRECTIONS

This section summarizes future research directions and clinical issues pertaining to childhood obesity treatment. We discuss body composition assessment, outgrowths of genetic research, treating massively obese children and adolescents, and the expanding scope of treatment outcomes.

Advances in Body Composition Assessment

Methods for precisely measured body composition in children have advanced in recent years (Goran, 1998). One example is dual energy X-ray absorptiometry (DXA), an X-ray based methodology for estimating fat mass in the legs, arms, trunk, and total body. We anticipate a greater use of these and other laboratory-based methods to monitor the effectiveness of behavioral interventions in the future.

Another relevant issue is that of body fat distribution and its relation to comorbidities in children and adolescents. Although data are quite limited, studies are exploring the hypothesis that fat distributed around the visceral organs—"intra-abdominal fat"—is more strongly associated with health complications than either total body fat or subcutaneous fat (Goran, 1997). Several recent studies have measured visceral adiposity using state-of-the-art methods such as magnetic resonance imaging (MRI) and computerized tomography (CT; Gower et al., 1998).

Outgrowths of Genetics Research

More than 10 years ago, Epstein and Cluss (1986) argued that a better understanding of the genetics of obesity might allow the tailoring of treatments "to the behavioral factors which are likely to have the most powerful effects . . . for children who are predisposed to become obese" (p. 332). Since that statement, there have been groundbreaking advances into the genetics of obesity and related phenotypes (Commuzzie & Allison, 1998). Three potential applications of genetics research for advancing the treatment of childhood obesity are (a) to provide psychological support for the obese child, (b) to predict which nonobese children will eventually become obese and target them for preventive efforts, and (c) to better select the appropriate treatments for the appropriate children.

Providing Psychological Support

The first potential application—to provide psychological support—is the one most currently available to clinicians. Obese children are subject to enormous stigmatization and social discrimination. This can be especially problematic if such stigmatization interferes with efforts to lose weight. It is conceivable that a greater understanding of genetics, in conjunction with other cognitive–behavioral strategies, might help obese children better cope with weight discrimination (Faith, Fontaine, Cheskin, & Allison, 2000). This may be the case because obese individuals are typically judged less harshly when their condition is attributed to external factors (such as genetic influences) rather than internal factors.

Predicting Obesity Onset

The second potential application of genetic advances is to predict which children will become obese and target them for intervention. At the current time, one can look to family history as a general index to predict if a child will become obese (Whitaker, Wright, Pepe, Seidel, & Dietz, 1997). Eventually, molecular genetic research identifying specific genetic polymorphisms (i.e., genetic differences) that influence body fat might allow "marker-assisted sampling" (Lynch & Walsh, 1998) of the children who may benefit the most from prevention efforts. By marker-assisted sampling, we mean sampling individuals for intervention on the basis of specific genes that are believed to influence obesity. Currently, the field has not yet identified polymorphisms that are common enough to be useful for this purpose, but this could be a promising area in the future.

Matching Treatments to Children

The third potential avenue for applying genetic information is to better select the right treatment for the right obese child. Although schemas for matching individuals to treatment have been proposed (Brownell, 1995), these conceptualizations predated the current genetic advances. Further advances may lead to pharmacological interventions for obese children fitting a specific genetic profile who fail to respond to behavioral treatment. To illustrate the potential of this approach, consider Table 13-4, which summarizes all of the currently identified and published cases of obesity as a result of mutations or polymorphisms in single genes (excluding syndromes

TABLE 13-4
Identified and Published Probable Cases of Single-Gene Obesities in
Humans (as of October 1998).

Reference	Gene	Number of Families Studied	Number of Cases
Jackson et al. (1997).	Prohormone convertase 1 (PC1)	1	1
Montague et al. (1997).	OB (LEP)	1	2
Strobel et al. (1998).	OB (LEP)	1	3
Clement et al. (1998).	OB-R (LEP-R)	1	3
Krude et al. (1988).	POMC (pre-pro-opiomelanocortin)	2	2
Ristow et al. (1988).	PPAR$_\gamma$2	4	4
Yeo et al. (1998)	MC4R	1	2
Vaisse et al. (1998).	MC4R	1	6

such as Prader-Willi syndrome; see Allison, Packer-Munter, Pietrobelli, Alfonso, & Faith, 1998). The number is quite small, and the clinical characteristics are varied. This marked variation suggests that a better understanding of the specific genes underlying specific clinical characteristics could yield targeted pharmacological interventions for those obese children who do not respond to behavior therapy.

An example of this point is the case of two massively obese girls for whom nonpharmacological intervention proved ineffective (Montague et al., 1997). Because their obesity was a result of a unique and genetically based inability to produce leptin (a protein produced primarily from fat cells), it was reasoned that injecting synthetic leptin should successfully treat the girls' obesity. One girl received such a treatment, which resulted in rapid and dramatic weight loss (Farooqi et al., 1998). This case study illustrates how molecular advances were used to develop a specific pharmacological intervention matched to a specific genetic polymorphism.

Treating Massively Obese Children and Adolescents

The greatest increments in childhood obesity, on a population level, are occurring among the heaviest children (Troiano & Flegal, 1998). Behavioral interventions will need to be tested among massively obese children to determine which strategies work the best for which children under which circumstances. In addition, there is limited information on the treatment of mild-, moderate-, or massively obese adolescents. As Jelalian and Saelens (1999) noted, "There is currently minimal documentation of treatment efficacy for children who present with comorbid psychopathology or are greater than 100% overweight" (p. 228).

Expanding the Scope of Outcome Variables

Given the diversity of health complications associated with obesity, intervention studies might expand outcome measures to include indexes of fitness, blood pressure, lipids, other health-related variables, as well as psychological well-being or interpersonal functioning. Including such measures would provide a fuller picture of the overall effectiveness of behavioral interventions.

CONCLUSION

Compared to the behavioral treatment of adult obesity, family-based interventions for childhood obesity have yielded much more encouraging results at short- and long-term follow-up (Epstein et al., 1998). Nonetheless, there is considerable interindividual variation in response to interventions such that not all children maintain weight loss, and the needs of the heaviest children still need to be addressed. Future developments in behavioral theory, body composition measurement, and insights into the genetics of obesity are expected to enhance the development of more effective intervention packages.

REFERENCES

Allison D. B., Packer-Munter, W., Pietrobelli, A., Alfonso, V. C., & Faith, M. S. (1998). Obesity and developmental disabilities: Pathogenesis and treatment. Journal of Developmental and Physical Disabilities, 10, 215–255.

Amador, M., Ramos, L. T., Morono, M., & Hermelo, M. P. (1990). Growth rate reduction during energy restriction in obese adolescents. *Experimental & Clinical Endocrinology, 96, 73–82.*

American Academy of Pediatrics. Statement on Cholesterol. (1992). *Pediatrics, 90, 469–473.*

Andersen, R. E., Crespo, C. J., Bartlett, S. J., Cheskin, L. J., & Pratt, M. (1998). Relationship of physical activity and television watching with body weight and level of fatness among children: Results from the third National Health and Nutrition Examination Survey. *Journal of the American Medical Association, 279, 938–942.*

Archibald, E. H., Harrison, J. E., & Pencharz, P. B. (1983). Effect of a weight-reducing high-protein diet on the body composition of obese adolescents. *American Journal of Diseases of Children, 137 , 658–662.*

Bandini, L. G., Vu, D., Must, A., Cyr, H., Goldberg, A., & Dietz, W. H. (1999). Comparison of high-calorie, low-nutrient-dense food consumption among obese and non-obese adolescents. *Obesity Research, 7, 438–443.*

Banis, H. T., Varni, J. W., Wallander, J. L., Korsch, B. M., Jay, S. M., Adler, R., Garcia-Temple, E., & Negrete, V. (1988). Psychological and social adjustment of obese children and their families. *Child Care Health Development, 14, 157–173.*

Barlow, S. E., & Dietz, W. H. (1998). Obesity Evaluation and Treatment: Expert Committee Recommendations. *Pediatrics, 102 (e. 29),* http://www.pediatrics .org/cgi/content/full/102/3/e29.

Becque, M. D., Katch, V. L., Rocchini, A. P., Marks, C. R., & Moorehead, C. (1988). Coronary risk incidence of obese adolescents: Reduction by exercise plus diet intervention. *Pediatrics, 81, 605–612.*

Blomquist, B., Borjeson, M., Larsson, Y., Persson, B., & Sterky, G. (1965). The effect of physical activity on the body measurements and work capacity of overweight boys. *Acta Paediatrica Scandinavica, 54, 566–572.*

Brown, M. R., Klish, W. J., Hollander, J., Campbell, M. A., & Forbes, G. B. (1983). A high protein, low calorie liquid diet in the treatment of very obese adolescents: long-term effect on lean body mass. *American Journal of Clinical Nutrition, 38*, 20–31.

Brownell, K. D. (1995). Matching individuals to treatments. In: Brownell, K. D. & Fairburn, C. G. (Eds.), *Eating disorders and obesity: A comprehensive handbook*, pp. 552–557. New York: Guilford Press.

Brownell, K. D., Kelman, J. H., & Stunkard, A. J. (1983). Treatment of obese children with and without their mothers: Changes in weight and blood pressure. *Pediatrics, 71*, 515–523.

Clement, K., Vaisse, C., Lahlou, N., Cabrol, S., Pelloux, V., Cassuto, D., Gourmelen, M., Dina, C., Chambaz, J., Lacorte, J. M., Basdvant, A., Bougneres, P., Lebouc, Y., Froguel, P., & Guy-Grand, B. (1998). A mutation in the human leptin receptor gene causes obesity and pituitary dysfunction. *Nature, 392*, 398–401.

Coates, T. J., Jeffery, R. W., Slinkard, L. A., Killen, J. D., & Danaher, B. G. (1982). Frequency of contact and monetary reward in weight loss, lipid change, and blood pressure reduction with adolescents. *Behavior Therapy, 13*(2), 175–185.

Coates, T. J., Killen, J. D., & Slinkard, L. A. (1982b). Parent participation in a treatment program for overweight adolescents. *International Journal of Eating Disorders, 1*, 37–48.

Cole, T. J., Bellizzi, M. C., Flegal, K. M., & Dietz, W. H. (2000). Establishing a standard definition for child overweight and obesity worldwide: international survey. *British Medical Journal, 320*, 1240–1243.

Comuzzie, A. G., & Allison, D. B. (1998). The search for human obesity genes. *Science, 280*, 1374–1377.

Dietz, W. H. (1983). Childhood obesity: susceptibility, cause, and management. *Journal of Pediatrics, 103*, 676–686.

Emes, C., Velde, B., Moreau, M., Murdoch, D. D., & Trussell, R. (1990). An activity based weight control program. *Adapted Physical Activity Quarterly, 7*, 314–324.

Endo, H., Takagi, Y., Nozue, T., Kuwahata, K., Uemasu, F., & Kobayashi, A. (1992). Beneficial effects of dietary intervention on serum lipid and apolipoprotein levels in obese children. *American Journal of Diseases of Children, 146*, 303–305.

Epstein, L. H., & Cluss, P. A. (1986). Behavioral genetics of childhood obesity. *Behavior Therapy, 17*, 324–334.

Epstein, L. H. & Goldfield, G. S. (1999). Physical activity in the treatment of childhood overweight and obesity: current evidence and research issues. *Medicine and Science in Sports and Exercise, 31*, S553–S559.

Epstein, L. H., Kuller, L. H., Wing, R. R., Valoski, A., & McCurley, J. (1989). The effect of weight control on lipid changes in obese children. *American Journal of Diseases of Children, 143*, 454–457.

Epstein, L. H., Myers, M. D., Raynor, H. A., & Saelens, B. E. (1998). Treatment of pediatric obesity. *Pediatrics, 101*, 554–570.

Epstein, L. H., Nudelman, S., & Wing, R. R. (1987). Long-term effects of family-based treatment for obesity on nontreated family members. *Behavior Therapy*, 2, 147–152.

Epstein, L. H., Paluch, R. A., Gordy, C. C., & Dorn, J. (2000). Decreasing sedentary behaviors in treating pediatric obesity. *Archives of Pediatric and Adolescent Medicine*, 154, 220–226.

Epstein, L. H., Saelens, B. E., & Giancola O'Brien, J. (1995). Effects of reinforcing increases in active behavior versus decreases in sedentary behavior for obese children. *International Journal of Behavioral Medicine*, 2, 41–50.

Epstein, L. H., & Squires, S. (1988). *The Stoplight Diet for Children: An Eight-Week Program for Parents and Children* . Boston: Little, Brown.

Epstein, L. H., Valoski, A. M., Kalarchian, M. A., & McCurley, J. (1995). Do children lose and maintain weight easier than adults: A comparison of child and parent weight changes from six months to ten years. *Obesity Research*, 3, 411–417.

Epstein, L. H., Valoski, A. M., Vara, L. S., McCurley, J., Wisniewski, L., Kalarchian, M. A., Klein, K. R., & Shrager, L. R. (1995). Effects of decreasing sedentary behavior and increasing activity on weight change in obese children. *Health Psychology*, 14, 109–115.

Epstein, L. H., Valoski, A., Wing, R. R., & McCurley, J. (1990). Ten-year follow-up of behavioral, family-based treatment for obese children. *Journal of the American Medical Association*, 264, 2519–2523.

Epstein, L. H., Valoski, A., Wing, R. R., & McCurley, J. (1994). Ten-year outcomes of behavioral family-based treatment for childhood obesity. *Health Psychology*, 13, 373–383.

Epstein, L. H., Wing, R. R., Koeske, R., Ossip, D., & Beck, S. (1982). A comparison of lifestyle change and programmed aerobic exercise on weight and fitness changes in obese children. *Behavior Therapy*, 13, 651–665.

Epstein, L. H., Wing, R. R., Koeske, R., & Valoski, A. (1984). Effects of diet plus exercise on weight change in parents and children. *Journal of Consulting and Clinical Psychology*, 52, 429–437.

Epstein, L. H., Wing, R. R., Koeske, R., & Valoski, A. (1985). A comparison of lifestyle exercise, aerobic exercise, and calisthenics on weight loss in obese children. *Behavior Therapy*, 16, 345–356.

Epstein, L. H., Wing, R. R., Penner, B. C., & Kress, M. J. (1985). Effect of diet and controlled exercise on weight loss in obese children. *Journal of Pediatrics*, 107, 358–361.

Epstein, L. H., Wing, R. R., Steranchak, L., Dickson, B., & Michelson, J. (1980). Comparison of family-based behavior modification and nutrition education for childhood obesity. *Journal of Pediatric Psychology*, 5(1), 25–36.

Epstein, L. H., Wisniewski, L., & Wing, R. (1994). Child and parent psychological problems influence child weight control. *Obesity Research*, 2, 509–515.

Faith M. S., & Allison, D. B. (1997). Barriers to weight control in children. *Weight Control Digest, 7,* 649–654.

Faith, M. S., Berman, N., Heo, M., Pietrobelli, A., Gallagher, D., Epstein, L. H., Eiden, M. T., & Allison, D. B. (in press). Evaluation of a simple home-based method to increase physical activity and decrease TV viewing in obese children. *Pediatrics.*

Faith, M. S., Fontaine, K. R., Cheskin, L. R., & Allison, D. B. (2000). Behavioral approaches to the problems of obesity. *Behavior Modification, 24,* 459–493.

Faith, M. S., Pietrobelli, A., Allison, D. B., & Heymsfield, S. B. (1997). Prevention of pediatric obesity. Examining the issues and forecasting research directions. In A. Bendich, & R. J. Deckelbaum (Eds.), *Preventive nutrition* (pp. 471–486). Totowa, NJ: Humana Press.

Faith, M. S., Pietrobelli, A., Nuñez, C., Heo, M., Heymsfield, S. B., & Allison, D. B. (1999). Evidence for independent genetic influences on fat mass and body mass index in a pediatric twin sample. *Pediatrics, 104,* 61–67.

Fanari, P., Somazzi, R., Nasrawi, F., Ticozzelli, P., Grugni, G., Agosti, R., & Longhini, E. (1993). Haemorheological changes in obese adolescents after short-term diet. *International Journal of Obesity, 17,* 487–494.

Farooqi, I. S., Jebb, S. A., Langmack, G., Lawrence, E., Cheetham, C. H.,, Prentice, A. M., Hughes, I. A., McCamish, M. A., & O'Rahilly, S. (1998). Effects of recombinant leptin therapy in a child with congenital leptin deficiency. *New England Journal of Medicine, 341,* 879–884.

Figueroa-Colon, R., von Almen, T. K., Franklin, F. A., Schuftan, C., & Suskind, R. M. (1993). Comparison of two hypocaloric diets in obese children. *American Journal of Diseases of Children, 147,* 160–166.

Fladmark, C., Ohlsson, T., Ryden, O., & Sveger, T. (1993). Prevention of progression of severe obesity in a group of obese schoolchildren treated with family therapy. *Pediatrics, 91,* 880–884.

Freedman, D. S., Dietz, W. H., Srinivasan, S. R., & Berenson, G. S. (1999). The relation of overweight to cardiovascular risk factors among children and adolescents: The Bogalusa Heart Study. *Pediatrics, 103,* 1175–1182.

Golan, M., Weizman, A., Apter, A., & Fainaru, M. (1998). Parents as the exclusive agents of change in the treatment of childhood obesity. *American Journal of Clinical Nutrition, 67,* 1130–1135.

Goran, M. I. (1997). Energy expenditure, body composition, and disease risk in children and adolescents. *Proceedings of the Nutrition Society, 56,* 195–209.

Goran, M. I. (1998). Measurement issues related to studies of childhood obesity: Assessment of body composition, body fat distribution, physical activity, and food intake. *Pediatrics, 101,* 505–518.

Gower, B. A., Nagy, T. R., Trowbridge, C. A., Dezenberg, C., & Goran, M. I. (1998). Fat distribution and insulin response in prepubertal African American and white children. *American Journal of Clinical Nutrition, 67,* 821–827.

Gutin, B., Cucuzzo, N., Islam, S., Smith, C., & Stachura, M. E. (1996). Physical training, lifestyle education, and coronary risk factors in obese girls. *Medicine and Science in Sports and Exercise, 28*(1), 19–23.

Haddock, C. K., Shadish, W. R., Klesges, R. C., & Stein, R. J. (1994). Treatments for childhood and adolescent obesity. *Annals of Behavioral Medicine, 16,* 235–244.

Hayden, H. A., Stein, R. I., Saelens, B. E., Zabinski, M., Ghaderi, A., Wilfley, D. E. (in preparation). Effects of teaching experiences among obese children versus non-overweight peers.

Hill, J. O., & Peters, J. C. (1998). Environmental contributions to the obesity epidemic. *Science, 280,* 1371–1374.

Hills, A. P., & Parker, A. W. (1988). Obesity management via diet and exercise intervention. *Child: Care, Health, and Development, 14,* 409–416.

Himes, J. H., & Dietz, W. H. (1994). Guidelines for overweight in adolescent preventive services: recommendations from an expert committee. *American Journal of Clinical Nutrition, 59,* 307–316.

Hoffman, R. P., Stumbo, P. J., Janz, K. F., & Nielsen, D. H. (1995). Altered insulin resistance is associated with increased dietary weight loss in obese children. *Hormone Research, 44,* 17–22.

Israel, A. C., Stolmaker, L., & Andrian, C. A. (1985). The effects of training parents in general child management skills on a behavioral weight loss program for children. *Behavior Therapy, 16*(2), 169–180.

Jeffery, R. W., Drewnowski, A., Epstein, L. H., Stunkard, A. J., Wilson, G. T., Wing, R. R., & Hill, D. R. (2000). Long-term maintenance of weight loss: Current status. *Health Psychology, 19* (Suppl.), 5–16.

Jelalian, E., & Saelens, B. E. (1999). Intervention for pediatric obesity: Treatments that work. *Journal of Pediatric Psychology, 24,* 223–248.

Johnson, S. L., & Birch, L. L. (1994). Parents' and children's adiposity and eating style. *Pediatrics, 94,* 653–661.

Johnson, W. G., Hinkel, L. K., Carr, R. E., Anderson, D. A., Lemmon, C. R., Engler, L. B., & Bergeron, K. C. (1997). Dietary and exercise interventions for juvenile obesity: long-term effects of behavioral and public health models. *Obesity Research, 5,* 257–261.

Katch, V., Becque, D., Marks, C., Moorehead, C., & Rocchini, A. (1988). Basal metabolism of obese adolescents: inconsistent diet and exercise effects. *American Journal of Clinical Nutrition, 48,* 565–569.

Kingsley, R. G., & Shapiro, J. (1977). A comparison of three behavioral programs for the control of obesity in children. *Behavior Therapy, 8,* 30–36.

Kirschenbaum, D. S., Harris, E. S., & Tomarken, A. J. (1984). Effects of parental involvement in behavioral weight loss therapy for preadolescents. *Behavior Therapy, 15,* 485–500.

Knip, M., & Nuutinen, O. (1993). Long-term effects of weight reduction on serum lipids and plasma insulin in obese children. *American Journal of Clinical Nutrition, 57,* 490–493.

Kohl, H. W., III, & Hobbs, K. E. (1998). Development of physical activity behaviors among children and adolescents. *Pediatrics, 101,* 549–554.

Kolody, B., & Sallis, J. F. (1995). A prospective study of ponderosity, body image, self-concept, and psychological variables in children. *Journal of Developmental & Behavioral Pediatrics, 16,* 1–5.

Krude, H., Biebermann, H., Luck, W., Horn, R., Brabant, G., & Gruters, A. (1998). Severe early-onset obesity, adrenal insufficiency and red hair pigmentation caused by POMC mutations in humans. *Nature Genetics, 19,* 155–157.

Lissau, I., & Sørensen, T. I. A. (1994). Parental neglect during childhood and increased risk of obesity in young adulthood. *Lancet, 343,* 324–327.

Lynch, M., & Walsh, B. (1998). *Genetics and analysis of quantitative traits.* Sunderland, MA: Sinauer Associates.

Marshall Hoerr, S. L., Nelson, R. A., & Essex-Sorlie, D. (1988). Treatment and follow-up of obesity in adolescent girls. *Journal of Adolescent Health Care, 9,* 28–37.

Montague, C. T., Farooqi, I. S., Whitehead, J. P., Soos, M. A., Rau, H., Warcham, N. J., Sweter, C. P., Digby, J. E., Mohammed, S. N., Hurst, J. A., Cheetham, C. H., Earley, A. R., Barnett, A. H., Prins, J. B., O'Rahilly, S. (1997). Congenital leptin deficiency is associated with severe early-onset obesity in humans. *Nature, 387,* 903–908.

Must, A., Dallal, G. E., Dietz, W. H. (1991). Reference data for obesity: 85th and 95th percentiles of body mass index (wt/ht^2) and triceps skinfold. *American Journal of Clinical Nutrition, 53,* 839–846.

National Cholesterol Education Program. Report of the Expert Panel on Blood Cholesterol Levels in Children and Adolescents. (1991). Washington, DC: U.S. Government Printing Office. (No. 91-2732)

National Institutes of Health, NHLBI. (1998). Clinical Guidelines on the Identification, Evaluation, and Treatment of Overweight and Obesity in Adults— The Evidence Report. *Obesity Research, 6,* 51S–209S.

Nuutinen, O. & Knip, M. (1992). Predictors of weight reduction in obese children. *European Journal of Clinical Nutrition, 46,* 785–794.

Pate, R., Trost, S., & Williams, C. (1998). Critique of existing guidelines for physical activity in young people. In S. Biddle, J. Sallis, & N. Cavill (Eds.), *Young and active? Young people and health-enhancing physical activity—Evidence and implications* (pp. 162–176). London: Health Education Authority.

Pena, M., Bacallao, J., Barta, L., Amador, M., & Johnston, F. E. (1989). Fiber and exercise in the treatment of obese adolescents. *Journal of Adolescent Health Care, 10,* 30–34.

Pietrobelli, A., Leone, M. A., Heymsfield, S. B., & Faith, M. S. (1998). Association of physical-activity-teasing with reported activity and activity-attitudes in a pediatric sample. *International Journal of Obesity, 22 (Suppl. 4),* S8.

Ristow, M., Muller-Wieland, D. Pfeiffer, A., Krone, W., Kahn, C. R. (1998). Obesity associated with a mutation in a genetic regulator of adipocyte differentiation. *New England Journal of Medicine, 339,* 953–959.

Rocchini, A. P., Katch, V., Anderson, J., Hinderliter, J., Becque, D., Martin, M., & Marks, C. (1988). Blood pressure in obese adolescents: Effect of weight loss. *Pediatrics, 82,* 16–23.

Rocchini, A. P., Katch, V., Schork, A., & Kelch, R. P. (1987). Insulin and blood pressure during weight loss in obese adolescents. *Hypertension, 10,* 267–273.

Rosenbaum, M., & Leibel, R. L. (1998). The physiology of body weight regulation: Relevance to the etiology of obesity in children. *Pediatrics, 101,* 525–539.

Sallis, J. F., (1995). A behavioral perspective on children's physical activity. In Y. W. Cheung & B. J. Richmond (Eds.), *Child health, nutrition, and physical activity* (pp. 125–138). Champaigne, IL: Human Kinetics.

Sallis, J. F., Prochaska, J. J., Taylor, W. C., Hill, J. O., & Geraci, J. F. (1999). Correlates of physical activity in a national sample of girls and boys in grades 4 through 12. *Health Psychology, 18,* 410–415.

Sasaki, J., Shindo, M., Tanaka, H., Ando, M., & Arakawa, K. (1987). A long-term aerobic exercise program decreases the obesity index and increases the high density lipoprotein cholesterol concentration in obese children. *International Journal of Obesity, 11,* 339–345.

Second Task Force on Blood Pressure Control in Children. (1987). Report on the second Task Force on Blood Pressure Control in Children—1987. *Pediatrics, 79,* 1–25.

Senediak, C., & Spence, S. H. (1985). Rapid versus gradual scheduling of therapeutic contact in a family based behavioural weight control programme for children. *Behavioural Psychotherapy, 13,* 265–287.

Stallings, V. A., Archibald, E. H., Pencharz, P. B., Harrison, J. E., & Bell, J. E. (1988). One-year follow-up of weight, total body potassium, and total body nitrogen in obese adolescents treated with the protein-sparing modified fast. *American Journal of Clinical Nutrition, 48,* 91–94.

Strobel, A., Issad, T., Camoin, L., Ozata, M. & Stosberg, A. D. (1998). A leptin missense mutation associated with hypogonadism and morbid obesity. *Nature Genetics, 18,* 213–215.

Suskind, R. M., Sothern, M. S., Farris, R. P., von Almen, T. K., Schumacher, H., Carlisle, L., Vargas, A., Escobar, O., Loftin, M., Fuchs, G., Brown, R., & Udall, J. N. (1993). Recent advances in the treatment of childhood obesity. *Annals of the New York Academy of Sciences, 699,* 181–199.

Troiano, R. P., & Flegal, K. M. (1998). Overweight children and adolescents: Description, epidemiology, and demographics. *Pediatrics, 101,* 497–504.

U.S. Department of Health and Human Services, (1996). *Physical activity and health: a report of the Surgeon General.* Atlanta, GA: Author.

Wabitsch, M., Braun, U., Heinze, E., Muche, R., Mayer, H., Teller, W., & Fusch, C. (1996). Body composition in 5-18-y-old obese children and adolescents before and after weight reduction as assessed by deuterium dilution and bioelectrical impedance analysis. *American Journal of Clinical Nutrition, 64,* 1.

Wadden, T. A., Stunkard, A. J., Rich, L., Rubin, C. J., Sweidel, G., & McKinney, S. (1990). Obesity in black adolescent girls: A controlled clinical trial of treatment by diet, behavior modification, and parental support. *Pediatrics, 85*, 345–352.

Whitaker, R. C., Wright, J. A., Pepe, M. S., Seidel, K. D., & Dietz, W. H. (1997). Predicting obesity in young adulthood from childhood and parental obesity. *New England Journal of Medicine, 337*, 869–873.

Wilson, G. T. (1994). Behavioral treatment of obesity: Thirty years and counting. *Advances in Behaviour Research & Therapy, 16*(1), 31–75.

Yeo, G. S. H., Farooqi, I. S., Aminian, S., Halsall, D. J., & O'Rahilly, S. (1998). A frameshift mutation in MC4R associated with dominantly inherited human obesity. *Nature Genetics, 20*, 111–112.

Zwiauer, K., Kerbl, B., & Widhalm, K. (1989). No reduction of high density lipoprotein2 during weight reduction in obese children and adolescents. *European Journal of Pediatrics, 149*, 192–193.

14

PLASTIC SURGERY IN CHILDREN AND ADOLESCENTS

DAVID B. SARWER

An increasing number of children and adolescents now undergo plastic surgery to alter their physical appearance. The American Society of Plastic Surgeons (ASPS, 1999), which represents 97% of all physicians certified by the American Board of Plastic Surgery, reported that 24,623 persons under the age of 18 underwent cosmetic procedures in 1998 (see Table 14-1). This represents an 80% increase in the number of procedures from 1996 and a 138% increase since 1994. These figures are an underestimation of the actual number of cosmetic surgeries performed annually, because many nonplastic surgeon physicians now perform cosmetic procedures. For example, the American Society for Aesthetic Plastic Surgery (ASAPS, 2000), which includes procedures performed by dermatologists, otolaryngologists, and plastic surgeons, reported that more than 175,000 adolescents underwent cosmetic procedures in 1999. (The difference in the numbers is largely accounted for by chemical peels used to treat acne and laser hair removal.) If other more or less permanent methods to alter one's appearance (i.e., tattoos, body piercing, branding, and orthodontia) are considered also, it is likely that more children and adolescents are modifying their appearance than at any other time in history.

Cosmetic surgery is designed to improve the appearance of an individual with a "normal" appearance, and includes procedures such as liposuction (fat removal), rhinoplasty (nose surgery), and breast augmentation. Each year, thousands of adolescents also undergo reconstructive surgical procedures such as cleft lip and palate, that are used to treat a person with an "abnormal" appearance in an attempt to return them to a "normal" appearance. Because of the lack of agreement as to what constitutes a "normal" appearance, the line between cosmetic and reconstructive procedures is often unclear.

TABLE 14-1
National Cosmetic Surgery Statistics for Adolescents

Procedure	1994	1996	1998
Breast augmentation	392	1172	1840
Breast lift	101	228	406
Breast reduction in men (gynecomastia)	1237	1319	1862
Buttock lift	6	0	0
Cheek implants	34	12	36
Chemical peel	0	157	491
Chin augmentation	73	61	204
Collagen injection	0	135	298
Dermabrasion	808	640	1317
Ear surgery (otoplasty)	2576	2470	4721
Eyelid surgery (blepharoplasty)	0	267	126
Facelift	0	0	34
Fat injections	90	86	244
Forehead lift	0	47	0
Laser skin resurfacing	N/A	404	1005
Liposuction	511	788	1645
Male-pattern baldness	0	29	0
Nose reshaping (rhinoplasty)	4311	4313	8074
Retin-A treatment	209	1417	2224
Thigh lift	0	0	19
Tummy tuck	0	130	56
Upper arm lift	0	0	19
Wrinkle injections	0	24	2
Total	10,348	13,699	24,623

Note: From the *1994, 1996, and 1998 Plastic Surgery Statistics by the American Society of Plastic Surgeons,* Arlington Heights, IL: Author. Copyright American Society of Plastic Surgeons. Reprinted with permission. All figures are projected based on a survey of the American Society of Plastic Surgeons (ASPS) members only. ASPS membership includes 97% of the plastic surgeons certified by the American Board of Plastic Surgery.

The motivation for both cosmetic and reconstructive surgery, however, is often the same—that by modifying their physical bodies, persons can improve their satisfaction with their appearance and body image. Thus both types of procedures have significant psychological consequences. Our understanding of the psychology of physical appearance has increased greatly in the past several decades. We have learned that, whether we like to admit it or not, our physical appearance matters. Physically attractive persons are often viewed more positively by others and are frequently the recipients of preferential interpersonal treatment (Bull & Rumsey, 1988; Feingold, 1992; Hatfield & Sprecher, 1986). More recently, we have learned a great deal about the "inside view" of physical appearance—our body image—and its contribution to psychological functioning (Cash & Pruzinsky, 1990; Thompson, 1996; Thompson, Heinberg, Altabe, & Tantleff-Dunn, 1999). These two areas of research have been used as a framework to understand the psychological issues in cosmetic and reconstructive surgery (Sarwer, Nordmann, & Herbert, in press; Sarwer, Wadden, Pertschuk, & Whitaker, 1998a).

There has long been a great deal of interest in the psychological characteristics of adults who undergo cosmetic surgery; however, very little is known about children and adolescents who surgically alter their appearance. Although adolescent cosmetic surgery is not new, it became a popular media topic during the summer of 1999. It was covered on at least two major television magazine shows and was a central feature of an article on cosmetic surgery in *Newsweek*. Each of these stories debated the appropriateness of cosmetic surgery on adolescents whose physical bodies are still maturing. An equally important issue is the potential effects of surgery on the developing *body image*. A particular concern is that adolescents, in their quest to improve their appearance, do not appreciate the relative permanent effects of surgery on their bodies. This is of particular importance in breast augmentation, because it appears that breast implants will need to be replaced several times over a woman's lifespan, thereby subjecting young women to several additional surgeries.

Another concern is the general public's misperceptions about cosmetic surgery. Many persons inaccurately view cosmetic surgery as medical treatments with minimal risks and few side effects that produce "Cinderella-like" transformations in patients. This perception is most likely gleaned from slick magazine advertisements that frequently use professional models as representations of postoperative results and promise dramatic improvements in self-esteem and quality of life. Another source of this misperception is television programs that often highlight the newest advances in the field of cosmetic surgery (e.g., the "lunchtime facelift") without fully discussing the risks and potential side effects of the procedure. Although teenagers and their parents may not view cosmetic surgery with the same casualness as they do orthodontic treatment (which, in some respects, is also cosmetic surgery), they frequently forget it is *surgery*—with all of the risks and potential complications of any invasive procedure.

This chapter will provide an overview of cosmetic and reconstructive surgery for children and adolescents. I will begin with a review of the psychological studies of cosmetic surgery patients, with an emphasis on more recent investigations that have focused on body image. I will review most common cosmetic and reconstructive surgical procedures for children and adolescents, and I will conclude with a discussion of patient assessment procedures for mental health professionals who encounter adolescent plastic surgery patients.

PSYCHOLOGICAL STUDIES OF COSMETIC SURGERY PATIENTS

Psychological investigations of cosmetic surgery patients have a history dating back to the 1940s (Sarwer, Wadden, et al., 1998a). The vast majority of these studies have focused on adults interested in cosmetic surgery; few papers have investigated adolescents and cosmetic surgery. Thus we must borrow from the adult literature and combine these findings with the few reports of adolescents to understand the psychological issues of teenagers who seek cosmetic surgery.

Studies of adult patients can be organized around two fundamental questions: (a) Do cosmetic surgery patients share certain psychological characteristics?; and (b) Do cosmetic surgery patients experience psychological change postoperatively? (Grossbart & Sarwer, 1999; Sarwer, in press; Sarwer, Pertschuk, Wadden, & Whitaker, 1998). Studies designed to address the first question have attempted to understand the psychological motivations of persons who seek cosmetic surgery. Investigations that have focused on the second question have attempted to confirm an intuitive assumption of cosmetic surgery—that a surgical change in appearance results in psychological benefit. These studies also have attempted to identify psychological factors related to a poor psychological outcome and, therefore, may contraindicate cosmetic surgery. The studies also can be organized by the type of surgical procedure; however, there does not appear to be a clear relationship between a given cosmetic procedure and specific psychological issues (Sarwer, Wadden et al., 1998a). Organizing the research around these two questions allows us to determine if these investigations have addressed the questions they set out to study.

Preoperative Studies of Cosmetic Surgery Patients

Preoperative studies of cosmetic surgery patients that have used clinical interviews as the primary assessment tool have, almost uniformly, found high rates of psychopathology in prospective patients. In several studies, a majority of patients who sought cosmetic surgery were diagnosed with a psychiatric disturbance (Edgerton, Jacobson, & Meyer, 1960; Marcus, 1984; Meyer, Jacobson, Edgerton, & Canter, 1960; Robin, Copas, Jack, Kaeser, & Thomas, 1988; Webb, Slaughter, Meyer, & Edgerton, 1965) or were described as experiencing increased symptoms of depression and anxiety, as well as low self-esteem (Beale, Lisper, & Palm, 1980; Ohlsen, Ponten, & Hambert, 1978; Sihm, Jagd, & Pers, 1978). For example, one interview investigation reported that 19.5% of patients had an Axis I disorder (predominantly mood and anxiety disorders) and 70% an Axis II disorder (predominantly narcissistic and borderline personality disorders; Napoleon, 1993).

Studies that have used standardized psychometric tests generally reported less psychological disturbance. Studies of patients who sought rhinoplasty and rhtydectomy (facelift) found relatively few symptoms of psychopathology (Goin, Burgoyne, Goin, & Staples, 1980; Goin & Rees, 1991; Wright & Wright, 1975). Similarly, two of three studies of breast augmentation patients found little evidence of psychopathology (Baker, Kolin, & Bartlett, 1974; Schlebusch, 1989; Shipley, O'Donnell, & Bader, 1977).

Both groups of investigations have several methodological shortcomings that raise questions about their validity (Sarwer, Pertschuk et al., 1998; Sarwer, Wadden et al., 1998a). Many of the interview investigations were conducted by psychiatrists working from a psychodynamic perspective. Thus the high levels of psychopathology in these studies may have reflected the theoretical biases of the interviewers. In other studies, the nature of the clinical interview was not described, and formal diagnostic criteria were not used. The psychometric studies also have methodological limitations, such as a failure to include control or comparison groups. As a result, the typical psychological presentation of cosmetic surgery patients cannot be reliably asserted (Sarwer, Pertschuk et al., 1998; Sarwer, Wadden et al., 1998a).

Postoperative Studies of Cosmetic Surgery Patients

Postoperative investigations of cosmetic surgery patients have focused on two issues: patient satisfaction and changes in psychological status. Studies of patient satisfaction following cosmetic surgery have been largely anecdotal, consisting primarily of surgeons' reports of their patients' satisfaction. These reports suggest that 70% or more of patients report satisfaction with their outcome (e.g. Park, Chetty, & Watson, 1996; Schlebusch & Marht, 1993; Young, Nemecek, & Nemecek, 1994).

Other studies have focused on the psychological changes following cosmetic surgery. The majority of postoperative interview investigations have reported that women experience psychological benefits from cosmetic surgery. Five of nine studies reported a generally favorable psychological outcome (Edgerton, Langman, & Pruzinsky, 1991; Goin, Goin, & Gianini, 1977; Marcus, 1984; Ohlsen et al., 1978; Robin et al., 1988), whereas two reported some negative consequences (Edgerton et al., 1960; Meyer et al., 1960), and two others noted no change or mixed results (Hay & Heather, 1973; Sihm et al., 1978). Similar to the preoperative interview investigations, these studies also had significant methodological shortcomings, including poor definitions of outcome, absence of preoperative interviews, and high attrition.

Of the seven studies that used standardized tests to assess psychological outcome, two showed favorable changes (Goin & Rees, 1991; Schlebusch

& Marht, 1993), three observed no change (Hollyman, Lacey, Whitfield, & Wilson, 1986; Slator & Harris, 1992; Wright & Wright, 1975), and two described an increase in depressive symptoms (Goin et al., 1980; Meyer & Ringberg, 1987). These psychometric investigations also had methodological problems. Whereas some used pre- and postoperative assessments, others only included postoperative assessments with comparisons to normative groups. These methodological concerns limit the confidence that can be placed in the claims that women experience psychological benefit from surgery (Pruzinsky, 1996; Sarwer, Pertschuk, et al., 1998; Sarwer, Wadden et al., 1998a).

Two recent studies, however, suggest that cosmetic surgery patients do experience psychological benefit postoperatively. Rankin, Borah, Perry, and Wey (1998) found that women reported significant improvements in depression and quality of life six months postoperatively as compared to preoperative levels. Similarly, Sarwer and colleagues (1998c) found that patients reported a significant reduction in the degree of dissatisfaction with the body feature altered by cosmetic surgery. Replication of these findings in studies that include nonsurgical control groups are needed to confidently conclude that cosmetic surgery leads to improvements in depression, quality of life, and body image.

Summary of the Research

Attempts at drawing firm conclusions from the psychological research in cosmetic surgery is difficult at best. Overall, the findings are contradictory and, as a result, my colleagues and I believe the existing research has failed to answer the main questions that have prompted the work (Sarwer, in press; Sarwer, Pertschuk, et al., 1998). Preoperative, interview-based investigations have suggested that patients are highly psychopathological, and studies that have used psychometric measures have found little psychopathology. Studies that have specifically looked at psychological change following surgery have, for the most part, suffered from many of the same methodological flaws as the preoperative studies. At this time, it may be premature to state confidently that cosmetic surgery leads to psychological benefit in a majority of patients (Sarwer, Pertschuk, et al., 1998; Sarwer, Wadden, et al., 1998a). More optimistically, with the exception of the patient who is actively psychotic (as well as patients who suffer from body dysmorphic disorder, as discussed next), there do not seem to be any absolute psychological contraindications to surgery (Sarwer, 1997; Sarwer, in press; Sarwer, Pertschuk, et al., 1998).

Nevertheless, studies that suggest that the majority of patients do not present with significant psychopathology and do experience psychological benefit from cosmetic surgery are more consistent with the experiences of surgeons in the present day. However, to accept that persons who request cosmetic surgery are no different from the general population does not make intuitive sense (Sarwer, Pertschuk, et al., 1998). Even among persons who can afford cosmetic procedures, only a minority pursue them. This led my colleagues and I to suggest that body image concerns may differentiate those who seek cosmetic surgery from those who do not (Sarwer, Pertschuk, et al., 1998; Sarwer, Wadden, et al., 1998a).

BODY IMAGE AND COSMETIC SURGERY

Within the past decade, body image has been considered an important psychological construct in understanding cosmetic surgery patients (Pruzinsky, 1993; Pruzinsky, 1996; Sarwer, Pertschuk, et al., 1998; Sarwer, Wadden, et al., 1998a). Pruzinsky and Edgerton (1990) have suggested that cosmetic surgery is body image surgery—that by modifying the body surgically, psychological improvement will occur. One consistent finding of the preoperative studies of cosmetic surgery patients is that women who seek cosmetic surgery have reported increased dissatisfaction with their bodies (e.g., Beale et al., 1980; Schlebusch, 1989), and improvements in body image were reported by the majority of patients postoperatively (e.g., Kilmann, Sattler, & Taylor, 1987; Schlebusch & Marht, 1993; Sihm et al., 1978; Young et al., 1994). It is only recently, however, that body image has been empirically studied in cosmetic surgery patients.

My colleagues and I theorized that body image dissatisfaction may be the motivational catalyst to the decision to seek cosmetic surgery (Sarwer, Wadden, et al., 1998a). A series of empirical investigations has supported this contention. In the first study (Sarwer, Wadden, Pertschuk, & Whitaker, 1998b), 100 women who sought a variety of procedures completed the Multidimensional Body-Self Relations Questionnaire (MBSRQ; Brown, Cash, & Mikulka, 1990; Cash, Winstead, & Janda, 1986) and the Body Dysmorphic Disorder Examination-Self Report (BDDE-SR; Rosen & Reiter, 1996) before their initial consultation. Results were compared to those of the normative samples for each of the measures. Prospective patients did not report greater investment or increased dissatisfaction with their overall body image compared to controls; however, they did report heightened dissatisfaction with the specific body feature for which they were pursuing surgery (as assessed by the BDDE-SR). Similar results were found in investigations of male cosmetic surgery patients and women who sought rhytidectomy and blepharoplasty (Pertschuk, Sarwer, Wadden, & Whitaker, 1998; Sarwer, Whitaker, Wadden, & Pertschuk, 1997). Together, these results suggested that patients had heightened dissatisfaction with the specific body feature considered for surgery rather than more global body dissatisfaction.

Three recent studies of breast surgery patients have expanded on these results. In the first investigation, breast augmentation and breast reduction patients were compared on the MBSRQ and BDDE-SR (Sarwer, Bartlett, Bucky, et al., 1998). Breast reduction patients reported greater dissatisfaction with both their breasts and overall body image, which may, in part, be explained by their increased body weight. More than 50% of both groups, however, reported significant behavioral change in response to negative feelings about their breasts, including avoidance of being seen undressed by others, checking the appearance of their breasts, and camouflaging the appearance of their breasts with clothing or special bras. This dissatisfaction also may have contributed to more general dysphoria, because in the year before surgery, more than 20% of both groups reported increased symptoms of anxiety and depression.

In the second investigation, women who sought breast augmentation were compared to an age-matched sample of small-breasted women not seeking augmentation surgery (Nordmann, 1998). Women who sought breast augmentation reported significantly greater dissatisfaction with their breasts, as well as greater body image discomfort in social situations. A subsequent study also compared women who sought breast augmentation to physically similar women not seeking surgery on body image, self-esteem, quality of life, and appearance-related teasing (Sarwer, unpublished data). As with previous studies, augmentation patients reported greater body image and breast dissatisfaction. Although the two groups did not differ on self-esteem and quality of life, augmentation patients did report greater investment in their appearance, more appearance-related teasing, and greater use of psychotherapy in the previous year.

Thus it appears that women who seek cosmetic surgery report different body image concerns than those not seeking surgery. Early investigations, which compared cosmetic surgery patients to normative samples, suggested that these concerns were limited to the feature considered for surgery. Studies of breast augmentation patients using physically similar women as controls, however, suggest that not only do these women have greater dissatisfaction with their breasts, they also have greater investment and dissatisfaction with their overall body image. In addition, they report a history of more appearance-related teasing. Augmentation patients' reports of more frequent use of psychotherapy also suggests that the body image dissatisfaction may be related to more general dysphoria, although this relationship awaits further study.

These studies raise an important question: Can someone be too dissatisfied with their body image for cosmetic surgery? Extreme body image dissatisfaction is a central component of body dysmorphic disorder (BDD). BDD is defined in the *DSM-IV* as a preoccupation with an imagined or slight defect in appearance that leads to significant impairment in functioning (American Psychiatric Association, 1994). Persons with BDD are often so preoccupied with a feature of their appearance that they will examine, check, or alter their appearance repeatedly, often preventing them from attending school, holding a job, or maintaining romantic and social relationships. Although any body area may be the focus of concern, the most commonly affected areas are the skin, hair, and nose (Phillips, 1996; Phillips & Diaz, 1997; Phillips, McElroy, Keck, Pope, & Hudson, 1993). Others have found that some overweight women also have a level of distress, preoccupation, and impairment consistent with BDD (Rosen, Reiter, & Orosan, 1995; Sarwer, Wadden, & Foster, 1998).

The average age of onset of BDD is 16 years old, suggesting that adolescence may be a particularly vulnerable time for the development of BDD (Phillips, 1996; Phillips & Diaz, 1997). BDD has many distinctive features that distinguishes it from more age-normative appearance concerns. Most persons engage in repetitive behaviors involving examining, hiding, or improving the defect. Others may engage in avoidance behaviors such as not looking at mirrors or refusing to leave the house. These behaviors may range in severity, but typically involve one or more hours a day (Phillips, 1996). Persons with BDD frequently attempt to correct their defect through cosmetic surgery or other medical treatments. A recent study found that 7% of female cosmetic surgery patients met diagnostic criteria for BDD (Sarwer, Wadden, 1998b), a prevalence greater than that thought to exist in the general population (2%). The prevalence of adolescents with BDD, both among persons presenting for cosmetic surgery and in the general population, is unknown.

BDD may be particularly difficult to diagnosis in cosmetic surgery patients (Sarwer, 1997; Sarwer, Wadden, et al., 1998b). Given the newness of BDD to American psychology and psychiatry (it was first introduced in *DSM-III-R* in 1987), many cosmetic surgeons are unfamiliar with the diagnosis. In addition, the objective of cosmetic surgery—to improve a "normal" appearance—also may make diagnosis difficult. Cosmetic surgery patients are frequently concerned with slight defects in their appearance. Such slight defects, however, are frequently judged as observable and correctable by the surgeon. As a result, judgment of a slight defect in appearance becomes highly subjective in these patients. Following surgery, persons with BDD often remain focused on the same feature or become focused on a different feature. In a series of 188 persons with BDD, 131 sought and 109 received nonpsychiatric treatments, including cosmetic surgery and dermatological care; 83% experienced an exacerbation of their symptoms (Phillips & Diaz, 1997). These reports suggest that BDD may contraindicate cosmetic surgery (Sarwer, 1997; Sarwer, in press).

Consider the following case of an adolescent with BDD who sought plastic surgery:

> John was a 17-year-old high school senior who was referred for psychological treatment by a plastic surgeon. He was a handsome young man who arrived at his initial consultation well-groomed. Over the past two years, John had become concerned about four moles on his face. The moles were of average size and not particularly noticeable, but John was convinced that they made him grotesquely ugly. He was so concerned with one on his cheek that he covered it with a small bandage, which drew even more attention to it. Early in high school, John was an A student and played on the basketball team. Over the past two years, however, he spent increasing amounts of time thinking about his facial appearance. At the time of the consultation with the surgeon, he was failing several classes and had stopped playing basketball. He reported skipping school several times a month because of his appearance. At home, he would spend hours focusing on his appearance— checking it in the mirror, asking his parents how he looked, or using the Internet to do research on plastic surgery. He reported seeing several plastic surgeons in an attempt to remove his moles. When he was unable to find a surgeon to treat him, he attempted to remove the moles himself with a razor blade.

In summary, body image has long been thought to play an important role in the decision to seek cosmetic surgery. Surprisingly, body image in cosmetic surgery patients has only been empirically studied, with psychometrically sound measures, in the past few years. These studies have suggested that persons who seek surgery report heightened body image dissatisfaction, particularly greater dissatisfaction with the feature to be surgically altered. These studies also have indicated that a minority of persons who seek surgery (7%) have extreme body image dissatisfaction characterized by BDD. Persons with BDD who undergo surgery do not appear to benefit from the procedures, leading some to suggest the BDD should be a contraindication to cosmetic surgery.

As with the more general studies of the psychological characteristics of cosmetic surgery patients, there has been little study of the body image concerns of adolescent cosmetic surgery patients. In some respects, this is not surprising, because adolescents still represent a small minority of patients in most cosmetic surgery practices. Given the increasing research interest in the psychological issues of cosmetic surgery, coupled with the rapid increase in the number of adolescents who seek surgery, it is likely that empirical studies of body image in adolescent patients will appear in the literature in the near future.

COSMETIC SURGICAL PROCEDURES

As can be seen in Table 14-1, children and adolescents undergo a wide range of cosmetic surgical procedures on both their faces and bodies. We will focus our discussion on the most common procedures.

Liposuction

The removal of fat cells through liposuction was the sixth most frequently performed cosmetic procedure for adolescents in 1998 (it is the most commonly performed procedure for adults). There are several misperceptions about liposuction. It is widely believed that liposuction is only used to remove excess fat from the torso. In reality, liposuction can be used to remove fat throughout the body. Another misconception is that liposuction results in weight loss. Liposuction typically produces little, if any, change in body weight, and thus is not an acceptable weight reduction treatment. Nevertheless, given liposuction's role as a tool to modify body shape, it is a procedure intricately tied to body image.

The greatest concern about liposuction in adolescents is the potential association with eating disorders. Willard, McDermott, and Woodhouse (1996) described two cases of women with bulimia who underwent liposuction in attempt to lose weight, only to experience an exacerbation of their bulimic symptoms postoperatively. Anorexia and bulimia likely occur among women (and men) who seek all forms of cosmetic surgery, because there are case reports of women with both disorders who have undergone breast augmentation, breast reduction, rhinoplasty, and chin augmentation (Losee, Serletti, Kreipe, & Caldwell, 1997; McIntosh, Britt, & Bulik, 1994; Yates, Shisslak, Allender, & Wollman, 1988). Adolescent liposuction patients should routinely be asked about their history of weight fluctuations, binge eating, amenorrhea, and dieting and purging behaviors.

The following case illustrates a typical presentation of an adolescent liposuction patient:

> Jessica was a 17-year-old recent high school graduate. She was 5'7" and weighed 160 lbs. She was interested in liposuction because she felt that her hips and thighs were out of proportion with the rest of her body. Jessica reported that she had been "pudgy" during junior high and the early part of high school. Over the past few years she had improved her diet—eating less junk food and eating more fruits and vegetables— and began jogging several times per week. Although she lost about 15 lbs, she remained concerned about deposits of fat on her hips and thighs. She felt self-conscious of her hips in summer clothes and swimsuits, as well as during sexual situations with her boyfriend. Following

liposuction, there was little change in her body weight, but she reported being less self-conscious with her hips and thighs.

Rhinoplasty

Rhinoplasty (nose reshaping) has long been the most frequently requested cosmetic procedure for adolescents. It is commonly performed to reduce the overall size of the nose, reshape the tip, or reduce the bridge of the nose. Psychologists and psychiatrists working from a psychodynamic perspective have vigorously exercised their theoretical muscle in interpreting adolescents' motivations for rhinoplasty. For example, a 16-year-old female rhinoplasty patient with a prominent nose resembling her father's might have had her desire for surgery interpreted as a somatic projection of an unconscious conflict with him. Given our current understanding of the importance of physical appearance in person perception and body image, a more straightforward and equally plausible interpretation of her interest in surgery is that she has an appropriate concern about an overly prominent feature that makes her feel self-conscious in certain situations.

Breast Augmentation

Cosmetic breast augmentation surgery for adolescent girls has increased by almost 370% from 1994 to 1998. Developmental and sociocultural factors that influence body image may help explain the rapid rise in breast augmentation surgery (Sarwer, Wadden, et al., 1998a). More frequent teasing about a lack of breast development was one characteristic that differentiated small-breasted women who sought augmentation surgery from those who did not (Sarwer, 2000). Mass media images of beauty also may contribute to the increasing popularity of this surgery. The image of lean yet full-breasted woman has dominated the mass media for the past decade (Sarwer et al., in press). This is true not only for adult models but also television and movie stars (such as Jennifer Love Hewitt) as well as musicians (such as Brittney Spears) who appeal to younger audiences.

Perhaps the greatest concern surrounding breast augmentation surgery is safety. Silicone breast implants have been banned from use for cosmetic procedures since 1992 because of concerns about the relationship with autoimmune disease. In the summer of 1999, the Institute of Medicine released its report on the safety of silicone implants and concluded that there was no relationship between the implants and autoimmune disease (IOM, 1999). However, the report also concluded that local and perioperative complications "occur frequently enough to be a cause for concern and to justify the conclusion that they are the primary safety issue." Many of these complications occur not only with silicone implants but also with saline implants that are currently used. These complications include capsular contracture (hardening of the breasts), mammographic interference, breast feeding difficulties, loss of nipple sensation, and hypertrophic scarring. Furthermore, the average life expectancy of a breast implant is 10 to 15 years (IOM, 1999). Thus an adolescent who undergoes breast augmentation is likely to undergo repeated surgical procedures (with the associated risks) to replace her implants throughout her lifetime.

Facial Implants

Adolescents will occasionally seek to enlarge their chin, jaw, cheeks, or brow with permanent implants. The two studies that have reported on the experiences of patients who have undergone these procedures have suggested that the majority of patients experienced psychological benefit from the procedures (Edgerton, Langman, & Pruzinsky, 1990, 1991). Edgerton and colleagues (1991) have suggested that these procedures also may benefit persons with a history of significant psychopathology (including thought disorders and depression), given that these patients are vigilantly managed by both the surgeon and a mental health professional.

Other Cosmetic Procedures

Children and adolescents also see plastic surgeons for a variety of less frequently performed cosmetic procedures. These procedures include surgical treatments for prominent ears (otoplasty), gynecomastia (male breast development), and several different treatments for acne. Although these conditions rarely, if ever, cause physical discomfort or affect physical functioning, the treatments are similar to reconstructive procedures, because they are designed to correct an abnormal appearance feature.

There has been little study of the psychological issues of persons who undergo these procedures. In one study of the psychological functioning of children who underwent otoplasty, psychological and social distress were the predominant motivators for surgery. The vast majority of children and parents were satisfied with the result, and 63% of parents reported that the child was happier and more confident postoperatively (Bradbury, Hewison, & Timmons, 1992). The relative ease, however, with which we can picture children with these conditions being teased about their appearance suggests the potentially damaging effects on body image and self-esteem.

RECONSTRUCTIVE SURGICAL PROCEDURES

The common perception of a plastic surgeon is a physician who performs solely cosmetic procedures. In reality, more than half of the procedures performed by ASPS members are reconstructive in nature (see Table 14-2). These procedures can range from treatment of developmental abnormalities to treatment of physical insults from illness or traumatic injury. We now turn to some of the most common reconstructive procedures for children and adolescents.

Breast Reduction

In 1998, the ASPS reported that 2823 adolescent girls underwent breast reduction surgery. There are no data on the average age of persons who underwent this surgery, however they often are in their late teens, because surgeons typically wait to perform surgery until breast development has stopped. Large breasts can result in significant physical discomfort, including neck, shoulder, and back pain, skin rashes, and grooving of the shoulders from brassiere straps. These women also report difficulty exercising and shopping for properly fitting clothes, as well as personal embarrassment because of their breast size (Glatt et al., 1999).

The ability of reduction mammaplasty to reduce or eliminate the physical symptoms of large breasts is well-documented. These women also experience significant improvements in body image postoperatively (Glatt et al., 1999). Regardless, insurance companies often deny coverage for the procedure on the grounds that it is "cosmetic" or require women to lose weight in an attempt to reduce their breast size. Several studies have found that women experience improvement in the physical discomfort associated with large breasts independent of their preoperative body weight, thereby demonstrating no rationale to recommend weight loss as an alternative to surgery (Dabbah, Lehman, Parker, Tantri, & Wagner, 1995; Glatt et al., 1999).

Maxillofacial Surgery

Maxillofacial surgery for craniofacial deformities and other birth defects involves the reconfiguration of both bone and soft tissue in highly complex and often risky surgeries. These procedures range from cleft lip and palate corrections to treatment of rare congenital conditions that dramatically distort facial appearance. Children with these conditions often undergo one or more major surgeries before the age of 5 and may undergo repeated revisions throughout adolescence. Unfortunately, many are left with significantly disfigured facial appearances.

Investigations of children born with craniofacial anomalies have shown decreased self-esteem, increased anxiety, behavioral problems, social withdrawal, and social interaction problems (for a review see, Endriga & Kapp-Simon, 1999). Psychological functioning has been found to improve after

TABLE 14-2
1998 Cosmetic and Reconstructive Statistics for Adolescents and Adults

Procedure	Adolescents	Total
Animal bite repair	N/A	10,152
Birth defect reconstruction	20,255	22,457
Breast augmentation	1840	132,378
Breast implant removal	N/A	43,681
Breast lift	406	31,525
Breast reconstruction	173	69,683
Breast reduction	2823	70,358
Breast reduction in men (gynecomastia)	1862	9023
Burn care	N/A	27,875
Buttock lift	0	1246
Cheek implants	36	2864
Chemical peel	491	66,002
Chin augmentation	204	4795
Collagen injection	298	45,851
Dermabrasion	1317	12,191
Ear surgery (otoplasty)	4721	8069
Eyelid surgery (blepharoplasty)	126	120,001
Facelift	34	70,947
Fat injections	244	25,437
Forehead lift	0	36,777
Hand surgery	N/A	160,671
Lacerations	N/A	72,818
Laser skin resurfacing	N/A	55,623
Liposuction	1645	172,079
Male-pattern baldness	0	2146
Maxillofacial surgery	N/A	22,516
Microsurgery	N/A	24,573
Nose reshaping (rhinoplasty)	8074	55,953
Retin-A treatment	2224	106,862
Scar revision	N/A	47,100
Subcutaneous mastectomy	191	1500
Thigh lift	19	3785
Tummy tuck (abdominoplasty)	56	46,597
Tumor removal	N/A	509,457
Upper arm lift	19	1939
Wrinkle injections	2	1463
Other reconstructive		116,620
Reconstructive endoscopic		2235
Total	47,060[a]	2,215,249

[a] Some Numbers are not Available for Adolescents.
Note: *1998 Plastic Surgery Statistics by the American Society of Plastic Surgeons* (Arlington Heights, IL: Author.) Copyright American Society of Plastic Surgeons. Reprinted with permission. All figures are projected based on a survey of the American Society of Plastic Surgeons (ASPS) members only. ASPS membership includes 97% of the plastic surgeons certified by the American Board of Plastic Surgery. Adolescent numbers are unavailable for several procedures; the total is based on the procedures tabulated.

surgical treatment; however, it does not necessarily return to normal levels (Pertschuk & Whitaker, 1988). A recent study of adolescents born with a craniofacial deformity found that these teenagers reported more frequent teasing about their facial appearance, which was correlated with lower self-esteem, greater symptoms of depression, and greater problems with attachment (Sarwer, Whitaker, Bartlett, & Wadden, 1999). Facially disfigured adults also report difficulties with body image, self-esteem, and quality of life, with more than one third reporting social or job discrimination (Sarwer et al., 1999).

Traumatic Injury and Cancer

Plastic surgeons also perform reconstructive surgeries following physical insults such as automobile accidents, burns, dog bites, and cancer. The effect of these insults on appearance can range greatly, and treatment may involve a series of surgeries over several years. In all but the rarest of cases, there is typically some degree of residual appearance deformity. There has been little formal study of body image in adolescents with these conditions. Nevertheless, it is easy to speculate that any bodily injury or insult has the potential to have a negative effect on body image.

PATIENT SELECTION FOR PLASTIC SURGERY

Mental health professionals may encounter adolescents interested in plastic surgery in a variety of contexts. Adolescent patients in a psychotherapy practice who have body image concerns may have considered (or have undergone) cosmetic surgery. Patients with posttraumatic stress disorder following an accident that disfigured their appearances may have to undergo reconstructive surgery. Surgeons also may ask a mental health professional to see a patient. These consultations typically occur in one of two contexts— to evaluate a patient before surgery or to assess psychological functioning postoperatively.

Preoperative Consultations

The vast majority of adult cosmetic surgery patients are thought to be psychologically appropriate for surgery and probably do not require a mental health consultation. These patients typically have specific appearance concerns and realistic postoperative expectations. Most cosmetic surgeons probably hold similar assumptions about their adolescent patients. Given the absence of evidence suggesting that adolescent patients have specific psychopathology or distinct psychological issues, this assumption is understandable.

A small minority of both adult and adolescent patients, however, may exhibit symptoms to the surgeon that warrant a psychological evaluation (Sarwer, 1997, in press). In addition to using the basic principles of cognitive–behavioral assessment, the assessment should focus on three additional areas: motivations and expectations, psychiatric history, and appearance concerns and body dysmorphic disorder.

Motivations and Expectations

It is important to determine the patient's motivation for surgery. Several researchers have attempted to categorize patients motivations as internal (undergoing the surgery to improve one's self-esteem) or external (undergoing the surgery for some secondary gain, such as starting a new romantic relationship; Goin et al., 1980; Meyer et al., 1960). Although a clear distinction between an internal and external motivation may be difficult, internally motivated patients are thought to be more likely to meet their goals for surgery (Edgerton et al., 1991).

Assessing patient motivation may be particularly important in adolescents. Some teenagers interested in cosmetic surgery may be driven by pressure from parents to improve their appearance, particularly in families in which one or both parents have had cosmetic surgery. To address this potential situation, the ASPS suggests that the teenager, and not the parent, must be the person who initiates the request for cosmetic surgery. Asking the adolescent when he or she first started thinking about surgery may help determine if the patient's interest in surgery is internally derived or strongly influenced by external pressures. Even if the adolescent's interest in surgery is internally derived, the parents' attitudes toward surgery should be assessed. Parents are occasionally not supportive of an adolescent's interest in surgery but have agreed to pursue it (and most often pay for it) simply to appease the teenager's repeated requests for surgery. This family dynamic may reflect some psychopathology in the teenager (such as BDD) or the family and therefore warrants further assessment before surgery.

In addition to parental influence, adolescents interested in cosmetic surgery may be influenced by the mass media, either through the unrealistic images of beauty or through stories promoting the benefits of cosmetic surgery. Adolescents also may feel some pressure from their peers to have surgery. Such pressure may be both direct and indirect. A peer may suggest cosmetic surgery to a teenager unhappy with his or her appearance or an adolescent may live in a community in which cosmetic surgery is seen as a "rite of passage" or is commonly given to an adolescent as a high school graduation present.

Pruzinsky (1997) has categorized postoperative expectations as surgical, psychological, and social. Surgical expectations address the specific concerns about the patient's appearance (discussed later). Psychological expectations include the possible psychological benefits, such as improvement in body image, that may occur postoperatively. Social expectations address the potential social benefits of cosmetic surgery. Many adolescents interested in cosmetic surgery believe that they will become more popular following surgery. Although plastic surgery can enhance physical appearance, it may not improve a person's popularity. Thus prospective patients should be aware that an improvement in appearance (which may or may not be noticeable) probably will not result in a change in the social responses of others.

Psychiatric Status and History

Assessing current psychological status, as would be done in any mental health consultation, is an important part of the consultation with the plastic surgery patient (Sarwer, in press). With the exception of BDD, there currently are no conclusive data on the prevalence of psychiatric diagnoses among plastic surgery patients. Given the increasing numbers of persons who now seek surgery, it is likely that all of the major psychiatric conditions occur. Nevertheless, particular attention should be paid to disorders with a body image component, such as eating disorders and somatoform disorders, as well as mood and anxiety disorders. The presence of these disorders, however, may not be an absolute contraindication for cosmetic surgery. In the absence of sound data on the relationship between psychopathology and surgical outcome, a patient's appropriateness for surgery should be made on a case by case basis and include careful collaboration between the mental health professional and surgeon.

A thorough psychiatric history should be obtained. Patients should be asked about diagnoses both past or present as well as ongoing treatment. Patients with a positive psychiatric history and who are not currently in treatment should be assessed carefully. A patient currently under psychiatric care should be asked if his or her mental health professional is aware of the interest in surgery. These professionals should be contacted to confirm that cosmetic surgery is appropriate. Patients who have not mentioned their interest in cosmetic surgery to their mental health provider, or do not allow him or her to be contacted, should be viewed with caution. Surgeons will often refuse to operate on patients who they believe are psychiatrically inappropriate for surgery.

Appearance Concerns and BDD

Assessment of appearance concerns and body image is a central component of an evaluation of the adolescent plastic surgery patient. Pruzinsky (1997) has suggested the use of Lazarus's BASIC ID (1981) with plastic surgery patients, which assesses seven dimensions of body image—behavior, affect, sensation, imagery, cognition, interpersonal, and biological. Many of the measures discussed by Gardner (chapter 8, this volume) also may be appropriate.

Prospective patients should be able to articulate specific concerns about their appearance that should be visible with little effort. Patients who are markedly distressed about slight defects that are not readily visible may be suffering from BDD. The degree of dissatisfaction also should be assessed. Asking about the amount of time spent thinking about a feature or the activities missed or avoided may indicate the degree of distress and impairment a person is experiencing and may help determine the presence of BDD.

Informed Consent

The issue of informed consent in cosmetic surgery is particularly interesting. In most cosmetic surgery cases, a patient with no illness or defect is asking a physician to perform a surgical operation that will create an injury or scar (which, it could be argued, is at odds with the Hippocratic oath of "Do no harm"). Furthermore, the procedure is undertaken with the objective of improving both aesthetic appearance and psychological well-being, although, as discussed previously, there is little evidence to suggest that this occurs. Pruzinsky (1997) has suggested that true informed consent in cosmetic surgery must include not only a discussion of the risks and benefits of surgery but also a discussion of body image concerns and expectations.

Perhaps somewhat surprisingly, there are currently no specific informed consent procedures for adolescents who undergo cosmetic surgery. Thus as with other medical procedures, if the adolescent is below a certain age (typically 18) he or she must have parental consent to undergo cosmetic surgery. Similarly, the ability to provide informed consent for cosmetic surgery as it is related to mental illness also falls under more general medical guidelines. This is an issue that warrants additional attention from the cosmetic surgery profession, because the issue of preexisting psychopathology is a frequent element in malpractice cases.

Postoperative Consultations

Mental health professionals also may be asked to consult with cosmetic surgery patients postoperatively. This typically occurs in one of three scenarios—the cosmetic surgery patient is dissatisfied with successful surgery, the reconstructive patient is having difficulty coping with some residual deformity following surgery, or the cosmetic or reconstructive patient is experiencing an exacerbation of psychopathology that was not detected preoperatively. Patients in each of these examples typically warrant psychotherapeutic care. Cognitive–behavioral models of body image therapy (e.g., Cash, 1996;

Rosen, 1996) are often useful with these individuals, although more diagnosis-specific treatments also may be required. Body image psychotherapy also may be useful for an adolescent who is determined by the surgeon to be inappropriate for surgery preoperatively.

In summary, mental health professionals may encounter adolescent plastic surgery patients in a variety of contexts. In addition to the basic principles of cognitive–behavioral assessment, the mental health professional should assess the patient's motivations and expectations for surgery as well as current psychiatric status and psychiatric history. This assessment should include an evaluation of the parents' thoughts about cosmetic surgery. Mental health professionals also should thoroughly assess the appearance concerns of adolescent patients, paying particular attention to symptoms of BDD. Cognitive–behavioral body image psychotherapy may be an appropriate alternative to cosmetic surgery or may be a useful adjunctive therapy for postoperative patients.

CONCLUSION

Cosmetic surgery is becoming an increasingly popular pursuit for adolescents who are dissatisfied with their physical appearance. As with many rapidly developing areas of Western culture, however, the hype surrounding adolescent cosmetic surgery (and cosmetic surgery in general) has already lapped thoughtful consideration of the appropriateness of cosmetic surgery on individuals whose bodies and body images are still developing. Over the past several decades, there has been a great deal of research on the psychological issues of adults who seek cosmetic surgery. Unfortunately, there has been scarcely any research on the psychological characteristics of adolescents who seek cosmetic surgery, nor has there been any research documenting the psychological changes that occur postoperatively. One could optimistically argue that adolescent patients are just like adults—that the majority are psychologically appropriate for surgery and may experience psychological benefit postoperatively. However, given the central role of body image in the pursuit of cosmetic surgery, coupled with the often turbulent nature of body image during adolescence, it is clear that more research in this area is needed before we can confidently state that cosmetic surgery is psychologically beneficial to the majority of adolescents who pursue it.

Several areas of research are perhaps most critical. First, we need to understand more fully the psychological motivations of adolescents interested in cosmetic surgery. As body image dissatisfaction is thought to motivate the pursuit of cosmetic surgery for adults, studies assessing body image dissatisfaction in younger patients are needed. In addition to body image dissatisfaction, factors such as parental or peer pressure and appearance-related teasing may influence the decision to seek surgery. Second, given that extreme body image dissatisfaction and BDD are often traced to adolescence, a better understanding of the relationship between extreme body image dissatisfaction, body dysmorphic disorder, and cosmetic surgery is needed. Third, additional research is needed to investigate further the effectiveness of cosmetic surgery as a treatment for body image dissatisfaction in both adolescents and adults. Given the effectiveness of cognitive–behavioral psychotherapy for body image dissatisfaction, a particularly interesting investigation would be a comparison of this approach to cosmetic surgery.

Given the increasing popularity of cosmetic surgery, it is likely that clinicians will encounter children and adolescents interested in changing their body image through surgery. In addition to using the basic principles of cognitive–behavioral assessment, preoperative assessments should focus on several additional areas. The adolescent's motivations and expectations for surgery (as well as those of the parents), psychiatric status and history, and body image concerns and BDD all should be assessed before cosmetic surgery. Mental health providers also may encounter adolescent cosmetic surgery patients postoperatively, a time in which cognitive–behavioral body image interventions (as well as diagnosis-specific interventions) may be useful. As plastic surgery continues to increase in popularity for both adolescents and adults, the relationship of body image and cosmetic surgery is likely to further develop as an interesting and informative area of body image study.

REFERENCES

American Psychiatric Association. (1994). *Diagnostic and statistical manual of mental disorders* (4th ed.). Washington, DC: Author.

American Society of Plastic Surgeons. (1999). *1998 plastic surgery procedural statistics*. Arlington Heights, IL: Author.

American Society for Aesthetic Plastic Surgery. (2000). *ASAPS 1999 Statistics on Cosmetic Surgery*. New York: Author.

Baker, J. L., Kolin, I. S., & Bartlett, E. S. (1974). Psychosexual dynamics of patients undergoing mammary augmentation. *Plastic and Reconstructive Surgery, 53*, 652–659.

Beale, S., Lisper, H., & Palm, B. (1980). A psychological study of patients seeking augmentation mammaplasty. *British Journal of Psychiatry, 136*, 133–138.

Bradbury, E. T., Hewison, J., & Timmons, M. J. (1992). Psychological and social outcome of prominent ear correction in children. *British Journal of Plastic Surgery, 45*, 97–100.

Brown, T. A., Cash, T. F., & Mikulka, P. J. (1990). Attitudinal body image assessment: Factor analysis of the Body-Self Relations Questionnaire. *Journal of Personality Assessment, 55,* 135–144.

Bull, R., & Rumsey, N. (1988). *The social psychology of facial appearance.* New York: Springer-Verlag.

Cash, T. F. (1996). The treatment of body-image disturbances. In J. K. Thompson (Ed.), *Body image, eating disorders, and obesity* (pp. 83–107). Washington, DC: American Psychological Association.

Cash, T. F., & Pruzinsky, T. (1990). *Body images: Development, deviance, and change.* New York: Guilford Press.

Cash, T. F., Winstead, B. A., & Janda, L. H. (1986). The great American shape-up: Body image survey report. *Psychology Today, 20,* 30–37.

Dabbah, A., Lehman, J. A., Parker, M. G., Tantri, D., & Wagner, D. S. (1995). Reduction mammaplasty: An outcome analysis. *Annals of Plastic Surgery, 35,* 337–341.

Edgerton, M. T., Jacobson, W. E., & Meyer, E. (1960). Surgical-psychiatric study of patients seeking plastic (cosmetic) surgery: Ninety-eight consecutive patients with minimal deformity. *British Journal of Plastic Surgery, 13,* 136–145.

Edgerton, M. T., Langman, M. W., Pruzinsky, T. (1990). Patients seeking symmetrical recontouring for "perceived" deformities in the width of the face and skull. *Aesthetic Plastic Surgery, 14,* 59–73.

Edgerton, M. T., Langman, M. W., & Pruzinsky, T. (1991). Plastic surgery and psychotherapy in the treatment of 100 psychologically disturbed patients. *Plastic and Reconstructive Surgery, 88,* 594–608.

Endriga, M. D., & Kapp-Simon, K. A. (1999). Psychological issues in craniofacial care: State of the art. *Cleft Palate-Craniofacial Journal, 36,* 3–11.

Feingold, A. (1992). Good looking people are not what we think. *Psychological Bulletin, 111,* 304–341.

Glatt, B. S., Sarwer, D. B., O'Hara, D. E., Hamori, C., Bucky, L. P., & LaRossa, D. (1999). A retrospective study of changes in physical symptoms and body image after reduction mammaplasty. *Plastic and Reconstructive Surgery, 103,* 76–82.

Goin, M. K., Burgoyne, R. W., Goin, J. M., & Staples, F. R. (1980). A prospective psychological study of 50 female face-lift patients. *Plastic and Reconstructive Surgery, 65,* 436–442.

Goin, M. K., Goin, J. M., & Gianini, M. H. (1977). The psychic consequences of a reduction mammaplasty. *Plastic and Reconstructive Surgery, 59,* 530–534.

Goin, M. K., & Rees, T. D. (1991). A prospective study of patients' psychological reactions to rhinoplasty. *Annals of Plastic Surgery, 27,* 210–215.

Grossbart, T. A., & Sarwer, D. B. (1999). Cosmetic surgery: Surgical tools—Psychosocial goals. *Seminars in Cutaneous Medicine and Surgery, 18,* 101–111.

Hatfield, E., & Sprecher, S. (1986). *Mirror, mirror . . . The importance of looks in everyday life.* Albany: SUNY Press.

Hay, G. G., & Heather, B. B. (1973). Changes in psychometric test results following cosmetic nasal operations. *British Journal of Psychiatry, 122,* 89–90.

Hollyman, J. A., Lacey, J. H., Whitfield, P. J., & Wilson, J. S. P. (1986). Surgery for the psyche: A longitudinal study of women undergoing reduction mammoplasty. *British Journal of Plastic Surgery, 39,* 222–224.

Institute of Medicine. (1999). *Safety of silicone implants.* Washington, DC: National Academy Press.

Killman, P. R., Sattler, J. I., & Taylor, J. (1987). The impact of augmentation mammaplasty: A follow-up study. *Plastic and Reconstructive Surgery, 80,* 374–378.

Lazarus, A. A. (1981). *The practice of multimodal therapy.* New York: McGraw-Hill.

Losee, J. E., Serletti, J. M., Kreipe, R. E., & Caldwell, E. H. (1997). Reduction mammaplasty in patients with bulimia nervosa. *Annals of Plastic Surgery, 39,* 443–446.

Marcus, P. (1984). Psychological aspects of cosmetic rhinoplasty. *British Journal of Plastic Surgery, 37,* 313–318.

McIntosh, V. V., Britt, E., & Bulik, C. M. (1994). Cosmetic breast augmentation and eating disorders. *New Zealand Medical Journal, 107,* 151–152.

Meyer, E., Jacobson, W. E., Edgerton, M. T., & Canter, A. (1960). Motivational patterns in patients seeking elective plastic surgery. *Psychosomatic Medicine, 22,* 193–202.

Meyer, L., & Ringberg, A. (1987). Augmentation mammaplasty-psychiatric and psychosocial characteristics and outcome in a group of Swedish women. *Scandinavian Journal of Plastic and Reconstructive Surgery, 21,* 199–208.

Napoleon, A. (1993). The presentation of personalities in plastic surgery. *Annals of Plastic Surgery, 31,* 193–208.

Newsweek. (1999). *The New Age of Cosmetic Surgery* (August 9), 52–59.

Nordmann, J. E. (1998). *Body image and self-esteem in women seeking breast augmentation.* Unpublished doctoral dissertation.

Ohlsen, L., Ponten, B., & Hambert, G. (1978). Augmentation mammaplasty: A surgical and psychiatric evaluation of the results. *Annals of Plastic Surgery, 2,* 42–52.

Park, A. J., Chetty, U., & Watson, A. C. H. (1996). Patient satisfaction following insertion of silicone breast implants. *British Journal of Plastic Surgery, 49,* 515–518.

Pertschuk, M. J., Sarwer, D. B., Wadden, T. A., & Whitaker, L. A. (1998). Body image dissatisfaction in male cosmetic surgery patients. *Aesthetic Plastic Surgery, 22,* 20–24.

Pertschuk, M. J., & Whitaker, L. A. (1988). Psychosocial outcome of craniofacial surgery in children. *Plastic and Reconstructive Surgery, 82,* 741–744.

Phillips, K. A. (1996). *The broken mirror: Understanding and treating body dysmorphic disorder.* New York: Oxford University Press.

Phillips, K. A., & Diaz, S. F. (1997). Gender differences in body dysmorphic disorder. *Journal of Nervous and Mental Disease, 185*, 570–577.

Phillips, K. A., McElroy, S. L., Keck, P. E., Pope, H. G., & Hudson, J. I. (1993). Body dysmorphic disorder: 30 cases of imagined ugliness. *American Journal of Psychiatry, 150*, 302–308.

Pruzinsky, T. (1993). Psychological factors in cosmetic plastic surgery: Recent developments in patient care. *Plastic Surgical Nursing, 13*, 64–71.

Pruzinsky, T. (1996). Cosmetic plastic surgery and body image: Critical factors in patient assessment. In J. K. Thompson (Ed.), *Body image, eating disorders, and obesity* (pp. 109–127). Washington, DC: American Psychological Association.

Pruzinsky, T. (1996). The psychology of plastic surgery: Advances in evaluating body image, quality of life, and psychopathology. In M. B. Habal, W. C. Lineaweaver, R. W. Parsons & J. E. Woods (Eds.), *Advances in plastic and reconstructive surgery* (Vol. 12, 153–170). Philadelphia: Mosby.

Pruzinsky, T., & Edgerton, M. T. (1990). Body image change in cosmetic plastic surgery. In T. F. Cash & T. Pruzinsky (Eds.), *Body images: Development, deviance, and change* (pp. 217–236). New York: Guilford Press.

Rankin, M., Borah, G. L., Perry, A. W., & Wey, P. D. (1998). Quality-of-life outcomes after cosmetic surgery. *Plastic and Reconstructive Surgery, 102*, 2139–2145.

Robin, A. A., Copas, J. B., Jack, A. B., Kaeser, A. C., & Thomas, P. J. (1988). Reshaping the psyche: The concurrent improvement in appearance and mental state after rhinoplasty. *British Journal of Psychiatry, 152*, 539–543.

Rosen, J. C. (1996). Body dysmorphic disorder: Assessment and treatment. In J. K. Thompson (Ed.), *Body image, eating disorders, and obesity* (pp. 149–170). Washington, DC: American Psychological Association.

Rosen, J. C., & Reiter, J. (1996). Development of the Body Dysmorphic Disorder Examination. *Behaviour Research and Therapy, 34*, 755–766.

Rosen, J. C., Reiter, J., & Orosan, P. (1995). Cognitive behavioral body image therapy for Body Dysmorphic Disorder. *Journal of Consulting and Clinical Psychology, 63*, 263–269.

Sarwer, D. B. (2000) An investigation of the psychological characteristics of cosmetic breast augmentation patients. Unpublished data.

Sarwer, D. B. (in press). Psychological considerations in cosmetic surgery. In R. M. Goldwyn & M. N. Cohen (Eds.), *The unfavorable result in plastic surgery* (3rd ed.) Lippincott Raven, Philadelphia.

Sarwer, D. B. (1997). The "obsessive" cosmetic surgery patient: A consideration of body image dissatisfaction and body dysmorphic disorder. *Plastic Surgical Nursing, 17*, 193–209.

Sarwer, D. B., Bartlett, S. P., Bucky, L. P., LaRossa, D., Low, D. W., Pertschuk, M. J., Wadden, T. A., & Whitaker, L. A. (1998). Bigger is not always better: Body image dissatisfaction in breast reduction and breast augmentation patients. *Plastic and Reconstructive Surgery, 101*, 1956–1961.

Sarwer, D. B., Bartlett, S. P., Whitaker, L. A., Paige, K. T., Pertschuk, M. J., & Wadden, T. A. (1999). Adult psychological functioning of individuals born with craniofacial anomalies. *Plastic and Reconstructive Surgery, 103*, 412–418.

Sarwer, D. B., Nordmann, J. E., & Herbert, J. D. (2000). Cosmetic breast augmentation surgery: A critical overview. *Journal of Women's Health and Gender-Based Medicine, 9*, 843–856.

Sarwer, D. B., Pertschuk, M. J., Wadden, T. A., & Whitaker, L. A. (1998). Psychological investigations of cosmetic surgery patients: A look back and a look ahead. *Plastic and Reconstructive Surgery, 101*, 1136–1142.

Sarwer, D. B., Wadden, T. A., & Foster, G. D. (1998). Assessment of body image dissatisfaction in obese women: Specificity, severity, and clinical significance. *Journal of Consulting and Clinical Psychology, 66*, 651–654.

Sarwer, D. B., Wadden, T. A., Pertschuk, M. J., & Whitaker, L. A. (1998a). The psychology of cosmetic surgery: A review and reconceptualization. *Clinical Psychology Review, 18*, 1–22.

Sarwer, D. B., Wadden, T. A., Pertschuk, M. J., & Whitaker, L. A. (1998b). Body image dissatisfaction and body dysmorphic disorder in 100 cosmetic surgery patients. *Plastic and Reconstructive Surgery, 101*, 1644–1649.

Sarwer, D. B., Wadden, T. A., Pertschuk, M. J., & Whitaker, L. A. (1998c, March 25–28). *Changes in body image following cosmetic surgery.* Paper presented at the Nineteenth Annual Meeting of the Society of Behavioral Medicine, New Orleans, LA.

Sarwer, D. B., Whitaker, L. A., Bartlett, S. P., & Wadden, T. A. (1999, March 3–6). *Psychological functioning of adolescents born with craniofacial anomalies.* Paper presented at the Twentieth Annual Meeting of the Society of Behavioral Medicine, San Diego, CA.

Sarwer, D. B., Whitaker, L. A., Wadden, T. A., & Pertschuk, M. J. (1997). Body image dissatisfaction in women seeking rhytidectomy or blepharoplasty. *Aesthetic Surgery Journal, 17*, 230–234.

Schlebusch, L., & Mahrt, I. (1993). Long-term psychological sequelea of augmentation mammoplasty. *South African Medical Journal, 83*, 267–271.

Shipley, R. H., O'Donnell, J. M., & Bader, K. F. (1977). Personality characteristics of women seeking breast augmentation. *Plastic and Reconstructive Surgery, 60*, 369–376.

Sihm, F., Jagd, M., & Pers, M. (1978). Psychological assessment before and after augmentation mammaplasty. *Scandinavian Journal of Plastic and Reconstructive Surgery, 12*, 295–298.

Slator, R., Harris, D. L. (1992). Are rhinoplasty patients potentially mad? *British Journal of Plastic Surgery, 45*, 307–310.

Thompson, J. K. (1996). *Body image, eating disorders, and obesity: An integrative guide for assessment and treatment.* Washington, DC: American Psychological Association.

Thompson, J. K., Heinberg, L. J., Altabe, M., & Tantleff-Dunn, S. (1999). *Exacting beauty: Theory, assessment, and treatment of body image disturbance*. Washington, DC: American Psychological Association.

Webb, W. L., Slaughter, R., Meyer, E., & Edgerton, M. (1965). Mechanisms of psychosocial adjustment in patients seeking "face-lift" operation. *Psychosomatic Medicine, 27*, 183–192.

Willard, S. G., McDermott, B. E., & Woodhouse, L. M. (1996). Lipoplasty in the bulimic patient. *Plastic and Reconstructive Surgery, 98*, 276–278.

Wright, M. R., & Wright, W. K. (1975). A psychological study of patients undergoing cosmetic surgery. *Archives of Otolaryngology, 101*, 145–151.

Yates, A., Shisslak, C. M., Allender, J. R., & Wollman, W. (1988). Plastic surgery and the bulimic patient. *International Journal of Eating Disorders, 7*, 557–560.

Young, V. L., Nemecek, J. R., & Nemecek, D. A. (1994). The efficacy of breast augmentation: Breast size increase, patient satisfaction, and psychological effects. *Plastic and Reconstructive Surgery, 94*, 958–969.

AUTHOR INDEX

Numbers in italics refer to listings in the reference sections.

Froguel, P., 331, *334*
Frohlich, K., 78, *83*
Fryer, S., 115, *120*
Fuchs, G., 321, *339*
Fuhrman, S., 276, 277, *284*
Fujishima, M. J., 177, *189*
Fulkerson, J., 19, *21*, 46, *43*, 60, *61*, 99, 100, 111, *121* 139, *144*, 223, *231*, 299, *310*
Fullan, M., 276, 277, *287*
Fullerton, D., 155, *165*
Furnham, A., 298, *308*
Fusch, C., 321, *339*

Gaetke, L., 173, *189*
Gaggar, A., 113, *124*
Gaines, S. O., 275, *287*
Galef, B. G., 27, *37*
Gallagher, D., 279, 290, 325, *336*
Gallagher, M. M., 70, *85*
Gallucci, W. T., 180, *188*
Galmann, M. C., 279, *289*
Garcia, H., 53, *59*
Garcia-Coll, C., 53, *59*
Garcia-Temple, E., 329, *333*
Gardner, E. A., 203, 205, 206, *209*
Gardner, J. D., 265, *287*
Gardner, R., 42, *43*, 44, *45*, *59*, 108, 110, *120*, 169, 193, 194, 196, 197, 198, 203, 204–205, 207, *209*, 359
Garfinkel, P., 49, *59*, 110, *120*, 133, 139, *143*, *147*, 155, *165*, 193, *210*, 222, *230*
Garner, D., 49, *59*, 67n, 88, 110, *120*, 133, *143*, 193, 198, 200, *210*, 222, 223, *230*, 295, *309*
Garner, M. V., 295, *309*
Garrahie, E. J., 33, *39*
Gaupmann, G., 177, *189*
Geller, J., 104, *121*, 133, 139, *144*
George, D. T., 178, 180, *188*, *189*
Geraci, J. F., 329, *339*
Gerald, L. B., 71, *85*
Gergen, P., 84, *92*
Gershunskaya, Y. B., *89*
Gersten, J. C., 68, *87*
Ghaderi, A., *337*
Ghadirian, A. M., 133, *146*
Ghee, K., 75, *83*, *93*
Giancola O'Brien, J., 325, *335*

Gianini, M. H., 345, *362*
Gibbons, S., 154, *163*
Gilbert, S., 2
Gilinsky, N. H., 177, *188*
Gillman, M., 3, *14–16*, 33, 39, 44, *59*
Gilroy, M., 217, *231*, 295, 300, 303, 307, 310
Gilsanz, V., 282, *287*
Ginsberg-Fellner, F., 265, *288*
Girgus, J., 47, *62*
Gittelsohn, J., 80, 85, 90, 92, 95, 96
Gladis, M., 303, *311*
Glatfelter, L., 33, *38*
Glatt, B. S., 354, *362*
Gleason, L., 276, *291*
Gleaves, D. H., 196, 205, *212*, *213*, 220, 221, 222, *232*, 231
Gleeson, C., 195, *208*
Gleghorn, A. A., 202, *210*
Glengery, A. M., 205, *212*
Glucksman, M. L., 202, *210*
Glueck, C. J., 33, *38*
Godart, N. T., 11, *15*
Goering, P., 155, *165*
Goin, J. M., 345, 346, 357, *362*
Goin, M. K., 345, 346, 357, *362*
Going, S. B., 90, 92, 95, 96
Golan, M., 326, 327, 328, *336*
Gold, E., 158, 162, *165*
Gold, P. W., 178, 180, 181, 185, *188*, *189*, *191*
Gold, R. S., 276, *287*
Goldberg, A., 324, *333*
Goldberg, J. A., 277, *288*
Goldberg, R. J., 264, 270, *286*
Goldberg, S., 194, *210*
Goldbloom, D., 155, *165*
Goldfield, A., 74, *85*
Goldfield, G. S., 323, 325, *334*
Golding, C., 44, 45, *65*
Goldsmith, H., 47, *60*
Gomez, Y., 70, 73, *84*
Gonzalez, I., 261n
Goodman, N., 74, *89*
Goodrick, G. K., 80, *85*
Goodyer, I., 217, *230*
Goran, M. I., 282, *287*, 330, *336*
Gordy, C. C., 325, *335*
Gore, S. A., 235, *293*
Goreczny, A. J., 196, *213*
Gorman, B., 222, *230*

Kahn, C. R., 331, *339*
Kakegamic, L., 80, *85*
Kalarchian, M. A., 319, 321, 322, 325, 327, 328, *335*
Kalat, J. W., 27, *38*
Kaminski, Z., 217, *229*
Kaplan, A., 139, *147*, 155, *165*
Kapp-Simon, K. A., 354, *362*
Karmel, M. P., 248, *256*
Kashubeck, S., 74, 75, 86, *95*
Kass, E. J., 182, *191*
Katch, V., 320, 321, 323, 325, *333*, *337*, *339*
Kater, K. J., 243 *257*
Katz, D. P., 265, *288*
Katz, R., 46, 58, 74, 83, 95, 98, 294, *309*
Katzman, M., 104, *121*, 133, 139, *144*
Kaye, W., 134, 139, *142*, *144*, 171, 178, 180, *188*, *188*, *189*
Kazdin, A., 103, 104, 105, 108, 109, *121*
Keane, F. B., 177, *189*
Kearney-Cooke, A., 48, 65, 158, 160, *165*, 301, *309*
Keck, P. E., 349, *364*
Keel, P. K., 111, *121*, 139, *144*, 223, *231*
Keeton, W. P., 194, 196, 206, *210*
Kegeles, S., 194, *208*
Kelch, R. L., 320, 325, *339*
Kelder, S. H., 263, 264, 270, *289*
Kelleem, J. M., 178, 179, *191*
Kellun, J. M., 179, *191*
Kelly, C., 54, 55, 60, 223, *231*
Kelly, K., 33, *38*
Kelman, J. H., 322, 326, *334*
Kemper, K. A., 74–75, 76, *86*
Kemper, R., 73, 74, 88, *93*
Kendler, K. S., 128, 140, *144*
Kendrick, J., 220, *231*
Kennedy, P. F., 51, *61*
Kennedy, S., 41, *59*, 155, *165*, 294, *309*
Kennel, K., 29, *39*
Kerbl, B., 320, *340*
Kern, D. L., 34, *38*
Kern, J., 134, *144*, 154, 156, 157, 158, *165*
Kerr, B. A., 299, *308*
Kessler, J. W., 136, 137, *146*
Kessler, R., 103, 104, 105, 108, *121*, 128, 140, *144*
Kevany, J., 195, *208*
Khoury, P., 33, *38*, 279, 285, *290*

Kidder, F., 302, *309*
Kiekhofer, M., 199–202, *210*
Killeen, J., 279, *288*
Killen, J., 5, 7, 12, *17*, 19, *21*, 41, 46, 49, 50, 51, 52, 53, 60, 64, 65, 99, 100, 159, 162, *166*, 198, 201, *211*, 224, 228, *232*, 252, *259*
Killen, J. D., 7, 12, *15*, 72, 75, 89, 95, 96, 108, 111, 112, 114, 115–116, *121*, *124*, 133, *146*, 235, 236, 240–241, 244, 245, 254, 255, 257, 261, 263, 266, 270, 288, 291, 320, 322, 327, *334*
Killman, P. R., 347, *363*
Kilpatrick, D., 155, *164*
Kim, U., 69, *83*
Kimm, S. Y., 72, *86*
Kinder, B. N., 205, *208*
King, M., 171, *188*
King, S. L., 75, 89, *95*
Kingsley, R. G., 328, *337*
Kinzl, J., 134, *144*, 154, *165*
Kirk, J., 294, 295, 305, *308*
Kirschenbaum, D. S., 131, *147*, 296, *310*, 326–327, 328, *337*
Kiss, A., 177, *189*, *191*
Kjolhede, C. L., 26, *37*
Klein, E., *261n*
Klein, K. R., 325, 327, *335*
Klerman, G. L., 296, *310*
Klesges, L. M., 32, *38*, 273, *288*
Klesges, R. C., 32, *38*, 227, *231*, 262, 273, 286, 287, *288*, 319, 321, 322, 324, *337*
Klibanski, A., 179, *190*
Klinnert, M., 47, *60*
Klish, W. J., 320, 324, *333*
Klonoff, E. A., 275, *288*
Klump, K. L., 111, *121*, 139, *144*, 223, *231*
Knapp, J. A., 71, *86*
Knibbs, J., 218, *230*
Knip, M., 320, 321, 328, *337*, *338*
Knittle, J. L., 265, *288*
Knowler, W. C., 70, *86*
Kobayashi, A., 320, 321, *334*
Kobayashi, N., 177, *189*
Koenig, T., 73, *83*
Koerner, J., 19, *21*
Koeske, R., 320, 322, 323, 325, 327, *335*
Koff, E., 41, 60, 199–202, *210*, 298, *309*

SUBJECT INDEX

Food avoidance emotional disorder, 13, 217–218
Food dislikes, 30–32
Food guide pyramid, 31, 324
Food monitoring, 226
Food preferences, 30, 273
Food refusal, 218
Food restrictions, 31–32
Forbidden foods, 31–32
Formula feeding, 24–26
Foster care, 150
Full of Ourselves program, 249
Functional dysphagia, 13

Gallstones, 178, 186
Gastric bypass surgery, 178, 186
Gastrointestinal assessment, 177–178
Gastroplasty, 186
Gender differences
    body image, 3, 44, 49–50, 53
    eating disorder contributor, 47
    family functioning, 132
    partial syndromes, 7
    prevention programs, 252–254
Genetics predisposition, 72–73, 329, 330–333
Group work intervention, 162
Growth, arrested, 179
Growth retardation, 11
Guided imagery, 301
Gynecomastia, 353

Harter Physical Appearance, 54
Harvard Eating Disorder Center, 249
Health and Human Services, Department of, 187
Health care use patterns, 81
Health Resources and Services Administration, 187
Hispanics, 43, 69, 70, 72, 132
Hormonal replacement, 179
Hospitalization, 184–186, 301–303
Hyperamylasemia, 178
Hyperlipidemia, 172
Hyperphagia, 183
Hypertension, 10, 172, 176
Hyperuricemia, 172
Hypocalcemia, 175, 182
Hypoestrogenemia, 180

Hypokalemia, 175, 183
Hypomagnesemia, 176, 182
Hyponatremia, 182
Hypophosphatemia, 175, 185
Hypoproteinemia, 182
Hypotension, 175

Incremental validity, 216
Indicated prevention, 238
Infant nutrition, 24–28
Informed assent–consent, 219, 359
Inpatient treatment, 301–303
Insight-oriented therapy, 303
Institute of Medicine, 352
Insulin resistance, 10
Intake regulation, 25, 30
Intergenerational eating behavior, 33
Internal consistency, 216
Interpersonal therapy, 116, 296, 305
Interrater reliability, 216
Interventions
    implementation assessments, 283
    implementation strategies, 275–278
    lifestyle, 314, 324
    obesity, 261–284, 313–333
    symptom-specific, 116–117
    timely, 81
Interview for Diagnosis of Eating Disorders (IDED), 221
Ipecac abuse, 176

Jejunoileal bypass, 186

Kid's Eating Disorder Survey (KEDS), 223–224
Kuder–Richardson Formula 20, 216

Laboratory evaluation, 180–183
    endocrine and metabolic, 180–181
    hemotologic and immunologic, 182
    renal, fluid, electrolytes, 181–182
Lanugo, 175
Laser hair removal, 341
Laxatives, 97, 152, 182
Leptin, 332
Leukopenia, 182
Life event studies, 106

Life skills training, 117
Lifestyle intervention, 314, 324, 325
Liposuction, 10, 341, 351–352
Literacy, 251–252
Lum Emotional Availability of Parents
    Scale (LEAP), 129

Macro-level environmental barriers,
    327–329
Magazines, 51, 114
Malnutrition, 175, 179
Marker-assisted sampling, 331
Maternal and Child Health Bureau,
    187
Maternal nutrition
    breast-feeding, 24–26, 27–28
    flavor exposure, 27
    formula feeding, 24–26
    prenatal, 24
Maxillofacial surgery, 354–356
McKnight Risk Factor Survey III (MFRS-
    III), 198, 201, 224–225, 228
Media influences, 51–52, 74, 352
Media literacy, 251–252
Mediators, 104
Medical complication assessment,
    175–180
Mentors, 117
Middle-school prevention curriculum,
    244–245
Modeling influences, 33, 136
Moderators, 104, 156–157
Morbid obesity, 172
Mother–daughter eating behaviors, 33,
    49
Motivation, 267–268
Movable Caliper Technique, 199
Multidimensional Body-Self Relations
    Questionnaire (MBSRQ), 347
Multiple-component interventions,
    264
Multiple regression analysis, 114, 115

National Center for Health Statistics
    growth charts, 316
National Heart, Lung, and Blood Insti-
    tute (NHLBI), 3, 264, 270, 272
Negative verbal commentary, 136–138
Neophobia, 27

NHLBI Strategy Development Workshop
    for Public Education on Weight
    and Obesity, 272
Nonalcoholic steatohepatitis, 178
Nonspecific vulnerability-stressor (NVS)
    model, 241
Nutritional education, 185

Obesity
    associated health problems, 10–12,
        176, 178, 179–180
    body satisfaction, 3–4
    detection and prevention, 11–12
    ethnic differences, 8, 69–73
    family functioning, 132
    gender differences, 8, 9
    physical assessment, 172–175
    prevalence, 8–9, 69–70
Obesity hypoventilation syndrome, 179
Obesity prevention, 261–284
    assessment, 280–281
    body composition measures,
        281–282
    control interventions, 278–279
    cultural appropriateness, 275
    current status, 262–264
    diet and activity, 282–283
    evaluation issues, 278
    high-risk children, 272
    implementation, 275–278, 283
    innovative, 272–275
    intervention development, 267–268
    intervention model, 266–267
    multiple component, 264
    parents and family, 264, 271–272
    physical education programs, 263,
        270
    preadolescent, 265–266
    primary outcome measures, 279
    reasons for, 261–262
    school curriculum programs,
        262–263
    school food service, 263–264,
        270–271
Obesity treatment
    barriers, 327–329
    behavioral, 313–333
    efficacy, 319–322
    future research, 329–332
    international guidelines, 316, 319

lifestyle, 314, 424
relapse, 322
screening process, 314–319
Oppositional disorder, 218
Orthopedic disorders, 10
Osteopenia, 178–179
Otoplasty, 353

Pancreas, 177–178
Pancreatitis, 177–178, 185
Pancytopenia, 182
Parent(s)
    body image influence, 48–50, 53, 136
    control in child feeding, 29–30
    eating preference modeling effects, 33–34
    excessive control, 30–32
    involvement in treatment, 322, 326–327
    overprotection, 131
    psychopathology, 133–134, 13
    weight perception attitudes, 134–136
Parental Bonding Inventory (PBI), 129
Parental Stress Index (PSI), 130
Parent–child control issues, 29–32
Parenting behavior, 133
Parenting psychopathology, 133–134
Parenting Scale, 130
Parenting skills training, 327
Parent intervention, 264, 271–272
Parotid enlargement, 178
Partial syndrome diagnosis, 6–7
Peer influence, 50–51, 74
Peer modeling, 50, 53
Peer support groups, 117
Peer-specific barriers, 327, 329
Perceptions of Parents Scale (POP), 129
Perceptual body-size distortion, 193
Perfectionism, 172, 254
Personal factors, 267
Pervasive refusal syndrome, 13, 218
Pharmacotherapy, 303, 332
Physical activity, 72, 282–283, 324–326, 329
Physical education (PE) interventions, 263
Physical exam, 173–175
Physical status assessment, 171–187
    differential diagnosis, 183

general appearance, 175
history, 172–173, 174
laboratory evaluation, 180–183
medical complications, 175–180
medical management, 183–187
Physical training, 300
Plastic surgery
    body image issues, 7, 347–350
    child and adolescent, 9–10, 341–361
    cosmetic, 351–353
    patient motivation and expectations, 357–358
    patient selection, 356–360
    psychological studies, 344–347
    reconstructive, 341, 353–356
Point of subjective equality (PSE), 205
Polydipsia, 182
Polyuria, 182
Posttraumatic stress disorder, 218
Prader-Willi syndrome, 332
Predictive validity, 216
Preferred body type, 73
Prevention, 11–12
    body image problems, 56–57, 237–256
    categories, 237–238
    child sexual abuse, 160–162
    described, 237
    eating disorder development, 34, 56–57, 116–117
    family functioning, 138–139
    goals, 239–240
    obesity, 261–284
    overview, 235–236
    primary prevention, 237–256
    rationale, 238–239
Prevention effect, 238
Prevention programs, 116–117
Primary outcome measures, 279–280
Primary prevention, 237–256
    conceptual issues, 237–240
    developmental perspective, 246–248
    ecological-empowerment perspective, 248–251
    idealized study checklist, 254
    literacy, critique, and activism, 251–252
    paradigms, 240–242
    race, gender, and class, 252–254
    research literature, 242–246
    universal versus targeted, 254

ABOUT THE EDITORS

J. Kevin Thompson received his doctoral training at the University of Georgia, where he obtained his PhD in 1982. He has been at the University of South Florida since 1985 and is a professor in the Department of Psychology. He has authored, coauthored, or edited three earlier books in the area of body image, eating disorders, and obesity (*Body Image Disturbance: Assessment and Treatment*, Pergamon Press, 1990; *Body Image, Eating Disorders, and Obesity: An Integrative Guide for Assessment and Treatment*, American Psychological Association, 1996; *Exacting Beauty: Theory Assessment and Treatment of Body Image Disturbance*, American Psychological Association, 1999). He has been on the editorial board of the *International Journal of Eating Disorders* since 1990, and joined the editorial board of *Eating Disorders: The Journal of Treatment and Prevention* in 2001.

Linda Smolak received her doctoral training at Temple University, where she obtained her PhD in 1980. She has been at Kenyon College since 1980, and is a professor in the Departments of Psychology and Women's and Gender Studies. She has coedited two other books in the area of body image and eating disorders (*The Developmental Psychopathology of Eating Disorders*, Erlbaum, 1996; *Eating Disorders: Innovations in Research and Practice*, American Psychological Association, 2001), and is coauthoring a book on prevention of eating disorders (*The Prevention of Eating Problems and Eating Disorders: Theory, Research, and Practice*, Erlbaum, in press). She is the author of numerous articles on the developmental psychopathology of eating disorders and has served as a consultant to the McKnight Risk Factor Study, the U.S. Office on Women's Health, and the Harvard Eating Disorders Center.